Trade, Health and the Environment

The trade conflicts that the European Union (EU) has faced within the EU or World Trade Organization (WTO) context demonstrate that the question of how to balance trade and other societal values in situations of uncertainty has not been solved by the regulatory model evolved by the EU in the aftermath of the BSE ('mad cow') crisis – one which privileges processes of depoliticisation and scientification. This book addresses the current key dilemmas around science, law and the regulation of trade, both on a regime level and in the context of particular industrial sectors, e.g. pharmaceuticals, climate change and nanotechnology. It will present possible future research avenues by looking at both theory and practice and learning from various disciplines (law and social sciences), legal realities (WTO, USA and EU) and actors (regulators, stakeholders, courts).

Marjolein B.A. van Asselt is Risk Governance chair, Faculty of Arts and Social Sciences, Maastricht University and member of the Scientific Council for Government Policy (WRR), The Hague, Netherlands.

Michelle Everson is Professor of European Law at Birkbeck, University of London, UK.

Ellen Vos is Professor of European Union Law at the Law Faculty of Maastricht University and co-director of the Maastricht Centre for European Law, Maastricht University, Netherlands.

Routledge Explorations in Environmental Studies

Nuclear Waste Management and Legitimacy
Nihilism and responsibility
Mats Andrén

Nuclear Power, Economic Development Discourse and the Environment
The case of India
Manu V. Mathai

Federalism of Wetlands
Ryan W. Taylor

Governing Sustainable Urban Renewal
Partnerships in action
Rory Shand

Employee Engagement with Sustainable Business
How to change the world whilst keeping your day job
Nadine Exter

The Political Economy of Global Warming
The terminal crisis
Del Weston

Communicating Environmental Patriotism
A rhetorical history of the American environmental movement
Anne Marie Todd

Environmental Justice in Developing Countries
Perspectives from Africa and Asia-Pacific
Rhuks Temitope Ako

Climage Change and Cultural Heritage
A race against time
Peter F. Smith

A Global Environmental Right
Stephen Turner

The Coming of Age of the Green Community
My neighbourhood, my planet
Erik Bichard

Fairness and Justice in Environmental Decision Making
Water under the bridge
Catherine Gross

Carbon Politics and the Failure of the Kyoto Protocol
Gerald Kutney

Trade, Health and the Environment
The European Union put to the test
Marjolein B.A. van Asselt, Michelle Everson and Ellen Vos

Trade, Health and the Environment

The European Union put to the test

Edited by
Marjolein B.A. van Asselt,
Michelle Everson and Ellen Vos

Routledge
Taylor & Francis Group
LONDON AND NEW YORK

earthscan
from Routledge

First published 2014
by Routledge
2 Park Square, Milton Park, Abingdon, Oxfordshire OX14 4RN

and by Routledge
711 Third Avenue, New York, NY 10017

Routledge is an imprint of the Taylor and Francis Group, an informa business

First issued in paperback 2015

British Library Cataloguing in Publication Data
A catalogue record for this book is available from the British Library

Library of Congress Cataloging-in-Publication Data
Asselt, M. B. A. van.
Trade, health and the environment : the European Union put to the test / Marjolein Van Asselt, Michelle Everson and Ellen Vos.
pages cm
1. European Union countries--Commerce. 2. Environmental protection--European Union countries. 3. Medical policy--European Union countries. I. Everson, Michelle. II. Vos, Ellen. III. Title.
HF3496.5.A87 2014
337.1'42--dc23
2013011567

ISBN 978-1-84971-362-7 (hbk)
ISBN 978-1-138-19260-7 (pbk)
ISBN 978-1-315-88678-7 (ebk)

Typeset in Times
by Taylor & Francis Books

Contents

Figures

Contributors

Marjolein B.A. van Asselt, Chair in Risk Governance at Maastricht University and member of the Scientific Council for Government Policy, the Hague, Netherlands.

Frederic Bouder, Assistant Professor, Department of Technology and Society Studies, Maastricht University, Netherlands.

Jos Cortenraad, journalist, BCcommunicatie & tekst, Meerssen, the Netherlands.

Bärbel Dorbeck-Jung, Professor of Regulation and Technology, University of Twente, Netherlands.

Michelle Everson, Professor of European Law, Director of University of London International Diploma in Law, Birkbeck, University of London, UK.

Maria Hage, Sustainability Coordinator, Municipality of Lingewaard, Netherlands.

Sofia Kaliarnta, PhD researcher at the Philosophy department, Delft University of Technology, Netherlands.

Kartika Liotard, Member of European Parliament, Confederal Group of the European United Left – Nordic Green Left, independent member, Brussels, Belgium.

Erik Millstone, Professor of Science Policy at SPRU – Science and Technology Policy Research, University of Sussex, UK.

Marjan Peeters, Professor of Environmental Policy and Law, Faculty of Law, Maastricht University, Netherlands.

Robert V. Percival, Robert F. Stanton Professor of Law and Director of the Environmental Law Programme at the University of Maryland Francis King Carey School of Law, USA.

Denise Prévost, Associate Professor of International Economic Law, Faculty of Law, Maastricht University, Netherlands.

Sabine Roeser, Professor of Ethics at Delft University of Technology, Netherlands.

Mariachiara Tallacchini, Professor of Legal Philosophy, Faculty of Economics and Law, Università Cattolica del Sacro Cuore, Piacenza, Italy; Professor of Bioethics, Faculty of Biotechnology, Università degli studi di Milano, Italy. Currently working for the European Commission, Institute for the Protection and Security of the Citizen of the Joint Research Centre, Ispra, Italy.

Ellen Vos, Professor of European Union Law, Faculty of Law and Co-Director of the Maastricht Centre for European Law, Maastricht University, Netherlands.

Acknowledgements

The first versions of a number of papers collected in this volume were presented and discussed at a conference entitled *European Integration Between Trade and Non Trade* held in Maastricht on 14–15 April 2010. The papers, which were presented by young researchers at the workshop that was held in addition to this conference, have been published in an edited volume by M.B.A. van Asselt, E. Versluis and E. Vos (eds), *Balancing between Trade and Risk. Integrating Legal and Social Science Perspectives* (Routledge/Earthscan, 2013).

The publication of this volume would not have been possible without the help of a number of colleagues. First and foremost we would like to express our thanks to all the contributors for their collaboration and commitment to the publication of this book. Special and enormous thanks go to our dear colleague Marina Jodogne who provided invaluable assistance through her able and patient work in the formatting and editing of this book. We would like to thank Kirstyn Inglis for doing a thorough language revision of all chapters. We would also like to express our gratitude to Marina Jodogne, Lidwien Hollander, Tessa Fox and Marijke Hermans who helped us with the organisation of the conference. The friendly, able and co-operative attitude of the colleagues of Taylor & Francis, in particular Charlotte Russell, Louisa Earls and Helena Hurd, was a constant encouragement. Last but not least, we would like to thank the Education, Audiovisual and Culture Executive Agency for financially supporting this research and publication project under the EU's Jean Monnet Programme.

Marjolein van Asselt, Michelle Everson
and Ellen Vos
Maastricht
December 2012

Abbreviations

AEMPS	Agencia Española de Medicamentos y Productos Sanitarios – Spanish Health Products Safety Agency
AFSSAPS	French Health Products Safety Agency
AIDS	Acquired immunodeficiency syndrome
BBC	British Broadcasting Corporation
BfR	Bundesinstitut für Risikobewertung
BSE	Bovine spongiform encephalopathy
BVLS	Bundesamt für Verbraucherschutz und Lebensmittel Sicherheit
CAC	Codex Alimentarius Commission
CBD	Convention on Biological Diversity
CBDR	Common but differentiated responsibilities
CDM	Clean development mechanism
CEC	Commission of the European Community
CFI	Court of First Instance
CHMP	Committee for Human Medicinal Products
CJEU	Court of Justice of the European Union
CMRs	chemicals that are carcinogenic, mutagenic or toxic for reproduction
CoC	Committee on Carcinogenicity
CPMP	Committee for Proprietary Medicinal Products
DG SANCO	Directorate General for Public Health and Consumer Protection
DIY	Do-it-yourself
DNA	Deoxyribonucleic acid
DQA	Data Quality Act
EC	European Commission
ECB	European Central Bank
ECHA	European Chemical Agency
ECJ	European Court of Justice
ECR	European Court Reports
EC SCVMPH	European Commission's Scientific Committee on Veterinary Measures relating to Public Health
EEA	European Environmental Agency
EFSA	European Food Safety Authority

EMA	European Medicines Agency
EMEA	European Medicines Evaluation Agency
EMS	ethyl methanesulfonate
EPA	Environmental Protection Agency
ERU	Emission reduction unit
EU	European Union
EU ETS	EU emissions trading scheme
FAO	Food and Agriculture Organization
FDA	Food and Drug Administration
FSA	Food Standards Agency
GATT	General Agreement on Tariffs and Trade
GM	Genetically modified
GMO	Genetically modified organism
HIV	Human immunodeficiency virus
HPV	Human papillomavirus
ICH	International Conference on Harmonisation of Technical Requirements for Registration of Pharmaceuticals for Human Use
IPCC	Intergovernmental Panel on Climate Change
IPPC	International Plant Protection Convention
IRGC	International Risk Governance Council
JI	Joint implementation
MAFF	Minister of Agriculture, Forestry and Fisheries
MEP	Member of the European Parliament
MMR	Measles, mumps and rubella
MoE	Ministry of Environment (Japan)
MSD SNC	Merck Sharp & Dohme-Chibret, société en nom collectif
MTBE	methyl tertiary butyl ether
NGO	Non-governmental organisation
NRC	National Research Council
OCU	Organización de consumidores y usuarios
OECD	Organisation for Economic Cooperation and Development
OIE	World Organisation for Animal Health
OSHA	Occupational Safety & Health Administration
OST	Office of Science and Technology
PCBs	polychlorinated biphenyls
PDUFA	Prescription Drug User Fee Acts
POPs	persistent organic pollutants
ppm	part/s per million
RAP	Risk assessment policy
RoHS	Restriction of Hazardous Substances directive
RRI	Responsible research and innovation
SE	*Status epilepticus*
SEC	[US] Securities and Exchange Commission
SPA	Sanitary and Phytosanitary Agreement

SPS	Sanitary and phytosanitary
STD	Sexually transmitted disease
SVHC	substances of very high concern
TBT	Technical barriers to trade
TFEU	Treaty on the Functioning of the European Union
TRT	Groupe interassociatif Traitements et Recherche Thérapeutique
UK	United Kingdom
UNEP	United Nations Environment Programme
UNFCCC	United Nations Framework Convention on Climate Change
US	United States
USA	United States of America
USTR	United States Trade Representative
VCLT	Vienna Convention on the Law of Treaties
vPvBs	very persistent or very bioaccumulative substances
WEEE	Waste Electrical and Electronic Equipment directive
WHO	World Health Organization
WMD	Weapons of mass destruction
WTO	World Trade Organization

Part I

Introduction and conclusion

Trade versus health and the environment?

Marjolein B.A. van Asselt, Michelle Everson and Ellen Vos

European integration processes are increasingly being confronted with the dilemma of how to balance the free trade imperative, as well as ever more intense economic integration, against non-economic societal values, such as safety and human and environmental health. Measures designed to protect these values inevitably impact upon trade. Accordingly, the dilemma is often shaped in the terms of trade versus health and the environment.

The BSE (bovine spongiform encephalopathy) crisis, as well as subsequent food crises, have been highly influential in shaping the mode in which the EU currently deals with the science that underlies its decision-making. Crisis has resulted in a significant change in what is considered to be a legitimate governmental use of science and has also resulted in a quest to secure far better 'quality' scientific advice, as well as to establish increased transparency and broader participation in science-based decision-making.

Today, however, the issue is not merely one of how to ensure that the science used in EU governance is sound. Instead, it also encompasses the manner in which scientific opinions are balanced against far wider ethical and social values. New approaches introduced by the EU in the wake of the BSE crisis sought to repair alleged deficiencies in EU risk regulation. The aim was to make a clearer separation between risk assessment and risk management, as well as to clarify the distinct roles of scientists and decision-makers. Consequently, new principles, models and rules shaping the production of scientific advice have been introduced, such as European agencies, the precautionary principle for health protection reasons, transparency and participation (see e.g. Ansell and Vogel 2006; Fisher 2009; Harremoës *et al.* 2002; Zander 2010).

At the same time, internal market and free trade concerns are becoming increasingly intermingled with health and other concerns that can create barriers to free trade. In the EU and World Trade Organization (WTO) context, both Member States and the EU are increasingly being required to provide a scientific justification for any deviations from free trade in favour of interests relating to the protection of health, the environment or ethical concerns. This obligation to justify what might be considered to be political decisions in terms of science and scientific evidence has been introduced as a means to ensure that measures adopted are inspired by genuine non-trade, rather than protectionist, motives and intentions. The position of science as 'neutral arbiter' has solidified. Yet, the majority of controversial cases in the ambit of the free trade versus protection of human health and the environment dilemma involve high levels of scientific uncertainty.

We argue that the dilemma of balancing trade and non-trade issues increasingly boils down to a question of how to regulate 'uncertain risks'. Our earlier work on the regulation of uncertain risks revealed a degree of 'scientification' of EU risk regulation (Everson and Vos 2009; Van Asselt and Vos 2006, 2008). Striking controversies, however, clearly demonstrate that the question of how to balance trade and other societal values in situations of uncertainty has not been solved by the current regulatory model evolved by the EU in the aftermath of the BSE crisis – one which privileges processes of depoliticization and scientification.

Frederic Bouder's identification of the development of a 'post-trust' environment in the regulation of pharmaceuticals[1] highlights public dissatisfaction with this model; as does the obscuring complexity of EU regimes designed to combat climate change (see Marjan Peeters[2] in this volume). The various contributions made by young scholars to our related volume, *Balancing between Trade and Risk* (Van Asselt, Versluis and Vos 2013), similarly confirm the limits to the current approach. Notwithstanding numerous efforts to design regulatory models for accommodating science, this problem continues to deserve our full academic attention.

Whilst the financial crisis does not form part of our study in this book, it nonetheless provides us with an important message: namely that not all risk can be modelled. Funtowicz and Ravetz have evolved a concept of 'radical uncertainty' in this context.[3] This theme is echoed in contributions to this volume (see, especially, the contributions by Mariachiara Tallacchini and by Erik Millstone) and indicates that much work needs to be done in fundamentally rethinking the role of science in risk regulation. Both identify a need for a certain degree of politicization (see also Everson and Vos 2009; Van Asselt and Vos 2006, 2008).

The problems emerging in controversies around trade, human health and the environment also relate to trust issues. As Bouder depicts in relation to pharmaceuticals, we are living in a 'post-trust society' where 'the critical voices of new opinion leaders and NGOs have become more trustworthy than those of government or scientists' (Bouder, p. 92). The concept of 'post trust' should not be equated with that of 'no trust'. Yet, it does indicate that we cannot simply assume a degree of trust in regulators and science. Who is trusted by whom is a critical question, but not necessarily an easy one to answer. Yet, it has become a critical question within decision-making processes focusing on socially controversial issues. Trust matters.

Theory also matters, but must likewise be sufficiently grounded in reality. Reintroducing the notion of 'politics' to the theoretical risk debate, Robert V. Percival[4] notes that a major current problem is that risk regimes also suffer from their failure to recognize the presence of 'power' within trade relations, or the fact that political interests play a major role in the complex balancing of science-based regulation of trade and other societal concerns. As a consequence, in the global and EU frameworks, problem-solving is delegated to the relevant courts, which are often unable to address the core problem of scientific uncertainty (see the contributions by Prévost and Vos). An inherently political process of the weighing-up of trade, safety and human and environmental interests should and cannot solely take place in courts. If we are concerned for the enduring health of the rule of law, we must be concerned that the legitimacy of courts is also challenged by processes of depoliticization and scientification.

Millstone explicitly challenges the role of scientific risk assessment within the regulatory process. He convincingly demonstrates how the process of risk assessment within current frameworks is a central point of passage in any decision-making process (see also Van Asselt, Versluis and Vos 2013 and Lee 2010), but accordingly also – in its focus on neutral application of science – heightens the concomitant problem whereby non-scientific socio-economic and ethical concerns are disregarded. Societal concerns can only be considered within science-based risk assessments where they can themselves be framed as 'risks'. As a consequence, the current balance in regulation appears to be tilted in favour of trade. Although the current regulatory regimes at the level of the Member States and at the EU and the global (WTO) level have been developed to protect free trade against purely protectionist measures, the question, which runs through this volume, is one of whether trade is – in practice – afforded too great a degree of protection at the expense of other societal values.

There is still much room for further research on the manner in which the EU balances trade interests against the protection of health and the environment. Above all, we still need to pay specific attention to the problem of scientific uncertainty within a multi-level system of governance. Which shortcomings beset this system, and how might we improve its functioning? A critical question asked throughout this volume is accordingly one of the degrees to which scientification needs likewise to be balanced by repoliticization: to which extent should non-scientific concerns be reintegrated within EU risk regulation and how might this be best achieved? In short: can and should we repoliticize decision-making on issues that involve trade, human health, environment and other societal concerns?

The book will present possible future research avenues by looking at both theory and practice and learning from various disciplines (law and social sciences), legal realities (WTO, USA and EU) and actors (regulators, stakeholders, courts). It particularly addresses the interplay between trade, health and the environment, both on a regime level and in the context of particular industrial sectors, e.g. pharmaceuticals, climate change and nanotechnology. In these fields, the EU is wrestling with the dilemma of how to balance the various interests at stake and, above all, with conflicts within its own development agenda, or *telos* – one which envisages the establishment by 2020 of an

Innovation Union and a European knowledge society, but which still posits the existence of a European Union which pays sufficient regard to health, safety and environmental and other social interests.

As trade concerns are central to the EU, both with regard to its internal market and in its relationships with other parts of the world, divergences and deadlocks concerning trade, health and the environment have very visibly put the EU to the test. How did the EU perform in this test? That is the question addressed in this book.

The book consists of five sections. Following this introduction and a conclusion included in Part I, Part II provides a broader context for the modelling of science and precaution. The contribution by Robert V. Percival draws lessons from US environmental law, showing the enormous political influence of regulated industries. He concludes that politics do matter in environmental regulation. This is even the case for the judiciary, which remains split between opponents and proponents of precautionary regulation, thus revealing the difficulties for the judiciary to deal with these issues and how politics may even creep into judicial decision-making. Erik Millstone analyses the role of scientific evidence and expertise in EU regulatory policy-making and their interactions with non-scientific considerations. He points to the limits of the so-called 'Red Book' model, developed in the USA, whereby policy-making is supposedly premised upon science rather than policy considerations. He calls for evolution of a co-dynamic model in which the relationship between risk assessment and risk management is at least two-sided. Mariachiara Tallacchini discusses the evolving meaning and role of the precautionary principle in European governance of emerging technologies and calls for a more diffused and participatory idea of precaution that networks individual and collective responsibilities.

Part III of the book involves the in-depth analysis of three case studies in the fields of pharmaceuticals, climate change and nanotechnologies. The contribution by Frederic Bouder reveals the 'post-trust' environment in which scientists and policy-makers have to operate, where expert-based decision-making is increasingly challenged. He provides a detailed analysis of the handling of scientific evidence in two specific cases, the anti-HIV (human immunodeficiency virus) drug Viracept and the anti-HPV (human papillomavirus) vaccine Gardasil, where societal perceptions and preferences played a key role in the balancing of risk assessment and protection measures. Bärbel Dorbeck-Jung analyses the regulatory activities by the EU to control therapeutic nanoproducts. She explores the governance responses to the regulatory problems of such products and examines them in the light of responsiveness and stakeholder and scientific legitimacy. The contribution by Marjan Peeters discusses the complex design of the Emission Trading Scheme adopted by the EU in its efforts to combat climate change. She highlights the lack of a scientific body to underpin the technical decision-making under this regime and the difficulties for accommodating competitive trade concerns within it. She further investigates how courts will deal with this highly complex regulatory framework. In doing so, this chapter provides an appropriate bridge to the next section.

Part IV deals with the role that courts have in judging on conflicts between trade and human health, environment and other concerns. The contributions by Denise Prévost and Ellen Vos illustrate how WTO panel(s) and the EU courts visibly struggle with the technicalities of disputes involving both science-based measures and high levels of scientific uncertainty. Both contributions show that, in practice, judicial authorities may 'promise' limited judicial review, but nonetheleless overstep their mandate and do not shy away from actively engaging in substantive review of the disputes at hand. The impact of risk scientification accordingly also echoes within the court room. Both contributions underline the need for interdisciplinary research on the role that courts can and should play vis-à-vis science-based measures. Repoliticization of regulation is also a way to improve the circumstances in which the court must rule and may result in less delegation of problem-solving to the courts.

The last section of the book, Part V, deals with practitioners' perspectives as well as an interview with a Member of the European Parliament. The contribution by Sofia Kaliarnta, Maria Hage and Sabine Roeser highlights the many problems relating to stakeholder participation in science-based decision-making, and they thus reflect on the stakeholder panels to the 2012 conference. They harvest practical considerations brought up by the participating stakeholders and emphasize the importance of trust and the emotional concerns of the public.

The interview with Kartika Liotard, with which we close this book, is of great interest as it reveals the various elements that the EU legislator faces in dealing with very politically sensitive dossiers, such as the amendment of the novel foods regulation. It perfectly illustrates the struggle around the interplays between trade, science, the precautionary principle and ethical concerns that has been addressed academically in other chapters. In this case, the gulf between trade interests and ethics exhibited within US government pressure on the EU to allow marketing of meat derived from cloned animals, and ethical concerns, was so great that the Council and the Parliament failed to come to an agreement. This account provides compelling reasons for us to take very seriously indeed the question of whether free trade interests have now been afforded far too great a degree of protection, to the detriment of other social values.

Through the analyses carried out by the individual contributors, this book thus seeks to give a vital contribution to the debate on science-based regulatory regimes and in particular the need to bring politics back in, including at the international level.

Notes

1 See Chapter 4 in this book.
2 See Chapter 6 in this book.

3 See the contribution by Tallacchini, Chapter 3.
4 See Chapter 1 in this volume.

References

Ansell, C. and Vogel, D. (eds) (2006) *What's the Beef? The Contested Governance of European Food Safety*, London: MIT Press.

Everson, M. and Vos, E. (2009) 'Scientification of Politics and Politicisation of Science', in M. Everson and E. Vos (eds), *Uncertain Risks Regulated*, London: Routledge/Cavendish Publishing, 1–17.

Fisher, E. (2009) *Risk Regulation and Administrative Constitutionalism*, London: Hart Publishing.

Funtowicz, S.O. and Ravetz, J.R. (1992) 'Risk Management as a Post-normal Science', *Risk Analysis*, 12(1): 95–97.

Harremoës, P., Vas, S., Stirling, A. and Wynne, B. (eds) (2002) *The Precautionary Principle in the 20th Century: Late Lessons from Early Warnings*, London: Earthscan.

Lee, M. (2010) 'Beyond Safety? The Broadening Scope of Risk Regulation', in: C. O'Cinneide (ed.), *Current Legal Problems 2009*, Oxford: Oxford University Press, 267–76.

Van Asselt, M.B.A. and Vos, E. (2006) 'Precautionary Principle and the Uncertainty Paradox', *Journal of Risk Research*, 313–36.

——(2008) 'Wrestling with Uncertainty: EU Regulation of GMOs and the Uncertainty Paradox', *Journal of Risk Research*, 11(1/2): 281–300.

Van Asselt, M.B.A., Versluis, E. and Vos, E. (eds) (2013) *Balancing between Trade and Risk: Integrating Legal and Social Science Perspectives*, London: Routledge.

Zander, J. (2010) *The Application of the Precautionary Principle in Practice: Comparative Dimensions*, Cambridge: Cambridge University Press.

The European Union put to the test

The quest for politics

Michelle Everson, Ellen Vos and Marjolein B.A. van Asselt

In the current World Trade Organization (WTO) world, it is assumed that global trade regulation is highly dependent on science. The establishment of a scientific basis is considered indispensable for decision-making and conflict resolution. This perspective also resonates in the following quote from Kaliarnta, Hage and Roeser (this volume, p. 243):

> Depending on science is the only way to go. Certainly in a WTO world, science [and] health effects are the only issues where you can find a baseline for some kind of common agreement, because we know our culture is different from culture in the Philippines. The only way to come to a common agreement is to use science.

This assumption has stimulated the current way in which the regulation of global trade, including trade of (potentially) risky products and technologies, takes place. The current legal regime of global trade regulation is highly dependent upon science for its functioning, decision-making and conflict resolution. Science is a corner stone, if not the girder, in the global regulation of trade. The WTO regime is organized in such a way that trade restrictions have to be grounded in scientific arguments and an important question to be answered in conflict resolution is whether trade measures have been (sufficiently) scientifically justified. For many this position of science is inevitable, uncontested and hence unquestionable. At the same time, however, as the contributions in this volume testify, there are also good reasons to rethink the relationship between science and global regulation, science and global law, science and the ethics and the concerns of an internationalized civil society and hence the position of science in regulatory regimes. These contributions also point to societal changes, such as changes in trust levels, to argue that it is difficult if not impossible for science to fulfil the role it is supposed to fulfil. Is the institutionalized principle that science is indispensable for the regulation of global trade a systematic error, which in an era characterized as 'post-trust' (Bouder, this volume) becomes increasingly problematic or even untenable?

The global science-based trade regime impacts on, if not shapes, decision-making and conflict resolution on other levels of social organization. Trade occupies the central place in the European Union, both with regard to its internal market and in its relationships with other parts of the world. As a consequence, conflicts concerning trade, health and environment have visibly put the European Union to the test (see also Chapter 1). The contributions to this volume divulge that the obligatory point-of-passage role of science and the scientification of trade regulation have to be rethought. In this concluding chapter, we aim to synthesize the key dilemmas around science, law and the regulation of trade.

A failure of science or a failure of responsibility?

Mariachiara Tallacchini in her contribution to this volume reiterates the uncomfortable place of hazard, uncertainty and incalculable risk within global complexes of science-based trade regulation. As scientific data prove uncertain, insufficient or susceptible to divergent interpretations, law bears the responsibility to fill the gaps left by science. One dimension of the discomfort between science and law pertains to the methodology of science, which, unlike the decision-oriented premises of law and regulation (see Vos in this volume), is, from its very inception, an indeterminate process, working not with absolute certainties, but with unproven premises of possible harm. Due to its epistemological mismatch, the 'uncertain' and provisional nature of scientific knowledge is not recognized in the legally oriented regime for the regulation of trade and risks. With regard to the regulation of the trade of innovative products, which are the most likely candidates for trade conflicts, uncertainty is even elevated as innovation generates uncertainty (Nowotny 2008). The predominance of science within global trading regimes is a contemporaneous reflection of the continuing global failure to govern or, even to accept, the uncertain character of both the benefits and risks of innovation.

Above all, science-based regulation limits itself to simply modelling risks, and hence assuming that risks can be modelled. In this way, the radical uncertainties are backgrounded, if not ignored. Actually, in the current global trade regime, risk assessment is a political act (see Van Asselt, Versluis and Vos 2013), as it suggests that there is sufficient scientific uncertainty to model the risks. Nonetheless, and to the degree that uncertainty still exists, the 'political' act of risk assessment also acts to depoliticize debate. As Julia Black has cogently observed: '[F]raming regulatory problems as risks allows regulators to argue that certain regulatory failures are not regulatory failures at all, but normal events, which are to be expected, and for which they are not to blame' (Black 2007: 58). Within this constellation, personal and social responsibility for uncertainty is denied. The obfuscating couplet of 'risk' and 'normality' instead makes us all ('complicit') victims in the face of fate (Everson 2012). Framing trade conflicts as risk issues dilutes responsibility:

> You need courage to make a decision and that is what at certain times is missing in politicians. They don't want to show any courage because they

> want to have the freedom to say: 'I cannot do anything else other than to accept the conclusion'. But that is not the politician's job. Therefore you need the courage to make a decision, notwithstanding the question of whether it's certain or not.
>
> (Kaliarnta, Hage and Roeser, this volume, p. 244)

So the core weaknesses of regulatory regimes, including the global trade regime, are not simply ones of a failure to properly institutionalize the scientific bases for our decision-making or the global inability to establish a regulatory system of oversight that is sufficiently sensitive to the spread of systemic risk (Black and Baldwin 2010). The core weaknesses are far more ones of our lack of responsibility, wilful self-deception or 'blind optimism' (Majone 2013) with regard to the misplaced faith which we have placed in the ability of indeterminate methodologies of science to master uncertainty. This misplaced faith in turn is reifying the uncertainty paradox[1] (Van Asselt and Vos 2006, 2008), which, as has been demonstrated in various case studies, causes regulatory complexities, if not unintelligibility, and provides a fruitful basis for what Beck (1986) has referred to as organized irresponsibility.

Mariachiara Tallacchini's contribution to this volume, amongst others, reminds us that some actors have long recognized, not least from within a scientific community (Everson and Vos 2009), the central place and problem of scientific uncertainty within global trade regimes. The consequence of the degree of authority that is ascribed to science by the law and decision-makers, and which has been termed the 'meta-legal authority of science' (Joerges 1997: 320), is that social and ethical interests must continue to struggle for attention (see also Van Asselt, Versluis and Vos 2013). Conversely, the lack of political readiness to accept responsibility for decision-making under conditions of uncertainty – and especially so, under conditions of 'radical uncertainty' (Van Asselt 2000; Tallacchini, this volume, p. 80) – may have retarded the evolution of, or public recognition for, a form of regulatory science that seeks to bridge the epistemological divide, incorporating a measure of public voice and/or public responsibility within scientific decision-making at the level of the identification of the premises of regulatory investigation (Bouder in this volume). If political responsibility would be assumed, science might be encouraged to develop different, more modest, however fruitful, ways to contribute to the governance of trade.

Scientification and the problem of power

Yet, the conflation of risk and uncertainty and the denial of political and public responsibility for 'uncertain decision-making' contributes to a preternatural absence of the discussion of the unwarranted influence of 'power' and (commercial) interests within much of recent regulatory debate. The fear that regulatory regimes might be subverted by powerful actors within regulated industries, or diverted to serve the needs and requirements of particularly powerful commercial interests, was a constant feature of regulatory debate in the 1970s (see, for example, Stiglitz *et al.* 1989). Most commonly enunciated as a danger of 'agency capture', the notion that powerful industrial interests would seek to subvert regulation to its own ends nonetheless began to disappear from academic literature in the late 1980s, with a few notable exceptions (Shapiro 1988). Regulatory debates began to coalesce with notions of governance, especially at the global level, in which private actors are primarily framed as stakeholders and in which the power question is less pronounced. Models of government founded in theories of command and control were slowly replaced by new forms of economic organization and novel understandings of consensual decision-making, in which the issue of ill-intentioned commercial power is hardly addressed or even unpopular. A new range of regulatory models, applicable and applied at national and international level, which seek to establish 'smart' or 'responsive' regulation, reflect a radical alteration in our perception of how steering capacities within the modern economy are exercised and to what end (Vibert 2011).

In a governance view, steering capacities cannot be assured through political fiat. Instead, steering is possible only where political capacity acts *within* a network of public–private relations. The blurring of the public and the private and the flattening of distinctions between governors and governed are not considered principally problematic, but are accepted. At the same time, however, this shift in modes of economic organization, and its regulation, has also entailed its own fundamental alteration within our understanding of government, as commercial interests that were once regarded to be, at best, 'troublesome' in character, have been recast as 'stakeholders' and partners in a joint enterprise, a process of 'good' governance, which ensures general welfare through processes of economic growth.

However, this assumption is inexorably challenged by financial crisis. Above all, in addition to clear instances of social abuse for financial gain (Block 2013), the particularly close relations between regulators and industry in the matter of the setting of economic solvency margins in the regulatory systems for financial services have been identified as intensifying and precipitating the rapid spread of systemic risk (Black 2010). Power, and its misuse, is therefore back as a topic for discussion on regulation and governance. Recent discussions on the dependence[2] and the lack of independence of the European agencies from industry and the problems of the 'revolving doors' (European Court of Auditors 2012; European Parliament 2012) underline this. As the important contribution to this volume by Robert V. Percival details, 30 years of market-orientedness have also impacted on the mode in which power may be exercised within trade regimes.

Robert V. Percival's analysis of US environmental law corrects one misperception and raises one conundrum. As Percival indicates, the precautionary principle is no stranger to US law than it is to European legal systems. Instead, courts within the US have, in fact, applied a precautionary principle, remarkably similar in character to the constitutionalized standard of protection more commonly thought to be a feature of the EU governance regime; and they first did so in the 1970s. However, and notwithstanding the great degree of independence afforded to the US Environmental Protection Agency, US regulatory influence on the global environmental stage is more commonly identified with rejection of precaution and a deep mistrust for the concomitant acceptance of lost-opportunity costs, which also fuels resistance to trade restrictions. Percival hints that this may be due to a prevailing paradigm of free trade, in which commercial interests also exercise considerable influence.

In other words, and expanding on the analysis, power interests do impact on the global regulatory regime, but do so in an indirect manner. Power, it would seem, is no longer a matter of 'purchasing' the regulator, but is far more a matter of the usurpation of the agenda for, and the framing of, the debate, such that the regulator and regulated no longer recognize that alternative opportunities for action exist (Lukes 2005). Global economic growth through trade would thus seem to be an imperative, which, despite constant challenges before the WTO, nonetheless achieves hegemonic status as it is presented as a fixed good, rather than one of a range of options. Economic imperatives and interests coalesce with science-based regulation. The seizing of the mind of the international trade regime has resulted in what may be referred to as depoliticization or scientification of the regulation of global trade.

Agenda-setting is a powerful force in human affairs and commercial interests have successfully used it to target the international trade regime in order to pursue their own deregulatory goals and interests. In its turn, scientification of regulation in an era in which governance is a leading icon, hides the exercise of industry power from view. This dimension and the effects of the scientification of trade regulation have not been granted sufficient attention. We are not principally contesting the idea of governance as a normative model for regulation, but we argue that it should not imply that important questions of power remain unasked. In new regulatory models, old questions of power need to be asked, not just by industries, but also by NGOs, the media and experts acting as stealth advocates (see also Pielke 2007 and Löfstedt *et al.* 2011).

Precaution has also become a controversial element within the internal EU trade environment, with its stronger emphasis upon social and ethical concerns (see Tallacchini and Millstone in this volume). The 'capture' of a supranational trade regime, designed also to respect non-trade interests and concerns, can perhaps also be argued to owe something to the evolution of a dominant rationality of 'scientification' and hence depoliticization (Everson and Vos 2009; see also Millstone in this volume). Due to depoliticization the results of the regulatory debate cannot be traced back to particular individuals or commercial interests. Instead, the power of rationality is exercised from within the trade regime itself, as scientification processes not only usurp the agenda for debate, but also the very terms in which it is carried out.

Re-establishment of political responsibility, not only with regard to the mastering of uncertainty, but also with due consideration for control of power within a science-based trade regime, is needed. However, the contributions to this volume reveal that it requires a much more complex matter of challenging a dominant rationality, which, in its unquestioning reliance upon the neutrality and 'objective rationality' of scientific risk assessment, similarly privileges the trade and economic imperative above non-economic concerns (see also Van Asselt, Versluis and Vos 2013; Everson 2012).

A crisis of science or a crisis of law?

Addressing this complex problem of political responsibility must thus surely be a matter of encouraging a meaningful debate, in order to accepting competing rationalities, in such a way that no single rationality is privileged. Within the current complex of science-based regulation of trade, the final arbiter between trade interests and non-trade concerns remains the law. This raises a further epistemological problem, as the legal order accordingly struggles, first, to enunciate uncertainty within its own methodological terms and, second, to recognize alternative interests or rationalities founded in politics and civil society, rather than the putative universalisms of science or economics.

The partial emergence of a principle of precaution within the global trade regime and, in particular, its concretization as a 'constitutionalized' principle within the EU legal order, might be greeted as a reassertion of political control within the trade regime or even as a principled assertion of the primacy of ethical and social concerns in the face of scientific uncertainty. Nevertheless, the precautionary approach has proven to be a disappointment in its legal operalization, not only because WTO panels have been reluctant to give it full recognition (see Prévost in this volume). Instead, as various contributions to this volume once again confirm (Peeters, Prévost and Vos), application of the principle of precaution within the adjudicative legal arena only heightens epistemological dissonance as the law struggles with the problems posed by risk and uncertainty within its own methodologies.

The contribution by Marjan Peeters raises a suspicion that normative enunciation of the precautionary principle is also representative of political failings, as issues that are too difficult to treat through political negotiation are shifted to the judicial arena. This actually reifies the role of the law as arbiter, while making it more demanding at the same time to fulfil this role. The notion of precaution is, by virtue of its indeterminate nature, highly challenging for legal methodology. Above all, within the context of post-national law, the need to fill the principle of precaution raises a danger that law will create its own substantive value of precaution.

In this regard, suspicions have been raised that post-national law, especially to the degree that legal enunciation of the principle of 'efficiency' reflects the growing power of the law and economics movement within the global legal order (Mattei and Nader 2008), has itself become a servant of deregulatory commercial interests. As detailed by Denise Prévost in this volume, the absolute or partial refusal of WTO panels to adopt the precautionary approach, as well as their preparedness to engage in substantive review of scientific findings and their hostility towards notions of scientific uncertainty, might be taken as proof that free trade interests have superseded the principle of precaution within the global legal order. Ellen Vos in this volume shows that the Court of Justice of the European Union (CJEU) also struggles with regard to its application of the principle of precaution. Most notably, the CJEU also seeks to engage in substantive review of scientific findings: a review which is necessarily frustrated as the Court paradoxically finds itself demanding *impossible* scientific proofs for scientific findings of uncertainty (Van Asselt and Vos 2006).

The CJEU's struggles with precaution hint at a far deeper crisis, or process of scientification, within modern legal rationalities. Post-national law is struggling to identify a non-naturalistic basis for its post-national legitimacy. The lure of the law and economics movement cannot be equated with the simple capture of law by economic interests. Instead, the marriage of law and economics, which is witnessed in legal promotion of efficiency principles, is one that promises law a universal and objective legitimacy within an economic science of market relationships. This claim can be and is strongly doubted, not least from within economically oriented doctrines of legal operation (Mestmäcker 2007). To the global trade order, however, the same universalizing aspirations surely also apply to the legal relationship with science. Science, with its universalist promise, offers law a universality of legitimate application. 'Indeterminate science' – or, the recognition that the premises of science are contingent and are always, by their very nature, uncertain – creates an epistemological dissonance within the legal system, which it has difficulty tolerating, let alone addressing.

Can science-based decision-making survive in the post-trust era?

As Frederic Bouder points out in his contribution to this volume, publics have changed in their trust in the scientific basis for decision-making. In Bouder's analysis, loss of trust is prevalent, and significant political consequences, in particular in the area of pharmaceutical regulation, are demonstrated. The spectre raised by public responses to scandals, such as those of substandard breast implants, is one of wholesale abandonment of the scientific basis for decision-making in this area. It can be argued that the global financial crisis has precipitated scepticism and even public hostility towards experts, who have dominated the regulatory sphere for so long, albeit that, in some cases, experts are preferred above politicians (see, e.g., the acceptance of technocratic government in Italy). The societal dynamics described in contributions to this volume raise the interesting issue of whether, and if so how, science-based decision-making can survive in a post-trust era.

At the same time, it is also clear that science can inject much-needed competence and intelligence into the regulatory system, which is otherwise far too vulnerable to the demands of politics (Jasanoff 1990). Demanding an evidential basis for decision-making, the use of science in international regulation has also emerged in a 'deliberative' guise (Joerges and Neyer 1997).

Science forces national authorities to justify the premises for their regulatory regimes. At one and the same time, the forensic qualities of scientific regimes can act to unmask ill-justified national protectionist interests and to force national governments to consider the interests of others excluded from national decision-making processes. As Christian Joerges (2013) has observed, the emergence of science as an evidential standard has done much to ameliorate the inevitably exclusionary tendencies of the nation state and to found a global civil society or democracy, not in impossible visions of the global collective, but in the pragmatic process of the balancing of the myriad of deliberatively justifiable national interests on the international stage.

This globally civilizing impact of evidential, science-based decision-making is without doubt inspirational and is, perhaps, justification enough for the effort to secure the use of science within international and supranational trading regimes. Yet, 'inclusion of the other' within national decision-making is not the only benefit to accrue to a role of science in regulation. Instead, in addition to its crucial contribution to forms of global citizenship, science and evidential decision-making have also done much to correct democratic deficits *within* the national setting. Output legitimacy does matter (Majone 2013). In particular, within the context of complex post-industrial societies facing complex and interrelated challenges of economic, social and ethical organization, traditional administrative modes of top-down executive government – both by virtue of their inexpert nature and as a result of their obscurantism – not only pose dangers in terms of inefficient or 'poor' decision-making, but may also mask power interests. By contrast, innovative models of science-based governance may act to reintegrate public concerns within executive decision-making, unmasking rather than concealing power and guaranteeing the quality of, and enhancing the inclusive character of, decision-making.

Beyond scientification: an impossible wish list?

This volume points out that the difficulties and problems inherent in the use of science-based decision-making within the global and European trade orders may not be laid at the door of science as such. Instead, the core problem resides in far more general failures: first, an inability to understand the methodologies of science at public and at political level; second, a related refusal to recognize uncertainty and the limits inherent in scientific methodology; and third, and vitally so, a reluctance to re-establish political responsibility. Addressing such problems is undoubtedly a daunting process. We have written elsewhere of the dangers posed by a silent threat of 'scientification' (Everson and Vos 2009).

This depoliticizing concept may be expanded in order to encompass a process, whereby the political will to engage with complex uncertainties is itself overcome by a misplaced faith in rationality, or the universalism promise of a scientific method, which absolves decision-makers from all responsibility for the consequences arising. Science is merely 'science', a 'mirror onto the world'

(Laski 1935): a universally oriented representation of it, which aids in our understanding of natural and social phenomena. Scientific methods seek to provide us with universal understandings, but science is not itself, intrinsically, universal. Nor is it a neutral instrument of public policy.

At the more pragmatic level of the establishment of science-based trade regimes therefore, the effort to overcome epistemological dissonance, or the failure to delimit scientific method, must accordingly focus upon the re-establishment of political responsibility for political actions. Remaining initially within the ambit of regime design, rather than operation, the primary building block in this effort must be one of re-establishing the distinction between what have been termed 'simple risks' and 'uncertain, ambiguous and/or complex risks', usually abbreviated to uncertain risks (Van Asselt and Renn 2011). Where simple risks to a certain extent can be modelled and calculated, different modes of appraising, assessing, managing and communicating are needed for uncertain risks.

At one and the same time a means of re-establishing political responsibility and a mode of controlling the 'mind-seizing' powers of the promise of universal rationality, the institutionalization of the distinction between simple and uncertain risk would be most easily achieved through vigorous assertion of the precautionary principle and, above all, assertion of its politicized rather than objective nature. Precaution is a political decision, for which political responsibility must be assumed, and not one which can be delegated to the substantive review of international courts, such as the CJEU or WTO panels. At the same time, explicit politicization of the precautionary principle would allow the globalizing legal order to escape the chimera of universalizing legal-scientific rationalities and to return to its primary function of the control of power (Mestmäcker 2007) at this interface between trade, environmental, social or ethical concerns. Reborn as a procedural, rather than absolute concept within constitutional law, the purpose of adjudication on precaution must surely be a simple one of testing the appropriateness of the scientific evidence relied upon and by procedural correctness maintained within political decision-making, which directly addresses the problem of uncertainty (see Vos, in this volume).

The primary re-establishment of political responsibility within global and supranational trade regimes in the overdue reiteration of the complex significance of uncertainty (Van Asselt 2005) will undoubtedly do much to restore public faith in global trade regimes and indeed is already playing its part in regulatory response to financial crisis:

> Financial economics is heading back towards the world as Keynes and Hayek knew it: where economic uncertainty was recognized as such, rather than mathematized and missold as controllable risks.
>
> (*Guardian* Editorial, 'On knowing too much', 10.09.2012)[3]

Nonetheless, where public faith in science-based decision-making also relates to its output legitimacy, or its ability to provide the correct and preferably 'good' regulatory results, negative public perception within the post-trust environment must be combated by a global trading regime which: first, secures the advantages of evidential decision-making, or efficiency and transparency; and second also combats scientification or depoliticization tendencies, including at the level of day-to-day decision-making.

To this degree, the notion of an 'efficient' global trading regulation must be viewed in a more nuanced light. The global efficiency advantages of the daily myriad of uncontested processes of science-based risk regulation are highlighted in Kaliarnta, Hage and Roeser (this volume). Nonetheless, and without prejudice to the efficiency of these processes, a mode must be found to respond to the recognition that the act of risk assessment can also be understood to be political in character, at least to the degree that, in the complex global regulatory arena of interrelated and ever evolving economic activities and concomitant environmental uncertainty, daily responses to possible hazard are also part of a complex and *political* process of risk framing and agenda setting (Van Asselt, Versluis and Vos 2013). In other words, trade regimes must recognize and respond properly to 'radical uncertainty' (Tallacchini, in this volume), withstand the daily powers of trade-based interests (Percival, in this volume) and also be made transparent to public concerns. Such transparency, however, or the incorporation of stakeholder interests within the decision-making process must likewise be put in its proper complex and nuanced context: transparency serves a variety of functions. It is not simply a question of procedure, of a tick-box mentality of ensuring the physical presence of social and political interests within science-based decision-making. Instead, transparency and stakeholder participation within supranational or global trading regimes must be understood as serving vital substantive aims of the daily politicization of trade regulation: enhancing its responsiveness to radical uncertainty (divergent scientific opinions), furnishing a political basis for risk assessment (inclusion of ethical and social concerns), balancing of trade and social concerns (unveiling protectionist interests) and, perhaps most controversially, re-establishing trust in science-based decision-making by including an emerging post-national civil society within the ambit of political responsibility for international and supranational trade regimes.

Concluding remarks: the ongoing research agenda

The trade conflicts that the EU has faced within the EU or WTO context, detailed in various contributions to this book, reveal the inability of the EU to deal with uncertain risks. The EU regulators operate under the shadow of the WTO requirement of science-based decisions, which makes the focus on science inevitable and problematic as regards uncertain risks. In this light it is unsurprising that the EU failed to properly solve the issue of meat from cloned animals, whilst today it is still struggling to settle the conflicts around genetically modified organisms. As noted, the combination of a demand for the reassertion of the primacy of political responsibility for global trading regimes and the effort to re-establish politics in the daily operation of trade regimes at international and supranational level resolves itself, in detail, into a wish list that may prove impossible to assert in practice, especially at the level of WTO–EU relations. Nevertheless, given the global importance of efforts to respond to post-trust tendencies and to re-establish evidential decision-making, without, however, falling victim to depoliticizing processes of scientification, the work included within this volume represents an important contribution to a demanding research agenda.

Certainly, the models of trade regulation presented within this volume have yet to be perfected and, above all, may be subject to criticism in the light of practitioner contributions and require detailed study of particular areas of regulation. Mariachiara Tallacchini's reworking of the precautionary principle as a response to radical uncertainty finds support in Bärbel Dorbeck-Jung's investigation of the new regime governing nanotechnologies within the EU: diverse social interests can be brought together to impact upon agenda-setting risk assessment. However, as Sofia Kaliarnta, Maria Hage and Sabine Roeser similarly note, regulators are quite often overwhelmed by the variety of interests with which they are presented. Which stakeholders should they consult and when? Erik Millstone searches for regulatory models where risk assessment is no longer an obligatory point of passage, model fuelling scientification and depoliticization, but where risk assessment serves as a resource, while at the same the limits of science are acknowledged. In this model, participation (also of a political and social character) may precipitate a sense of 'inclusion' once a final risk assessment is established on the basis of a collection of diverging substantive assessments of what constitutes a risk. Finally, Bärbel Dorbeck-Jung's faith in the notion of responsive regulation may be justified in terms, for example, of increasing the global trade regime's ability to identify and react to new and hence uncertain risks.

With this volume we hope to have given a constructive contribution to the debate on how to regulate trade in general and in particular with regard to innovative products and technologies that are accompanied not only by (uncertain) benefits, but also by (potential) risks. At the same time, however, we are aware of the complexity of the debate and underline the need for ongoing and interdisciplinary research on this issue. Above all, as the interview with Kartika Liotard demonstrates, conflicts between trade interests and ethical concerns do have an enormous impact upon the structures of the EU. The need for the development of sensible structures, wherein competing interests can be transparently balanced, is an urgent one.

In our title and in our introduction we stress that Europe is being put to the test with regard to scientific uncertainty. In our conclusion, however, we have no firm answer as to whether Europe has met this test. Above all, when the European dilemma is placed in the far broader context of the global regime, we are left with a further conundrum: will Europe be able to change in the direction to which we aspire on its own, or are changes in the international trade regime needed before Europe can innovate?

Notes

1 Although uncertainty is acknowledged, not only by regulators, but also by courts, the role of science and experts is always framed in terms of providing certainty about uncertain risks (Van Asselt and Vos 2006, 2008).

2 See Van Asselt and Vos (2008) for an example of agencies' dependency on industry in the regulation of genetically modified organisms (GMOs).

3 In response to UK proposals to split 'casino' and 'high-street' banking business.

References

Beck, U. (1986) *Risk Society: Towards a New Modernity*, London: Sage.

Black, J. (2007) 'Tensions in the Regulatory State', *Public Law*, 58–73.

——(2010) 'Restructuring Global and EU Financial Regulation: Capacities, Coordination and Learning', LSE Law, Society and Economy Working Papers 18/2010, London School of Economics and Political Science.

Black, J. and Baldwin, R. (2010) 'Really Responsive Risk-Based Regulation', *Law & Policy*, 32(2): 181–213.

Block, F. (2013) 'Relational Work and the Law: Recapturing the Legal Realist Critique of Market Fundamentalism', *Journal of Law & Society*, forthcoming.

European Court of Auditors (2012) *Management of Conflict of Interest in Selected EU Agencies*, Special Report No. 15 2012.

European Parliament (2012) *European Parliament Decision of 10 May 2012 on Discharge in Respect of the Implementation of the Budget of the European Medicines Agency for the Financial Year 2010* (C7–0281/2011 – 2011/2220[DEC]).

Everson, M. (2012) 'A Technology of Expertise: EU Financial Services Agencies', LSE 'Europe in Question' Discussion Paper Series, LEQS Paper No. 49/2012.

——(2013) 'Je t'accuse: The Fault of (European) Law in (Economic) Political and Social Crisis Law in Crisis', *Law & Critique*, forthcoming.

Everson, M. and Vos, E.I.L. (eds) (2009) *Uncertain Risks Regulated*, London: Routledge/Cavendish Publishing.

Jasanoff, S. (1990) *The Fifth Branch: Science Advisers as Policy Makers*, Cambridge: Harvard University Press.

Joerges, Ch. (1997) 'Scientific Expertise in Social Regulation and the European Court of Justice: Legal Framework for Denationalised Governance Structures', in: C. Joerges, K.H. Ladeur and E. Vos (eds), *Integrating Scientific Expertise into Regulatory Decision-Making – National Experiences and European Innovations*, Baden-Baden: Nomos, pp. 295–324.

——(2013) 'What is Left of the Integration through Law Project? A Reconstruction in Conflicts-Law Perspectives', in: S. Kadelbach (ed.), *Legal Cultures, Legal Transfer, and Legal Pluralism*, Frankfurt/New York: Campus, forthcoming.

Joerges, Ch. and Neyer, J. (1997) 'Transforming Strategic Interaction into Deliberative Problem-solving: European Comitology in the Foodstuff Sector', *Journal of European Public Policy*, 4: 609–25.

Laski, H. (1935) *Studies in Law and Politics*, reproduced in P. Hirst (1993) *The Pluralist Theory of the State*, London: Routledge.

Löfstedt, R., Bouder, F., Wardman, J.K. and Chakraborty, S. (2011) 'The Changing Nature of Regulation and Communication of Risk in Europe', *Journal of Risk Research* – Special issue, 'Uncertainty, Precaution and Risk Governance', 14(4): 409–29.

Lukes, S. (2005) *Power: A Radical View*, 2nd edn, London: Palgrave Macmillan.
Majone, G. (2013) *The EU in Comparative Context: Regional Integration and Political Transaction Costs*, Cambridge: Cambridge University Press, forthcoming.
Mattei, U. and Nader, L. (2008) *Plunder: When the Rule of Law is Illegal*, Oxford: Blackwell.
Mestmäcker, E-J. (2007) *A Legal Theory Without Law – Posner v. Hayek on Economic Analysis of Law* (Beiträge zur Ordnungstheorie und Ordnungspolitik series), Tübingen: Mohr Siebeck.
Nowotny, H. (2008) *Insatiable Curiosity: Innovation in a Fragile Future*, Boston: MIT Press.
Pielke Jr., R.A. (2007) *The Honest Broker: Making Sense of Science in Policy and Politics*, New York: Cambridge University Press.
Shapiro, M. (1988) *Who Guards the Guardians? Judicial Control of Administration*, Athens: University of Georgia Press.
Stiglitz, J. *et al.* (1989) *The Economic Role of the State: The Road to Nowhere?* Oxford: Basil Blackwell.
Van Asselt, M.B.A. (2000) *Perspectives on Uncertainty and Risk: The PRIMA Approach to Decision Support*, Dordrecht: Kluwer Academic Publishers.
——(2005) 'The Complex Significance of Uncertainty in a Risk Era: Logics, Manners and Strategies in Use', *International Journal for Risk Assessment and Management*, 5(2/3/4): 125–58.
Van Asselt, M.B.A. and Vos, E. (2006) 'Precautionary Principle and the Uncertainty Paradox', *Journal of Risk Research*, 313–36.
——(2008) 'Wrestling with Uncertainty: EU Regulation of GMOs and the Uncertainty Paradox', *Journal of Risk Research*, 11(1/2): 281–300.
Van Asselt, M.B.A. and Renn, O. (2011) 'Risk Governance', *Journal of Risk Research* – special issue 'Uncertainty, Precaution and Risk Governance', 14(4): 431–49.
Van Asselt, M.B.A., Versluis, E. and Vos, E. (eds) (2013) *Balancing between Trade and Risk: Integrating Legal and Social Science Perspectives*, London: Routledge.
Vibert, F. (2011) 'Regulation in an Age of Austerity: Reframing International Regulatory Policies', LSE Working Paper, WP 03/2011 2011.

Part II

Science and precaution in regulatory decision-making

1 Risk, uncertainty and precaution

Lessons from the history of US environmental law

Robert V. Percival

One of the most important functions of government is to protect public health and the environment from exposure to environmental risk. Through the enactment of environmental laws governments have established regulatory programmes that seek to provide comprehensive protection against environmental harm. Yet regulatory policy inevitably must confront considerable uncertainty in assessing risks and determining how to control them most effectively. As society struggles to forge rough consensus over appropriate approaches to regulation in the face of this uncertainty, decisions to regulate or not to regulate individual products, chemicals or pollutants often generate enormous controversy.

The precautionary principle wisely counsels that lack of full scientific certainty should not preclude the adoption of prudent precautionary measures to prevent harm. Although the precautionary principle has been widely embraced, it is often misunderstood and has even become a focus of controversy (Percival 2006). Regulatory policy generally seeks to prevent harm before it occurs, but the reality is that it usually has been more reactive than precautionary, responding only after harm has become manifest (Percival 1998; Percival *et al.* 2009). As regulators seek to improve their responses to new and emerging environmental risks, it is useful to consider what lessons can be learned from past experience with regulatory policy.

This chapter reviews controversies over regulatory policy through the lens of history. First it discusses the precautionary principle and why it is valuable even if it does not purport to answer the question of how stringent regulatory policy should be. Then it considers recent studies that assess whether regulatory policy is more precautionary in the United States (US) or the European Union (EU) and why it is difficult to make confident, comparative conclusions. The chapter then examines the history of how precaution has been incorporated into US environmental law. It demonstrates that, despite the law's promise to prevent harm before it occurs, regulatory policy has been largely reactive, concentrating primarily on highly visible problems only after harm has become manifest. After reviewing the state of contemporary regulatory politics in the US, the chapter analyses lessons that can be learned to improve future regulatory policy.

The precautionary principle and global environmental law

Globalization and expanding world trade are creating new pressures to harmonize environmental standards. Countries increasingly are borrowing legal and regulatory policy innovations from one another, moving toward greater harmonization of regulatory policies. As traditional distinctions between domestic and international law and private and public law are blurring, I have argued that a new kind of 'global environmental law' is emerging (Percival 2009; Yang and Percival 2009; Percival 2011). Non-governmental organizations (NGOs) and national regulatory officials increasingly coordinate their activities on a global scale. Even countries with very different legal and political traditions are borrowing legal and regulatory innovations from each other. For example, the EU's programme requiring registration, evaluation, authorization and restriction of chemicals (REACH) is becoming highly influential in shaping approaches to chemical regulation in countries outside the EU (see Part II).

The precautionary principle

As global environmental law has developed, one of the most broadly adopted concepts has been the precautionary principle. Although there are different formulations of the precautionary principle, the most widely embraced is the one articulated in Principle 15 of the Rio Declaration, signed by representatives of 178 nations at the United Nations Summit on Environment and Development (UNCED) in 1992. This states:

> In order to protect the environment, the precautionary approach shall be widely applied by States according to their capabilities. Where there are threats of serious or irreversible damage, lack of full scientific certainty shall not be used as a reason for postponing cost-effective measures to prevent environmental degradation.[1]

This version of the precautionary principle does not purport to dictate how precautionary regulatory policy should be. Rather it states only that, if there are threats of significant harm, scientific uncertainty should not serve as an excuse to reject cost-effective, preventive measures. It does not specify how significant the harm must be to trigger a regulatory response or what particular preventive measures should be undertaken to address it. Thus, the precautionary principle should not be viewed as an effort to establish any particular, prescriptive decision rule.

The Rio Declaration's statement of the precautionary principle has been widely embraced in subsequent international agreements. Some argue that the principle now is so widely accepted that it should be recognized as customary international law. Others disagree (Zander 2010). Language virtually identical to the Rio Declaration's articulation of the precautionary principle was incorporated into the 1992 Framework Convention on Climate Change[2] and in the Preamble to the Convention on Biological Diversity.[3] The EU has expressly endorsed the precautionary principle and incorporated it in some of its regulatory directives. The Maastricht Treaty of 1992 adopted the precautionary principle without explaining what it provides, and today Article 191(2) of the Treaty on the Functioning of the EU refers to the precautionary principle as part of environmental policy.

In February 2000 the European Commission issued a Communication on the Precautionary Principle to explain in considerable detail its views concerning what the principle is and how it should be applied in EU environmental policy decisions.[4] The US government has been reluctant to embrace the precautionary principle, even though it generally is consistent with the thrust of most US environmental laws, as discussed below.

Criticisms of the precautionary principle

The precautionary principle has come under fire from critics who believe that it will exacerbate what they perceive as overly stringent regulatory policies. Frank Cross argues that 'the precautionary principle is deeply perverse in its implications for the environment and human welfare' (Cross 1996). Bjørn Lomborg argues that, if it is used to strengthen environmental regulations, 'the precautionary principle is actually all about making worse decisions than we need to' (Lomborg 2001). Robert Hahn and Cass Sunstein argue that 'taken seriously, the precautionary principle can be paralyzing, providing no direction at all' (Hahn and Sunstein 2005). Sunstein argues that the precautionary principle is incoherent, potentially paralyzing, and that it will lead regulators to make bad choices (Sunstein 2005). Implicit in their arguments is the notion that society faces greater peril from overly precautionary regulations than from risks whose effect on human health and the environment is not fully understood at present.

To a large extent critics of the precautionary principle (e.g. Cross 1996; Hahn and Sunstein 2005; Sunstein 2005) are attacking a straw man. Because the precautionary principle does not purport to dictate how stringent precautionary regulatory policy should be, it cannot fairly be blamed for perceived instances of overregulation, as I previously have argued (Percival 2006). The essential notion embodied in the precautionary principle – that uncertainty should not be used as an excuse to eschew cost-effective preventive measures – is unassailable. It does not require that innovation come to a halt whenever any risks may be conjured. Properly understood, the precautionary principle is neither incoherent nor paralyzing; nor is it a prescription for overregulation. Rather, it cautions that regulatory policy should be proactive in responding to uncertainty concerning potentially serious threats to human health and the environment, mindful of the potential consequences for future generations.

Critics of the precautionary principle concede that the formulation articulated in the Rio Declaration is unobjectionable, but they point to the 'Wingspread Statement on the Precautionary Principle', drafted by a group of academics attending a conference in January 1998. The Wingspread Statement includes the sentence: 'When an activity raises threats of harm to human health or the environment, precautionary measures should be taken even if some cause and effect relationships are not established scientifically.' They use the Wingspread Statement as a straw man to imply that proponents of the precautionary principle seek to prohibit any activity that has the potential to cause harm. However, this is a gross distortion of both the Wingspread Statement and the precautionary principle. It has not been embraced by the larger environmental community or regulatory policymakers. The precautionary principle does not mandate that regulators ban or forgo all new technologies. Instead it supports a nuanced range of regulatory responses and 'a flexible degree of risk aversion' (Applegate 2002). Its critics' claim that society should not ignore potential negative consequences of precautionary regulation 'is a trivial observation for no serious proponent of the precautionary principle disagrees with it' (Kysar 2010). The critics' 'crudely absolutist' caricature of the precautionary principle is simply inaccurate because the principle is 'merely one aspect of a much more elaborate regulatory process in which the precautionary principle is applied with a view toward proportionality of response and adaptability over time' (Kysar 2010).

The most vociferous critics of the precautionary principle argue that cost-benefit analysis is a superior decision tool for regulatory policy because it promises objectivity (e.g. Graham and Wiener 1995; Sunstein 2005). Unlike the precautionary principle, which does not purport to dictate how precautionary regulation should be, cost-benefit analysis counsels that regulation should not be so stringent as to generate compliance costs that exceed the benefits of regulation. Yet the conceptual and empirical difficulty of estimating regulatory costs and benefits actually renders cost-benefit analysis to be a highly uncertain decision tool, albeit one that at its core lacks both 'the virtues of humility and self-awareness that lie at [the] core' of the precautionary principle (Kysar 2010: 250).

Critics of the precautionary principle believe that it will lead to over-regulation and that it may even cause more harm than it prevents. They argue that it will deprive society of 'opportunity benefits' that could prevent even greater harm, or that regulation that it inspires will induce substitution of products or activities that pose even greater risks than those caused by the regulatory target (Cross 1996; Graham and Wiener 1995). Yet there is no basis for assuming that risks that are sufficiently salient to spawn precautionary regulation are systematically more likely to be less risky than the unknown risks of potential substitutes. 'Risk-risk' trade-off analysis is flawed as a decision tool because it focuses only on ancillary risks generated by regulation while ignoring regulation's ancillary benefits (Rascoff and Revesz 2002). The ancillary benefits of regulation (e.g. the Montreal Protocol's phase-out of ozone-depleting substances also reducing greenhouse gases) often are highly significant and there is no reason to believe that they systematically would be less than any ancillary risks of regulation.

In his book *The Laws of Fear* Cass Sunstein argues that the public is overly fearful of certain immediate risks that are statistically less dangerous than what could substitute for them if regulators respond to public demands for precaution (Sunstein 2005). But Sunstein's account ignores the great difficulty of generating political support for regulations that impose immediate, and often visible, costs in order to produce diffuse, and less visible, future benefits (Dana 2003). Embrace of the precautionary principle actually may help overcome political obstacles to collective action to protect against environmental risks. Even Sunstein concedes that some form of the precautionary principle can be useful in responding to risks that are too uncertain to be amenable to cost-benefit analysis, such as particular catastrophic risks and the destruction of biodiversity.

The precautionary principle does not purport to dictate how precautionary regulatory policy should be. Instead it is directed only at deeming a particular argument ('lack of full scientific certainty') as unacceptable as a justification for postponing cost-effective actions to prevent serious or irreversible harm (Sandin *et al.* 2002). Decisions concerning how much protection to afford public health and the environment are embodied in the environmental laws that countries adopt, which represent the authoritative declarations of how precautionary regulatory policy should be. These laws generally do not prescribe any all-encompassing decision rule for setting regulatory policy. Instead they embrace a wide range of regulatory approaches while identifying a host of relevant factors for officials to consider in making regulatory decisions (Percival 2009).

The notion that embrace of the precautionary principle will result in overregulation also is amply refuted by the European Commission's Communication outlining guidelines for using the precautionary principle.[5] The Communication, which was subsequently endorsed by both the European Parliament and the EU Council of Ministers, emphasized flexibility in applying the precautionary principle to combat 'potentially dangerous effects deriving from a phenomenon, product or process [that] have been identified', when 'scientific evaluation does not allow the risk to be determined with sufficient certainty'. The Communication advised that regulatory responses to risk should be 'proportional', 'non-discriminatory' and 'consistent with similar measures already taken'. It endorsed the use of cost-benefit analysis to inform regulatory decisions and it also recognized the importance of reviewing interim regulatory measures in light of new scientific evidence.

As contributors to Michelle Everson and Ellen Vos's book *Uncertain Risks Regulated* emphasize, various countries and institutions apply the precautionary principle in different ways when addressing particular sources of environmental risk (Everson and Vos 2009). This is not surprising in light of the different social, cultural, economic and political factors that influence what risks are targeted by regulatory policy in different countries. As countries increasingly borrow regulatory innovations from one another, cross-cultural differences in regulatory policy are narrowing and the precautionary principle is becoming increasingly popular even though it does not purport to provide any specific decision rule to answer the 'How safe is "safe?"' question.

Comparative studies of regulatory policy

In recent years a rich literature has developed comparing regulatory policies in different countries and assessing the influence of the precautionary principle. In addition to the literature cited above (Everson and Vos 2009; Zander 2010), David Vogel's study of *The Politics of Precaution* (Vogel 2012) and Jonathan Wiener's anthology on *The Reality of Precaution* (Wiener *et al.* 2011) provide detailed analyses of how regulatory policy in the US and EU have responded to a wide range of environmental and safety risks. Both are excellent books that present valuable data, while reaching distinctly different conclusions concerning whether regulatory policy is more precautionary in the EU or the US.

Wiener's 'regulatory parity' thesis

Wiener concludes that, even though the EU has more explicitly embraced the precautionary principle, its member states are not more precautionary than the US in addressing health, safety, environmental and security risks. Based on several case studies comparing the history of regulation in the EU and the US and a quantitative analysis of a sample of 100 risks, Wiener believes that 'Europe and the United States have maintained rough parity across all risks over the past four decades' (Wiener *et al.* 2011: 521). Europe is more precautionary than the US in dealing with some risks; the US is more precautionary in dealing with others. Wiener concludes that the US is now more precautionary than the EU in dealing with the risks of mad cow disease, diesel engine exhaust, particulate air pollution, environmental tobacco smoke, biodiversity loss and terrorism. The EU is now more precautionary in responding to the risks of growth hormones in beef, genetically modified foods, stratospheric ozone destruction, climate change and chemical risks.

Wiener frames his conclusion as a surprise in light of the EU's more explicit embrace of the precautionary principle. Yet, even if one accepts the notion of rough parity in regulatory stringency between the US and EU, it does not contradict the notion that the EU more faithfully adheres to the precautionary principle in its regulatory policy. The relative stringency of regulation is not necessarily an accurate indicator of fidelity to the precautionary principle because the principle does not purport to dictate how stringent regulatory policy should be (Percival 2006).

To be sure, a nation that frequently succumbs to the argument that uncertainty precludes all regulatory action is likely to have less stringent regulations than a nation that faithfully embraces the precautionary principle. But countries in the former ('reactive') category may adopt stringent regulatory responses in reaction to highly visible disasters (e.g. terrorist attacks or a nuclear accident like the Fukushima Daiichi tragedy) that are less likely to occur in countries in the latter ('precautionary') category.

Vogel and the 'flip-flop' toward greater precaution in the EU

In his book *The Politics of Precaution: Regulating Health, Safety, and Environmental Risks in Europe and the United States* (Vogel 2012) David Vogel concludes that, although the US was more precautionary than Europe during the 1970s and early 1980s, the EU today is more precautionary than the US in dealing with risks to human health and the environment. Vogel emphasizes tighter EU regulation of chemical substances, greenhouse gas emissions, agriculture, food and consumer products.

According to Vogel, this shift is the result of political changes in both countries. He cites three factors. First, '[d]uring the last two decades, Europeans have perceived *more* health, safety, and environmental risks caused by business to be both credible and politically unacceptable than have Americans' (Vogel 2012: 34). Second, the politics of regulatory policy in the US has become more 'polarized along ideological and partisan lines' (Vogel 2012: 35) as politicians supported by business interests have sought to demonize regulation. Third, greater emphasis on risk assessment and less deferential judicial review in the US has 'increased the level of scientific evidence necessary to justify new risk regulations'. Recent developments in the US, including the debate over regulatory policy during the 2012 US presidential campaign, provide powerful support for Vogel's second and third arguments.

Comparative regulatory policy: an assessment

Globalization and regulatory diversity

Both Wiener's and Vogel's studies provide powerful support for the notion that globalization is having a profound effect on the evolution of environmental law. In particular, they emphasize that neither the EU nor the US should be viewed as a regulatory monolith. In the US the state of California has adopted more aggressive policies to control climate change and exposure to toxic chemicals than the federal government. These policies have been modelled on the regulatory approach of the EU (Vogel 2012: 16). Vogel acknowledges that 'the nature and mechanisms of global regulatory emulation and policy diffusion have shifted', but he concludes that 'the EU, rather than the American federal government', is now the entity playing the most 'important role in strengthening the risk regulations of many of its trading partners'. He argues that the 'California effect' has become the 'EU effect' with other countries now importing regulatory innovations from the EU, rather than from California.

Wiener also acknowledges the diversity of approaches to regulation employed by California and different EU members. He concedes that the EU now regulates chemicals more stringently than the US, but he questions whether there has been any fundamental 'flop' toward greater regulatory stringency in respect of chemicals in the EU. Wiener appears to seriously underestimate the significance of the EU's REACH (Registration, Evaluation, Authorisation and Restriction of Chemicals) programme as well as EU directives on electronic waste[6] and hazardous substances in electronics and electrical equipment.[7] These programmes represent enormous advances in precautionary regulation that have become highly influential in moving global regulatory policy in a more precautionary direction. REACH requires pre-market toxicity testing of chemicals, both old and new, and it creates incentives to substitute safer chemicals without requiring elaborate proof that harm actually has occurred. The Directives on Wastes from Electronics and Electrical Equipment (WEEE) and Restrictions of Hazardous Substances (RoHS) seek to reduce the presence of toxic chemicals in various products and to ensure their safe disposal.

The global reach of REACH

The EU's REACH programme has had a profound effect on chemical regulation worldwide. It established the European Chemical Agency (ECHA) to manage and coordinate chemical regulation and it requires registration of all chemical substances used in the EU, evaluation of those that may be harmful and authorization for substances believed to pose the greatest risks. A data-gathering process is required of all chemicals, both old and new, that are produced in or sold in quantities greater than one metric ton per year. This must be completed between 2007 and 2018, beginning with substances of very high concern (SVHC), substances known to be very toxic to aquatic organisms and substances supplied in quantities greater than 1,000 metric tons per year. By 1 June 2018 all substances supplied in quantities greater than 1 metric ton per year must be registered. Unregistered substances may not be manufactured in the EU or exported to the EU after 1 June 2018.

All chemical registration applications must be accompanied by a technical dossier and a comprehensive set of information on the chemical's properties, and registration applications for chemicals produced in quantities above 10 metric tons per year must be accompanied by a Chemical Safety Report. Authorization is required only for SVHC. These substances include those that cause cancer or mutations or disrupt reproductive processes (CMRs); persistent, bioaccumulative or toxic substances (PBTs); very persistent or very bioaccumulative substances (vPvBs); persistent organic pollutants (POPs); and other chronic hazards. SVHC must be specifically authorized before they can be used and their manufacturers must find safer replacement substances or ensure that they are 'adequately controlled'. If a SVHC is sold, the manufacturer must prove that the benefits outweigh the risks. Thus, manufacturers are faced with a strong incentive to find safer substitutes rather than endure the authorization process or have their products banned from the market entirely.

Because it applies to foreign manufacturers of products sold in the EU, REACH has had a significant influence throughout the world. Dow Chemical, which estimates that compliance with REACH will cost it between US $100 million and $250 million over 11 years, announced in 2008 that it has decided to prepare REACH-qualifying dossiers for all its chemical products, not just those sold in the EU (Vogel 2012: 169). REACH is a model for California's Green Chemistry Initiative, although California's approach is not as comprehensive as the EU's.[8] Inspired by REACH, Massachusetts in 2008 unanimously passed a 'safer alternatives' law to encourage safer substitutions for ten toxic chemicals.

In January 2010 China introduced its updated chemical notification programme, Measures on Environmental Management of New Chemical Substances, or Order 7. Order 7 became effective on 15 October 2010. Turkey has enacted chemical regulation legislation that resembles REACH; it came into force in January 2010. The law prioritizes testing of substances based on their potential effects on health and the environment and subjects substances with carcinogenic and mutagenic effects to 'specific scrutiny'.

Although Wiener's study questions the relevance of REACH to the precautionary principle, REACH promotes precautionary regulation in two fundamental respects. First, it shifts the burden of proving safety to manufacturers of chemicals (Naiki 2010). Second, it requires them to search for safer substitutes for chemicals shown to pose the greatest risks. When it adopted REACH, the

> European Parliament specifically rejected the United States' model of chemical regulation by adopt[ing] the precautionary principle; REACH, in effect, preempts complete scientific proof of the harm of a chemical by placing the burden of proving a chemical's safety on the industry.
>
> (Benedetto 2010)

REACH responds to uncertainty by mandating data gathering to reduce it. In 2001 the European Environmental Agency completed an inquiry into why government regulators failed to prevent more than a dozen significant environmental problems caused by radiation exposure, benzene, asbestos, PCBs (polychlorinated biphenyls), MTBE (methyl tertiary butyl ether) and other harmful substances (European Environmental Agency 2001). Its report, 'Late Lessons from Early Warnings', emphasized the importance of long-term monitoring and research to reduce ignorance concerning chronic environmental hazards, including those that may cause significant harm with a considerable latency period. REACH's chemical testing programme represents a giant step in this direction. '[M]ore data on chemicals have been assembled and made available to the supply chain and to the public at large than ever before,' as a result of REACH, which 'stimulates risk-management measures and chemical substitutions that enhance safety' (Abelkop *et al.* 2012: 11043).

The EU also has been a pioneer in promoting the notion of producer responsibility for waste and the importance of reducing the generation of toxic residues from electronic products. The EU's RoHS has affected product regulation on a global scale. China, Korea, Taiwan and Japan promptly responded to RoHS by adjusting product designs to eliminate the six toxic chemicals banned under RoHS to ensure continued access to the EU market.

The influence of historical differences between civil and common law regimes

Professor Noga Morag-Levine has conducted extensive research into the historical roots of differences in patterns of risk regulation between common law (the United Kingdom (UK) and the US) and civil law (continental Europe) countries (Morag-Levine 2011). She argues that contemporary regulatory policy differences between the EU and the US actually can be traced to centuries of divergences between Europe's civil law tradition and the common law tradition inherited by the US from the UK (Morag-Levine 2011). Professor Morag-Levine argues that European countries with a civil law tradition favour technology-based regulation as a product of their greater receptivity to the precautionary principle. She maintains that this is a more effective approach to preventing environmental harm than 'the American regulatory paradigm', which 'aspires to scientific determination of the level of pollution mitigation required' (Morag-Levine 2003: 180).

While precautionary regulation emerged in Britain with the adoption of the Alkali Act in 1863, Morag-Levine argues that this Act was directly inspired by French and other continental regulatory models developed under the civil law tradition. This makes it 'easier to reconcile the civil law character of precautionary regulation with the evident presence of that instrument in Victorian Britain' (Morag-Levine 2011: 1). Since the 1980s, differences between British and continental approaches to regulation have narrowed significantly, but Morag-Levine maintains that the historical roots of these divergences still have considerable explanatory power in understanding contemporary differences between US and EU regulatory policy.

US environmental law may in fact be somewhat more precautionary than Morag-Levine's description (Percival 2004), but her conclusion that continental Europe historically has been more precautionary than the US has considerable historical support. Her research into the historical roots of current regulatory policy differences suggests that divergences in legal traditions may remain an obstacle to greater harmonization of global regulatory policy. Although it is difficult to make confident conclusions concerning whether regulatory policy is more precautionary in the US or the EU, comparative study of this history can yield some rich lessons for improving future regulatory policy.

A brief history of precaution in US regulatory policy

This section summarizes the history of environmental risk regulation in the US, which I have discussed in more detail in previous work (Percival 2006). In the nineteenth and early twentieth centuries regulatory policy focused only on the most noticeable environmental risks such as exploding steamship boilers (Rabin 1986) or smelter pollution that visibly altered the surrounding landscape (Percival *et al.* 2009). Highly publicized incidents of harm (e.g. workers dying in the first tetraethyl lead manufacturing plant or deaths from radiation exposure of workers using radium to paint watch dials) generated public clamour for action. Prior to the advent of comprehensive, national regulatory programmes to protect public health, the official response to such incidents was to convene conferences of experts. However, regulatory policy rarely was able to prevent harm from less visible risks posed by chronic, low-level exposures to toxic substances such as lead. Common law liability actions provided some measure of redress for pollution that caused the most obvious environmental harm to private property, but the common law ultimately proved to be too crude a vehicle for safeguarding public health when humans are exposed to multiple environmental risks from numerous sources.

During the decade of the 1970s, the US Congress adopted a series of comprehensive regulatory programmes to protect public health and the environment. These programmes were the product of an extraordinary outpouring of public support for environmental protection, fuelled by the publication of Rachel Carson's *Silent Spring* (Carson 1962), which helped inspire the first Earth Day in April 1970. The initial generation of regulatory programmes to protect the environment incorporated a variety of approaches to determining how precautionary regulatory policy should be – including technology-based regulation, health-based regulation and risk-benefit balancing. Regulations issued to implement these new statutes spawned a host of legal challenges from regulated industries. US courts hearing these challenges initially endorsed precautionary regulation,[9] while expressing concern about how precautionary regulatory policy should be.

In December 1973, US Environmental Protection Agency (EPA) issued its first regulations limiting the amount of tetraethyl lead that could be added to gasoline to 0.5 gpg (grams (of lead) per gallon of gasoline) for all gasoline produced. Lead-additive manufacturers challenged EPA's decision in court. In December 1974, a three-judge panel of the US Court of Appeals for the District of Columbia Circuit struck down the regulations by a 2:1 vote. The court held that there was insufficient evidence to prove that lead emissions 'will endanger the public health or welfare', as required by the Clean Air Act, because it found that 'the case against auto lead emissions is a speculative and inconclusive one at best'. The EPA appealed this decision to the full court, which agreed to rehear the case. In March 1976, the court by a 5:4 vote reversed the three-judge panel's decision and upheld the lead standard.[10]

In a decision that stands as a landmark in its endorsement of precautionary regulation, the court ruled that there was sufficient evidence to regulate lead additives even though it could not be proven with certainty that they endanger public health. The court emphasized the precautionary nature of the Clean Air Act's regulatory mandate. 'Regulatory action may be taken before the threatened harm occurs; indeed the very existence of ... precautionary legislation would seem to demand that regulatory action precede, and, optimally, prevent, the perceived threat.'

The tetraethyl lead manufacturers argued that there was no definitive proof that emissions of lead from gasoline caused harm. They maintained that EPA was required to present some 'dispositive study' to demonstrate that lead additives in gasoline had caused lead poisoning in individuals. The court acknowledged the lack of 'hard proof of any danger', but it rejected the notion that such proof was necessary before precautionary regulation could be implemented.

> Undoubtedly, certainty is the scientific ideal – to the extent that even science can be certain of its truth. But certainty in the complexities of environmental medicine may be achievable only after the fact … . Awaiting certainty will often allow for only reactive, not preventive regulation.[11]

After reviewing the 10,000-page record, the court rejected the industry's claim that a 'dispositive study' had to support EPA's determination, noting that '[b]y its nature, scientific evidence is cumulative'. The court noted the difficulties inherent in determining whether or not lead emissions endanger health,including the existence of multiple sources of human exposure to lead and the difficulties of conducting controlled experiments on humans. However, it upheld EPA's regulation by emphasizing the precautionary purpose of the statute:

> Where a statute is precautionary in nature, the evidence difficult to come by, uncertain, or conflicting because it is on the frontiers of scientific knowledge, the regulations designed to protect public health, and the decision that of an expert administrator, we will not demand rigorous step-by-step proof of cause and effect. Such proof may be impossible to obtain if the precautionary purpose of the statute is to be served.

The *Ethyl* decision remains a landmark in environmental law because of its endorsement of the precautionary principle long before it became a staple of global environmental policy. The decision established that precautionary regulation could be based 'on the inconclusive but suggestive results of numerous studies' indicating that exposure to a substance could endanger health even in the absence of conclusive proof that such adverse health effects actually had occurred. It also indicated that courts would be deferential in reviewing the judgment of the EPA Administrator in assessing the significance of scientific evidence.

Four years later, when confronted with the petroleum industry's claim that tighter limits on worker exposure to benzene would cripple the industry while providing scant benefit to public health, the US Supreme Court mandated that, prior to regulating workplace hazards, the US Occupational Health and Safety Administration (OSHA) should use risk assessment to determine that the risks to be regulated were 'significant' and could be appreciably reduced by regulation.[12] The Court did not specify any specific threshold of 'significance', but it indicated that it probably would lie somewhere between a 1 in 1000 risk that would be considered significant and a 1 in 1 billion risk that probably would not. A plurality of the Court concluded that a statutory command to establish a standard that 'most adequately assures, to the extent feasible, on the basis of the best available evidence', that 'no worker suffers material impairment of health of functional capacity', did not automatically require reducing exposure to carcinogens to the lowest feasible level. Instead the Court conditioned precautionary regulation on the making of threshold findings that such regulation would appreciably reduce risks that appear to be substantial.

The Court's plurality decision did not represent a wholesale rejection of the precautionary approach to regulation. In fact the Court expressly endorsed the notion that conservative default assumptions could be used in risk assessment (so long as 'they are supported by a body of reputable scientific thought'). The Court also specified that risk assessment need not be quantitative, particularly when uncertainty precludes confident quantitative assessments of risk.

By requiring OSHA to assess risks and to determine that they are 'significant' enough to warrant regulation, the Supreme Court fashioned its own kind of 'regulatory common law'. It placed a greater burden on agencies seeking to adopt precautionary regulation, but ultimately this has not proven to be a significant barrier to regulation. In the wake of the Supreme Court's *Industrial Union* ('*Benzene*') decision, US regulatory agencies have relied heavily on risk assessments to justify regulatory decisions even though many risks are impossible to assess with precision. Risk assessment models are most highly developed for carcinogens that pose health risks in probabilistic fashion, but ecological risks and non-cancer health effects are far more difficult to model (US Environmental Protection Agency 1987). Enormous uncertainties also surround the risks of new and emerging technologies, such as biotechnology and nanotechnology.

The Supreme Court's decision ultimately meant that workers had to tolerate exposure to dangerous levels of benzene for nearly a decade longer than OSHA initially had intended when it promulgated an emergency temporary standard in 1977. That standard had been invalidated by a lower court that held that the agency had failed to demonstrate the need to act on an emergency basis. Although it was not until 1987 that OSHA ultimately lowered the permissible exposure limit for benzene to the very level it had sought to adopt a decade earlier, by then the evidence of the significant risks posed by benzene had become so overwhelming that OSHA's decision was not even challenged in court.

The enactment of environmental legislation often has required some 'trigger event', usually a highly publicized incident of visible environmental harm that generates immediate public concern (Percival 1998). Examples include the 'Superfund' legislation adopted in 1980 after highly publicized contamination of homes in Love Canal by previously buried hazardous wastes, the Emergency Planning and Community Right to Know Act adopted in 1986 in response to the Bhopal tragedy and the Oil Pollution Act of 1990 adopted in response to the Exxon Valdez oil spill.

As Vogel cogently demonstrates, US regulatory policy depends in large part on the policy preferences of political leaders (Vogel 2012: 34). Because President Reagan was ideologically opposed to regulation, Congressional distrust of his executive agencies spawned a backlash that led Congress to strengthen the US environmental laws during the 1980s. When it reauthorized the federal regulatory statutes, Congress added new provisions specifying actions that regulatory agencies must take coupled with statutory deadlines for completing them. It also adopted far-reaching legislation in 1986 requiring companies to make annual public disclosures concerning their emissions of toxic chemicals.[13] During the same year California voters adopted the highly precautionary Proposition 65, which prohibits companies from exposing humans without warning to significant risks from carcinogens or reproductive toxins and which places the burden of proof on companies to show that risks are insignificant.

Even though nearly all US environmental statutes authorize regulation prior to definitive proof of harm, it is easier to identify hazards and to predict harm *after* it occurs. In part due to enormous political pressures from the regulated community, federal agencies usually wait for proof of harm before adopting regulations. Most of the chemicals that have been stringently regulated in the US became the focus of regulatory attention only after highly publicized incidents in which they caused visible and substantial harm (Percival 2006). This reflects the facts that regulation is most politically salient when it responds to highly visible harm that has already occurred. Rather than realizing its promise of preventive regulation, US environmental policy usually has been saddled with the far more difficult task of remediating environmental contamination after it has occurred.

The European Environmental Agency's *Late Lessons from Early Warnings* study is one of the few studies to examine why society has failed to prevent chronic environmental harm from toxic substances, such as lead and asbestos, that long were known to be extremely hazardous. Because the neurological harm caused by exposure to lead is largely invisible, efforts to control lead exposure were only successful after decades of damage to public health. This stands in sharp contrast to the regulatory response to the stratospheric ozone depletion problem, a rare instance in which truly precautionary regulation was undertaken solely in response to a seemingly compelling scientific theory before actual harm to public health had been demonstrated (Benedick 1991).

As noted above, the judicial system has played an important role in developing US environmental policy through judicial review of agency regulatory decisions. The US Administrative Procedure Act and the federal environmental statutes generally authorize judicial review of agency action at the behest of anyone adversely affected by it. Although the US Supreme Court has instructed lower courts to defer to agency interpretations of ambiguous regulatory statutes,[14] significant regulatory initiatives have been derailed by the courts. In 1989, after a decade-long investigation, the EPA issued a regulation phasing out nearly all remaining uses of asbestos. The agency concluded that only a phase-out 'will adequately control' the life cycle of asbestos exposure risks that occur whenever the substance is mined, used in manufacturing, released into the environment through deteriorating asbestos-containing products or disposed of.[15] Despite the well-documented dangers of asbestos, this regulation was struck down by a reviewing court which concluded that the agency had failed to perform sufficiently detailed cost-benefit analyses of banning not only each particular use of asbestos, but also of all intermediate alternatives short of a ban. The court required such highly detailed proof, on a product-by-product basis, that benefits outweighed costs, as to render the Toxic Substances Control Act virtually impotent as a regulatory tool.[16]

The *Corrosion Proof Fittings* court applied a kind of reverse precautionary principle. Its decision essentially declared that, for a substance known to cause serious and irreversible damage to health, lack of certainty concerning the costs and benefits of all regulatory alternatives should be used as a reason for not regulating it. The court echoed critics of the precautionary principle who charge that precautionary regulation may create greater risks than it prevents, by chastising EPA for failing to perform detailed analyses of the risks of any potential substitutes for asbestos. Surprisingly, however, the court upheld the government's ban on new uses of asbestos without requiring *any* cost-benefit analysis, noting that 'EPA cannot possibly evaluate the costs and benefits of banning unknown, uninvented products'.[17] This represented a rare endorsement of truly precautionary regulation by permitting future products to be banned even before there was clear evidence to confirm that they actually caused harm.

While the *Corrosion Proof Fittings* decision effectively precluded EPA from banning existing uses of asbestos, most other developed countries have done so and the WTO has upheld such bans in light of the demonstrated dangers of asbestos. As of August 2012, 54 countries, including most EU members, have banned asbestos.[18] In September 2000, a WTO dispute resolution panel upheld France's ban on imports of chrysotile asbestos, rejecting arguments by Canada that it was an unjustified restriction on trade, an argument that representatives of the Canadian asbestos industry had raised unsuccessfully during the EPA rulemaking.[19] The panel concluded that the risks of asbestos had been so thoroughly researched that the ban was justified as necessary to protect human health.

Despite overwhelming proof of harm to health caused by tobacco products, when the US Food and Drug Administration sought to regulate them stringently, the US Supreme Court by a 5:4 vote rejected the agency's finding that cigarettes were 'drug delivery devices' for nicotine that could be regulated by the agency.[20] The Court refused to apply the *Chevron* doctrine of judicial deference to agency interpretations of ambiguous statutory directives because it did not believe that Congress intended to allow the FDA to regulate tobacco.

Despite some judicial reversals of important regulatory initiatives, the regulatory infrastructure of US environmental law generally has survived persistent legal attacks. In 2001 the US Supreme Court unanimously rejected an industry argument that unless the Clean Air Act was interpreted to require that regulations be based on cost-benefit analysis it would be an unconstitutional delegation of legislative authority to the executive.[21] In 2007 the Court by a 5:4 vote ordered EPA to reconsider its refusal to regulate greenhouse gas (GHG) emissions as arbitrary and capricious.[22] As a result of this decision, the US EPA was able to promulgate regulations controlling GHG emissions under the existing Clean Air Act, even though efforts to enact new legislation establishing a comprehensive, national cap-and-trade programme had failed. In June 2012 a panel of the US Court of Appeals for the DC Circuit unanimously rejected all industry challenges to these regulations in a decision deferring to EPA's findings concerning the contribution of GHG emissions to global warming and climate change.[23]

Yet ideological splits over the wisdom of environmental regulation persist in the US judiciary. In August 2012 a panel of the US Court of Appeals for the DC Circuit invalidated EPA's latest effort to control interstate air pollution in a controversial 2:1 decision.[24] The Court's decision was the second time in four years that EPA's effort to tighten such standards was rejected in court.[25] It came despite EPA's estimates that the new regulations would prevent between 13,000 and 34,000 premature deaths each year, generating annual benefits of between US $120 billion and $280 billion at a projected annual cost of $2.4 billion. The Court's decision has been sharply criticized as the product of 'a new breed of activist judges [who] are waging a determined and largely successful war on federal regulatory agencies' through the use of 'legal sophistry, procedural hair-splitting and scientific conjecture' (Pearlstein 2012).

The US Congress also is sharply split on issues of precautionary regulation. The Republican takeover of the US House of Representatives in the 2010 elections produced the most anti-environmental house of Congress in US history. In the 20 months that it was in session before adjourning on 21 September 2012, the 112th Congress has seen 315 anti-environmental measures pass the House.[26] Nearly all these measures have failed to become law because they cannot win passage in the US Senate, which is controlled by Democrats more sympathetic to environmental regulation. Due to the partisan split in the two houses of Congress it has become virtually impossible for Congress to enact any new environmental legislation.

Conclusion: lessons from the history of US regulatory policy

It is far easier to generate political support for controlling risks that cause immediate and highly visible harm than it is for regulating less visible risks that cause harm far into the future. This is well illustrated by the history of US regulatory policy. The first federal regulatory intervention in the US to protect public health was undertaken in 1832 to stop steamship boilers from exploding. In 1915 the US Supreme Court issued its first injunction to control pollution in order to reduce highly visible damage that emissions from copper smelters in Tennessee had caused by destroying all vegetation in a huge swathe of land extending far into the state of Georgia.[27]

With the exception of the remarkable public response to the theory that CFCs could deplete the ozone lawyer, which led EPA to ban ozone-depleting substances in the early 1970s, US regulatory policy has been largely reactive, rather than precautionary. Regulation generally has responded only after harm has become manifest. While the dangers of lead and asbestos were well known to scientists in the early twentieth century, regulatory policy did not respond to them for decades, even as enormous harm to public health accumulated, because the harm they caused was not immediately visible (Percival 2006). The eventual, reactive regulatory responses to the hazards of gasoline lead additives and worker exposure to asbestos have produced enormous benefits to public health, albeit belatedly. Despite this history, US regulatory policy has not aggressively focused on potentially emerging risks posed by the products of biotechnology or nanotechnology (Lin 2007).

Political theory teaches that it is a veritable miracle that the US has such comprehensive and durable environmental statutes. 'It is much easier to understand why environmental laws are needed than it is to comprehend how they came to be adopted' (Percival 1998). Mancur Olson's classic work *The Logic of Collective Action* argues that the political process will not favour collective action to impose concentrated costs on well-organized industry groups in order to prevent diffuse harms to the public (Olson 1965). Yet this theory seemingly is contradicted by the remarkable burst of legislative activity to protect the environment by the US Congress during the 1970s and 1980s. As noted above many of these statutes were the product of a highly publicized 'trigger' event, such as Earth Day, Love Canal, the Bhopal tragedy and the *Exxon Valdez* oil spill (Percival 1998).

Today, however, even highly publicized environmental disasters such as the April 2010 Deepwater Horizon oil spill in the Gulf of Mexico and the March 2011 Fukushima Daiichi nuclear disaster in Japan have not generated any legislative response. The 1989 *Exxon Valdez* oil spill in Alaska broke more than a decade of legislative gridlock over oil pollution legislation, resulting in the adoption by Congress of the Oil Pollution Act of 1990 ('OPA90'). Yet, because legislators always seem to respond to the last disaster, OPA90 focused almost entirely on the kind of oil spill that had just occurred – a spill from a tanker transporting oil. The law did not focus on pollution from offshore oil platforms, the genesis of the Deepwater Horizon disaster. Indeed, OPA90 actually limits liability for oil spills from offshore facilities to US $75 million plus removal costs.[28] Yet, in the wake of the Deepwater Horizon disaster, efforts to repeal this cap failed to pass either house of Congress. One could view these developments as another indication of a perceived 'crisis' – this time the global financial crisis – serving as a 'trigger' for reactive policies, this time policies founded on the false dichotomy that regulation inevitably hurts the economy.

What does seem clear is that the bipartisan consensus concerning the importance of environmental protection that spawned ambitious US environmental legislation during the 1970s and 1980s has now disappeared. During the 2012 US presidential election campaign, the political parties and the electorate were sharply split in their views concerning regulatory policy. Republicans blamed environmental regulation for high unemployment and slow economic growth, while Democrats generally tried to change the subject. Yet, until the 2008 global financial crisis, which produced the greatest economic downturn next to the Great Depression, the US economy prospered despite stringent environmental regulation. Extractive industries, newly freed from the restrictions of campaign finance laws by the Supreme Court's decision that they have a First Amendment free speech right to spend directly on election campaigns,[29] flooded the airwaves with ads blaming high unemployment on environmental regulation. Opponents of regulation usually describe it as 'job-killing' and never as 'life-saving'.

Despite all-time record temperatures and hurricanes that have caused unprecedented devastation to coastal areas, climate change has disappeared from US political discourse. During the 2012 US presidential election, climate change was never once mentioned during three 90-minute debates between the presidential candidates. President Obama's re-election in November 2012 and his political party's gains in both houses of Congress indicate that his opponents' anti-regulatory rhetoric was not decisive with voters. But there is little prospect of new bipartisan agreement on environmental measures, though legislation purporting to bar US airlines from paying EU emissions charges was signed into law on November 27. Thus, Vogel's theory that the US has become less precautionary than the EU because of political polarization is amply supported by recent events.

The political process rarely rewards government officials for focusing on problems that have not been obvious enough to generate demands for immediate action. Vogel explains the EU's adoption of REACH as reflecting 'not only the influence of the precautionary principle, but also several highly visible food safety failures in Europe, as well as the ongoing debate over the safety of GMOs' (Vogel 2012: 177). By adopting the REACH programme the EU set in motion a long-term process for uncovering chemical risks that will greatly facilitate precautionary regulation. Although the US has long resisted adopting a similar testing programme for chemicals, there is one rare example of US officials trying to discover risks in advance of harm. For several years the National Aeronautics and Space Administration (NASA) has been searching for 'Near Earth objects', such as asteroids, that may pose a danger of colliding with Earth.[30]

Vogel also argues that the US is less precautionary than the EU because greater emphasis on risk assessment and less deferential US judicial review has 'increased the level of scientific evidence necessary to justify new risk regulations' (Vogel 2012). While there is some recent evidence to support this claim, the Supreme Court's encouragement of risk assessment in its 1980 '*Benzene*' decision has not greatly handicapped regulatory agencies. Even the *Ethyl Corporation* court expressly endorsed risk assessment in its 1976 decision endorsing precautionary regulation. The very year after it decided the '*Benzene*' case, the US Supreme Court upheld OSHA regulations to protect workers from exposure to cotton dust because they were supported by an agency risk assessment.[31] The Court rejected the argument that OSHA was required to base its decisions on cost-benefit analysis, wisely eschewing an effort to paralyze regulatory action.

Yet Vogel clearly is correct that the US judiciary has impeded precautionary regulation in several cases, including the decision to strike down regulation of tobacco by the federal Food and Drug Administration,[32] the invalidation of EPA's asbestos phase-out regulations[33] and the August 2012 decision striking down EPA's latest effort to tighten controls on interstate air pollution.[34] Like Congress, the judiciary remains closely split between opponents and proponents of precautionary regulation. The opponents have been particularly active in striking down regulations issued in response to the Dodd-Frank Wall Street Financial Reform legislation, seizing on vague language in the statutory charter of the Securities and Exchange Commission (SEC) to demand that SEC rules meet ever more stringent cost-benefit tests.[35]

The enormous (and growing) political clout of regulated industries in the US essentially guarantees that US regulatory agencies cannot adopt overly precautionary policies that significantly overregulate industry. Thus, it is hardly surprising that it has been virtually impossible to identify instances in which precaution has produced significant overregulation by US agencies. While one can identify some US regulatory policies that are more stringent in controlling particular risks than in the EU, the EU clearly has been more innovative in embracing precautionary regulation through programmes like REACH, WEEE and RoHS. These programmes have been enormously influential in the development of regulatory policy throughout the world. Thus, despite current retrenchment in the US, the forces of globalization and the EU's warmer embrace of the precautionary principle ultimately may move the world in a more precautionary direction.

Notes

1 United Nations Environment Programme, Rio Declaration on Environment and Development, Principle 15 (1992) (available at: www.unep.org/Documents.Multilingual/Default.asp?documentid=78& articleid = 1163).
2 Article 3(3), United Nations Framework Convention on Climate Change, 31 I.L. N. 849 (1992).
3 Preamble to the Convention on Biological Diversity 1992.
4 Communication from the Commission on the Precautionary Principle (Commission of the European Communities 2000: 1).
5 Commission of the European Communities, Communication from the Commission on the Precautionary Principle, February 2, 2000.
6 Directive on Wastes from Electronics and Electrical Equipment (WEEE).
7 Directive on Restriction of Hazardous Substances (RoHS).

8 RSJ Technical Consulting, 'What is California Green Chemistry?' (2010), available at: www.rsjtechnical.com/ WhatisCaliforniaREACH.htm, accessed on 23 November 2012.
9 *Ethyl Corporation* v. *EPA*, 541 F.2d 1 (D.C. Cir. 1976) (en banc).
10 Ibid.
11 Ibid.: 24–25.
12 *Industrial Union Dept., AFL-CIO* v. *American Petroleum Institute*, 448 U.S. 607 (1980).
13 Emergency Planning and Community Right to Know Act, 42 U.S.C. §§ 11001–11050 (1986).
14 *Chevron USA* v. *Natural Resources Defense Council* 1984.
15 U.S. Environmental Protection Agency, Asbestos: Manufacture, Importation, Processing, and Distribution in Commerce Prohibitions, 54 Fed. Reg. 29,460 (1989).
16 *Corrosion Proof Fittings* v. *EPA*, 947 F.2d 1201 (5th Cir. 1991).
17 Ibid.
18 International Ban Asbestos Secretariat, Current Asbestos Bans and Restrictions (Revised 26 August 2012) (http://ibasecretariat.org/alpha_ban_list.php, accessed on 23 November 2012).
19 World Trade Organization, European Communities – Measures Affecting Asbestos and Asbestos-Containing Products (WT/DSI35/R, 18 September 2000).
20 *FDA* v. *Brown & Williamson Tobacco Corporation*, 529 U.S. 120 (2000).
21 *Whitman* v. *American Trucking Associations*, 531 U.S. 457 (2001).
22 *Massachusetts* v. *EPA*, 549 U.S. 497 (2007).
23 *Coalition for Responsible Regulation, Inc.* v. *EPA*, 684 F.3d 102 (D.C. Cir. 2012).
24 *EME Homer City Generation, L.P.* v. *Environmental Protection Agency*, 2012 WL 3570721 (D.C. Cir. Aug. 21, 2012).
25 *North Carolina* v. *EPA*, 531 F.3d 896 (D.C. Cir. 2008).
26 Database of Anti-Environment Votes in the 112th Congress, updated September 21, 2012, available at: http://democrats.energycommerce.house.gov/index.php?q=legislative-database-anti-environment&legislation=All&topic=All&statute=All&agency=All, accessed on 23 November 2012.
27 *Georgia* v. *Tennessee Copper Co.*, 237 U.S. 474 (1915).
28 33 U.S.C. 2704(a)(3).
29 *Citizens United* v. *Federal Election Commission*, 558 U.S. 50 (2010).
30 National Aeronautics and Space Administration, Near Earth Object Program, available at: http://neo.jpl.nasa.gov, accessed on 23 November 2012.
31 *American Textile Manufacturers Institute* v. *Donovan*, 452 U.S. 488 (1981).
32 *FDA* v. *Brown & Williamson Tobacco Corporation*, 529 U.S. 120 (2000).
33 *Corrosion Proof Fittings* v. *EPA*, 947 F.2d 1201 (5th Cir. 1991).
34 *EME Homer City Generation, L.P.* v. *Environmental Protection Agency*, 2012 WL 3570721 (D.C. Cir. Aug. 21, 2012).
35 *Business Roundtable* v. *Securities and Exchange Commission*, 647 F.3d 1144 (D.C. Cir. 2011).

References

Abelkop, A., Botos, A., Wise, L. and Graham, J. (2012) 'Regulating Industrial Chemicals: Lessons for US Lawmakers from the European Union's REACH Program', *Environmental Law Reporter*, 42(11): 11042–65.

Applegate, J.S. (2002) 'The Taming of the Precautionary Principle', *William & Mary Environmental Law and Policy Review*, 27(1): 13–78.

Benedetto, C. (2010) 'Is the European Laboratory over-Reach-Ing? The Experimentation, Reaction and Product Yielded by the European Union's Registration, Evaluation, and Authorization of Chemicals', *Villanova Environmental Law Journal*, 21(1): 75–110.

Benedick, R.E. (1991) *Ozone Diplomacy: New Directions in Safeguarding the Planet*, Cambridge: Harvard University Press.

Carson, R. (1962) *Silent Spring*, Boston: Houghton Mifflin Co.

Commission of the European Communities (2000) 'Communication from the Commission on the Precautionary Principle', COM (2000)1, available at: http://ec.europa.eu/dgs/health_consumer/library/pub/pub07_en.pdf.

Cross, F.B. (1996) 'Paradoxical Perils of the Precautionary Principle', *Washington and Lee Law Review*, 53(3): 851–925.

Dana, D.A. (2003) 'A Behavioral Economic Defense of the Precautionary Principle', *Northwestern University Law Review*, 97(3): 1315–45.

European Environmental Agency (2001) *Late Lessons from Early Warnings: The Precautionary Principle 1896–2000*, Copenhagen: Office for Official Publications of the European Communities.

Everson, M. and Vos, E. (eds) (2009) *Uncertain Risks Regulated*, London: Routledge.

Graham, J.D. and Wiener, J. (1995) *Risk Versus Risk: Tradeoffs in Protecting Health and the Environment*, Cambridge: Harvard University Press.

Hahn, R.W. and Sunstein, C.R. (2005) 'The Precautionary Principle as a Basis for Decisionmaking', *The Economists' Voice*, 2(2): 1–7.

Kysar, D.A. (2010) *Regulating from Nowhere: Environmental Law and the Search for Objectivity*, New Haven and London: Yale University Press.

Lin, A.C. (2007) 'Size Matters: Regulating Nanotechnology', *Harvard Environmental Law Review*, 31: 349–408.

Lomborg, B. (2001) *The Skeptical Environmentalist: Measuring the Real State of the World*, Cambridge: Cambridge University Press.

Morag-Levine, N. (2003) *Chasing the Wind: Regulating Air Pollution in the Common Law State*, Princeton, NJ: Princeton University Press.

——(2011) 'Is Precautionary Regulation a Civil Law Instrument? Lessons from the History of the Alkali Act', *Journal of Environmental Law*, 23(1): 1–43.

Naiki, Y. (2010) 'Assessing Policy Reach: Japan's Chemical Policy Reform in Response to the EU's REACH Regulation', *Journal of Environmental Law*, 22(2): 171–95.

Olson, M. (1965) *The Logic of Collective Action: Public Goods and the Theory of Groups*, Cambridge: Harvard College.

Pearlstein, S. (2012) 'The Judicial Jihad Against the Regulatory State', *Washington Post*, 13 October 2012.

Percival, R.V. (1998) 'Environmental Legislation and the Problem of Collective Action', *Duke Environmental Law & Policy Forum*, 9: 9–28.

——(2004) 'Chasing the Wind: Regulating Air Pollution in the Common Law State', *Law and Politics Book Review*, 14(1) (available online: www.bsos.umd.edu/gvpt/lpbr/subpages/reviews/Morag-Levine104.htm).

——(2006) 'Who's Afraid of the Precautionary Principle?', *Pace Environmental Law Review*, 23(1): 21–81.

——(2009) 'The Globalization of Environmental Law', *Pace Environmental Law Review*, 26(2): 451–64.

——(2011) 'Global Law and the Environment', *Washington Law Review*, 86: 579–634.

Percival, R.V., Schroeder, C.H., Miller, A.S. and Leape, J.P. (2009) *Environmental Regulation: Law, Science and Policy*, 6th edn, New York: Wolters Kluwer Law & Business.

Rabin, R.L. (1986) 'Federal Regulation in Historical Perspective', *Stanford Law Review*, 38(5): 1189–326.

Rascoff, S.J. and Revesz, R.L. (2002) 'The Biases of Risk Tradeoff Analysis: Toward Parity in Environmental and Health-and-Safety Regulation', *The University of Chicago Law Review*, 69(4): 1763–836.

Sandin, P., Peterson, M., Hansson, S.O., Ruden, C. and Juthe, A. (2002) 'Five Charges Against the Precautionary Principle', *Journal of Risk Research*, 5: 287–99.

Sunstein, C.R. (2005) *The Laws of Fear: Beyond the Precautionary Principle*, Cambridge: Cambridge University Press.

US Environmental Protection Agency (1987) *Unfinished Business: A Comparative Assessment of Environmental Problems.*

Vogel, D. (2012) *The Politics of Precaution: Regulating Health, Safety, and Environmental Risks in Europe and the United States*, Princeton, NJ: Princeton University Press.

Wiener, J.B., Rogers, M.D., Hammitt, J.K. and Sand, P.H. (eds) (2011) *The Reality of Precaution: Comparing Risk Regulation in the United States and Europe*, RFF Press.

Yang, T. and Percival, R.V. (2009) 'The Emergence of Global Environmental Law', *Ecology Law Quarterly*, 36(3): 615–64.

Zander, J. (2010) *The Application of the Precautionary Principle in Practice: Comparative Dimensions*, Cambridge: Cambridge University Press.

2 Science and decision-making

Can we both distinguish and reconcile science and politics?

Erik Millstone

Introduction

During the early 1990s, as the European Community, and later the European Union (EU), endeavoured to 'complete the Single Market', and as the World Trade Organization (WTO) was established, many economists and trade policy analysts hoped and expected that national differences between technical standards providing consumer and environmental protection, such as those covering food safety, would be diminished or even eradicated. Such convergence was anticipated by those who assumed that standards could and would be set solely or predominantly by reference to 'sound science'. Such convergence has, to say the least, been incomplete and in the case of genetically modified (GM) crops in the EU the prospect of convergence has sharply receded. This chapter first analyses the role of scientific evidence and expertise in regulatory policy-making and their interactions with non-scientific considerations, such as economic and political factors. It then uses that analytical framework to explain why regulatory convergence has not been achieved and outlines the conditions under which greater convergence might occur, or under which continued diversity may be sustainable.

Modelling science in policy

The role of science in public policy-making has been analysed and legitimated by reference to a range of ideas and models, but almost all of them have proved problematic and controversial. In discussions about agricultural biotechnology, those contests have been especially vigorous. The historical evolution of different ways of understanding the role of science in public policy will be outlined using four schematic models. Each of the models was developed to provide answers to the question: How can we understand the role of scientific evidence, understanding and advice in risk policy-making? The models have been understood, and used explicitly, both descriptively and prescriptively.

Weberian decisionism

The first model dates back to the late nineteenth century and the ideas developed by Max Weber and Emile Durkheim. Weber and Durkheim recognised the radical historical novelty represented by industrial societies that were then erupting around them. They argued that such societies could only function with increasingly bureaucratic forms of governance and that industrial and industrialising societies required and developed new forms of administration and policy-making. Their model resonated with the Aristotelian contrast between 'ends' and 'means', and his account of 'practical reason'. They stipulated that policy-makers, i.e. elected representatives, should select and define goals and 'ends', while the role of bureaucrats and technical experts was to select and implement the appropriate means to achieving those ends. Weber and Durkheim argued against nineteenth-century neo-Platonists; they were not advocating a bureaucratised technocracy, but warning against it. In response to what they perceived as the dangers inherent in the increasing influence of officials and experts, they argued that the proper role of bureaucrats should always be a subordinate one. The deliberations and judgements of bureaucrats (and by extension expert advisors) should always be framed by the policy goals and objectives that should properly be set by politically accountable representatives, rather than by unaccountable officials. Their model of the role of experts in policy-making has come to be known as a 'decisionist' model. It portrays the deliberations and judgements of the bureaucrats as framed by, and as secondary to, prior goal-setting policy decisions. A graphic representation of their decisionist model is given in Figure 2.1.

Weber and Durkheim argued that policy-making could be made more rational and scientific than it had been, but only partly. Their decisionist model presupposes a strict and clear division of labour between what Habermas referred to as 'the objectively informed and technically schooled general staffs of the bureaucracy' (including the experts) on the one hand and political leaders on the other (Habermas 1971: 83). Weber argued that policy-making could never be decided solely by the facts, since, although the choice of 'means' may be rationalised, the choice amongst the 'ends', the objectives of policy and the underlying values, remain irredeemably subjective (Weber 1958: 308 ff.).

On this type of decisionist model there are two discrete sets of deliberations and two corresponding lines of accountability. Democratically accountable ministers should be responsible to their electorates for choosing policy goals. Bureaucrats and experts, on the other hand, should be accountable to ministers for effectively pursuing the goals set from above, and to other experts for the

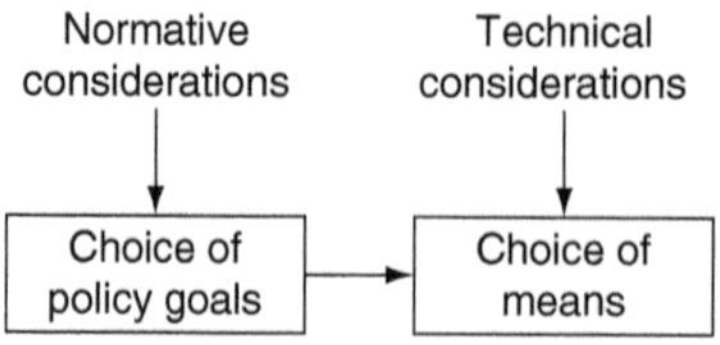

Figure 2.1 Weber and Durkheim's *decisionist* model

knowledge and judgements that they bring to bear in the discharge of their responsibilities.

This model is currently exemplified, for example, in the UK in the way in which the Bank of England's official base interest rate is set. The finance minister (or the Chancellor of the Exchequer) is responsible for the politically based judgement concerning the range within which a chosen indicator of the rate of inflation may vary, while the Monetary Policy Committee of the Bank of England, which is composed of expert economists, sets interest rates to try to ensure that the Chancellor's inflation target is met.

Weber anticipated that, in industrial societies, official decision-making would increasingly appeal to judgements based on ostensibly accurate observations and calculations and that expert advisors would play increasingly important roles in decision-making in bureaucratic institutions. Industrial societies certainly did become more bureaucratic in the nineteenth century, but it was not until the twentieth century that scientific experts came to make more than a marginal contribution to policy-making.

The division of labour envisaged in the Weberian decisionist model is not, however, unproblematic. In a relatively static pre-industrial society, political goal-setting might be independent of up-to-date scientific knowledge and technological change, but in a rapidly changing, technologically dynamic society, those responsible for goal-setting may need a great deal of scientific and technical advice before they can select all their policy goals. They need advice about the potential benefits and risks arising from new technologies, knowledges and uncertainties, because without that information and advice policy-makers might not even know which areas of policy need to be developed, nor which policy options might be available. Without scientific advice, politicians would never have known that emissions of Chloro-Fluoro-Carbons were damaging the ozone layer or that greenhouse gases might be destabilising our climate. In such circumstances, the simple division of labour between those that choose the ends of policy and those that select the means for attaining those ends becomes increasingly unrealistic.

As the decisionist model was increasingly seen as problematic, especially as science became pivotal to policy judgements about technological innovations, an alternative 'technocratic model' was developed, especially in France by the positivists. That approach suggested that policy could and should be based on and only on scientific expertise.

Positivism and 'technocracy'

A radically different and competing account of the role of experts in policy-making was derived from the arguments developed by positivists Henri de Saint-Simon and Auguste Comte; they were not warning against technocracy, but enthusiastically recommending it. They adopted especially optimistic assumptions about the progress, accuracy and adequacy of science and argued that public administration by impartial experts could and should replace governance by those with partial biases, ignorance and vested interests. The technocratic model of policy-making, as it is widely termed, has often been encapsulated in the claim that policy should be based on, and only on, 'sound science'. As Peter Weingart explained: 'In this "technocratic" model … the politician becomes fully dependent on the expert. Politics is replaced by a scientifically rationalised administration' (Weingart 1999: 154).

The assumption of technocracy, that scientific and technical considerations are not just necessary but also sufficient for policy decision-making, implies that responsibility for policy-making can and should be allocated to an elite of scientific and technical experts; they and they alone are in possession of the relevant knowledge and understanding. From this perspective, the responsibilities of elected representatives and government ministers are confined to recruiting the elite experts and ensuring that their advice is followed.

Technocratic ideas began to acquire some currency in policy circles in the first half of the twentieth century, especially in the USA. In 1926, Leonard White wrote about the role of technical experts in the US political system, saying: 'These men are not merely useful to legislators overwhelmed by the increasing flood of bills; they are simply indispensable. They are the government' (White 1926). A graphic representation of the conceptual structure of the technocratic model is given in Figure 2.2.

This model presupposes that the science and the facts are entirely objective and socially and politically neutral and that all the facts can readily be gathered. Technocratic narratives are therefore potentially very vulnerable to criticisms that the evidential base and the understanding of experts are incomplete, unreliable, equivocal or biased. Scientific uncertainty, evidence of conflicts of interest and disputes amongst the experts undermine the plausibility of the technocratic model and the credibility of participants, processes and outcomes.

Public policy-makers, especially government ministers and officials at the European Commission, often have claimed that their policies to regulate risks are always and only based on 'sound science'. Similar tactics have been adopted in numerous otherwise diverse jurisdictions, such as Iran, Japan, Kenya, the People's Republic of China and the USA.

The UK administration was not alone amongst jurisdictions and governments in presuming that science-based risk assessments could deliver uniform judgements and therefore regulatory convergence and the eradication of unnecessary barriers to trade. As the subsequent discussion will show,

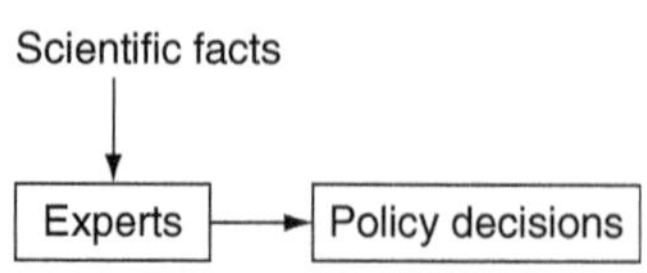

Figure 2.2 The technocratic model: 'policy is based (only) on sound science'

however, many policy-makers have failed to appreciate (or at any rate explicitly acknowledge) that the judgements of and advice from different groups of experts will depend not just on the field under consideration but also on the characteristics of the questions asked of them. Different groups of expert advisors have reached different conclusions and given different advice, not because a few do 'good science' and the others do 'bad science', but because they have been asked different questions.

Versions of the technocratic model continue to be invoked rhetorically by various groups and for several reasons, even though it has been torpedoed below the water-line by the obvious fact that scientific evidence is often incomplete, equivocal and uncertain and that the selection and interpretation of evidence is frequently contested. It is repeatedly invoked, first, because it may help to portray potentially controversial issues in depoliticised terms. Second, it may be used to facilitate what Hood and Rothstein have characterised as 'blame avoidance', in other words to portray government ministers as devoid of responsibility for controversial decisions (Hood and Rothstein 2001). As the UK Secretary of State for Health explained to the first Chair of the newly established Food Standards Agency (FSA) in their initial meeting: 'Professor, I want you to realise that I shall never hesitate to use you as my shield'.

Ironically, while the Chair of the FSA recognised that the organisation was born of the BSE (bovine spongiform encephalopathy or mad cow disease) saga, on that occasion the minister was reproducing the approach adopted by UK ministers in the two previous administrations when seeking to defend their policies on BSE, by trying to assign all the responsibility to the scientists (van Zwanenberg and Millstone 2005). Until the crisis of March 1996 UK Ministers and EU officials had repeatedly claimed that, in relation to BSE, they were doing what, and only what, their expert advisors recommended: even though that was always a misrepresentation. In the UK, for example, from 1985 until the start of 1996, officials tried to ensure that ministers only received advice from scientists who would provide the kind of advice that ministers and officials had already indicated that they wanted to receive. Instead of providing evidence-based policy-making they engaged in policy-based evidence-selection, while invoking technocratic narratives to conceal the underlying realities. The continuing popularity of the technocratic model in the rhetoric of senior policy-makers should not be mistaken for evidence of the truth of those portrayals. On the contrary, those who articulate that rhetoric most enthusiastically are often best placed to know how poorly their rhetoric matches the underlying reality. To maintain a facade of plausibility, technocratic regimes often chose not to disclose some or even much of the evidence and information available to them, because if all the evidence and information was in the public domain the uncertainties, equivocalities and ambiguities in the science would be undeniable.

Although technocratic narratives continue to have some currency, they have often been undermined when the uncertainties that characterise the scientific basis of policy-making are revealed. For example, the range of uncertainty in the magnitude of the carcinogenic risk to the US population from consuming the artificial sweetener 'saccharin' has been quantitatively estimated. In the early 1980s a panel of the US National Research Council reviewed all the available English-language evidence with a bearing on the putative carcinogenicity of saccharin and estimated that, over the next 70 years, the number of extra cases of cancer that the prevailing average rate of saccharin consumption might provoke in the population of the USA could range from as few as 0.22 cases (which would correspond to one case every some 320 years) to as many as 1,144,000 per year (US National Academy of Sciences 1978). The scale of that uncertainty may not have been untypical, but what was unusual was that efforts had been made to estimate and then publish that scale. The local impacts of climate change, or the environmental consequences of cultivating GM crops, are also uncertain and contested, although policies on such issues often continue to be portrayed as if legitimated solely or primarily by reference to reliable scientific facts.

Technocratic portrayals of policy-making are moreover always misleading, not just because, even if *per impossibile* all scientific uncertainties could be eliminated, scientific facts could never alone decide policy issues because such issues are irredeemably normative as well as factual. Policy judgements about the acceptability of technological novelties typically adjudicate trade-offs concerning the acceptability of risks (as well as uncertainties) in exchange for anticipated benefits. Scientific facts also cannot decide those trade-offs because they depend on socially variable and contestable evaluative and normative judgements.

The **Red Book** *model*

The plausibility of the technocratic model in the USA was undermined by the Freedom of Information Acts of 1966 and 1974 because, once the evidence, by reference to which policies were ostensibly being decided, entered the public domain, uncertainties could no longer be concealed. In response to the challenges posed by that development, and by judicial decisions such as that in the so-called 'benzene' case, a new model was developed in the USA in 1970s and early 1980s.

The regulatory dispute about occupational exposures to benzene in industrial conditions focussed on a proposal from the US Occupational Safety & Health Administration (or OSHA) to lower its standard for the maximum permitted air-borne concentration of benzene from 10 parts per million (ppm) to 1 ppm, after evidence emerged indicating that occupational exposures to benzene were linked to increased rates of leukaemia. OSHA's view was not that 1 ppm was a level below which the risk was negligible, but rather that 1 ppm was the lowest level that was then achievable and close to the minimum level of detection with the monitoring equipment then available. The trade association which led the opposition to this regulation was the American Petroleum Institute, which took its case all the way to the US Supreme Court, where the court ruled in its favour.[1] The court ruled that OSHA had 'exceeded its authority by reducing permissible exposure limits to benzene at industrial worksites without making a threshold determination that a significant risk was present at the original level' (Mounts 1980: 53). The court argued that OSHA had failed to provide an adequate scientific case to justify the proposed standard. The court introduced, moreover, a particular expression, namely a scientific 'risk assessment', arguing that the analysis on which the proposed regulation was based did not constitute a risk assessment of anticipated exposures.

The US federal government responded by developing a new analysis of the role of science in policy-making, cast in a new vocabulary. The process by which science-based risk policies were decided came to be represented as a two-stage process. The first stage is called 'risk assessment', the responsibility for which is attributed to scientific experts and which is routinely portrayed as if purely scientific. The second stage came to be known as 'risk management', during which non-scientific considerations can legitimately contribute to the deliberations and decision-making of policy-makers. The revised model was then formalised in 1983 by the US National Research Council in its so-called *Red Book* (also known as *Risk Assessment in the Federal Government: managing the process*). The so-called *Red Book* model is represented graphically in Figure 2.3.

An important feature of this model is that it is unidirectional; it claims that science influences policy-making, while portraying scientific advisors to policy-makers as if they were entirely free of any influences from non-scientific realms. This model represents 'science' as the starting point of all risk and technology policy-making processes, and the science as preceding, and entirely independent of, any and all policy considerations. Scientific deliberations constituting risk assessments are represented as if they occur in a political vacuum. While risk management policy-making is informed by, and based on an expert scientific risk assessment, the arrow only goes one way; science influences policy-making, but supposedly policy considerations do not influence the science. Policy-making deliberations only commence once scientific experts have completed their deliberations and made their determinations, so policy-making could not have influenced the science. The suggestion is that science is, in effect, on everybody's side because it is on no-one's side.

Figure 2.3 The *Red Book* model

This model has become the dominant official orthodoxy not just in the USA and EU, but also at the WTO. The presumed division of labour between scientific experts and the policy-makers may be superficially plausible, and commonly invoked, but it is problematic both conceptually and empirically. Conceptually the model is bizarre because, when it is benchmarked against the contrast between 'ends' and 'means', it can only be interpreted as implying that scientific experts can take responsibility for identifying and selecting the ends and goals of policy, while the responsibilities of policy-makers are confined to selecting first the expert advisors and last the means by which those goals should be achieved. That representation of the roles of governmental policy-makers and expert advisory bodies is profoundly counter-intuitive. We expect the ship's captain to set the course and the engineers and crew to deliver the chosen course, not the other way round.

This model has, nonetheless, travelled well. It was serviceable in the USA because it provided regulatory agencies with structures, processes and narratives that could withstand civil litigation and judicial scrutiny, at least some of the time (Jasanoff 1995). It was useful to policy-makers because it helps them to represent their decisions as 'science-based', and therefore those bases are incontestable by anyone other than expert scientists. It was also highly serviceable for the scientists selectively enrolled as expert advisors, because it flatters their epistemological and social credentials, portraying them as authoritative and responsible. The US government worked hard to disseminate the model by persuading the Organisation for Economic Cooperation and Development (OECD) to adopt that approach in its comparative reviews of policy-making in its Member States. The USA's longer-term strategy was to persuade the EU, and subsequently other jurisdictions too, to adopt this model both rhetorically and operationally. The motivation for doing so was not primarily focussed on issues concerning risks to, for example, consumer, occupational or environmental health, but because of trade policy concerns.

Non-tariff barriers to trade, of a technical type, were hampering flows of international trade, while trade policy-makers and their advisors were assuming that increasing the scale of international trade would increase aggregate value, wealth and welfare. The presence and operation of technical rules restricting the characteristics of products and processes do not, in themselves, constitute barriers to trade. If all jurisdictions were to share the same set of regulations, then products and processes deemed acceptably safe and lawful anywhere could lawfully be sold everywhere. Trade barriers were, however, conspicuous because in the prevailing circumstances numerous jurisdictions had set different standards. The presumed solution was to establish and operate a set of institutionalised regimes to deliver a convergent set of standards that could ultimately deliver a regulatory 'level playing field'.

In the negotiations that led to the establishment of the WTO in 1994 a set of treaties were concluded in which the provisions concerning so-called 'technical barriers to trade' were worded in *Red Book* terminology. It is probable that many trade policy negotiators, and presumably corporate executives too, hoped and expected that once the WTO became operational, steady progress towards the full convergence of regulatory standards, set by reference to 'sound science', would readily be achieved. The assumption was that the science is known to be sufficiently 'sound' for the evidence and the experts consistently to 'speak with one voice', that is to say to exhibit high levels of consensus. That line of reasoning assumed that a risk assessment is always possible, reliable, sufficient, specific and precise. Those expectations have, however, been conspicuously frustrated. In part that has been a consequence of some of the shortcomings of the *Red Book* model, as well as an outcome of a set of unanticipated events.

Despite the abandonment of a technocratic model in large parts of the US government and its replacement with the *Red Book* model in the 1980s, technocratic models and narratives survived in Europe into the late 1990s. Technocratic models were, however, undermined in the UK, following the BSE crisis that erupted in March 1996, and similar changes unfolded a few years later in many continental European countries (Millstone 2009). From the first official recognition of BSE in the UK in December 1986 until the crisis of March 1996, the British authorities, followed by the European Commission, endeavoured to portray BSE policy-making in orthodox technocratic terms. The policy line was that the available science, as known, understood and interpreted by elite experts, showed that BSE posed no risks to human health (van Zwanenberg and Millstone 2005: chapters 4 and 5). That narrative was, unfortunately, misleading because neither the science nor the small group of chosen experts indicated that BSE was risk-free. The evidence was incomplete and equivocal, and the science was profoundly uncertain. The experts indicated that the risks from BSE were probably slight, as long as several conditions were satisfied, but they could not be sure whether or not those conditions were in practice met.

When the UK government's expert advisory committee on BSE informed ministers in February 1996 that evidence had emerged indicating that BSE was causing a fatal and untreatable illness in a group of unexpectedly young people, it became self-evident that the previous technocratic narrative had been misleading. Evidence eventually emerged that showed that, instead of science-based policy-making, the British and European authorities had engaged in policy-based selection and interpretation of some of the science, namely those parts that constituted no threat to their chosen policy narrative, while discounting or ignoring the rest. That explains in part why the BSE crises, along with other food safety policy problems, provoked a wave of reform in the UK and EU, as well as in other countries where BSE had been problematic, such as Switzerland and Japan (van Zwanenberg and Millstone 2005; Millstone 2009). One conspicuous refrain in those processes of reform was the adoption of vocabulary derived directly from the *Red Book*. For example, the White Paper from the European Commission, in which the proposal for the creation of what became the European Food Safety Authority (or EFSA) was articulated, was worded explicitly in terms of a need to separate science from policy-making and achieving it by locating responsibility for 'scientific risk assessments' in an institutional location distinct from the body with responsibility for 'risk-management policy-making' (Commission of the European Community 2000).

Problems with the **Red Book** *model*

Ironically, by the time European policy-makers eventually adopted *Red Book* vocabulary and prescriptions, the underlying model had lost much of its plausibility. A substantial body of science policy research, regulatory studies research and work by sociologists of scientific knowledge had demonstrated that the deliberations and judgements of official expert scientific advisory bodies never operate in a policy vacuum and that they are always framed by some prior policy-related assumptions (Wynne 1992; Funtowicz and Ravetz 1993; Levidow *et al.* 1997; van Zwanenberg and Millstone 2000). Those studies showed that, in controversial policy contexts, the scientific community never speaks with just one consensual voice and that the available evidence is never complete, definitive or unequivocal. It also showed that scientific considerations on their own can never settle policy issues. On the contrary, policy judgements influence for example the particular choice of questions that scientific experts address, and which they ignore. They influence the range of evidence deemed relevant, and which is discounted or ignored. They also influence judgements about how much of which kinds of evidence may be deemed necessary or sufficient for permitting, restricting or banning particular products or processes. That body of research showed that those kinds of choices routinely depend on prior socially variable, contestable and contested framing assumptions. Those assumptions are matters on which scientific advisors have no particular authority, and their expertise cannot legitimate the choices of assumptions that frame their deliberations, judgements and conclusions. Those judgements are furthermore unavoidably evaluative, and in a democracy the responsibility for making those choices and judgements should be with electorally accountable policy-makers, e.g. government ministers, rather than democratically unaccountable scientists (Millstone 2007).

The range of risks included within the scope of risk assessments are not determined by fixed sets of scientific parameters, and continuing opportunities for changes in their scope have not been exhausted. For example, in most jurisdictions the official assessments of the risks from the use of mobile phones focus just on the possible thermal effects of the microwave radiation that they exchange with base stations, but in the foreseeable future they may be extended to include electromagnetic effects. Similarly, the official assessments of the risks from the use of chemical food additives as emulsifiers focus just on their possible toxicological effects, but in the future they may be extended to include nutritional effects, for example on intakes of oils and fats and their consequent impact on obesity and public health nutrition. Before the banking crisis of 2008, the UK authorities assessed the viability and sustainability of banks individually and in isolation. Since that crisis, the scope of their terms of reference has been explicitly extended to include systemic risks arising from the interdependence of banks on each other. When the European Central Bank (ECB) was established in 1998 its remit was specifically focused on controlling the average rate of inflation in the Eurozone by making appropriate adjustments to interest rates. More recently, and particularly in 2011 as the euro crisis unfolded, it was clear that the remit of the ECB had been deliberately extended to trying to avoid a recession in the Eurozone and wider EU, as well as trying to stabilise the finances of EU Member States and of EU-based private sector financial institutions.

In practice, policy-makers are often well aware of the political sensitivities of the precise wording of the questions that they ask of their expert advisors, and often much care and time is taken (behind the scenes) to craft the terms of reference given to those advisors, even though the policy-makers and their expert advisors routinely proclaim the complete separation of science from politics, using the vocabulary and rhetoric of the *Red Book* model.

The co-dynamic model

The conceptual and analytic lessons of those studies and findings can be embodied in one further model of science in policy, which in this context is termed the 'co-dynamic model'. A graphic representation of this model is provided in Figure 2.4. My contention is that this model provides a more accurate and comprehensive representation of science-based policy-making than any of the preceding models, but not that this model is exhaustive or definitive. It can, however, provide considerable descriptive and analytical power and indicates guidelines for reforming institutional structures and practices.

This model has several distinctive advantageous features. First, instead of attempting to portray scientific deliberations as if they took place in a policy vacuum, the influence of the policy context is acknowledged explicitly in a way that enables such issues to be addressed by institutions and processes that are

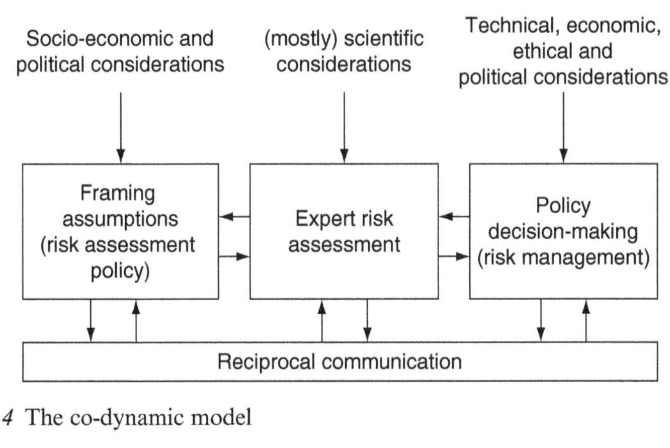

Figure 2.4 The co-dynamic model

accountable and therefore may be legitimate. Second, scientific deliberations are understood as 'sandwiched' between two sets of policy deliberations: one up-stream and one down-stream. The down-stream risk management decisions can be understood, as in the *Red Book* model, as the adjudication of, for example, trade-offs between anticipated risks and benefits. The *Red Book* model correctly highlighted the importance of those considerations, and the nature of those down-stream decisions, but it failed to acknowledge the no less important contribution of the up-stream framing assumptions. Third, the arrows of communication between the expert risk assessors and both the up-stream and down-stream risk management policy-makers go both ways. That means, for example, that while expert advisors and risk assessors may have contributions to make to deliberating on the chosen up-stream assumptions that frame their deliberations, responsibility for setting those up-stream assumptions should lie with risk managers rather than with risk assessors; the issues are policy matters that science cannot settle.

My argument is not that science-based risk policy-making is currently officially represented in accordance with this model, but rather that despite the fact that most policy-making institutions and procedures continue to be officially portrayed as if they operated *Red Book* (or sometimes even technocratic) models, those representations are never correct because they are always incomplete, and especially because the decisions that they fail to mention are often the most important ones. The corollary of this analysis is that, if science-based policy-making were reformed so that the institutions functioned in ways that explicitly endeavoured to correspond with this co-dynamic model, then policy-making institutions and procedures would enhance their democratic and scientific legitimacy; until then their legitimacy in those respects will remain problematic.

Evidence that, in current regimes, ostensibly scientific bodies are taking responsibility for policy decisions can readily be located. For example, even though responsibility for setting guidance on risk assessments of GM crops should lie with the European Commission or the Council of Ministers, since they have authority over policy matters, in practice it is the EFSA that has set and issued all the relevant guidance, without the prior advice and consent of the Commission or the Parliament (EFSA 2010).

Despite the continuing popularity of *Red Book* narratives in official circles, one globally pivotal international organisation, namely the Codex Alimentarius Commission (or 'Codex' for short), has in effect adopted a variant of the co-dynamic model. While it is relatively straightforward to show that Codex has explicitly adopted terminology and procedures that are incompatible with both technocratic and *Red Book* models, but which match closely to the co-dynamic model, it is far harder to explain why that innovation occurred, or to forecast the long-term implications (Millstone 2009).

Codex was formed in 1963 from the joint membership of the World Health Organization and the United Nations Food and Agriculture Organization; it is an inter-governmental body with a remit to set food safety standards for internationally traded agricultural commodities and food products. Until the WTO was activated in 1994, Codex standards had only been advisory; they had had no statutory force. Member States were at liberty to adopt them or not as they chose. Under the WTO regime, however, Codex standards set legal global minimum standards for internationally traded food products. All WTO Member States can lawfully refuse to accept imports that fail to meet Codex standards, but disputes can arise when importers refuse to accept products that meet Codex standards but not the national standards of the potential importer (Millstone 2000).

The text of the relevant agreement (the Sanitary and Phytosanitary Agreement) was couched in orthodox *Red Book* terms; it was widely understood as assuming or implying that agreed scientific risk assessments do and will provide sound scientific bases for globally agreed standards. In practice the convergence of national standards in line with Codex standards has seriously disappointed those who enthused about a 'level regulatory playing field' (Millstone and van Zwanenberg 2003). Instead, diversity is more conspicuous than uniformity, and in the particularly contested domain of GM crops and foods, regimes are becoming increasingly diverse (Commission of the European Community 2010a, 2010b).

An innovation at Codex: 'risk assessment policy'

A remarkable innovation at Codex, which suggested that *Red Book* and technocratic models were being repudiated and replaced with a co-dynamic model, was formally adopted in 2003. This innovation was encapsulated in a newly introduced provision of a document called the *Codex Procedural Manual*. Prior to 2003, 12 earlier versions had been developed and adopted, the thirteenth version, however, contained an entirely novel set of provisions, and they referred to the newly introduced concept of 'risk assessment policy'. The thirteenth edition of the Codex *Procedural Manual* characterises '*Risk Assessment Policy*' in the following terms:

- Determination of risk assessment policy should be included as a specific component of risk management.
- Risk assessment policy should be established by risk managers in advance of risk assessment, in consultation with risk assessors and all other interested parties. This procedure aims at ensuring that the risk assessment is systematic, complete, unbiased and transparent.
- The mandate given by risk managers to risk assessors should be as clear as possible.
- Where necessary, risk managers should ask risk assessors to evaluate the potential changes in risk resulting from different risk management options.

(CAC 2003: Appendix IV, paras 13–16)

Those provisions constituted a repudiation of the assumption, shared by both the technocratic and *Red Book* models, that science operates in a policy-free space. The wording makes it clear that risk managers have responsibility for making key policy judgements 'in advance of risk assessment', and those risk assessment policies refer to what in the co-dynamic model was termed 'up-stream framing assumptions'. The text also stipulates that 'Risk assessment policy should be established by risk managers ... in consultation with risk assessors and all other interested parties', in other words, the expert scientists may have a contribution to make to deliberations that precede risk assessment policy-making, but so too may 'all other interested parties'. It implies therefore that, if in practice risk assessment policies are decided by risk assessors, those practices would not conform to these provisions.

The implications of those developments may be profound, although their significance is not yet widely appreciated; indeed, it is not obvious that all those present at the meeting at which those provisions were adopted fully understood that to which they were agreeing. Their importance was, however, reinforced when at the July 2007 plenary meeting of the Codex Alimentarius Commission (CAC), the text of a similar document called the *Working Principles for Risk Analysis for Food Safety for Application by Governments* was formally adopted (CAC 2007: 9, paras 56–60). Under the provisions of that document, all Codex Member States and regional jurisdictions like the European Commission accepted an obligation on their domestic risk managers to provide their risk assessors with explicit risk assessment policies prior to the start of the deliberations of those risk assessors. The text that the Codex Member States adopted on 'risk assessment policy' is identical to that in the *Codex Procedural Manual*, cited above.

In two studies of the similarities and differences amongst the risk assessment policies as between different jurisdictions, and across different types of food-borne risks, it emerged that at least three main different types of risk assessment policies can be identified (Millstone *et al.* 2004; Millstone *et al.* 2008). Those three main types of risk assessment policies have been termed as: *substantive*, *procedural* and *interpretative* risk assessment policies, which have been characterised as follows:

- *Substantive* risk assessment policies are concerned with delineating which potential changes and effects are to be included within the scope of risk assessments and which are outside their scope, and which kinds of evidence are admissible and which are not. For example, when the risks posed by food additives are considered, does the assessment focus solely on toxicological issues or should it be extended also to consider possible impacts on public health nutrition?
- *Procedural* risk assessment policies are concerned with the processes by which risk assessments are conducted and reported. For example, should risk assessment deliberations be conducted in open or closed meetings, and how should risk assessors respond to uncertainties?
- *Interpretative* risk assessment policies are concerned with the ways in which data are interpreted. Data and documents do not interpret themselves;

> interpretation often involves judgements and assumptions. For example, are laboratory rodents treated as good or as poor models for the effects of chemicals on humans – and for all types of lesions at all sites, or only for some? Judgements about how much of which kinds of evidence may be deemed necessary or sufficient for permitting, restricting or banning particular products or processes are also matters for interpretative risk assessment policies.

Even though Codex itself and its Member States have collectively committed themselves to operating in accordance with the provisions outlined above, there is little evidence to suggest that any of them are consistently or explicitly implementing those commitments (Millstone 2009). Nonetheless the models set out above, and the Codex text relating to 'risk assessment policy', provide a set of analytical concepts that may be used to describe and characterise and evaluate policy-making institutions, practices and regimes. Furthermore, they can provide an analysis of the ways in which regulatory policies and trade policies have interacted and of the ways in which those patterns of interaction may change.

By enumerating the differences amongst various countries in those three types of risk assessment policies in respect of particular regulatory debates, it is possible forensically to analyse the sources of key tensions amongst different jurisdictions and so explain the source of the differences in their risk assessments and policy judgements, and thereby explain the source of inter-jurisdictional trade disputes over the acceptability of those types of commodities. But it can do more, and highlight the conditions under which their risk assessments and policy judgements could converge, or alternatively reach some sort of WTO-dispute-proof sustainable divergence. Those tasks will be approached by outlining comparative accounts of those three types of risk assessment policies in respect of official appraisals of two sets of putative food-borne risks. The first set of comparisons is now primarily of historical interest and relates to the putative risks from the use of synthetic growth-promoting hormones in beef production. The second set of issues is of more contemporary interest and concerns the putative risks from GM crops and foods.

The beef hormones dispute

The dispute about beef hormones between the USA and Europe was long lasting and acrimonious. Synthetic hormones are permitted for use in beef production in the USA but have been banned in Europe since the mid-1980s. The import of US beef into Europe is also banned, unless it can be certified as produced without these hormones. The US government, in the form of the Department of Agriculture and the Food and Drug Administration (FDA), has evaluated the hormones and deemed them, and the beef produced with their use, to be acceptably safe, as has the Codex Alimentarius Commission. The USA repeatedly complained, but the European ban on imports of US beef remained. In the mid-1990s the US government took the EU to a dispute at the WTO. In 1997, a WTO Dispute Panel found against the Europeans, and the WTO's Appellate Body confirmed most aspects of that Panel's judgement (WTO 1997). The US government then exercised its right to impose financial penalties, at a rate of some US $160 million a year, on selected European imports, and used the revenue to compensate US beef farmers for their lost sales.

Many commentators, on both sides of the Atlantic, initially interpreted the outcome of that dispute as implying that regulatory standards can and will be harmonised by reference to internationally agreed scientific judgements. If the details of the case are scrutinised more carefully, a very different picture emerges. The WTO Dispute Panel and Appellate Body found in favour of the USA on the grounds that the EU had failed to conduct a proper and appropriate science-based risk assessment. The WTO did not rule, however, that the use of synthetic beef hormones was risk-free, or that beef produced using synthetic hormones is acceptably safe. Nor did it rule that the EU had no scientific evidence, but merely that the EU had not followed the rules concerning the conduct of, and requirements for, an appropriate science-based risk assessment.

The judgement went against the EU because the scientific evidence of risk that the European Commission provided derived from studies of direct human exposure to hormone products, for example in pharmaceutical formulations, and not from studies of the likely effects on consumers of ingesting beef produced using the hormones. As the Appellate Board stated, the evidence:

> constitute[s] general studies which do indeed show the existence of a general risk of cancer; but they do not focus on and do not address the particular kind of risk here at stake – the carcinogenic or genotoxic potential of the residues of those hormones found in meat derived from cattle to which the hormones had been administered for growth promotion purposes … . Those general studies are, in other words, relevant but do not appear to be sufficiently specific to the case at hand.
>
> (WTO Appellate Body 1998: para 200)

In other words, the scientific evidence used by the Europeans to justify their measure was too indirect.

The EU's response was not to lift the ban on US beef but to commission further scientific studies intended to provide more direct and relevant evidence and to plan to conduct revised risk assessments once the results of these studies emerge. Commission officials then gathered sufficient evidence to enable them to conduct new risk assessments, and they deliberately chose to ask a different set of questions from those asked in the USA. The US authorities asked, in effect, if it was acceptably safe for beef produced using hormones to be consumed by average healthy adults. In 1999, the European Commission's Scientific Committee on Veterinary Measures relating to Public Health concluded that, while beef produced using synthetic hormones might be safe for healthy adults, it was not acceptably safe for prepubertal children, the elderly and those who were immunologically compromised (EC SCVMPH 1999). The Commission then argued that the most straightforward way of protecting those vulnerable groups was to ban the use of growth promoting hormones in beef and the import of beef that had been so produced. Subsequently and consequently, the US authorities and the WTO recognised that the EU's new scientific risk assessment did meet the requirements of the WTO rules, and so the financial penalties are no longer levied and, instead of regulatory convergence, the USA and the EU have reached a state of sustainable diversity. The EU has sustained its ban on beef hormones because it chose to ask a significantly different set of questions about the risks posed by beef hormones than were addressed by the US authorities. In other words, the substantive risk assessment policy adopted in the EU after the 1998 ruling from the WTO Appellate Body was different from that which the USA adopts and from that which the EU had itself previously considered. Lessons from the beef hormones case have been carried over in the EU to affect its approach to policies on GM crops and foods.

Substantive risk assessment policies concerning GM foods and crops

As indicated above, substantive risk assessment policy issues are concerned with deciding what kinds of changes and effects should be included within, and excluded from, the scope of official risk assessments. For reasons connected with the contrasting politics of the USA and Europe, the scope of official assessments of the risks of GM foods in Europe has been consistently wider than those in the USA, although both have evolved, in part because of their interactions with each other. In the USA, GM foods are officially deemed safe just as long as chemical analyses of the GM foodstuff, focussing on, e.g., levels of protein, carbohydrates, vitamins and minerals, are within the range found in their non-GM counterparts; in those cases they are said to be 'substantially equivalent' and acceptably safe without any further testing (OECD 1993). While the European authorities and several EU Member States adopted that tactic in the 1990s, they subsequently shifted their position. The current policy is that chemical analyses on their own are not sufficient and can at most provide a starting point for a risk assessment, but not a conclusion to it (Millstone *et al.* 1999; Levidow *et al.* 2007). In the EU and elsewhere, too, official risk assessments of the safety of GM foods require more than just data from chemical analyses; they also require some biological and toxicological data and often also immunological data to illuminate issues of potential allergenicity.

In the USA, throughout the 1990s, risk assessments of the environmental impacts of the commercial cultivation of genetically modified crops only deemed as adverse environmental effects those changes that would harm the commercial prospects of US farmers; all others were discounted and portrayed merely as 'adaptations' (House of Lords 1998). In Europe, on the other hand, under the provision of a Directive issued in 1990, the scope of official risk assessments of GM crops included effects on flora and fauna that could disrupt both agricultural and non-agricultural environments (EC 1990).

Subsequently the scope of scientific deliberations on both sides of the Atlantic expanded in response to pressure from consumer, environmental and scientific groups. In the EU the scope was explicitly widened in 2001 to include not just direct and short-term effects but also some indirect and long-term effects (EC 2001). When evidence emerged in the USA in 1999 indicating that the cultivation of a GM maize might adversely affect the Monarch butterfly, the US authorities widened the scope of their deliberations about the possible environmental effects of cultivating such crops to include some of those possible effects (Losey *et al.* 1999; Jasanoff 2000; Levidow and Carr 2000).

In recent years several documents have emerged from EU bodies setting out the types and minimum quantities of data that would need to be submitted to the body responsible for conducting official risk assessments, namely the EFSA. Those data requirements are clearly a sub-set of what, in this context, is being termed 'substantive risk assessment policy'. The provisions of the Codex agreement on the topic indicate that responsibility for setting those policies should lie with risk managers, which at the EU level corresponds to the Directorate General for Public Health and Consumer Protection (also known as DG SANCO) and the members of the relevant Ministerial Council; the fact that DG SANCO has left the task to EFSA suggests that the EU practices have yet fully to conform to the agreement reached at Codex in 2007.

In Japan official documents have indicated that the scope of assessment of the environmental risks of cultivating GM crops may be extended to cover the range of putative effects that should be addressed in the EU, but also that putative adverse effects on soil micro-organisms should be considered. In India, the scope of official risk assessments has recently been modified to take account of the putative effects on the livelihoods of smallholder farmers, while in Argentina there is evidence that the Argentinian expert advisory body considers the potential impact on agricultural exports of cultivating GM crops for sale to markets to which the import of some GM crops is prohibited or restricted (Millstone *et al.* 2008).

Procedural risk assessment policies

While many issues of substantive risk assessment policies have been implicit, rather than explicit, procedural risk assessment policy issues have in several jurisdictions been addressed more explicitly. In the USA a variety of explicit procedural risk assessment policies have been established by regulatory agencies and Congress. Even on issues where specific procedural guidance does not exist, some legal statutes guide and restrict the procedures with which US risk assessors can frame their assessments and gather, select and interpret data. Some of the key assumptions that frame and underpin risk assessments are explicit in US institutions and procedures, partly as a consequence of the requirements of US statutes but also because of attempts on the part of regulatory agencies to anticipate or avoid legal challenges.

For example, the US *Administrative Procedures Act 1946* imposes constraints on agencies' regulatory discretion by stipulating mandatory consultation procedures. Regulatory agencies must give advance notice of draft regulations as well as opportunities for comments by interested parties. This requirement has generated adjudicatory procedures with broad scope for participation, often testing evidence in adversarial hearings (Brickman *et al.* 1985). More recently, in 2001, Congress passed The Data Quality Act (or DQA), which imposed procedural obligations on US government regulatory agencies such as the FDA and the Environmental Protection Agency (EPA) to provide some procedural guidance, that corresponds to risk assessment policy, to their risk assessors (US Congress 2001). The DQA was, however, also widely interpreted as an attempt to impose a deregulatory and an anti-regulatory agenda, because it set relatively high evidential standards before regulatory measures may be introduced (Weiss 2004).

Regulatory decisions in the USA are also routinely subject to judicial review, and the courts may overturn decisions deemed 'arbitrary, capricious, an abuse of discretion, or otherwise not in accordance with law' (Jasanoff 1995). Moreover the courts may overturn any decision not supported by 'substantial evidence'. In making such a judgement, courts may review the evidence cited and draw on expert witnesses. This threat of litigation has provided a strong incentive for agencies to adopt consultative procedures, as well as to formalise risk assessment methods that can be defended in adversarial judicial contexts.

As Jasanoff has shown in her analysis of the role of expert scientific advisors in US risk policy-making regimes, there is a tendency in the USA for both risk assessors and risk managers to portray many of their key risk assessment policy judgements as if they were fundamentally scientific. The purpose of so doing may, as Jasanoff suggests, be to try to insulate those sensitive issues from judicial or Congressional scrutiny (Jasanoff 1990). That tactic can also be interpreted as an attempt to invoke a decisionist *Red Book* model, so that risk assessments can be portrayed as emerging from a policy-free zone.

In the aftermath of the BSE crises (of 1996 in the UK and of the end of the century in continental European countries), the European Commission issued a raft of documents stipulating the procedures that should be followed by European risk assessors. In 2002 at least four separate documents emerged from the Commission intended to improve regulation and governance (Commission of the European Community 2002a, 2002b, 2002c, 2002d). The text of those documents provides some procedural guidance to expert risk assessment bodies that advise Commission-based policy-makers. They therefore constitute examples where Commission risk management policy-makers have provided some explicit up-stream procedural risk assessment policy guidance, although without labelling it in those terms, and without consulting all interested parties. Moreover, they persist in trying to portray their 'risk assessors' and 'risk assessments' as entirely independent of all policy-making considerations.

In other cases, however, some procedural risk assessment policy guidance to EU risk assessors has also been published by a group of risk assessors, namely the European Commission's Scientific Steering Committee, which issued its 'First Report on the Harmonisation of Risk Assessment Procedures' in 2000. In that case, the procedural guidance came to subordinate risk assessors from more senior risk assessors rather than from risk managers.

In the UK, in the aftermath of the BSE crisis of March 1996, the Office of Science and Technology (OST – headed by the government's Chief Scientific Advisor) provided explicit procedural risk assessment policy guidance to expert advisory committees across all government departments (OST 1997, OST 2000, OST 2005). In April 2002, the UK Food Standards Agency published a review of the conduct of its scientific advisory committees; its conclusions and recommendations included some detailed procedural guidance (FSA 2002). That guidance covered, for example, issues of data confidentiality and openness, and the treatment of scientific uncertainties, assumptions and unorthodox scientific views. It was not referred to by the FSA as 'risk assessment policy', but it did provide generic advice to any and all of its committees in advance of their appraisal of particular risks and so constitutes some up-stream procedural RAP guidance. The FSA's advice was also developed in open prior consultation with a wide range of stakeholders, unlike the earlier OST guidance.

The FSA guidelines stipulated that its expert committees should routinely provide an audit trail: 'showing how the committee reached its decisions' (FSA 2002: 22). This document also stipulated that:

> When reporting outcomes, committees should make explicit the level and type of uncertainty (both limitations on the quality of the available data and lack of knowledge) associated with their advice … . Where significant uncertainty exists, committees should advise on the steps that might be taken to reduce this in future.
>
> (FSA 2002: 25)

In practice, however, FSA expert committees rarely make explicit statements about scientific 'uncertainty', especially not when making safety claims, which are usually unqualified and unconditional. When discounting evidence of possible adverse effects, however, possible uncertainties are enthusiastically highlighted (CoC 2006). Uncertainties concerning possible false negatives are hardly ever highlighted.

In the case of Germany, and its consideration of the putative risks from GM foods, some procedural risk assessment guidance has been published by the body with explicit responsibility for risk assessments, namely the *Bundesinstitut für Risikobewertung* (or BfR) rather than by risk managers (although the German authorities do not use the expression 'risk assessment policy', or its German equivalent). That guidance was developed by BfR staff and then presented to risk managers at the *Bundesamt für Verbraucherschutz und Lebensmittel Sicherheit* (or BVLS), in effect as a *fait accompli*. Stakeholders and interested parties were almost entirely excluded from establishing that procedural risk assessment policy guidance. In general, stakeholder involvement is understood by the BfR as something that happens after finalising an assessment and does not include influencing or involvement in the risk assessment question or process (BfR 2005).

In Japan, several procedural risk assessment policy guidance documents setting out data collection methods have been published for legally mandated risk assessments of GM foods and crops by the Japanese Food Safety Commission, i.e. by risk assessors rather than risk managers. For GM foods, the principal document is *Standards for the Safety Assessment of Genetically Modified Foods (Seeds Plants)* (FSC 2004). For GM crops, however, procedural guidance documents have been published by risk managers, including *Guidance on Implementation of Assessment of Adverse Effects on Biological Diversity of Type 1 Use of Living Modified Organisms and the Application of Approval for the Production and Distribution of GMOs under the Jurisdiction of Minister of Agriculture, Forestry and Fisheries* (MAFF Japan 2004; MoE undated). Those documents are not referred to as 'risk assessment policy', but they do provide some procedural guidance.

Interpretative risk assessment policies

There have been several contexts and occasions in which risk managers have provided their risk assessors with some explicit guidance on how the evidence to be considered should be interpreted. The passage of the Delaney Amendment by the US Congress imposed some constraints on the exercise of the discretion of the FDA (Delaney 1959). It stipulated that: 'the Food and Drug Administration shall not approve for use in food any chemical additive found to induce cancer in man, or, after tests, found to induce cancer in animals' (Ibid.). Subsequently, detailed guidance has been provided from time to time to FDA risk assessors on how animal toxicological data should be interpreted in respect of humans, which has included stipulations that estimated added lifetime risks of less than 1 in a million can be deemed sufficiently slight to be socially acceptable (US Federal Register 1987). Guidance on how to deal with some uncertainties has also been provided, which typically asks the experts to estimate the magnitudes of the uncertainties that confront them.

In the UK, the FSA has not provided interpretative risk assessment policy guidance to its advisory committees over and above that implied by the procedural guidance discussed above. Similar comments apply also to France, Germany, Japan and Argentina, from which it follows that in all those contexts decisions about interpretative risk assessment policy issues have been, and are being, decided by expert advisory committees that function as risk assessors rather than by policy-makers acting as risk managers. Consequently, the supposed separation of scientific deliberations from policy considerations is marked more frequently in the breach than in the observance.

Intra-EU disagreements

One of the many factors that complicates policy-making in the EU on GM foods and crops is that, as well as trans-Atlantic differences in risk assessment policies, there are also divergences on these matters amongst EU Member States. For example, Austria adopts a different set of interpretative criteria than are adopted by several other countries. The Austrian approach is to require that the environmental impact of cultivating GM crops should be no greater than that which is consequent on organic cultivation, which is connected to the fact that (at least until the most recent round of increases in the EU's membership) there were more organic farms in Austria than in the remainder of the EU Member States added together (Torgersen and Seifert 2000). In most other EU Member States, it can be sufficient if their environmental impact is no worse than that consequent on conventional high agrichemical-input-based farming. In that context, different questions are being asked, and the available data are being interpreted and benchmarked against significantly different criteria.

By 2010 the patience of the President of the EU Commission had worn thin, because it had proved increasingly difficult to obtain a qualified majority of votes in the Council of Ministers to either authorise the sale of new GM crops or to ban them. In response, the Commission proposed amending Directive 2001/18 so as to allow decisions about authorising the commercial cultivation to individual Member States, just so long as they had been acceptable by the European Food Safety Authority (EFSA 2010). The lack of sufficient consensus amongst EU Member States over that controversial policy area can be directly attributed to the differences in risk assessment policy assumptions that had been adopted by the Member States.

Implications and conclusions

The foregoing discussion has shown that the main reason why different groups of official expert advisors, and in particular scientific risk assessors, reach divergent conclusions and deliver conflicting advice is not because they are reviewing identical bodies of evidence while interpreting them differently, nor because some are doing 'good science' while others are doing 'bad science'. Those different outcomes are a consequence of the fact that they are asking and answering different questions and consequently gathering, reviewing and interpreting differing bodies of evidence, and often judging those bodies of evidence against different criteria.

In the case of beef hormones, the EU learnt that it can request and accept advice from its expert scientific advisors that is framed in terms that are significantly different from those adopted by the US authorities, or for that matter the authorities of any other jurisdiction. As a result, the advice the EU received can support a significantly different policy outcome and regulatory regime from those adopted by countries with which the EU trades.

In relation to policy-making on GM crops, the European Commission initially tried to sustain a contradictory set of claims. In the context of WTO disputes, the European Commission argued at the WTO Dispute Panel that science does not necessarily speak with just one voice and that, on the contrary, different conclusions can legitimately be reached on opposite sides of the Atlantic. In respect of GM crops within the EU, however, the Commission tried to maintain that science could speak with only one voice, and risk assessments that fail to coincide with those published by EFSA were simply wrong. That tactic eventually proved unsustainable, because not just the Austrians, but other Member States too learnt that they can decide for themselves the precise terms of reference that they give to their own expert advisory risk assessment bodies. Those bodies adopt their own preferred risk assessment policy assumptions, and consequently different national bodies can and do provide conflicting conclusions and advice. Instead of EFSA resolving the cacophony of voices, and providing a harmonised and consensual assessment of the risks and benefits of GM crops, EFSA has added to the cacophony.

That analysis does not entail that risk assessments in different jurisdictions will unendingly continue to diverge from each other; it implies, rather, that, if convergence is to be achieved, a necessary condition for its attainment would be a prior set of deliberations, negotiations and agreements on a shared set of risk assessment policy judgements.

To the extent that risk assessment policies differ over *substantive* issues, the scope of their deliberations would not coincide. The most straightforward way of ensuring that they did coincide would then be to agree that their overall scope would be constituted by the sum of the scopes of the individual approaches. If everyone's concerns are included from the start, they cannot argue that the issues over which they were especially concerned had not been addressed.

Agreement over *procedural* risk assessment policies need not be especially difficult to achieve, if the discussions were predicated on shared assumptions about openness, independence and accountability.

Negotiations aimed at achieving agreement over the *interpretative* aspects of risk assessment policy might be the most challenging of the three sets of discussions, but making those assumptions explicit, and then comparing them with each other, in open and accountable ways, might go a very long way to providing policy-making regimes that effectively achieved and reconciled both scientific and democratic legitimacy. Moreover, the resultant regimes should then be EU-wide and WTO-dispute-proof.

The foregoing discussion has revealed how the co-dynamic model can serve several purposes. First, it can help to explain why and where regulatory disputes have arisen, by reference to contrasting risk assessment policy assumptions.

Second, it can enable us to identify the conditions under which convergence might be attainable. Third, the model indicates a set of structural and procedural conditions under which science-based regulatory policy-making processes could be reformed to enhance their scientific and democratic legitimacy.

Meeting those conditions would, moreover not only enhance the domestic legitimacy of policy regimes: they would also render them 'WTO-proof'. Risk assessment policies are therefore pivotal to understanding the role of science in policy-making, the causes of regulatory trade disputes and the conditions under which regulatory diversity can be sustainable and those under which regulatory convergence might be enhanced.

Note

1 See Industrial Union Department, *AFL-CIO* v. *American Petroleum Institute*, 448 US 607 (1980).

Bibliography

BfR (2005) *Guidance Document – The Format for Health Assessment Documents.*

Brickman, R., Jasanoff, S. and Ilgen, T. (1985) *Controlling Chemicals: The Politics of Regulation in Europe and the USA*, Ithaca: Cornell University Press.

CAC (2003) Codex Alimentarius Commission, *Procedural Manual*, 13th edition; available as ftp://ftp.fao.org/codex/Publications/ProcManuals/Manual_13e.pdf, accessed October 2011.

——(2007) *Working Principles for Risk Analysis for Food Safety for Application by Governments*; available at www.fao.org/docrep/010/a1550t/a1550t00.htm> and as ftp://ftp.fao.org/codex/Publications/Booklets/Risk/Risk_EN_FR_ES.pdf, accessed October 2011.

CoC (2006) *Minutes of Committee on Carcinogenicity*, 2 March; available at www.advisorybodies.doh.gov.uk/coc/meetings/coc061.htm, accessed 6 June 2007.

Commission of the European Community (2000) *White Paper on Food Safety in the European Union*, COM(99) 719, 12 January; available at http://ec.europa.eu/dgs/health_consumer/library/pub/pub06_en.pdf, accessed October 2011.

——(2002a) 'Communication from the Commission towards a Reinforced Culture of Consultation and Dialogue: General Principles and Minimum Standards for Consultation of Interested Parties by the Commission', COM(2002) 704.

——(2002b) Communication from the Commission 'On the Collection and Use of Expertise by the Commission: Principles and Guidelines', COM(2002) 713.

——(2002c) Communication of the Commission 'On Ompact Assessment', COM (2002) 276; Communication from the Commission 'Action Plan Simplifying and Improving the Regulatory Environment', COM(2002) 278.

——(2002d) Communication from the Commission 'The Operating Framework for the European Regulatory Agencies', COM(2002) 718.

——(2010a) 'Commission Announces Upcoming Proposal on Choice for Member States To Cultivate or Not To Cultivate GMOs and Approves 5 Decisions on GMOs', Brussels, 3 March; available at http://ec.europa.eu/malta/news/commission_announces_upcoming_proposal_gmos_mt.htm. accessed March 2010 and 25 September 2011.

——(2010b), *Proposed Amendment to Directive 2001/18 Regulation 1829/2003*; available at http://eur-lex.europa.eu/LexUriServ/LexUriServ.do?uri=OJ:L:2010:053:0011:0014:EN:PDF, accessed October 2011.

Delaney (1959) *The Delaney Clause*, named after Congressman James Delaney of New York which amended the Federal Food, Drugs, and Cosmetic Act in 1958.

EC (1990) Directive 90/220 of the European Parliament and of the Council 'On the Deliberate Release into the Environment of Genetically Modified Organisms'.

——(2001) Directive 2001/18/EC of the European Parliament and of the Council 'On the Deliberate Release into the Environment of Genetically Modified Organisms and Repealing Council Directive 90/220/EEC'.

EC SCVMPH (1999) 'Opinion of the Scientific Committee on Veterinary Measures relating to Public Health Assessment of Potential Risks to Human Health from Hormone Residues in Bovine Meat and Meat Products', Document XXIV/B3/SC4, 30 April.

EFSA (2010) 'Guidance on the Environmental Risk Assessment of Genetically Modified Plants, European Food Safety Authority Panel on Genetically Modified Organisms', *EFSA Journal*, 8(11): 1879, pages 1–111; available at *www.efsa.europa.eu/de/efsajournal/doc/1879.pdf*, accessed October 2011.

FSA (2002) *Report on the Review of Scientific Committees*, Food Standards Agency, 15 April 2002; available at www.food.gov.uk/multimedia/pdfs/publication/fsa02_03_04rep.pdf, accessed October 2011.

FSC (2004) *Standards for the Safety Assessment of Genetically Modified Foods (Seeds Plants)*, Japan Food Safety Commission, Tokyo, 29 January.

Funtowicz, S. and Ravetz, J. (1993) 'Science for the Post-Normal Age', *Futures*, 25: 739–55.

Habermas, J. (1971) 'The Scientization of Politics and Public Opinion', first published in *Technik und Wissenschaft als Ideologie*, Frankfurt am Main: Suhrkamp Verlag, 1968 and translated into English in *Toward a Rational Society*, Boston, MA: Beacon Press, pp. 62–80.

Hood, C. and Rothstein, H. (2001) 'Risk Regulation under Pressure: Problem Solving or Blame Shifting?', *Administration and Society*, 33(1): 21–53.

House of Lords (1998) *EC Regulation of Genetic Modification in Agriculture*, Second Report of the Select Committee on the European Communities, Session 1998–99, HL 11-I, London: The Stationery Office.

Jasanoff, S. (1990) *The Fifth Branch: Science Advisors as Policy-Makers*, Cambridge, MA: Harvard University Press.

——(1995) *Science at the Bar: Law, Science and Technology in America*, Cambridge, MA: Harvard University Press.

——(2000) 'Between Risk and Precaution – Reassessing the Future of GM Crops', *Journal of Risk Research*, 3(3): 277–82.

——(2005) *Designs on Nature – Science and Democracy in Europe and the United States*, Princeton, NJ: Princeton University Press.

Levidow, L. and Carr, S. (2000) 'Unsound Science? Trans-Atlantic Regulatory Disputes over GM Crops', *International Journal of Biotechnology*, 2: 257–73.

Levidow, L. and Murphy, J. (2003) 'Reframing Regulatory Science: Trans-Atlantic Conflicts over GM Crops', *Cahiers d'économie et sociologie rurales*, 68–69: 48–74.

Levidow, L., Murphy, J. and Carr, S. (2007) 'Recasting "Substantial Equivalence": Transatlantic Governance of GM Food', *Science Technology and Human Values*, 32 (1): 26–64.

Levidow, L., Carr, S., Wield, D. and von Schomberg, R. (1997) 'European Biotechnology Regulation: Framing the Risk Assessment of a Herbicide-Tolerant Crop', *Science, Technology and Human Values*, 22: 472–505.

Losey, J.E., Rayor, L.S. and Carter, M.E. (1999) 'Transgenic Pollen Harms Monarch Larvae', *Nature*, 399(6733): 214.

MAFF Japan (2004) *The Application of Approval for the Production and Distribution of GMOs under the Jurisdiction of Minister of Agriculture, Forestry and Fisheries*, Notification of the Food Safety and Consumers Bureau of Ministry of Agriculture, Forestry and Fisheries (MAFF), No. 15-5839.

Millstone, E. (2000) 'Food Safety and Consumer Protection in a Globalised Economy', *Swiss Political Science Review*, 6(3): 109–18.

——(2007) 'Can Food Safety Policy-making be both Scientifically and Democratically Legitimated? If so, how?', *Journal of Agricultural and Environmental Ethics*, 20: 483–508.

——(2009) 'Science, Risk and Governance: Radical Rhetorics and the Realities of Reform', *Research Policy*, 38(4): 624–36.

Millstone, E. and van Zwanenberg, P. (2003) 'Food and Agricultural Biotechnology Policy: How Much Autonomy Can Developing Countries Exercise?', *Development Policy Review*, 21(5-6): 655–67.

Millstone, E., Brunner, E. and Mayer, S. (1999) 'Beyond the "Substantial Equivalence" of GM Foods', *Nature*, 401: 525–26.

Millstone, E., van Zwanenberg, P., Marris, C., Levidow, L. and Torgersen, H. (2004) *Science in Trade Disputes Related to Potential Risk: Comparative Case Studies*, Seville: Institute for Prospective Technological Studies: European Science and Technology Observatory Technical Report Series; available at http://esto.jrc.es/detailshort.cfm?ID_report=1203, accessed October 2011.

Millstone, E., van Zwanenberg, P., Levidow, L., Spök, A., Hirakawa, H. and Matsuo, M. (2008) *Risk-assessment Policies: Differences Across Jurisdictions*, Seville: Institute for Prospective Technological Studies, EUR Number: 23259 EN, April; available at http://ipts.jrc.ec.europa.eu/publications/pub.cfm?id=1562, accessed October 2011.

MoE (undated), Ministry of Environment Japan, *Guidance on Implementation of Assessment of Adverse Effect on Biological Diversity of Type 1 Use of Living Modified Organisms*, from Ministry of Environment, Ministry of Finance, Ministry of Education, Culture, Sports, Science and Technology, Ministry of Health, Labour and Welfare, Ministry of Economy, Trade and Industry (METI), Ministry of Agriculture, Forestry and Fisheries; available as www.bch.biodic.go.jp/download/en_law/en_assessment_guidence.doc from www.bch.biodic.go.jp/english/law.html, accessed 6 June 2007.

Mounts, G.J. (1980) 'OSHA Standards: the Burden of Proof', *Monthly Labor Review*, 103(9): 53–6.

OECD (1993) *Safety Evaluation of Foods Derived by Modern Biotechnology*, Paris: OECD.

OST (1997) *The Use of Scientific Advice in Policy Making*, UK Office of Science and Technology, London: HMSO.

——(2000) *Scientific Advice and Policy Making*, London: HMSO.

——(2005) *Scientific Analysis in Policy Making*, London: Office of Science and Technology (revision of OST, 2000, *Scientific Advice and Policy Making*).

Torgersen, H. and Seifert, F. (2000) 'Austria: Precautionary Blockage of Agricultural Biotechnology', *Journal of Risk Research*, 3(3): 209–17.

US Congress (2001) *Data Quality Act*, Section 515 of the Consolidated Appropriations Act, 2001, Pub.L. 106-554; available at http://frwebgate.access.gpo.gov/cgi-bin/getdoc.cgi?dbname=106_cong_public_laws& docid = f:publ554.106, accessed October 2011.

US Federal Register (1987) 52 FR 49586, Dec. 31, as amended at 67 FR 78174, Dec. 23, 2002; available at http://a257.g.akamaitech.net/7/257/2422/12feb20041500/edocket.access.gpo.gov/cfr_2004/aprqtr/pdf/21cfr500.82.pdf, accessed 6 June 2007.

US National Academy of Sciences (1978) *Saccharin: Technical Assessment of Risks and Benefits*, Washington, DC: Government Printing Office.

van Zwanenberg, P. and Millstone, E. (2000) 'Beyond Skeptical Relativism: eEvaluating the Social Constructions of Expert Risk Assessments', *Science, Technology & Human Values*, 25(3): 259–82.

——(2005) *BSE: Risk, Science and Governance*, Oxford: Oxford University Press.

Weber, M. (1958) *Gesammelte politischen Schriften*, 2nd edn, Tübingen: Mohr Verlag.

Weingart, P. (1999) 'Scientific Expertise and Political Accountability: Paradoxes of Science in Politics', *Science and Public Policy*, 151–61.

Weiss, R. (2004) 'Data Quality Law is Nemesis of Regulation', *Washington Post*, 16 August.

White, L. (1926) *Introduction to the Study of Public Administration*, New York: Macmillan.

WTO (1997) 'EC Measures Concerning Meat and Meat Products (Hormones) Complaint by the United States – Report of the Panel', WT/DS26/R/USA, 18 August, Geneva: WTO.

WTO Appellate Body (1998) *EC Measures Concerning Meat and Meat Products (Hormones)*, AB-1997-4, Document number 98-0099, 16 January.

Wynne, B. (1992) 'Uncertainty and Environmental Learning: Reconceiving Science and Policy in the Preventative Paradigm', *Global Environmental Change*, 2(2): 111–27.

3 Between uncertainty and responsibility

Precaution and the complex journey towards reflexive innovation

Mariachiara Tallacchini

Introduction

In the context of the European regulation of science and technology, the precautionary principle has been used to provide a wide protection of the health of human beings, animals, plants and the environment. Initially aimed at framing potential risks as actual risks because 'lack of full scientific certainty' may lead to 'threats of serious or irreversible damage', the precautionary principle has gradually evolved toward a more complex and stratified concept. In fact, while its major epistemological achievement consisted in shifting the focus from certainty to uncertainty in the vision of science, and from a neutral legal attitude towards scientific uncertainty to a positive bias towards safety, its limits were shown in its paternalistic and discretional implementation, and in its failure to describe uncertainty as integral to the daily life of technological societies.

Increasingly, the relationship between science and society has moved towards a situation where uncertain knowledge is the rule. Uncertainty has become a general term to refer to a broad variety of situations connected to knowledge complexities (Wynne *et al.* 2007; Stirling 2010): lack of data, ongoing or incomplete information, ignorance, unresolved ambiguities, unexpected developments and outcomes, and other forms of unpredictability.

In dealing with emerging (and re-emerging) technologies (Tallacchini 2011a, 2011b), European institutions have gone through an enduring learning process about how and when to regulate, in order not to make the mistake of responding too early to a technology, to fail to adequately address its nature or to act too late and miss the opportunity to intervene (Von Schomberg and Davies 2010: 8). During this process toward better – or smarter (Rübig 2012) – regulation, the EU has developed a specific regulatory approach that recognizes the political embeddedness of science (Shepherd 2000; Vos 2008) and, increasingly, at least in principle, the importance of public participation and engagement (Hagendijk and Irwin 2006; Wynne *et al.* 2007). More recently, this 'European approach' (CEC 2012) has also been proposed as a fair global model for the governance of science (CEC 2009, 2012).[1]

Indeed, in the passage from biotechnology to nanotechnology, and now (at least prospectively) to synthetic biology, the original concept of precaution has been enriched with new elements of reflection. On the one hand, the idea of an 'extended participatory model' in the relationships between science and society has been introduced as a general method to gather all relevant knowledge by engaging all potentially interested citizens and to make it available to policy-making. On the other hand, precaution has been (re-)integrated in the principle of responsibility that should inform research and innovation with emerging technologies. In this respect, the inclusion of the precautionary principle in the Nanocode of conduct for responsible research on nanosciences and nanotechnologies (CEC 2008) illustrates how precaution is no longer enforced as a veto-power belonging to institutions and associated with top-down policies. Instead, it is increasingly envisioned as a more distributed social practice that researchers, Member States and all stakeholders can and should directly endorse as part of responsible behaviour: a principle shared by sound science, good practices and public ethics.

All these developments proceeding towards more aware and careful innovation are definitely consistent with widely agreed expectations about global governance of science and technology (CEC 2009; Suresh 2011). However, it is a matter of debate over to what extent and how responsible innovation can be implemented effectively, and whether it is capable of preventing catastrophic outcomes (Dupuy 2004, 2011).

Even though these concerns cannot be easily addressed and set aside, it may still be argued that the very same idea of collectively practising responsibility as an epistemic, moral and political principle has the potential to promote an innovative and valuable culture of social commitment. This chapter explores the changes in the meaning and role of the precautionary principle, highlighting them as a co-production between science, democracy and law.

Policy models for regulatory science

The leading role that science is playing in economic and social development has caused politics and the law, on the one hand, to be colonized by an increasing amount of scientific knowledge and, on the other hand, to engage in techno-science regulation. Many decisions concerning public policy strongly depend on scientific knowledge, requiring the State's powers – the organs of government, legislative power and the judiciary – to be directly involved in science-related regulatory choices and to equip themselves with experts (committees and boards of experts, expert witnesses, risk assessors). Furthermore, in connection with the increasing impact of science and technology on society, legal systems initiated a broad regulatory activity towards scientific products and procedures. The interplay between science and society – and its political and legal institutions – has become so strong that it deeply affects institutional dynamics, the roles of the different stakeholders and the positions of individual citizens.

Science dealing directly with public policy was recognized quite early as being a distinct activity from both pure science and applied science (OTA

1986; Shepherd 2000). Pure science is mainly guided by the researcher's curiosity, while applied science is guided by a project and its goal to achieve particular outcomes. In contrast, policy-related science must help to define the problems which, as they have to find a social application, are linked to broad judgments that eventually demand a political choice even where they appear to be purely scientific or technical problems.

'Science in policy' and 'policy for science' – as depicted at the beginning of science policy theoretical analysis (Brooks 1968) – had already shown the links between the inevitable presence of scientific knowledge in regulatory matters and the open and uncertain character of scientific knowledge itself, requiring policy choices to fill the gaps. While policy-makers have to be better informed about science, experts involved in policy-making – advisors, members of technical boards, expert witnesses in trials – form an integral part of the political–scientific process.

The complexities resulting from the mixing of science and the rules that govern civil life have given rise to concerns about the most adequate ways of governing science in democratic societies, leading toward a rethinking of the idea of the State under the rule of law.

Three models of science policy

With some simplifications, three main science policy models have been described which show the historical developments of the relationships between science and political decision-making (Funtowicz and Strand 2007). Although quite different, they can be found as coexisting and competing even within the same regulatory environment. These models can be defined as 'science-based', 'precautionary', and 'extended participatory'.

While the first model stands by itself in maintaining a strong division between science and policy, and in denying the legitimacy of the specific features of science when framed for policy purposes, the other two share some basic assumptions about the blurred boundaries between facts and values as well as between descriptive and normative languages.

Science-based policy

Since the origins of modern thought, political and legal philosophy have emphasized the neutrality and objectivity of scientific method, which seem to be lacking irremediably in political and legal thought. The unique opportunity and example that science has offered to social disciplines in order to free them from values and subjective opinions, have been widely explored by legal scholars and political scientists as ways both to shaping legal systems according to the rules of logic and to founding the social contract on scientific bases. From this perspective, science is considered both as a methodological idea and a reality separated from society, a self-contained form of knowledge with no links to social practices (Tallacchini 2002).

By and large, this approach has also influenced the legal regulation of scientific activities and products. Law related to science has been framed as technical rules, meaning that science brings norms their contents – namely, knowledge validated by the scientific community – and law plays a neutral role in science, acting rather as a mechanism for enforcement.

The image of the scientific community corresponding to this model is the idealized 'Republic of science' depicted by Michael Polanyi (and in a similar way by Robert Merton) (Polanyi 1962; Merton 1968). According to this model, scientists form a perfect community of peers, self-governing through shared and freely discussed knowledge, with no coercive mechanisms or authority other than knowledge itself.

Science and its experts should naturally prevail over society in the name of the authority of knowledge.[2] The science-based model shows its main character in claiming to be more rigorously and objectively informed by scientific facts and theories: decisions are legitimized by the assumed validity of science. Validity and morality are intrinsically connected in the scientific community. Validity is part of the 'ethos' that, according to Merton, while expressing the reliability of scientific method, also shapes scientists' moral integrity (Merton 1968: 613). The morality of the scientific community (Merton 1968) has represented one of the most important reasons to exempt science, when science policy was first shaped in the USA after World War II (Bush 1945), from those legal and political controls that should apply to all powers in democratic societies. In this vision, 'science speaks truth to power' (Wildavsky 1979): namely, it is a precondition for legitimate politics and can only thrive in a politically free environment. However, the hypothesis of the separation of science from the other social systems, incorporated in this model, fails at least to consider that such a concept is implausible when analyzed in the context of institutional procedures and social practices, where science, policy and the law merge and reciprocally legitimize their respective forms of knowledge.

The precautionary model

The understanding of regulatory science – science framed for regulatory purposes – as a technical and neutral tool has been showed to be unrealistic. 'One does not have to believe rigidly in the constructivist account of science or adopt the most radical form of ontological skepticism', Jasanoff has argued, to conclude that:

> regulatory science is particularly susceptible to divergent, socially conditioned interpretations. … In regulatory science … standards for assessing quality tend to be more fluid, controversial and sensitive to political factors. … Further, regulatory science is often constrained by strict time limitations that impede scientific consensus-building. At the same time, the stakes are so much higher in regulatory than in research science that different

> interest groups have incentives to press for divergent, politically congenial interpretations of the available facts.
>
> (Jasanoff 1995: 281–82)

However, the uncertainties arising, first from environmental problems and later from the consequences of new technologies (OTA 1986; Jasanoff 2011), with scientific positions and predictions becoming more divided and controversial, have become major rationales for a different vision.

Contemporary scientific knowledge has been described as increasingly characterized by uncertainty (O'Riordan and Cameron 1994). Such uncertainty is the daily condition that shapes scientific work and affects technologies and their social consequences. As scientific data prove uncertain, insufficient or susceptible to sharply diverging interpretations, law bears the responsibility to fill the gaps left by science: the intrinsic incompleteness and open-ended indeterminacy of scientific knowledge can hardly match with the needs to adopt social choices, public policies and legal decisions.

The expression 'scientific uncertainty' has been used to refer to different cognitive conditions: complexity of knowledge, lack of data, unpredictability of results and the stochastic character of predictions. Lack of knowledge has been defined for policy purposes through different concepts: risk, uncertainty, ignorance and indeterminacy. In decisions under conditions of risk, the main variables of a problem are known and the respective probability of different outcomes is quantified. In contrast, in decisions under conditions of uncertainty, even if the main variables of a system are known, the probability of an event cannot be quantified. Ignorance is the situation dealing with 'unknown unknowns' (Wynne 1992; Van Asselt 2000; EEA 2001; Wynne *et al.* 2007). As the variables of a problem are not identified, the potential negative outcomes remain unknown and unpredictable unless new cognitive elements emerge (EEA 2001). Finally, indeterminacy is the concept summarizing the fundamentally open and conditional character of all knowledge, particularly its contextual meaning and its socio-cultural determination (Wynne *et al.* 2007).

How to legally frame uncertainty was a problem at the root of the precautionary principle when it was first internationally established in 1992 – as the precautionary approach – by Principle 15 of the Rio Declaration on Environment and Development:

> In order to protect the environment, the precautionary approach shall be widely applied by States according to their capabilities. Where there are threats of serious or irreversible damages, lack of full scientific certainty shall not be used as a reason for postponing cost-effective measures to prevent environment degradations.

Starting with the Maastricht Treaty (Article 130 R, para. 2, and later Article 174 EC Treaty), the precautionary principle has been shaped as an autonomous concept, distinct from the idea of risk assessment – now received by the Treaty on the Functioning of the European Union (TFEU) (Title XX, Environment, Article 191). The European interpretation of precaution was developed assuming that the law may protect against a potential risk even before a causal link for a risk has been established. In fact, scientific evidence may be achieved too late, and what constitutes an acceptable risk remains a political decision. From this perspective, the law is not exclusively bound to scientific knowledge in order to protect citizens. As scholarly work on precaution outlined very early in theoretically shaping precaution, the main element separating risk assessment and the precautionary principle centres on their different attitudes toward safety. While the former 'is information intensive and rational, [...] and often does take a neutral attitude towards uncertainty', 'the precautionary principle is not neutral towards uncertainty – it is biased in favour of safety' (Bodansky 1994: 209).

As is known, in risk analysis, two different kinds of error may occur in decisions taken under uncertainty: errors of type-I occur when one rejects a true null hypothesis (a claim of no effect); errors of type-II occur when one fails to reject a false null hypothesis. In assessing technological impacts, in a situation of uncertainty where both types of error cannot be avoided, when we minimize a type-I error, we minimize the error of rejecting a harmless development; when we minimize a type-II error, we minimize the error of accepting a harmful development. The former depends on an excessive scientific optimism, the latter on an excessive prudence. Precaution aims at minimizing risks for people.

These assumptions informed the European Commission *Communication on the Precautionary Principle in 2000*. Precaution was openly framed as a 'general principle' governing all European health policies ('environment, human, animal or plant health') and as an 'eminently political responsibility' about 'what is an "acceptable" level of risk for society' in connection with 'the high level of protection chosen for the Community' (CEC 2000).

Despite its political importance, the Commission Communication has been widely criticized for its paternalistic and top-down approach, and for the discretionary power given to authorities. Other criticisms address the ambiguities inherent in the principle and its applications. In 2002, a formulation very close to precautionary principle arguments was provided by Donald Rumsfeld to invoke a preemptive war with Iraq, due to the potential existence of WMD (weapons of mass destruction) (Saltelli and Funtowicz 2004). In 2003, within the European (Council of Europe and the European Communities) regulation of clinical experimentation of xenotransplants, the principle was evoked to legitimize precautionary constraints against patients, instead of protecting them from a potentially risky biomedical technology (Tallacchini 2011a). In 2004 the World Trade Organization (WTO), in the US *v.* EU trial concerning GMOs (genetically modified organisms), interpreted the European interpretation of precaution as a vested form of economic protectionism (Winickoff *et al.* 2005).

Several different factors have also contributed to a revision of precaution, especially in the EU context. In 2001, in the middle of a variety of health and food crises, the European Commission had to adopt an *Action Plan* for a closer relationship between science and society after European citizens' distrust toward science and technology became apparent (CEC 2002). Roughly at the same period, the effort to establish a knowledge-based economy and society under the Lisbon Strategy[3] called for a more reflective approach to scientific uncertainties resulting from the complex dynamics of emerging technologies. A better foundation of precaution, based on a more democratic and participatory approach to science policy, was needed.

The extended participatory model

In the early 1990s, Jerry Ravetz and Silvio Funtowicz introduced the expression 'post-normal science' to refer to situations where 'typically facts are uncertain, values in dispute, stakes high, and decisions urgent' (Funtowicz and Ravetz 1991, 1993; Funtowicz 2001).

Contemporary technoscience and its social impact nearly always give rise to post-normal conditions: in other words, post-normal science usually represents the normal situation in most of scientific social choices. From this point of view, conceptually speaking the precautionary principle as defined in the Rio Declaration is superseded. The implicit assumption that the 'lack of scientific certainty' justifying a precautionary approach would remain an exceptional, circumstantial and temporary condition that is absent from scientists' daily work has been widely challenged. The incremental model of science, where truth is reached sooner or later, is over: post-normal science is the norm.

The increasing speed at which emerging technologies develop and reciprocally connect has only served to make 'post-normality' more relevant. In discussing the challenges of nanotechnology, the epistemologist Jean-Pierre Dupuy outlined the most radical vision of uncertainty, which is not envisaged in the current meaning of the precautionary principle:

> The key notion here is that of informational incompressibility, which is a form of essential unpredictability. In keeping with von Neumann's intuitions on complexity, a complex process is defined today as one for which the simplest model is the process itself. The only way to determine the future of the system is to run it: there are no shortcuts. This is a radical uncertainty.
>
> (Dupuy 2004: 80)[4]

Uncertainties depending on the social implementation of new technologies require that broader conversations be opened up with scientists and citizens, their both being subjects of potentially relevant knowledge for decision-making and responsible actors in society.

The so-called 'extended participatory' model (or extended peer-review) (Liberatore and Funtowicz 2003; Stirling 2010) is based on a more general democratization of scientific expertise and public participation in science-based public policy.

This vision of the relationship between science and society does not refuse to acknowledge the privileged character of scientific language. Science may speak particularly reliable words, but it does not have the power to have the final say as to social choices.

The good governance of science is a problem of democracy and 'public reason' (Jasanoff 2012): every social decision must be screened in different places and through a plurality of knowledge, comparisons and transactions (Jasanoff 2004, 2011). Moreover, law becomes the place where different knowledge and languages are discussed and confronted.

It would be reductionist to interpret such a position as an antiscientific one. On the contrary, it is a question of favouring a deeper comprehension of the complex links between science and society, determining more adequate ways and procedures in scientific and technological choices at the root of social and civil transformations. 'If democracy is only seen as majority voting, and expertise as a self-referential system in which only peers can recognize and judge each other', Liberatore and Funtowicz clarified, then:

> clearly democratizing expertise, is a contradiction in terms. When such premises are challenged however, the contradiction disappears, while different issues still need to be addressed. … Science (seen as that activity performed by technicians and experts) is considered as a part of 'the relevant knowledge' and it is included only as a part of the probative evidence of a process. The ideal of rigorous scientific demonstration is thus replaced by an ideal of open public dialogue. Inside the knowledge production process, citizens become both critics and creators. Their contribution has not to be identified as 'local', 'practical', 'ethical', or 'spiritual' knowledge, but it has to be considered and accepted as a plurality of rightful and co-ordinated perspectives with their own meanings and value structures.

The outcome of this co-production of knowledge is a renovated kind of 'experience democracy' (Liberatore and Funtowicz 2003: 147). The European Commission endorsed this approach in the *White Paper on Governance* (CEC 2001) and has worked on the actual meaning and contents of governance since. This document expressed the need for deepening democracy in Europe, especially in the domain of science governance, where the democratic deficit is mostly felt by Europeans. As the EU has been shaken by several emergencies linked to inadequate and inefficient regulating measures in scientific fields, European reflection about science governance was meant not only to address the political need to re-establish citizens' trust towards science but also to work out a European way to regulate policy-related science.

The changes in the relationship between science and society are modifying the institutional structures, citizens' rights and the social contract deeply. If political rights granted to citizens in liberal democracies have been traditionally expressed through elections, the need to increase public knowledge and transparency about institutional procedures and decision-making has changed the traditional forms of participation to government and governance (Leach *et al.* 2005).

Although both Liberatore and Funtowicz's extended expertise model and Dupuy's radical critique of epistemic uncertainty seemed more aimed at showing the limits of the notion of precaution, and at overcoming it, the precautionary principle has been developed by scholarly analysis and policy-making towards more democratic practices.

Precaution as responsibility (for research and innovation)

In its early developments, the precautionary principle has been the object of much criticism, especially within specific scientific communities, as it was perceived as a kind of obscurantism and an instrumental support of irrational public fears, creating obstacles to innovation.

The reasons for this sceptical view were real and depended on how precaution had been theoretically conceived by the philosopher considered to be the main founder of the precautionary principle, Hans Jonas, and on the connection he had established between precaution and responsibility (Jonas 1984). Jonas rooted precaution in the feeling of fear towards the unknown consequences of innovation. This fear should guide humanity as a heuristic ('the heuristic of fear') in order to prevent technological threats. When confronted with scientific uncertainty and potentially irreversible damage to the environment, responsibility would require that we prioritize the worst-case scenario when taking action. In other words, a prophecy of doom has always to be preferred over a prophecy of hope, if humanity wishes to avoid a catastrophic end.

However, as seen above, uncertainty is not just a synonym for non-rationality or irrationality, and precaution as a policy-tool has lately developed towards becoming an epistemological approach to complex issues requiring more democracy. The task of creating an epistemic statute for the lack of knowledge may proceed hand in hand with a behaviour of active scientific wisdom, self-reflexivity, awareness of the value-laden dimensions of science, the intentions of making choices more legitimate and shared. In a similar way, responsibility should be rethought and reframed in order to connect individual and collective responsibility in terms of shared decisions and commitments (Von Schomberg 2007).

The current understanding of precaution goes beyond the idea of an emergency principle about science, while the concept of responsibility is expanding beyond liability and accountability. Precaution is democratically understood and endorsed as a form of responsible action, while responsibility is now depicted in worldwide policies on emerging technologies as the normative tool that brings precaution to individuals, making them self-reflexive about their actions.

This tendency to reframe precaution also as an individual (and not only as an institutional) principle together with responsibility has several reasons, connected to the changes brought about by new technologies (such as nanotechnology and synthetic biology) and to how these are reshaping both the scientific community and society.

After having launched a *European Strategy for Nanotechnology* in 2004, followed by an *Action Plan (2005–2009)* (CEC 2004, 2005), in 2008 the Commission approved, through a non-binding Recommendation, a code of conduct for responsible nanosciences and nanotechnologies research. The code invites: 'all stakeholders to act responsibly and co-operate with each other, in a safe, ethical and effective framework, supporting sustainable economic, social and environmental development'; and provides 'Member States, employers, research funders, researchers and more generally all individuals and civil society organisations involved or interested in nanosciences and nanotechnologies research with guidelines favouring a responsible and open approach to N&n research in the Community' (CEC 2008: 3–4).

The 'integrated, safe and responsible approach' was already at the core of the EU policy for nanotechnology, based on 'the high level of public health, safety, consumers and workers protection, and environmental protection chosen by the Community': the very same conditions allowing the precautionary principle to be invoked.

The soft law code is going to play a new role as a complementary instrument to legislation. As emerging technologies may develop in unexpected ways and several aspects cannot be anticipated, integrating the existing and the future legal provisions with norms providing guidance for individual behaviour is a way to overcome the gaps left by the law (Von Schomberg and Davies 2010). Appeal to responsibility as a precautionary attitude toward research is part of this guidance.

One of the major legal issues with nanosciences and technologies concerns the wide range of disparate topics that nanolegislation should cover, as nanos may range from the domains of physics and mechanics to food, cosmetics and medicine. Precaution and responsibility have the potential for transversally entering the field, indicating general principles and ethical boundaries valid for all research (Lee 2012), while leaving room for specific adaptations and personal commitment.

This more 'individualized' perspective in rethinking the precautionary principle goes even further with the peculiarities of synthetic biology (Tallacchini 2011b) and the tendencies towards DIY (do-it-yourself) technologies. In so-called post-academic, deinstitutionalized sciences – another expression of post-normality – scientists tend not to be rooted in single disciplines (and their ethical codes), not to belong to scientific and academic institutions; also, citizens are more likely to cultivate science and technology in 'amateur' ways:

> This will require mechanisms for amateurs to increase their knowledge and skills, access to a community of experts, the development of a code

> of ethics, responsible oversight and leadership on issues that are unique to doing biology outside of traditional professional settings.[5]

Responsibility and precaution here acquire a different and further meaning and role. In an almost completely prospective sector such as synbio, belonging more to imagination than to reality, potentially hosting a dispersed crowd of professional and amateur scientists, these principles may provide a fundamentally informal normative network (Von Schomberg and Davies 2010).

What's next? Scenarios of doom and hope versus exercises for a shared future

Since its beginnings and along the way, precaution has undergone dramatic changes in its foundations and ways of implementation. Started primarily as a prudential attitude towards technological unknowns, through time the precautionary principle has become epistemologically more sophisticated and politically more democratic. Also, it has shifted from a top-down, paternalistic form of citizens' protection to an instrument for citizens' empowerment. Most of its ambiguities have been progressively solved, allowing it to move on and to better express its potential value.

However, and despite all these positive developments, whether or not precaution and responsibility will be likely to develop safer technoscience is a matter of debate. According to supporters of 'Responsible Research and Innovation' (RRI) (CEC 2012; Von Schomberg 2012), the new EU science policy 'mantra' of responsibility – meant as, and embedded in, precaution – represents a key notion to deal with uncertain technologies and a desirable path in the attempt to normalize them:

> Responsible Research and Innovation is a transparent, interactive process by which societal actors and innovators become mutually responsive to each other with a view to the (ethical) acceptability, sustainability and societal desirability of the innovation process and its marketable products (in order to allow a proper embedding of scientific and technological advances in our society).
>
> (Von Schomberg 2012: 51)

The new vision of Europe, building on and developing post-Lisbon Treaty strategies for creating a European knowledge society, has been defined as the Innovation Union. As outlined in the *Europe 2020 Strategy*, 'this is a vision of Europe as an economy that is smart, sustainable and inclusive. The Innovation Union aims to turn ideas into jobs, generate green growth and promote social progress.'[6] However, 'to the extent that research and innovation are not ends in themselves but anchored in human rights and linked to public goods, European policy seeks robust and effective mechanisms for the governance of science and innovation' (CEC 2012: 4). Therefore, the ideal of Responsible

Research and Innovation requires 'a combination of the three themes of ethical acceptability, risk management, and human benefit' (CEC 2012: 8).

From this perspective, responsibility should imply taking care of all technological potential outcomes, well beyond a simplistic risk-benefit analysis, as not all outcomes fall within these two categories. Responsibility should involve more than just liability or accountability, and it should also look to care and responsiveness. Responsibility should overcome the individual dimension, and there is a need to build an operational legal concept of collective responsibility.

However, according to a different view, there are reasons to remain sceptical towards the idea of responsibility. After having shown how useless precaution becomes when we look at ontological, and not merely epistemic, uncertainty in dealing with the complexities of the nanoscale, Dupuy has argued that the concept of responsibility can be dangerous and mischievous, as it may induce a form of technological pride:

> We know today that prideful humanism which gives the modern world its incredible dynamism imperils the very continuation of the human adventure. We are living henceforth in the shadow of future catastrophes that, taken as a system, will perhaps provoke the disappearance of the species. Our responsibility is enormous, since we are the sole cause of what is happening to us. But our sense of responsibility has every chance of increasing inordinately the pride that got us here. Persuading ourselves that the salvation of the world is in our hands and that humanity is obligated to be its own saviour, we run the risk of throwing ourselves further into this headlong rush, this panic movement, which world history resembles more each day.
>
> (Dupuy 2011)

While these opposite scenarios of doom and hope fight for plausibility, the relevance of the epistemic, moral and political developments of precaution and responsibility seems to depend on something other than predictability and control of technological outcomes. Even though 'normal accidents' – as Charles Perrow named the systemic complexities that make technological failures inevitable (Perrow 1984) – will be increasingly likely to happen, still the creation of a culture of diffuse and shared responsibility has the potential to make a big difference. How we discuss and prioritize our knowledge and values, and how we can learn to face all forms of uncertainty by learning mutual respect and solidarity, represents a different social and political approach to reducing uncertainty. These shared humanistic and civic exercises have an intrinsic potential to trigger a more reflexive journey toward the future.

Notes

1 The 'European approach' is described as 'anchored in the human rights tradition and especially those enshrined in the *Charter of Fundamental Rights of the European Union* and the Treaty of Lisbon: dignity, freedoms, equality, solidarity, citizen's rights, justice, and sustainability' (CEC 2012: 4).

2 'The authority of scientific opinion remains essentially mutual; it is established between scientists, not above them. Scientists exercise their authority over each other. Admittedly, the body of scientists, as a whole, does uphold the authority of science over the public' (Polanyi 1962: 60).

3 http://consilium.europa.eu/ueDocs/cms_Data/docs/pressData/en/ec/00100-r1.en0.htm (last accessed in May 2012).

4 In Dupuy's view, the introduction of subjective probabilities in statistics has allowed the reduction of uncertainty to the concept of quantifiable risk, because subjective probabilities no longer correspond to any sort of regularity found in nature, but simply to the coherence displayed by a given agent's choices.

> A risk can in principle be quantified in terms of objective probabilities based on observable frequencies; when such quantification is not possible, one enters the realm of uncertainty. It is easy to see that the introduction of subjective probabilities erases the distinction between uncertainty and risk, between risk and the risk of risk, between precaution and prevention. No difference remains compared to the case where objective probabilities are available from the outset. Uncertainty owing to lack of knowledge is brought down to the same plane as intrinsic uncertainty due to the random nature of the event under consideration. … In truth, one observes that applications of the 'precautionary principle' generally boil down to little more than a glorified version of 'cost-benefit' analysis.
>
> (Dupuy 2004: 78–9)

5 An Institution for the Do-It-Yourself Biologist, DIY-BIO, http://diybio.org (last accessed in May 2012).

6 See http://ec.europa.eu/europe2020/index_en.htm (last accessed in July 2012).

Bibliography

Bodansky, D. (1994) 'The Precautionary Principle in US Environmental Law', in T. O'Riordan and J. Cameron (eds), *Interpreting the Precautionary Principle*, London: Earthscan, pp. 203–28.

Brooks, H. (1968) *The Government of Science*, Cambridge, MA: MIT Press.

Bush, V. (1945) *Science – The Endless Frontier*, 40th Anniversary Edition, Washington, DC: National Science Foundation.

CEC (Commission of the European Communities) (2000) *Communication from the Commission on the Precautionary Principle*, Brussels, 2.2.2000, COM(2000) 1.

——(2001) *European Governance. A White Paper*, Brussels, 25.7.2001, COM(2001) 428 final.

——(2002) *Science and Society Action Plan*, Luxembourg: Office for Official Publications of the European Communities.

——(2004) *Communication from the Commission. Towards a European Strategy for Nanotechnology*, Luxembourg: Office for Official Publications of the European Communities.

——(2005) *Nanoscience and Nanotechnologies: An Action Plan for Europe 2005–2009. Communication of the Commission to the Council, and the Economic and Social Committee*, Luxembourg: Office for Official Publications of the European Communities.

——(2008) *Commission Recommendation of 07/02/2008 on a Code of Conduct for Responsible Nanosciences and Nanotechnologies Research, 424 final*, Brussels: Commission of the European Communities.

——(2009) *Global Governance of Science Report of the Expert Group on Global Governance of Science to the Science*, Luxembourg: Office for Official Publications of the European Communities.

——(2012) *Ethical and Regulatory Challenges to Science and Research Policy at the Global Level*, Luxembourg: Office for Official Publications of the European Communities.

Dupuy, J.P. (2004) 'Complexity and Uncertainty: A Prudential Approach to Nanotechnology', in European Commission, *A Preliminary Risk Analysis on the Basis of a Workshop Organized by the Health and Consumer Protection, Directorate General of the European Commission, in Brussels 1–2 March 2004.*

——(2011) 'Mourning the Future', Paper presented at the 'Catastrophe Practice' workshop, New School of Social Research, New York, 2 February 2011, available at www.wisdomportal.com/ReneGirard/MourningTheFuture.html (accessed in May 2012).

EEA (European Environmental Agency) (2001) *Late Lessons from Early Warnings: The Precautionary Principle 1896–2000*, available at www.eea.europa.eu/publications/environmental_issue_report_2001_22 (accessed in May 2012).

Funtowicz, S. (2001) 'Post-normal Science. Science and Governance under Conditions of Complexity', in M. Tallacchini and R. Doubleday (eds), *Science Policy and the Law: Relationships Among Institutions, Experts, and the Public*, Milan: Notizie di Politeia, XVII(62): 77–85.

Funtowicz, S. and Ravetz, J.R. (1991) 'A New Scientific Methodology for Global Environmental Issues', in R. Costanza (ed.), *The Ecological Economics*, New York: Columbia University Press, pp. 137–52.

——(1993) 'Science for the Post-Normal Age', *Futures*, 25: 735–55.

Funtowicz, S. and Strand, R. (2007) 'Models of Science and Policy', in T. Traavik and L.C. Lim (eds), *Biosafety First: Holistic Approaches to Risk and Uncertainty in Genetic Engineering and Genetically Modified Organisms*, Trondheim: Tapir, pp. 263–78.

Hagendijk, R. and Irwin, A. (2006) 'Public Deliberation and Governance: Engaging with Science and Technology in Contemporary Europe', *Minerva*, 44: 167–84.

Jasanoff, S. (1995) *Science at the Bar*, Cambridge, MA: Harvard University Press.

——(2004) *States of Knowledge: The Co-production of Science and Social Order*, New York: Routledge.

——(2011) 'Constitutional Moments in Governing Science and Technology', *Sci Eng Ethics*, 17: 621–38.

——(2012) *Science and Public Reason*, Oxon: Routledge.

Jonas, H. (1984) *The Imperative of Responsibility. Search of an Ethics for the Technological Age*, Chicago, IL: University of Chicago Press (Frankfurt a.M. 1979).

Leach, M., Scoones, I. and Wynne, B. (eds) (2005) *Science and Citizens. Globalization and the Challenge of Engagement*, London/New York: Zed Books.

Lee, G.R. (2012) 'Look at Mother Nature on the Run in the 21st Century: Responsibility, Research and Innovation', *Transnational Environmental Law*, 1(1): 105–17.

Liberatore, A. and Funtowicz, S. (eds) (2003) 'Special Issue on Democratising Expertise, Expertising Democracy', *Science and Public Policy*, 3(30): 146–232.

Merton, R.K. (1968) *Science and Democratic Social Structure. Social Theory and Social Structure*, New York: Free Press.

O'Riordan, T. and Cameron, J. (eds) (1994) *Interpreting the Precautionary Principle*, London: Earthscan.

OTA (US Congress, Office of Technology Assessment) (1986) *The Regulatory Environment for Science – A Technical Memorandum*, OTA-TM-SET-34, Washington, DC: US Government Printing Office.

Perrow, C. (1984) *Normal Accidents: Living with High-Risk Technologies*, New York: Basic Books.

Polanyi, M. (1962) 'The Republic of Science', *Minerva*, I: 54–73.

Rübig, P. (2012) 'The Changing Face of Risk Governance: Moving from Precaution to Smarter Regulation', *European Journal of Risk Regulation*, 2: 145–46.

Saltelli, A. and Funtowicz, S. (2004) 'The Precautionary Principle: Implications for Risk Management Strategies', *International Journal of Occupational Medicine and Environmental Health*, 17(1): 47–58.

Shepherd, I. (ed.) (2000) 'Science and Governance in the European Union. A Contribution to the Debate', 9 March 2000, Brussels, EUR 19554 EN.

Stirling, A. (2010) 'Keep It Complex', *Nature*, 468: 1029–31.

Suresh, S. (2011) 'Moving Toward Global Science', *Science*, 333: 802.

Tallacchini, M. (2002) 'Epistemology of the European Identity', *The Journal of Biolaw & Business, Supplement Series Bioethix*, 60–66.

——(2011a) 'Risks and Rights in Xenotransplantation', in S. Jasanoff (ed.), *Reframing Rights. Bioconstitutionalism in the Genetic Age*, Cambridge, MA: MIT Press, pp. 170–92.

——(2011b) '"Meta-framing" and "Re-connecting": What is New in Synthetic Biology and What Can Be Reflected on from the Past?', Washington, DC: National Academy of Engineering, 30 September 2010, Workshop on Synthetic Biology and Engineering Ethics, available at http://onlineethics.org/Projects/PastProjects/26661/SynBioWorkshop/SynBioParticipants/CommentsMTallacchini.aspx (accessed in July 2012).

Van Asselt, M.B.A. (2000) *Perspectives on Uncertainty and Risk: The PRIMA Approach to Decision Support*, Dordrecht: Kluwer, PhD thesis.

Von Schomberg, R. (2007) 'From the Ethics of Technology towards an Ethics of Knowledge Policy and Knowledge Assessment', a working document from the European Commission Services, Luxembourg: Office for Official Publications of the European Communities.

——(2012) 'Prospects for Technology Assessment in a Framework of Responsible Research and Innovation', in M. Dusseldorp and R. Beecroft (eds), *Technikfolgen abschätzen lehren: Bildungspotenziale transdisziplinärer Methoden*, Wiesbaden: Springer VS Verlag, pp. 39–61.

Von Schomberg, R. and Davies, S. (eds) (2010) *Understanding Public Debate on Nanotechnologies. Options for Framing Public Policy*, Luxembourg: Publication Office of the European Union.

Vos, E. (ed.) (2008) *European Risk Governance. Its Science, its Inclusiveness and its Effectiveness*, Mannheim: CONNEX Report Series No. 06, available at www.mzes.uni-mannheim.de/projekte/typo3/site/index.php?id=642 (accessed in July 2012).

Wildavsky, A. (1979) *Speaking Truth to Power*, Boston, MA: Little, Brown and Co.

Winickoff, D.E., Jasanoff, S., Busch, L., Grove-White, R. and Wynne, B. (2005) 'Adjudicating the GM Food Wars: Science, Risk, and Democracy in the World Trade Law', *The Yale Journal of International Law*, 30: 81–123.

Wynne, B. (1992) 'Uncertainty and Environmental Learning: Reconceiving Science and Policy in the Preventive Paradigm', *Global Environmental Change*, 2(22): 111–27.

Wynne, B., Felt, U., Callon, M., Eduarda Gonçalves, M., Jasanoff, S., Jepsen, M., Joly, P.-B., Konopasek, Z., May, S., Neubauer, C., Rip, A., Siune, K., Stirling, A. and Tallacchini, M. (2007) *Taking European Knowledge Society Seriously. European Commission DG Research Science, Economy and Society*, Luxembourg: Publication Office of the European Communities.

Part III

Regulatory practice: Pharmaceuticals, nanotechnology and climate change

4 Handling pharmaceutical risks in post-trust society

Science-based decision making under strain?

Frederic Bouder

Introduction

Decisions to ban or restrict particular products or technologies often involve risk-related claims, for example in the case of hormones in beef or genetically modified organisms (GMOs). Such disputes have triggered comparisons about the nature of the risk assessments conducted on both sides of the Atlantic, in particular the question of which trade block might be more precautionary, or whether one trade block is inherently more precautionary (Löfstedt and Vogel 2001; Wiener and Rogers 2002; Wiener *et al.* 2011; Vogel 2012). The programme of the topical conference organised at Maastricht University on 14–15 April 2010 highlighted, in the author's view rightly so, the fact that 'European and WTO rules put a focus on science in their attempt to ensure that measures adopted by Member States and/or the EU are inspired by genuine non-trade rather than protectionist motives and intentions'. This chapter takes a closer look at the process put in place to mobilise science and translate genuine non-trade concerns into workable measures in a sector of high value for the global economy and public health, namely, pharmaceuticals.

According to the European Commission Directorate-General for Trade, the EU is the second largest manufacturer of pharmaceuticals, with 31.1 per cent of world output (2008). The pharmaceutical sector is the fifth largest sector in the Union and employs over 600,000 people. Europe is a net exporter, with a trade surplus of €35 billion in 2009. The US market receives a third of these exports. On the other hand, regulatory decisions involve a difficult balancing of benefits and risks to human health, which takes place at global, (Vogel 1998; Abraham and Lawton Smith 2003; Harman 2004), European (Permanand 2006) and national levels. The meeting of global public health objectives, for example the eradication of major diseases (e.g. HIV – human immunodeficiency virus) and the promotion of immunisation programmes, requires the balancing of speedy circulation and distribution of pharmaceutical products with approaches to deal with drug-related risks. The Erice Declaration of 1997 (Hugman 2006) offers an insight into how science may be mobilised to deal with pharmaceutical risks, when it calls for 'independent expertise to ensure that safety information on all available medicines is adequately collected, impartially evaluated, and made accessible to all'.

Meeting this requirement has been the source of a good deal of confusion at the core of the European decision-making system when the European Parliament refused to sign off the 2009 budget of the European Medicines Agency (EMA) after Members of the European Parliament (MEPs) criticised the EMA over conflicts of interests (Watson 2011). The result has been to strengthen the trend towards more transparency and disclosure (Löfstedt and Bouder 2013). Critical questions may be raised: how do pharmaceutical regulators use scientific evidence in the 'real' world of risk decisions? In particular, how do governments mobilise and use knowledge when they are confronted by imminent perils? What are the consequences for 'the protection of human health and the environment'?

This chapter draws on evidence from seven case studies developed between 2003 and 2010. Two of these looked at the regulation of MMR (measles, mumps and rubella) and Hepatitis B vaccines (Bouder 2006), one studied cardiovascular biomarkers (Bouder 2007), one analysed impurities in pharmaceuticals (Bouder 2008), and finally three case studies looked at the quality and safety issues in a weight-control drug, an anti-HPV (human papillomavirus) vaccine and an anti-HIV medicine (EMA 2011). This chapter is divided into three parts. The first part draws on the background of the seven case studies to analyse the changing nature of the context in which policy decisions are taken. Scientists and policy makers are confronted by a 'post-trust environment' where expert-based decision making is increasingly challenged. The second part focuses on two of the studied cases, those on the anti-HIV drug Viracept and the anti-HPV vaccine Gardasil, where genuine non-trade protection measures have been at odds with public health and global supply objectives. The third and final part presents an analysis of the cases and some recommendations as to how to handle protection measures more effectively.

Pharmaceutical regulation in post-trust environment

Trust is primarily built through a sense of fairness, competence and efficiency (Albin 1993; Renn and Levine 1991; Linnerooth-Bayer and Fitzgerald 1996; Löfstedt 2005; Renn *et al.* 1995; Renn, Webler and Kastenholz 1996; Viscusi 1998; Young 1994). The public is likely to lose faith in the scientific robustness of public risk decisions when influential players disagree, when established authorities contradict each other or when they seem to collude with each other. Without trust, patients and the general public no longer rely on official sources of expertise to accept or protect themselves against risks. Typically, this leads to what Löfstedt calls a 'post-trust society' (Löfstedt 2005). In the post-trust society, the critical voices of new opinion leaders and non-governmental organisations (NGOs) become more trustworthy than government or scientists.

A number of scandals, which took place at the end of the twentieth century, have had a defining impact on European risk regulation, particularly those involving bovine spongiform encephalopathy (BSE), tainted blood in France and dioxins in Belgian chickens. In addition to major economic consequences (Vos 2000; OECD 2003) their long-lasting effect has been increased public distrust of authorities and industry (Löfstedt 2004, 2005). Yet, for a long time the pharmaceutical area seemed relatively immune to scandal. Medicines are a matter of life and death, and it is not surprising that risk events involving pharmaceuticals have triggered swift protective measures (Vogel 1998), which have reassured the public and prevented controversies from developing.

The global regulatory framework for pharmaceuticals is the direct legacy of the US Food and Drug Administration (FDA)'s precautionary action in the face of a historic tragedy. In the late 1950s and early 1960s, a tranquilliser called Thalidomide, developed by German pharmaceutical company Grünenthal, was prescribed to pregnant women for morning sickness. The risks involved had not been properly assessed, which led to almost 10,000 birth defects worldwide. Although Thalidomide had been prescribed around the world, the drug never received FDA approval. The FDA had effectively prevented the disaster from reaching US shores and was determined to prevent any similar disaster in the future. The Kefauver–Harris amendments that were passed in October 1962 require that drugs be proven to be effective scientifically before being allowed to reach the market (Pellzman 1974; Hilts 2003). The Kefauver–Harris amendments also authorised the FDA to set standards for every stage of new drug testing, from the laboratory to human trials (Daemmrich 2003).

Since the 1970s this approach has become the international norm for drug approval. The result, a step-by-step approval process that takes about 6 to 8 years, has created its own problems. In the 1980s for example, vocal patient groups actively lobbied for faster access to drugs to contain or eradicate illnesses such as AIDS (acquired immunodeficiency syndrome) or cancer. This movement was especially strong in the USA and – to a lesser degree – Europe (Daemmrich 2003; Epstein 1996: 293–94). Patient organisations have also pushed for fast-track approvals in areas with low return on investment, such as rare diseases. In Europe, possible restrictions on access to drugs (on the basis of risk/benefit and cost/benefit analyses), especially anti-cancer and anti-Alzheimer medicines, have also been highly controversial.

Since the 1990s two parallel developments have taken place. On the one hand, AIDS activists and other pressure groups have driven relaxed regulations and, in the USA, the Prescription Drug User Fee Acts (PDUFA) have been designed to speed up drug approvals. On the other hand, a large number of drugs have been withdrawn for safety reasons by the FDA and/or the EMA (Löfstedt 2010). The review of EMA annual reports shows for example that 140 products were withdrawn between 1995 and 2008 under the centralised procedure.

It is against this ambivalent background that worries, heightened by several withdrawals, have developed. New opinion leaders, especially journalists, alternative scientists and members of advocacy groups, have been increasingly critical and vocal (for an illuminating discussion, see Löfstedt 2007, 2010). Worries about the safety of pharmaceuticals of mass consumption, such as pain killers (Löfstedt 2007), anti-diabetes drugs (Löfstedt 2010) and vaccines (Bouder 2006; EMA 2011) have developed into major controversies. A distinct effect of the post-trust society is that, on both sides of the Atlantic, the competence and independence of pharmaceutical regulators is increasingly being called into question. The high-profile withdrawal of the painkiller Vioxx and subsequent controversy around the safety of this class of drugs – the so-called Cox2 inhibitors – may have played a trigger role. Löfstedt has posited a post-Cox2 environment in which Industry and to some extent regulators are no longer trusted (Löfstedt 2007). Later cases, such as the controversy about the safety of the antidiabetic drug Avandia, seem to validate Löfstedt's hypothesis. In this case the scandal was actively driven by a combination of major consumer, stakeholder and political distrust of large pharmaceutical corporations (so-called 'big pharma') and to some extent the FDA (Löfstedt 2010).

Although some of these worries had an established scientific basis, others lacked any basis in evidence. The UK controversy about the MMR vaccine offers a good example of the possible amplification (Kasperson *et al.* 1988; Pidgeon *et al.* 2003; Kasperson and Kasperson 2005) of 'crackpot science' in post-trust society. A flawed study indirectly suggested that the triple vaccine against measles mumps and rubella (MMR) might cause autism (Wakefield *et al.* 1998). The media's high level of coverage of the issue resulted in a public scare (Fitzpatrick 2004; Horton 2004). The media scare led many parents to stop giving the jab to their children. On the part of parents it was a rational action, choosing to be safe rather than sorry. Their action is consistent with a number of *decision heuristics* well known of cognitive scientists, which apply here (Ritov and Baron 1990; Ball *et al.* 1998; Bostrom 1996):

- *compression*: overestimating the frequency of rare risks, such as the vaccine risk, and underestimating the frequency of common risks, such as measles;
- *availability* of negative information reported by the media compared to scientific sources of information that are less accessible;
- *omission bias*: positive actions, such as giving a vaccine, are perceived as more harmful than omission;
- *freeloading*: parents relying on high vaccination rates and herd immunity, which protects unvaccinated children.

Despite their inherent logic these individual choices have had a disastrous effect on public health. The sharp drop in vaccination rates has led to subsequent measles outbreaks. In May 2011 the BBC reported a tenfold rise in measles cases across the UK (Roxby 2011). The outcome will be long-lasting negative consequences and an increase in mortality.

When they feel under strain, regulators may not resist the temptation for knee-jerk reactions. In France, for example, a public scare developed in the late 1990s around the hypothetical relationship between the Hepatitis B vaccine and multiple sclerosis (Bouder 2006). Despite the weakness of the evidence (Ascherio *et al.* 2001; Hernan *et al.* 2004; Ritvo *et al.* 2005), the French Health Minister invoked the precautionary principle and stopped the vaccination campaign. This action was taken despite the opposition of patient organisations, especially ACT UP, an AIDS activist organisation. Arguably, the fear of living through a second tainted blood scandal, after politicians had failed to protect haemophiliacs against HIV contamination, played a major role (Bouder 2006). This example draws attention to the role that national histories, politics and opinion play in the definition of protection measures.

Keeping protection science-based? The cases of anti-HIV and anti-HPV products.

This part offers a succinct presentation of two 'safety alerts' (for a complete discussion see EMA 2011), which offer an illuminating example of the practical challenges posed by post-trust environments. Both cases illustrate how regulators have found it particularly challenging to balance expectations about the robustness of the scientific assessment process with the implementation of precautionary measures designed to reassure various sections of the public. The cases analysed are:

- the contamination of an anti-HIV drug (Viracept) by a genotoxic impurity and its subsequent suspension, withdrawal and reintroduction;
- a scare around the safety of the anti-HPV vaccine Gardasil.

In principle, after a precautionary ban has been imposed, more evidence should be found to reach an informed decision (Klinke and Renn 2002; Sunstein 2003; Charnley and Rogers 2011). The evidence-gathering stage may or may not lead to a reassessment of the precautionary decision. The cases are therefore presented in two phases: the precautionary decision and post-alert evidence gathering.

Viracept

Viracept is an antiviral medicine produced by Roche and used in combination with other antiviral medicines to treat adults, adolescents and children who are infected with HIV-1. This product was first introduced onto the market in 1998. It was prescribed mostly to pregnant women and children because of its high tolerability. In May 2007 patients reported an unpleasant smell, some nausea and vomiting. Roche, which had already detected the formation of an impurity known as ethyl methanesulfonate (EMS), informed the European Commission of the contamination. Although the company had been able to identify the impurity formation, Roche scientists still needed to identify the root causes of the contamination.

Ethyl mesilate is known to be 'genotoxic', i.e. it is harmful to DNA (deoxyribonucleic acid), the genetic material in cells. At sufficient levels it may trigger cancer. The contaminated batches were used to make Viracept tablets that were distributed around the world to a total of 29 countries including six within the European Union (France, Germany, Italy, Portugal, Spain and the United Kingdom). The USA, Canada and Japan were not affected because, in these countries, the drug is manufactured by another company (Pfizer) according to a different procedure. Most patients were found in developing countries and Eastern Europe, because later-generation treatments were usually prescribed in Western Europe. In all, an estimated 20,000 to 25,000 patients had been exposed to EMS. It was argued that, in the worst cases, patients may have taken highly contaminated Viracept for months (at least from March until June).

Precautionary measures

The carcinogenic nature of the impurity, combined with its large circulation, prompted immediate action. On 6 June 2007, Roche and the EMA announced that, in agreement with Swissmedic, the Swiss medicines agency, Viracept was to be recalled in Europe and some other world regions. A recall is a procedure through which a medicine may be removed from the market. The EMA issued a press release (Ref. EMEA/251718/2007) where it framed the risk as a 'known genotoxic substance', 'difficult to measure' and 'under further evaluation'. Roche published an Investor Update where it explained that 'affected tablets showed they contain higher than normal levels of methane sulfonic acid ethylester'. Roche immediately recalled all batches of Viracept from the European market and informed prescribing doctors about the incident. The recall was more difficult to enforce in other parts of the world for two main reasons. One reason is that, in developing countries, the distribution of Viracept was done through NGOs. This additional layer made it more difficult to identify doctors and patients. On the other hand, international mechanisms, including the World Health Organization (WHO), were not very effective in helping with the enforcement of the global recall.

Following the precautionary recall of Viracept, the EMA went a step further. The decision to suspend the marketing authorisation of pharmaceuticals lies with the EU Commission. On 21 June, the Agency announced that, because the quality and safety could not be ensured, it was recommending to the European Commission to suspend the marketing authorisation for Viracept.

Patient organisations have been at the forefront of debates about HIV/AIDS since the 1980s. Therefore it would have been unthinkable for the regulator and Roche to manage this event behind closed doors. Roche informed its patient network immediately and some European countries also mobilised their network of HIV/AIDS organisations. France was especially proactive, which is not surprising because the French regulators have had a very difficult relationship with HIV/AIDS groups since the tainted blood scandal and, as a result, anything related to HIV is taken very seriously. The French Health Products

Safety Agency (AFSSAPS) involved a coalition of eight leading organisations (Groupe interassociatif Traitements et Recherche Thérapeutique – TRT-5). TRT-5 and AFSSAPS meet two–three times a year to review and update information issues. TRT-5 involvement remained outside the EMA risk-handling process, but the coalition stayed in close contact with AFSSAPS. They also held separate conversations with Roche France.

The initial alert was strong enough to prompt high concerns among patient groups, including doubts about Roche's and the regulator's ability to detect safety issues. By mid-July, the European Commission's decision was still pending. Delays in the decision to suspend heightened patients' worries. Should it be interpreted as a sign of incompetence? Did it mean that the regulators were having second thoughts about the seriousness of the risk? On 18 July 2007, TRT-5 wrote a letter to the EMA, AFSSAPS and two EC Commissioners expressing their worries, using strong statements such as '[this raises] important questions regarding the quality of drugs authorised by EMA' and 'We do not accept that such crises should happen again'.

TRT-5 also considered going to the press and launching a media campaign. It is only the fact that the EMA had involved a known and well-respected member of the European AIDS Treatment Group that prevented an escalation. This individual became the interface between the organisation and the patient community. According to one respondent interviewed for this study: 'Knowing that a patients' advocate was involved reassured everybody'.

The EMA published *Further Questions and Answers* on 26 July 2007, where it reinforced its view that the 'EMA's recommendation to the European Commission that Viracept's marketing authorisation be suspended still applies'.[1] The document also heightened its message about the seriousness of the risk, speaking this time of high levels of ethyl mesylate. The marketing authorisation for Viracept was finally suspended on 7 August 2007, almost 7 weeks after the EMA's call for suspension.

Evidence gathering

Roche's Investor Update of 6 June 2007 promised a detailed chemical analysis. The EMA's press release was more generic and spoke of 'further investigation into the production process for Viracept to identify the exact reason for the contamination'. The EMA was concerned with two main issues. The first issue had to do with the contamination process. Was it incidental or was it systemic? As soon as the contamination was known, the EMA launched an investigation to identify the causes of the contamination. Swissmedic, in collaboration with the EMA, organised an inspection of the Basel active substance manufacturing site on 11 June 2007. The results were presented to the EMA on 19 June 2007. Experts found that the risk was systemic and resulted from 'the cleaning of a tank with the wrong type of alcohol' to use the words of one respondent. Roche was asked to adapt its manufacturing process and a reinspection of the site was planned to check on Roche's compliance.

The second issue was the health impact. At the time of the recall, the regulator was unsure of the potential consequences for patients. The EMA held a meeting of toxicology experts on 13 June 2007 and the scientific body of the EMA, the CHMP,[2] which meets on a monthly basis, looked into the issue the following week. The conclusion of this assessment, published in the EMA *Questions and Answers* of 21 June 2007,[3] was that there was 'currently insufficient data to establish which dose of ethyl mesylate may be toxic to humans'. The CHMP requested Roche to:

- identify the group of patients who had been exposed to contaminated batches of Viracept in order to establish registries; and
- carry out toxicological studies.

In order to establish registries, CHMP recommended that the exposure of specific categories of patients be monitored:

- those exposed to high levels of contaminant in the batches of Viracept released since March 2007;
- all pregnant women who have ever been exposed to Viracept; and
- all children who have ever been exposed to Viracept, including those exposed *in utero*.

Some countries were in favour of registries, including France and the UK, while others were more sceptical. Roche, on the other hand, argued that registries were neither realistic nor feasible.

The toxicological studies have been described as 'in-depth studies into the effects of EMS'. The studies were conducted on mice, as existing toxicology data on EMS did not permit an adequate patient risk assessment (Pozniak *et al.* 2009). The positive results of a reinspection of the Basel site as well as reassuring toxicological studies changed the regulator's perspective. A joint EU–Swissmedic reinspection was organised at the Basel active substance manufacturing site from 5 to 7 September 2007. Roche had met the requirements of the action plan defined in June, which reassured the regulators. The results were presented to the CHMP on 17 September 2007.

Toxicology studies took almost a year to bring results. The process involved back-and-forth interactions between the EMA and Roche, experts' panel meetings and public meetings where third parties were also involved. On 17 June 2008 Roche provided the EMA with an updated risk assessment (Müller *et al.* 2009; Müller and Singer 2009). It was considered that, based on extrapolation of mice to humans, the levels of EMS were too low to present a serious health risk. On 24 July 2008 CHMP issued a follow-up *Question and Answers* document, where it validated the studies:

> Company experts have used special models that allow results from animal studies to be extrapolated to humans. This has allowed them to calculate

> the threshold value for patients who have been exposed to ethyl mesilate (2 mg per kilogram and per day).

Furthermore, 'These animal studies have shown that there is a threshold level below which ethyl mesilate does not have a harmful effect on the DNA (25 mg per kilogram and per day in the mouse)'.[4]

Some patient representatives interviewed for this study have complained about the technical nature of the data conveyed. The difficulty for non-specialists to make full sense of the science hampered their capacity to assess the methodology and the results of the toxicology studies. Generally, however, they had sufficient levels of confidence in the process – led by the EMA, carried out by Roche and involving patient representatives – to buy into the conclusions of the research.

These results changed the CHMP's and the EMA's opinions on the usefulness of registries. The EMA finally decided that there should be no registries, thanks to the reassuring conclusions of the toxicological studies. On 20 September 2007 the EMA informed the public that 'The Committee was satisfied by the actions taken by the company and by the outcome of the inspection, which confirmed that the necessary measures had been put in place', and that:

> Patients who took Viracept tablets at the highest level of contamination were exposed to levels of ethyl mesilate of about 0.05 mg per kilogram per day. As these levels are below the threshold, the CHMP concluded that patients exposed to contaminated Viracept are not at an increased risk of developing cancer, and that they do not need to be followed up as was previously planned.[5]

The safety alert was technically over and Roche informed the public on 20 September 2007 that Viracept was recommended for reintroduction and, on 19 October 2007, that the European licence was re-established by the European Commission. The EMA did not announce these decisions but published some follow-up *Questions and Answers* 9 months later, on 24 July 2008.

Reactions of regulators in member countries have been more diverse. Some were satisfied. Others were of the opinion that the complete set of data from toxicology studies came too late. These divergences also demonstrate the complexity of consensus seeking in the EU context. National regulators may still disagree on the risk, even after a formal common position has been taken. For instance some national regulators still argue that registries should not have been abandoned. France even tried to set up patients' registries after the idea was ruled out by CHMP. One respondent from Roche suggested, for example, that:

> France was not happy and was not ready to accept CHMP's decision. They still wanted to monitor patients who took over 100ppm through

> French AIDS centres. Roche wrote a letter to France saying that it was EMA's decision for Europe. Then there were discussions between us, the EMA and AFSSAPS. AFSSAPS had difficulties accepting it.

Patient organisations did not present a unified view of the management of the crisis. Although they were generally satisfied with the degree of their involvement, some expressed concerns about the 'strain on resources' on them for what turned out to be a negligible risk. One member of a patient organisation suggested that, to him, it had been 'much ado about nothing'.

Gardasil

The European public assessment report of Gardasil (Sanofi Pasteur MSD SNC) available on the EMA's website[6] states that this vaccine is administered to prevent cervical cancers and other pre-cervical cancers that are triggered by various STDs (sexually transmitted diseases) related to human papillomavirus (HPV) types 6, 11, 16 and 18. Gardasil and its twin-vaccine Cervarix (GlaxoSmithKline) are administered to teenage girls. When the market authorisation was granted, Gardasil presented no major concerns in respect of immunological reactions and disorders. By 2008, 1.5 million patients had been vaccinated. In January 2008, the European Medicines Evaluation Agency (EMEA) received reports of deaths in women who had previously received Gardasil, including two reports concerning the sudden and unexpected deaths of two young women in Germany and Austria. On 24 January 2008, the Agency used its website to reassure the public by means of a press release.[7]

On Friday 6 February 2009, two girls from the Spanish province of Valencia were admitted to hospital. Both girls came from the same area and had been vaccinated with the same batch of Gardasil. They were put into the same room. The girls were very agitated and both suffered repeated and prolonged seizures and loss of consciousness. Doctors diagnosed *status epilepticus* (SE), which is a life-threatening condition that resembles epilepsy and in which the brain is in a state of persistent seizure. They decided to induce coma to put the girls' brains to sleep.

Precautionary measures

The Valencia province's health authorities alerted the Spanish Ministry of Health (Ministerio de Sanidad y Consumo) without delay. Although staff members of the Spanish Medicine Agency (AEMPS, Agencia Española de Medicamentos y Productos Sanitarios)[8] were convinced that a safety issue was highly unlikely, the provincial and central health authorities agreed to withdraw the batch. The immobilisation of the batch in Spain, which represented 75,582 doses, became effective from 10 am on Monday, 9 February 2009. The General Directorate of the Spanish Ministry of Health, which is the Spanish regulator of pharmaceuticals, issued a press release in which it announced its precautionary decision. According to officials in the Spanish pharmaceutical agency, the recall in the Valencia province strengthened the idea that the vaccine was responsible for what had happened. The event was immediately followed by extensive media and internet discussions (*El Mundo* 2009a, 2009b; *El País* 2009). These discussions included a detailed account of the girls' health and various testimonies concerning the vaccine that were mostly hostile (EMA 2011).

Immediate discussions took place – behind closed doors – between the regulator and the manufacturer. The next day, on 10 February, Sanofi Pasteur stopped the entire batch as a precautionary measure. In common with their colleagues in the AEMPS, the members of the CHMP – responsible for preparing the EMA's opinions on all questions concerning medicines for human use – were not convinced about the biological relationship between the product and the effects observed. On 19 February 2009, the EMA uploaded a press release on its website, EMEA/CHMP/103339/2009. This document suggested that:

> the cases are unlikely to be related to vaccination with Gardasil … . Therefore the Committee is recommending that vaccination with Gardasil should continue in accordance with national vaccination programmes in Member States.

The same document, however, did not rule out the risk:

> The CHMP and its Pharmacovigilance Working Party are investigating this situation further. The marketing authorisation holder has been requested to provide a full analysis of the batch, as well as further information on the vaccine's side effects, any similar cases, and possible ways in which Gardasil could be linked to the cases seen in Spain. Following assessment of all of the available data, the CHMP will determine whether further action is needed. … As part of its continuous monitoring of medicines, the CHMP recommended an update of the Product Information for Gardasil in January 2009, to reinforce information on syncope (fainting) as a side effect of vaccination with Gardasil, indicating that it is sometimes accompanied by tonic-clonic movements (movements resembling a seizure). This opinion has been forwarded to the European Commission, for the adoption of an EU-wide decision.

Evidence gathering

Sanofi Pasteur conducted the investigation. As expected, negative results followed. Reassuring information also came from the Centre for Disease Control and Prevention. The EMA, however, did not issue a new online communication. Spanish authorities, on the other hand, still faced fierce criticism in the media, on television and in the press (*El Mundo* 2009c, 2009d, 2009e).

One important factor is that the Spanish Health Ministry, which maintained a degree of secrecy throughout the alert, could not really count on any third parties to support a scientific assessment of the risk. Gardasil is expensive. Each vaccination costs several hundred euros. Prior to the scare, the price aspect already generated considerable opposition from different corners of Spanish society. Grassroots organisations involved in sexual health prevention argued that the vaccine was a waste of public resources and that conventional prevention measures would be as effective. In Spain, provincial governments are responsible for healthcare, while the central government makes crucial decisions about public health policies, including vaccination policy. Provincial governments, being responsible for financing the vaccination programme, were also concerned about the financial implications. Finally, regulators and industry could not rely on influential third parties to speak out for the vaccine.

Consumers and patient organisations were highly critical of the aggressive vaccination campaign. For example, the 250,000-member-strong consumer organisation OCU (Organización de consumidores y usuarios) supported the vaccination campaign in principle but opposed what it perceived as an aggressive marketing campaign. In its publication *OCU Compra Maestra 336* of April 2009, OCU explained at page 8 its position on the alert generated by the two suspicious cases (*Respetan los derechos del paciente*?). At that moment, OCU stated:

- that patients should be informed about the balance between benefit/risk of Gardasil before the vaccination;
- that patients should be informed that Gardasil was a new drug and that it is of utmost importance to declare any possible risks associated with it;
- that they would defend the importance of informing the patients and their right to a free choice.

Faced with this difficult situation, the Spanish Health Ministry launched their own initiative in the form of an ad hoc expert committee to investigate the issue. The committee members were renowned medical experts (including immunologists, epidemiologists, etc.). The committee visited the hospital where these events had taken place and conducted a thorough inquiry that found no trace of a biological link between the vaccine and the cases observed. On 9 April 2009, these results were communicated to the Ministry of Health in a document that remained confidential. A more succinct report explaining the Public Health aspects of the issue was published and made available on the internet. The report used the expression 'psychogenic convulsions' and it suggested a close relationship with the vaccinations but indicated that there was no evidence of a biological relationship. After the release of the conclusions of the investigation committee, the media controversy ceased overnight, while the internet controversy faded away soon after.

On 24 April, the AEMPS officially released the immobilised batch of Gardasil NH52670 and announced in a press release that:

> Batch NH52670 of the said medicine does not present any quality defect, and the benefit-risk ratio of the vaccine for human papilloma virus has not suffered any variation, and continues being favourable.

Handling scientific evidence in the post-trust environment

The general patterns of the Viracept and Gardasil episodes are consistent with earlier reviews of pharmaceutical crises (Löfstedt 2007, 2010; Bouder 2006, 2007, 2008). The cases bear some defining characteristics which suggest that a 'post-trust environment' was at play:

- New actors have emerged (HIV activists, consumer organisations, anti-vaccination groups) who play an undeniably important role in shaping the outcome of crisis events.
- The media are the key channel that publicises the demands of these groups, with the potential for amplification of even minuscule risks.

In France, because of the legacy of the tainted blood and Hepatitis B scandals (Bouder 2006), any risk related to sexual health and HIV/AIDS is a minefield. When the safety of Viracept was questioned, well-organised HIV/AIDS groups were able to mobilise quickly and put pressure on Roche and AFSSAPS, which in turn pushed for precaution at EU level. The press and patient groups were also applying significant pressure in other parts of Europe. For example, an EMA embargo on outside communication was breached by a Member State because the delays were too long. In the post-trust environment, activists, consumer organisations and other non-governmental/nonprofit groups are likely to be more trusted than traditional authorities (Löfstedt 2005). The regulators' authority or scientific evidence is no longer accepted without question. In the Gardasil case it took an independent investigation from scientists operating at arm's length from public authorities to reassure the media and stop the controversy.

When a safety alert signal is detected, the post-trust environment heightens the inherent sense of urgency that the regulator needs to face up to. In both cases the active involvement of various groups and the media persuaded the regulators that protection measures should be taken without delay. Interestingly, in the Gardasil case, the Spanish Health Ministry wanted tougher action than that advised by the medical agency. The EMA called for a reinforcement of the information on fainting as a side effect of vaccination, which in principle would imply a causal relationship between vaccination and syncope. In this case, the further away from the risk, the tougher the regulator got. In the Viracept case the commitment to precaution brought practical difficulties at the implementation stage. Arguably, the EMA expected the suspension of Viracept to be followed by prompt action from the EU Commission. Yet, it took several weeks before the Commission acted upon the Agency's recommendation.

The cases confirm earlier observations (e.g. with the MMR vaccine) that escalating public scares may have a tangible negative impact on public health. One key question regarding the Viracept and Gardasil cases is of course: Were public pressures addressed in a way that minimises such negative outcomes? This question requires a balanced answer. EMS is known to be genotoxic and therefore may trigger cancers. Seizures can also be life-threatening. Yet, in both cases experts had a high level of confidence that the situation was one of low risk. Tough measures may have protected the regulator against criticism and strengthened its position. Yet they also had negative knock-on effects. The Gardasil controversy has resulted in a significant drop in vaccination rates in Spain, especially in the province of Valencia where Gardasil is the vaccine of choice (as opposed to Cervarix). Figures from the health authorities in Valencia show that the HPV vaccine coverage in the Valencia region went down by more than 10 per cent as a result of the crisis. The crisis originated when the cohort of girls were being vaccinated with the second dose and the major impact was noted with the third dose: first dose: 85.23 per cent; second dose: 81.10 per cent; and third dose: 70.99 per cent.

Similarly, tough action on Viracept created a point of non-return for the drug. Despite its reintroduction, prescriptions have not followed suit and in effect Viracept is now very rarely prescribed. It is a classic case of stigmatisation as a result of precautionary measures (Sunstein 2003). When the contamination took place, Viracept was reaching the end of its patent time limit and alternatives were available in Western Europe. It could be argued that Roche would not have given up on a high-profile blockbuster or that regulators would have been more cautious in the absence of therapeutic alternatives. Yet, the phasing out of Viracept has caused serious public health difficulties outside Western Europe. When it was recalled, Viracept was still prescribed to a significant number of patients in Eastern Europe, Russia and many developing countries. Several patients involved in the case study highlighted that the complexity and opacity of the supply chain outside Europe – batches are usually purchased by NGOs and then are difficult to track – as well as weak international coordination, do not lead to clarity as to how many lives may have been impaired or lost as a result of the drug's withdrawal. It was for example reported that some Russian doctors stopped prescribing the drug without offering any alternatives.

The Viracept and Gardasil cases confirm that, in crisis situations, the balancing of scientific evidence against other factors, including societal expectations as well as the management of societal input, remained largely intuitive. The regulator's intuition may be right: some decisions did go in the direction of building confidence. In the Viracept case, one major trust-building action by the EMA was to involve a highly respected patient representative. This person acted as a mediator between the regulator, the industry and other patient organisations.

This is consistent with the fact that involving highly trusted individuals as early as possible can help in solving risk communication disputes amicably (Löfstedt 2005). Given the sensitivity of the issue in some Member States, including France, this help proved precious. In the Gardasil case, launching an independent investigation carried out by independent scientists was also consistent with the postulate that involving independent third parties builds trust (Löfstedt 2005).

Yet, the intuitive approach to precaution neglected other aspects. In the case of Gardasil, the strength of anti-vaccine feelings and the weakness of pro-vaccine feelings were likely to heighten the resistance to the vaccination campaign. Alongside negative feelings and heuristics (see Ball *et al.* 1998; Bostrom 1996), certain positive decision heuristics also play in favour of vaccination. Take, for example, altruism. Parents are motivated by altruistic feelings. Spanish authorities might have done well to invest in trying to understand how altruism might play out in this case. Gardasil is administered to teenage girls, unlike many vaccines. The risk (which the vaccination is designed to prevent, of HPV) is much less likely to materialise than, for example, smallpox. In addition, the vaccination relates to sexual health and we know from research on unwanted pregnancies that taboos are powerful in this area (Bok and Morales 1998; Crosby and Yarber 2001); they constitute a limitation to behavioural change. For parents, giving Gardasil to their daughters is not an obvious choice because it requires them to accept that their daughters may become sexually active very soon. Exploring these factors might have helped to build stronger support for the vaccination campaign and, if not to prevent overreactions, at least to address them.

Conclusions and recommendations

In the author's view, defining and maintaining the right balance between scientific assessment and protection measures requires that regulators pay far more attention to societal perceptions and preferences. What the case studies clearly show is that the process of handling science in a post-trust environment can be seriously damaged when it is not accompanied by effective benefit/risk communication. On the other hand, two-way and proactive risk communication helps stakeholders agree on the right course of action. For decades scholars have formulated precise recommendation to improve risk communication. The Leiss volumes are a well-known example, detailing what works and what is counterproductive (Leiss and Chociolko 1994; Leiss 2001; Powell and Leiss 1997). In the past decade or so, dedicated efforts have been made to introduce risk perception and communication research into the medical field (Slovic *et al.* 1989; Slovic *et al.* 1991; Bostrom 1996; Ball, Evans and Bostrom 1998; Fischhoff 1999; Alaszewski and Horlick-Jones 2003; Löfstedt 2007; Slovic *et al.* 2007; EMA 2011). Risk decision making has also attracted considerable attention (NRC 1983, 1996; IRGC 2005; Renn 2008; Renn and Walker 2008).

Yet, with respect to precautionary measures, academics have concentrated on what should be done – that is to say, cases where precaution is needed or where it is not needed – rather than how protection measures should be operationalised. At the same time it is clear that the traditional approach to pharmaceutical risk management has encountered a number of limitations (Bouder 2008), which will need to be addressed:

- Drug approval and the post-marketing surveillance of pharmaceuticals are safety rather than risk/benefit oriented. They tend to focus on detecting signals of possible harm (in other word hazards) rather than estimating magnitude and likelihood of harm (risks). When a crisis arises, case research suggests that this approach does not always support a proportionate response.
- These safety-oriented models are expert-based and do not integrate the subjective preferences of the actors themselves (risk producers, risk bearers, etc.), which becomes an issue when these actors do not agree on desirable outcomes.

In view of these limitations, and based on the Viracept and Gardasil cases, as well as earlier similar examples, three main recommendations may be formulated, as described below.

Recommendation: learn from risk analysis to better prepare for crisis situations

The risk research community has developed specific approaches that facilitate and organise the use of scientific knowledge for risk decisions, including essential aspects such as whether or not a risk may be deemed 'acceptable' (NRC 1983; Douglas 1985; Renn 2007). Conventional risk analysis approaches may not be sufficient to deal with high levels of uncertainty (Stirling 1998; Klinke and Renn 2002; Van Asselt 2005; Van Asselt and Vos 2006; Van Asselt and Renn 2011). In the Viracept and Gardasil cases, however, the degree of scientific confidence was high and risks were relatively well known. Yet, the institutional response suffered from the fact that risk analysis methods were not used. One of the recommendations put forward by the EMA study of influential stakeholders' expectations and attitudes – which includes the Viracept and Gardasil cases – (EMA 2011) is that an external risk communication advisory board, composed of experts from the risk communication and medical field, would help integrate risk communication research into everyday processes. The same logic may be applied to risk assessment with a view to integrating risk analysis and crisis management. It may not come in the form of a stand-alone 'risk analysis board' but of dedicated training led by scholars with a well-known expertise in risk analysis.

Recommendation: develop a strategic view of precaution

In the midst of a safety alert regulators have little time to engage in debating the balancing of the benefits and risks of their decisions. Regulators suspended Viracept and stopped Gardasil on intuitive grounds. This suggests that, when faced with urgency and exposed to external criticism and societal demands, pharmaceutical regulators tend to neglect the need for a due process. Regulators should invest in taking a more strategic look at crisis management. The issue is much more than one of public relations and how to avoid full-blown controversies. Regulators need to define very precisely when and how precaution may be initiated. The general provision of Paragraph 2 of Article 191 of the Lisbon Treaty states that 'preventive action should be taken' and does not leave regulators with very clear guidance. In a post-trust environment where controversies are likely to develop, regulators should be acquainted with the latest thinking about risk governance (Van Asselt and Renn 2011).

Recommendation: methods to analyse and meaningfully integrate society's views

Taking cognitive science on board would help decision makers to take stock of society's 'irrationalities' and sensitivities. These cognitive factors often contradict experts' intuitions and assumptions (Freudenburg 1988). For example, medical experts need to better understand well-established science about perception, affect and trust (Fischhoff *et al.* 1978; Slovic 1987; Slovic *et al.* 1985; Slovic 1993; Renn and Levine 1991). Integrating this knowledge into decisions is particularly important because, when left ignorant, organisations may amplify risks (Freudenburg 1992).

When trust is low regulators are often inclined to seek stakeholders' views. The resulting consultation mechanisms should be carefully designed as ad hoc mechanisms are likely to backslash (Löfstedt *et al.* 2011). Patient organisations should be systematically involved on sensitive issues. In such areas they should be involved early in the assessment phase. This involvement should become routine in distinct areas where patient organisations have expressed known concerns, where risk perceptions are negative or where intense media coverage is likely to trigger risk amplification.

Paying serious attention to these recommendations will help to develop a more nuanced perspective on protection and how it can be 'science-based'. This approach will help pharmaceutical regulators to overcome the ineffective opposition of 'science' – typically seen by them as a method of routine regulation – and 'precaution' – typically used as a reaction to bad events.

Notes

1 EMA/337440/2007, available at www.ema.europa.eu/humandocs/PDFs/EPAR/Viracept/33744007en.pdf, accessed in August.

2 The European Medicines Evaluation Agency (EMA) was established in 1995 by the European Commission. Technical and scientific support for International Conference on Harmonisation of Technical Requirements for Registration of Pharmaceuticals for Human Use (ICH) activities is provided by the Committee for Human Medicinal Products (CHMP) (formerly the Committee for Proprietary Medicinal Products, CPMP) of the EMA.

3 EMA/276379/2007, available at www.ema.europa.eu/humandocs/PDFs/EPAR/Viracept/27637907en.pdf, accessed in August 2011.
4 EMA/CHMP/375807/2008, available at www.ema.europa.eu/humandocs/PDFs/EPAR/Viracept/Q&A_Viracept_37580708en.pdf, accessed in August 2011.
5 EMEA/CHMP/375807/2008, available at www.ema.europa.eu/humandocs/PDFs/EPAR/Viracept/Q&A_Viracept_37580708en.pdf, accessed in August 2011.
6 Available at www.ema.europa.eu/docs/en_GB/document_library/EPAR_-_Summary_for_the_public/human/000703/WC500021146.pdf, accessed in August 2011.
7 Available at www.ema.europa.eu/humandocs/PDFs/EPAR/gardasil/Gardasil_-press_release.pdf, accessed in August 2011.
8 The Agency operates under the authority of the Ministry of Health.

References

Abraham, J. and Lawton Smith, H. (eds) (2003) *Regulation of the Pharmaceutical Industry*, Basingstoke: Palgrave Macmillan.

Alaszewski, A. and Horlick-Jones, T. (2003) 'How can Doctors Communicate Information about Risk more Effectively?', *British Medical Journal*, 327: 728–31.

Albin, C. (1993) 'The Role of Fairness in Negotiation', *Negotiation Journal*, 9: 223–44.

Ascherio, A., Zhang, S.M., Hernan, M.A., Olek, M.J., Coplan, P.M., Brodovicz, K. and Walker, A.M. (2001) 'Hepatitis B Vaccination and the Risk of Multiple Sclerosis', *New England Journal of Medicine*, 344(5): 327–32.

Ball, L.K., Evans, G. and Bostrom, A. (1998) 'Risky Business: Challenges in Vaccine Risk Communication', *Pediatrics*, 101: 453–58.

Bok, M. and Morales, J. (1998) 'Just Say No to Drugs and Sex: A Formula for Disaster', *Journal of HIV/AIDS Prevention & Education for Adolescents & Children*, 2(2): 88–94.

Bostrom, A. (1996) *Vaccine Risk Communication: Lessons from Risk Perception, Decision Making and Environmental Risk Communication*. Research paper based on a presentation at the Vaccine Safety Forum, IOM. Available at: www.fplc.edu/RISK/vol8/spring/bostrom.htm, accessed on 24 April 2005.

Bouder, F. (2006) 'A Contribution to Transnational Risk Analysis: Comparative Analysis of Risk Perception Related to Human Health Issues', in I.K. Richter, S. Sabine Berking and R. Müller-Schmid (eds), *Risk Society and the Culture of Precaution*, Basingstoke: Palgrave Macmillan, pp. 1967–83.

——(2007) 'Regulating Risks Resulting from the Lengthening of the QT Interval: A Regulatory Tennis Game across the Atlantic', *Journal of Risk Research*, 10(3): 385–412.

——(2008) 'Regulating Impurities in Pharmaceutical Products: A Tolerability of Risk Approach?', *Expert Review of Clinical Pharmacology*, 1(2): 241–50.

Charnley, G. and Rogers, M.D. (2011) 'Frameworks for Risk Assessment, Uncertainty, and Precaution', in J.B. Wiener, M.D. Rogers, J.K. Hammitt and P. Sand (eds), *The Reality of Precaution. Comparing Risk Regulation in the United States and Europe*, Washington, DC/London: Resources for the Future, pp. 361–74.

Crosby, R.A. and Yarber, W.L. (2001) 'Perceived versus Actual Knowledge about Correct Condom Use among US Adolescents: Results from a National Study', *Journal of Adolescent Health*, 28: 415–20.

Daemmrich, A. (2003) 'Regulatory Laws and Political Culture in the United States and Germany', in J. Abraham and H. Lawton Smith (eds), *Regulation of the Pharmaceutical Industry*, Basingstoke: Palgrave Macmillan, pp. 11–41.

Douglas, M. (1985) *Risk Acceptability According to the Social Sciences*, New York: Russell Sage Foundation.

El Mundo (2009a) 'Sanidad inmoviliza un lote de vacunas contra el papilomavirus tras reacciones en dos niñas' [Sanitary Immobilisation of a Batch of Vaccine against Papillomavirus following Reactions in Teenage Girls], 9 February 2009.

——(2009b) 'Dos vacunas para una misma infección' [Two Vaccines for the Same Infection], 9 February 2009.

——(2009c) 'Farmacoviligancia ha registrado 45 reacciones adversas graves a la vacuna del papilomavirus' [Pharmacovigilance has Registered 45 Severe Adverse Reactions from the Vaccine against Papillomavirus], 12 February 2009.

——(2009d) 'Vuelve a la UCI una de las jóvenes valencianas afectadas por la vacuna del papilomavirus' [One of the Young Girls Affected by the Papillomavirus Vaccine Returns to Intensive Care Unit], 23 February 2009.

——(2009e) 'Las familias de las ninas ingresadas en la UCI estudian presentar una denuncia' [The Families of the Girls sent to Intensive Care Unit are Introducing a Claim], 2 March 2009.

El País (2009) 'Hospitalizadas dos niñas en Valencia tras ser vacunadas contra el virus del papiloma humano Sanidad inmoviliza el lote sospechoso de haber causado "efectos adversos"' [The Two Girls Hospitalised in a Valencia Hospital after being Vaccinated against the Virus of the Human Papilloma Raise Fears of 'Adverse Effects'], 9 February 2009.

Epstein, S. (1996) *Impure Science: AIDS, Activism and the Politics of Knowledge*, Berkeley, CA: University of California Press.

European Medicines Agency (EMA) (2011) *Benefit/Risk Communication by the European Medicines Agency: A Study of Influential Stakeholders' Expectations and Attitudes*, 15 March. Available at www.ema.europa.eu/docs/en_GB/document_library/Report/2011/05/WC500106865.pdf, accessed on 25 August 2012.

Fischhoff, B. (1999) 'What Do Patients Want? Help in Making Effective Choices', *Effective Clinical Practice*, 2: 198–200.

Fischhoff, B., Slovic, P. and Lichtenstein, S. (1978) 'How Safe is Safe Enough? A Psychometric Study of Attitudes towards Technological Risks and Benefits', *Policy Sciences*, 9: 127–52.

Fitzpatrick, M. (2004) *MMR and Autism: What Patients Need to Know*, London: Routledge.

Freudenburg, W.R. (1988) 'Perceived Risk, Real Risk: Social Science and Art of Probabilistic Risk Assessment', *Science*, 239: 44–9.

——(1992) 'Nothing Recedes Like Success? Risk Analysis and the Organizational Amplification of Risk', *Risk Issues in Health and Safety*, 3: 1–35.

Harman, R. (2004) 'Why the International Harmonisation Process is Increasingly Important', *The Pharmaceutical Journal*, 273(7312): 224–26.

Hernan, M.A., Jick, S.S., Olek, M.J. and Jick, H. (2004) 'Recombinant Hepatitis B Vaccine and the Risk of Multiple Sclerosis: A Prospective Study', *Neurology*, 63(5): 838–42.

Hilts, P.J. (2003) *Protecting America's Health. The FDA, Business, and One Hundred Years of Regulation*, New York: Knopf.

Horton, R. (2004) *MMR: Science and Fiction*, London: Granta Books.

Hugman, B. (2006) 'The Erice Declaration', *Drug Safety*, 29(1): 91–3.

International Risk Governance Council (IRGC) (2005) *Risk Governance: Towards an Integrative Approach*, White Paper No. 1, O. Renn with an Annexe by P. Graham, Geneva: IRGC.

Kasperson, J.X. and Kasperson, R.E. (2005) *The Social Contours of Risk: Publics, Risk Communication and the Social Amplification of Risk.* Vol. I., London/Sterling, VA: Earthscan.

Kasperson, R.E., Renn, O., Slovic, P., Brown, H.S., Emel, J., Goble, R., Kasperson, J.X. and Ratick, S. (1988) 'The Social Amplification of Risk: A Conceptual Framework', *Risk Analysis,* 8(2): 177–87.

Klinke, A. and Renn, O. (2002) 'A New Approach to Risk Evaluation and Management: Risk-Based, Precaution-Based and Discourse-Based Strategies', *Risk Analysis,* 22(6): 1071–94.

Leiss, W. (2001) *In the Chamber of Risks: Understanding Risk Controversies,* Montreal: McGill-Queen's University Press.

Leiss, W. and Chociolko, C. (1994) *Risk and Responsibility,* Montreal: McGill-Queen's University Press.

Linnerooth-Bayer, J. and Fitzgerald, K.B. (1996) 'Conflicting Views on Fair Siting Processes: Evidence from Austria and the United States', *Risk: Health, Safety and Environment,* 7: 9–134.

Löfstedt, R.E. (2004) 'Risk Communication and Management in the Twenty-first Century', *International Public Management Journal,* 7(3): 335–46.

——(2005) *Risk Management in Post-Trust Societies,* Basingstoke: Palgrave Macmillan.

——(2007) 'The Impact of the Cox-2 Inhibitor Issue on Perceptions of the Pharmaceutical Industry: Contents Analysis and Communication Implications', *Journal of Health Communication,* 12(5): 471–91.

——(2010) 'Risk Communication: The Avandia Case, A Pilot Study', *Expert Review of Clinical Pharmacology,* 3(1): 31–41.

Löfstedt, R.E. and Bouder, F. (2013 forthcoming) 'New Transparency Policies: Risk Communication's Doom?', in J. Arvai and L. Rivers (eds), *Effective Risk Communication,* Earthscan Risk in Society.

Löfstedt, R.E. and Vogel, D. (2001) 'The Changing Character of Regulation: A Comparison between Europe and the United States', *Risk Analysis,* 21(3): 399–405.

Löfstedt, R.E., Bouder, F., Wardman, J. and Chakraborty, S. (2011) 'The Changing Nature of Communication and Regulation of Risk in Europe', *Journal of Risk Research,* 14(4): 409–29.

Müller, L. and Singer, T. (2009) 'EMS in Viracept – The Course of Events in 2007 and 2008 from the Non-clinical Safety Point of View', *Toxicology Letters,* 190: 243–47.

Müller, L., Gocke, E., Lave, T. and Pfister, T. (2009) 'Ethyl Methanesulfonate Toxicity in Viracept – A Comprehensive Human Risk Assessment Based on Threshold Data for Genotoxicity', *Toxicology Letters,* 190: 317–29.

National Research Council (NRC) (1983) *Risk Assessment in the Federal Government: Managing the Process,* Washington, DC: National Academy Press.

——(1996) *Understanding Risk,* Washington, DC: National Academy Press.

OECD (2003) *Emerging Systemic Risks. Final report to the OECD Futures Project,* Paris: OECD.

Pellzman, S. (1974) *Regulation of Pharmaceutical Innovation: The 1962 Amendments,* Washington, DC: American Enterprise Institute.

Permanand, G. (2006) *EU Pharmaceutical Regulation. The Politics of Policy-making,* Manchester: Manchester University Press.

Pidgeon, N., Kasperson, R. and Slovic, P. (eds) (2003) *The Social Amplification of Risk,* New York: Cambridge University Press.

Powell, D. and Leiss, W. (1997) *Mad Cows and Mother's Milk*, Montreal: McGill-Queen's University Press.

Pozniak, A., Müller, L., Salgo, M., Jones, J.K., Larson, P. and Tweats, D. (2009) 'Elevated Ethyl Methanesulfonate (EMS) in Nelfinavir Mesylate (Viracept, Roche): Overview', *AIDS Research and Therapy*, 6: 6–18.

Renn, O. (2007) 'Concepts', in F. Bouder, D. Slavin and R.E. Löfstedt (eds), *The Tolerability of Risk: A New Framework for Risk Management*, London/Sterling, VA: Earthscan, pp. 5–83.

——(2008) *Risk Governance. Coping with Uncertainty in a Complex World*, London: Earthscan.

Renn, O. and Levine, D. (1991) 'Credibility and Trust in Risk Communication', in R.E. Kasperson and P.J. Stallen (eds), *Communicating Risk to the Public: International Perspectives*, Amsterdam: Kluwer, pp. 175–218.

Renn, O. and Walker, K. (2008) 'Lessons Learnt. A Re-Assessment of the IRGC Framework on Risk Governance', in O. Renn and K. Walker (eds), *The IRGC Risk Governance Framework: Concepts and Practice*, Heidelberg/New York: Springer, pp. 331–67.

Renn, O., Webler, T. and Wiedeman, P. (eds) (1995) *Fairness and Competence in Citizen Participation*, Dordrecht: Kluwer.

Renn, O., Webler, T. and Kastenholz, H. (1996) 'Procedural and Substantive Fairness in Landfill Siting', *Risk: Health, Safety and Environment*, 7: 145–68.

Ritov, I. and Baron, J. (1990) 'Reluctance to Vaccinate: Omission Bias and Ambiguity', *Journal of Behavioural Decision Making*, 3: 263–77.

Ritvo, P., Wilson, K., Willms, D. and Upshur, R. (2005) 'Vaccines in the Public Eye', *Nature Medicine*, 11(4): 20–24.

Roxby, P. (2011) 'Measles Outbreak Prompts Plea to Vaccinate Children', BBC News, 27 May. Available at www.bbc.co.uk/news/health-13561766, accessed on 25 August 2012.

Slovic, P. (1987) 'Perception of Risk', *Science*, 236: 280–85.

——(1993) 'Perceived Risk, Trust and Democracy', *Risk Analysis*, 13: 675–82.

Slovic, P., Fischhoff, B. and Lichtenstein, S. (1985) 'Characterizing Perceived Risk', in R.W. Kates, C. Hohenemser and J. Kasperson (eds), *Perilous Progress: Managing the Hazards of Technology*, Boulder, CO: Westview, pp. 91–125.

Slovic, P., Kraus, N., Lappe, H. and Malmfors, T. (1989) 'Risk Perception of Prescription Drugs: Report on a Survey in Sweden', *Pharmaceutical Medicine*, 4: 43–65.

Slovic, P., Kraus, N., Lappe, H. and Major, M. (1991) 'Risk Perception of Prescription Drugs: Report on a Survey in Canada', *Canadian Journal of Public Health*, 82: S15–S20.

Slovic, P., Finucane, E., Peters, D. and MacGregor, R. (2002) 'The Affect Heuristic', in T. Gilovich, D. Griffin and D. Kahneman (eds), *Intuitive Judgment: Heuristics and Biases*, Boston, MA: Cambridge University Press, pp. 397–420.

Slovic, P., Peters, E., Grana, J., Berger, S. and Dieck, G.S. (2007) 'Risk Perception of Prescription Drugs: Results on a National Survey', *Drug Information Journal*, 41(1): 81–100.

Stirling, A. (1998) 'Risk at a Turning Point?', *Journal of Risk Research*, 1(2): 97–109.

Sunstein, C. (2003) 'Beyond the Precautionary Principle', Public Law and Legal Theory Working Paper No. 38, Chicago, IL: Law School, University of Chicago. Available at http://law.uchicago.edu/Lawecon/index.html, accessed on 25 August 2012.

Van Asselt, M.B.A. (2005) 'The Complex Significance of Uncertainty in a Risk Era: Logics, Manners and Strategies in Use', *International Journal for Risk Assessment and Management* (special issue on uncertainty), 5(2/3/4): 125–58.

Van Asselt, M.B.A. and Renn, O. (2011) 'Risk Governance', *Journal of Risk Research*, 14(4): 431–49.

Van Asselt, M.B.A. and Vos, E. (2006) 'The Precautionary Principle and the Uncertainty Paradox', *Journal for Risk Research*, 9(4): 313–36.

Viscusi, W.K. (1998) *Rational Risk Policy*, Oxford: Oxford University Press.

Vogel, D. (1998) 'The Globalisation of Pharmaceutical Regulation', *Governance: An International Journal of Policy and Administration*, 11(1): 1–22.

——(2012) *The Politics of Precaution, Regulating Health, Safety and Environmental Risks in Europe and the United States*, Princeton, NJ: Princeton University Press.

Vos, E. (2000) 'EU Food Safety Regulation in the Aftermath of the BSE Crisis', *Journal of Consumer Policy*, 23: 227–55.

Wakefield, A.J., Murch, S.H., Anthony, A., Linnel, J., Casson, D.M., Malik, M., Berelowitz, M., Dhillon, A.P., Thomson, M.A., Harvey, P., Valentine, A., Davies, S.E. and Walker-Smith, J.A. (1998) 'Ileallymphoid-nodular Hyperplasia, Non-specific Colitis, and Pervasive Developmental Disorder in Children', *Lancet*, 351: 637–42.

Watson, R. (2011) 'MEPs Criticise European Medicines Agency over Staffing and Conflicts of Interest', *BMJ*, 342: d3081, 17 May.

Wiener, J.B. and Rogers, M.D. (2002) 'Comparing Precaution in the United States and Europe', *Journal of Risk Research*, 5(4): 317–49.

Wiener, J.B., Rogers, M.D., Hammitt, J.K. and Sand, P. (2011) *The Reality of Precaution. Comparing Risk Regulation in the United States and Europe*, Washington, DC/London: Resources for the Future.

Young, H.P. (1994) *Equity: In Theory and Practice*, Princeton, NJ: Princeton University Press.

5 Responsive governance of uncertain risks in the European Union

Some lessons from nanotechnologies

Bärbel Dorbeck-Jung

Introduction

European governance of nanotechnologies[1] is fascinating because it illuminates the possibilities and limits of regulating uncertain risks and especially so because, although there is no evidence on the benefits and risks of nanotechnologies as yet, European regulators are required to take action. They cannot afford to wait until the effects of technological applications are known. European regulators are committed to responsible nanotechnological development (EC 2005) and to precautionary action (EC 2000; Haum *et al.* 2004). Numerous commentators have concluded that applications of nanotechnologies will penetrate and permeate through nearly all sectors and spheres of life (IRGC 2006: 19). Although many of these accounts are focusing on new, advanced and coming applications, nano-enabled products are already on the market. In March 2011 the well-known inventory of the US Woodrow Wilson Centre noted that it now includes 1,317 consumer products and that it has grown by nearly 521 per cent since it was released in March 2006 (Woodrow Wilson Center 2011).

The unknown benefits and risks of nanotechnologies raise the crucial question of how such a promising but speculative technology can be regulated effectively and legitimately. This chapter analyses regulatory activities that are taking place in the European Union (EU) to control therapeutic nanoproducts. Nanomedical governance is particularly interesting because of the large body of existing regulation, ongoing changes and new modes of governance, as well as because of its high importance on the European and global nanotechnological agenda. This chapter first sets the scene by providing an overview of nano(medical) applications, including their potential benefits and risks. The second section discusses the model of responsive regulation that serves as an analytical frame. In the third section we describe the existing nano(medical) regulation. The fourth section deals with regulatory problems of therapeutic nanoproducts. The analysis of governance responses is provided in the fifth section and leads to tentative conclusions on the lessons to be learnt in order to enhance the effectiveness and legitimacy of a regulatory technology that has to cope with uncertain benefits and risks.

Potential benefits and risks of nano(medical) development

There is much rhetoric and speculation about the benefits and risks of current and coming activities with engineered nanoparticles.[2] Analyses by the scientific committees of the EU, its Member States, the USA and the OECD have identified many knowledge gaps concerning the benefits and risks of nanomaterials to humans and the environment (SCENIHR 2007; Zijverden and Sips 2008). Numerous benefits for society are expected, including contributing to faster electronics, CO_2 reduction, the move to less fuel consumption and cost savings, the improved functionality of materials, better delivery of medicated skin products, better surveillance techniques, self-cleaning, anti-bacteria and anti-fouling household products and stronger and more durable textiles (Roco and Bainbridge 2001, 2005; IRGC 2006). Influential accounts agree that strong patient benefits can be expected in the field of nanomedicine (EMA 2010b).

Nanomedicine is developing rapidly in the EU. It is defined as the application of nanotechnologies for the diagnosis, treatment or prevention of diseases and for preserving and improving human health.[3] Nanomedicine spans diagnostics, therapeutics and regenerative medicine. In the field of nanomedicine, major breakthroughs are being made in terms of smart drug delivery systems, bio-diagnostics and the early discovery of diseases, improved implants and the visualization of cells, tissues, or organs, and in targeting tissues and organs for regeneration and repair. Product development and marketing is mainly in the area of therapeutics, with a strong focus on controlled drug delivery. One survey in 2006 identified 23 nanoscale drug delivery systems worldwide that had already been launched in the market (Wagner *et al.* 2006). To date, 18 nanopharmaceuticals have been evaluated by the European Medicines Agency for approval (EMA 2010b). Other nano-enabled applications include advanced therapies medicinal products, medical devices and combination products. In the field of drug delivery, dozens of products are being developed. Estimates indicate that by 2015 about half of drug delivery systems will be based on nanotechnology (Zijverden and Sips 2008).

In addition to drug delivery systems, major breakthroughs are expected in the areas of bio-diagnostics and early discovery of diseases, improved implants, visualization of cells, tissues, or organs, and targeting tissues and organs for regeneration and repair. A new generation of polymer therapeutics has emerged which uses self-assembling nanomaterials for delivery of drugs and genes, and imaging molecules (EMA 2010b: 17). These materials are also used in combination with cell-based therapies. Rutledge Ellis-Behnke, an eminent neuroscientist, speaks of the 'nanomics revolution'. He is convinced that this revolution goes far beyond manipulating living tissues. He notes that

> *the nanomics revolution* delves into *molecular manipulation* that will change what we wear and how we live … . Tissue engineering no longer involves simply taking a cell, placing it in a particular scaffold, putting it back in the body and hoping that everything will reconnect and function

> properly. It is the ability to *influence* an environment either by adding, subtracting or manipulating that environment to allow it to be more conducive for its purpose.
>
> (EMA 2010b 7)

Although many commentators refer to the Asbestos Case, there is no evidence that nanoparticles might have similar devastating effects. In the risk debate it is crucial to distinguish between *free nanoparticles* that are released into the body or the environment and *fixed nanoparticles.* Since no specific hazards are expected from activities with fixed nanoparticles, the focus of risk assessment and regulatory activities lies on free nanoparticles. So far, toxicological studies have indicated that free nanoparticles might penetrate through blood and brain barriers or remain lodged in capillaries (Linkov *et al.* 2008; Poland *et al.* 2008; Kandlikar *et al.* 2007; Nel *et al.* 2006). The small size of nanoparticles results in a relatively large surface area that is accompanied by an increase of surface activity (Geertsma *et al.* 2007). This may or may not lead to increased reactivity towards cells and organs, resulting in toxic responses (EMA 2010b: 11). Research has shown that nanoparticles less than 100 nanometer (nm) can enter cells; at less than 40 nm they can enter a cell nucleus; and at less than 35 nm they can pass the blood-brain barrier (Lundqvist *et al.* 2008). These particles could also have an impact on the immune system. Another risk challenge is related to uncertainties about the biocompatibility of products in which nanoparticles have been used (Zijverden and Sips 2008).[4]

Analytical frame: the model of responsive regulation

According to the theory of the social welfare state, public regulators are required to facilitate positive (nanotechnological) development under the condition that risks to constitutionally protected concerns be minimal (Franzius 2001; Kloepfer 2002; Dorbeck-Jung 2007). The EU commitment to responsible nanotechnological development implies the balancing of efforts to maximize the technology's positive contributions and to minimize its negative consequences (CRNNI 2006). This broad definition raises questions concerning what constitutes 'positive contributions' and 'negative consequences' and how to optimize the positive. Referring to the rationale of the European Union Treaties, von Schomberg (2011) proposes to define responsible research and innovation as a 'transparent, interactive process by which societal actors and innovators become mutually responsive to each other with a view to the (ethical) acceptability, sustainability and societal desirability of the innovation process and its marketable products'. Accordingly, positive contributions include the support of nanotechnological advance and its contribution to a competitive social market economy and to the other goals of the Treaties. Negative consequences relate to damage to human health, the environment, equality and fundamental rights. Minimizing negative consequences serves also to maximize the normative targets of the EU Treaties.

Von Schomberg's definition of responsible research and innovation identifies transparency and responsiveness as core principles of good governance. Where the regulation of an emerging technology having uncertain benefits and risks and public regulators depend on the regulated parties' knowledge and regulatory capacity, responsiveness is an important departure point for regulatory strategies (Levi-Faur and Comaneshter 2007; Dorbeck-Jung 2007, 2011). As Kearnes and Rip (2009) put it:

> The primary uncertainty regarding the trajectory of nanotechnology and its possible risks and broader societal consequences have given rise to the proposition that policymakers and regulators need to identify frameworks of governance that are adaptive and anticipatory, yet which recognize the limits of prediction.

Responsiveness is not only required to cope prudently with technology-related uncertainties, but also to tackle control-related uncertainties (Borrás 2006). Regulatory uncertainties refer to whether the regulated parties will comply with regulation, whether control measures can create trust and, finally, whether they will contribute to responsible development.

To answer the question of how promising but highly speculative emerging technologies can be regulated, we build on the analytical frames of responsive regulation (Nonet and Selznick 1978; Ayres and Braithwaite 1992; Selznick 1992; Dorbeck-Jung 2007, 2011; Black and Baldwin 2010). The theoretical building blocks that have been proposed by Black and Baldwin focus on dynamics, interaction and learning processes. Regarding the fast development of nanotechnologies and the uncertain effects thereof, regulatory learning in the light of the limits of evidence-based models of regulation seems to be the most appropriate approach. Responsive regulation commits regulatory institutions to (Nonet and Selznick 1978; Trubek *et al.* 2008: 1):

- enlarge their scope of inquiry to embrace knowledge and the social contexts and effects of regulatory decisions;
- employ a style of reasoning that reaches beyond mere rule-following by focusing on social consequences; and
- test alternative strategies for the implementation of mandates and reconstruct those mandates in the light of what is learned.

The core idea of responsive regulation is that regulatory effectiveness and legitimacy can be enhanced by critical responses to regulatory concerns, changing structures and institutional environments. Critical responses include attempts to strike a balance between conflicting interests and conflicting normative requirements. In the case of the regulation of emerging technologies with uncertain effects, responsive regulators build on empirical knowledge on technological benefits and risks as well as on the successes and failures of (technological) regulation. They are aware of the limits of evidence-based regulation in the context of considerable uncertainties. They promote vigilance, collaboration with stakeholders and continuous adaptation of regulation in case of regulatory gaps.

In the EU, regulatory governance is committed to the principles of participation, transparency, accountability, legality, impartiality, proportionality and effectiveness (EC 2001; van Kersbergen and van Waarden 2004; Curtin and Wessel 2005; Dorbeck-Jung 2008). These are crucial 'rules-of-the-game' that legitimate private, public and multi-actor regulation serving public policy goals. In social theory the notion of legitimacy is related to the acceptance of collective action. According to Schmitte (2001), legitimacy is about:

> a shared expectation among actors in an arrangement of asymmetric power, such that the actions of those who rule are accepted voluntarily by those who are ruled because the latter are convinced that the actions of the former conform to pre-established norms.

Under pre-established norms, traditional legal theory focuses on legality, while political philosophy emphasizes the criteria of democratic decision-making. In modern governance these focuses are extended and merged. One of the reasons for the extension is that regulatory activities, as in the case of nanosciences and nanotechnologies, often involve private actors.

In the multi-level and multi-actor context of EU regulatory governance, the approach to legitimacy cannot merely reproduce the model of the nation State with its focus on legality and democracy. The requirements of the modern welfare State have led to a general withdrawal of the legislature in favour of the administration and non-governmental actors (Vos 1999: 94). As a consequence, a surrogate political process has emerged to ensure the fair representation of the affected actors. Increased accountability, transparency and stronger participation are proposed to compensate for the 'democratic deficit'. In this context the question of whether private regulators are also committed to these criteria of decision-making arises. According to the broader view of organizational legitimacy, private regulators are bound to similar principles of corporate governance when they regulate their own affairs (Rosenbaum and Shepherd 2000; Woods 2000).[5] When private regulation is employed to achieve public policy goals, a governmental responsibility applies, providing for the acceptance of the whole governance arrangement. Private regulation is then taking place in the 'shadow of hierarchy' (Héritier and Lehmkuhl 2008): thus, the principles of (public) good governance apply to the whole governance arrangement.

Responsive regulators do not focus only on the 'rules-of-the-game' (input legitimacy), but also on whether and how they are used in regulatory practice (throughput legitimacy), as well as on the outcomes of regulation (output legitimacy).[6] In the case of emerging technologies with uncertain benefits and risks the outcomes of regulation strongly depend on broad and effective participation of stakeholders (on stakeholder legitimacy, see Masis Report

2009;[7] Forsberg 2011), as well as on how the scientific basis and environment is evaluated (scientific legitimacy). Scientific legitimacy relies on the robustness of the involved scientific expertise, as well as on the academic background, areas of expertise and independence of the experts. Since experts are stakeholders and other stakeholders than experts can participate in knowledge creation (Everson and Vos 2009; Masis 2009), stakeholder legitimacy and scientific legitimacy are intertwined. In the fifth section we explore whether the emerging governance responses related to therapeutic nanoproducts can be regarded as responsive and what can be said about the stakeholder and scientific legitimacy.

Regulatory landscape of therapeutic nanoproducts

From the very beginning the European Commission has taken an incremental regulatory approach to the regulation of nanomaterials. It has reviewed existing legislation with the intention to adapt it, if necessary, to specific nanotechnological requirements (EC 2008a). The EC review concluded that, although nanomaterials are not mentioned specifically in Union legislation, current legislation in principle covers the potential health, safety and environmental risks. However, in 2009, the European Parliament demanded regulatory constraints for placing products with engineered nanomaterials on the EU market. It asked for the introduction of a comprehensive science-based definition of nanomaterials in Union legislation. It called on the Commission to promote the adoption of a harmonized definition of nanomaterials at the international level and to adapt the relevant European legislative framework accordingly.

In the EU a large and complex body of regulation is in place to achieve responsible development of nanoscience and nanotechnologies. This paper focuses on regulatory governance arrangements that serve to achieve the efficacy, safety and effectiveness of therapeutic nanoproducts. We use a broad view on regulation to include the control of human conduct or social affairs through rules that are set, implemented and enforced by public and/or private organizations.[8] Consequently, this investigation covers legislation ('hard regulation') but also other rules which, although not legally binding, are attracted to contribute to the achievement of policy goals ('soft regulation'[9]). In the case of nanotechnologies, examples of soft regulation include industry and government codes of conduct, information-reporting schemes, guidelines, recommendations and communications of regulatory bodies, as well as benchmarks and certification schemes. Figure 5.1 gives an overview of the existing hard and soft regulation that applies to nano-enabled products. The figure distinguishes between general and nano-specific legislation as well as between general and nano-specific public and private soft instruments.

The overview indicates that there is hardly any *nano-specific* legislation in the European Union. To date at the EU level, the only nano-specific legislation is contained in Regulation EC/1223/2009 on Cosmetic Products. Nano-specific legislation is currently discussed and prepared in the implementation of the

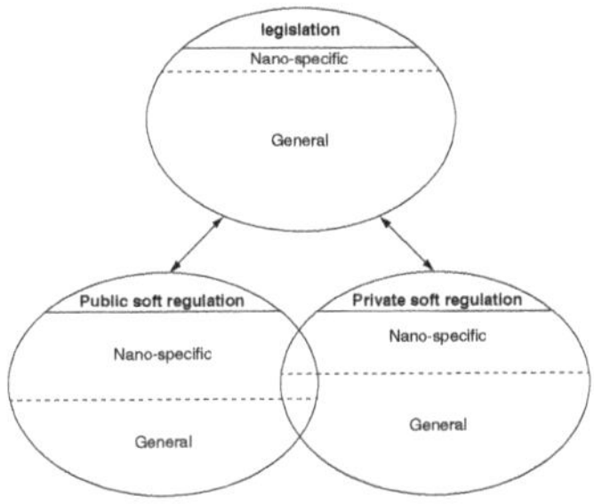

Figure 5.1 Overview of hard and soft regulation applicable to nanosciences and nanotechnologies

REACH (Registration, Evaluation, Authorisation and Restriction of Chemicals).[10] It is underway in the legislation for the regulation of novel foods.[11] Relevant *general legislation* is found in the domains of product safety, occupational health and safety, environment, privacy and civil liberties, intellectual property and liability (Hodge *et al.* 2007).

With regard to therapeutic nanoproducts no specific legislation has been established in the EU: rather, the current regulatory system of medical products is applicable. This system is composed of two main regimes (medicinal products and medical devices) which have specific or additional provisions for specific applications. Due to the broad scope and the variety of regulatory activities, as well as the forms and levels of regulation, the regulatory system under which therapeutic nanoproducts fall is very complex. It covers the whole product life cycle: the stages of research and development, marketing (including manufacturing) and post-marketing controls (including vigilance and waste disposal). With regard to 'hard law', general European drugs legislation[12] applies to all therapeutic nanoproducts that are classified as medicinal products.[13] In addition, where therapeutic nanoproducts are characterized as advanced therapies medicinal products (ATMPs[14]), additional provisions apply (Regulation EC/1394/2007). This is also the case with medicinal products for pediatric use (Regulation EC/1901/2006) and orphan drugs (Regulation EC/141/2000). Furthermore, where medical devices[15] use nanomaterials, the medical devices regulation may apply.[16] Therapeutic nanoproducts can also fall under Regulation (EC) No 1907/2006 on the Registration, Evaluation, Authorisation and Restriction of Chemical Substances (REACH).[17] Furthermore, to activities of science, development and manufacturing of therapeutic nanoproducts a large body of regulation on occupational health and safety applies. To reduce the complexity of the investigation, this chapter focuses on the European medical product regulation system.

Figure 5.1 indicates that *nano-specific soft regulation* has been established by public and private regulators. There are some overlapping regulatory activities in cases where these regulators co-regulate (e.g. safety standards; see Dorbeck-Jung 2008) and where they use the same instruments (e.g. the EC

Code of Conduct for Responsible Nanosciences and Nanotechnologies Research (EC 2008b) and the BASF nano-specific code of conduct[18]). Regarding therapeutic nanoproducts, specific guidance has been prepared by the European Working Group on medical devices (N& ET 2007). In addition to nano-specific soft regulation, *general soft regulation* like the EC Communication on the Precautionary Principle (EC 2000), the As-Low-As-Reasonably Achievable (ALARA) principle, general safety, quality and efficacy standards, general codes of conduct and benchmarks are applicable.

In regulatory governance of therapeutic nanoproducts, four different categories of stakeholders are involved: first, technology suppliers; second, technology users; third, regulators; and fourth, other groups (e.g. insurance stakeholders and civil society).[19] With regard to technology suppliers including nanoscientists, product developers and manufacturers the European Technology Platform Nanomedicine (ETPN) and the European Foundation for Clinical Nanomedicine (CLINAM) are active in regulatory debates. At their conferences attention is paid to regulatory issues. Regulators that have taken an active regulatory stance, are: the European Medicines Agency (EMA), the European Commission (DG Health and Consumers), its Scientific Committee on Emerging and Newly Identified Health Risks (SCENIHR), the European Working Group on New and Emerging Technologies in Medical Devices (N& ET Working Group). Technology users (patients and physicians) and a number of regulators (the national competent bodies, the International Conference on Harmonization of Technical Requirements for Registration of Pharmaceuticals for Human Use (ICH), the European Directorate for the Quality of Medicines and Health Care (EDQM at the Council of Europe) and the World Health Organization) have not yet been actively involved in regulatory governance activities related to therapeutic nanoproducts.

Regulatory activities and regulatory problems

In collaboration with DG Health and Consumers, the EMA has initiated numerous activities to explore regulatory problems of therapeutic nanoproducts. In 2006, the EMA's Scientific Committee (CHMP) launched a reflection paper on nanotechnology-based medicinal products for human use (EMA 2006). Later the EMA established an ad hoc CHMP Expert Group which organized a workshop in 2009. The EMA's Innovation Task Force provides a forum for early exploration of regulatory implications. The Small and Medium Size Enterprises (SME) Office offers regulatory support. Since 2006 the EMA actively participates in the dialogue platform of regulators from the EU, the USA, Canada and Australia. This platform serves to share experience and understanding across regulatory frameworks including food, medical devices, cosmetics and pharmaceuticals. In September 2010 the first international workshop on nanomedicines was held with the EMA. Later in 2010 key representatives of the EMA and DG Health and Consumers participated in the Annual Conference of the ETPN. In 2011, the EMA organized sessions on regulatory issues at the 4th

Conference on Clinical Nanomedicine. The competent bodies of the Member States have joined the EMA's activities on therapeutic nanoproducts.

In the area of medical devices one nano-specific governance activity has taken place. At the Medical Devices Expert Group (MDEG) meeting in October 2004 the Commission proposed a Working Group on New and Emerging Technologies (N& ET Working Group) to be formed with a focus on new and emerging technologies such as robotic surgery, nanotechnology and minimally invasive surgery. In 2007, the N& ET Working Group issued recommendations on nanotechnological applications (N& ET 2007). These recommendations are under revision. Further notable activities which are providing regulatory insights for therapeutic nanoproducts are: the 2007 European Group of Ethics in Science and New Technologies (EGE) *Opinion on the Ethical Aspects of Nanomedicine* (EGE 2007), the NanoMed Round Table project,[20] the opinions of SCENIHR (2007, 2008, 2010) and the results of the European Commission's annual Nanotechnology Safety for Success Dialogues. Moreover, ETPN and CLINAM are paying attention to regulatory topics at their annual conferences and in their policies.

According to the EMA, the existing evaluation system for pharmaceuticals is robust enough to accommodate nanodrugs (EMA 2010b). This conclusion is based on the 2006 reflection paper of its scientific committee on nanotechnology-based medicinal products for human use. The CHMP noted then that the evaluation and prevention of potential hazards related to the use of any nanomedicinal products is foreseen under existing pharmaceutical legislation. The conclusion refers also to the 18 nanopharmaceuticals that passed the centralized authorization procedure without any problems related to their nano-component. Likewise, the N& ET Working Group concluded that the medical device legislation is suitable to deal with medical devices utilizing nanotechnologies. Here, the main argument was that the legal provisions on risk management are appropriate to address all kinds of risks. However, referring to the 2006 Opinion of SCENIHR, the N& ET Working Group recommended that regulatory guidance be developed for collecting information on the experience with medical devices utilizing nanotechnology (including risk assessment), as well as specific requirements for post-marketing control.

The EMA is also well aware of the regulatory challenges that coming nanomedical applications are posing. The CHMP 2006 reflection paper admits that:

> it is likely that many novel applications of nanotechnology will span the regulatory boundaries between medicinal products and medical devices …. It is likely that the evaluation of products of such novel technology will require special consideration.
>
> (EMA 2006: 4)

To cope with these challenges identified in the CHMP reflection paper, the 2009 and 2010 EMA workshops concluded that it is essential to ensure dialogue at an early stage with the Agency, sponsors and stakeholders. Furthermore, the 2010 EMA Workshop recommended pooling knowledge and expertise at a global level and across disciplines. At the workshop, regulatory gaps were identified with regard to the definition of nanomedical products, the regulatory classification of combination products and nano-specific safety and quality standards, as well as validated risk assessment methods and the environmental impact analysis.

Although the European Commission adopted a recommendation on the definition of nanomaterials in October 2011 (EC 2011), legal definitions are still lacking. Commentators agree that definitions are important as 'they assist in establishing the subject matter and scope of what is to be regulated' (Hodge *et al.* 2010). Definitions of nanomaterials and nanomedicinal products are essential to provide regulatory and commercial certainty (Bergeson and Auer 2011). A similar conclusion can be drawn with regard to the classification of combination products. Experts agree that these products pose major regulatory challenges (Gaspar 2010). Highly discussed are nano-enabled drug delivery systems that integrate medical devices and pharmaceuticals. In this context the question arises as to which regulatory regime applies. Since an approval according to the medicinal products regulation is accompanied by stricter regulatory obligations than a notification according to the medical devices regime, the classification of the combined product does matter in regulatory practice. Furthermore, nanomedical applications challenge the internal logics of the various medical product regulation regimes. For example, the commercialization of more advanced and sophisticated nanodevices that offer a range of different applications, while using various materials and coatings, is likely to blur the distinction that the medical devices system makes between a medical device and an *in vitro* device, which are regulated by different directives and different harmonized standards (D'Silva and Bowman 2011). As a consequence, the generally accepted approach of treating such products primarily as *in vitro* devices is challenged. It is also argued that the blurring of these traditional boundaries has the potential to question the competences of the notified bodies that are charged with the assessment and authorization of these borderline products (D'Silva and Bowman 2011).

More generally, the lack of expertise on the properties and effects of nanomedical products challenges the regulatory capacity of the competent authorities. These shortcomings are induced by the gaps of scientific knowledge and inappropriate risk assessment methodologies. Safety regulation cannot be updated because the risks cannot yet be determined. Existing risk assessment criteria rely on mass metrics. They do not yet cover agglomeration, particle size, shape and surface reactivity, all of which are essential for the risk evaluation of nanomaterials. The available methods are said to be not appropriate for accurate mass balance and to distinguish between discrete nanopharmaceuticals and aggregates. The levels of nanopharmaceuticals in blood and tissues are difficult to measure (Gaspar 2010: 305). Specific guidance on quality, safety and efficacy of emerging therapeutical nanoproducts cannot be set up because reliable testing methods have not yet been developed, which in turn is due to the 'nanosize' and the unique behaviour of nano-systems in biological structures. Scientific problems of measurement and risk assessment induce also challenges to the environment impact analysis.

In short, regulators agree that regulatory problems of therapeutic nano-products occur mainly in the implementation of existing regulations. They think that appropriate governance responses focus on instruments of soft regulation (amongst which nano-specific safety and quality standards, and specific guidance for the environmental impact analysis). In the next section we explore whether the emerging governance responses can be regarded as responsive and what can be said about stakeholder and scientific legitimacy.

Analysis of governance responses

Responsiveness

According to the conceptualization of responsiveness the analysis explores whether the governance activities include ongoing tests of the robustness of the existing rules and the monitoring of scientific development, and whether existing regulation is adapted in case of regulatory gaps. It pays specific attention to how regulatory activities are underpinned and how regulatory actors govern nanotherapeutical innovation.

The robustness of the European pharmaceuticals regulation was tested in the explorative activities for the CHMP reflection paper on nanotechnology-based medicinal products and in the context of both EMA workshops. These activities were accompanied by further reflection on the evaluation processes of the 18 nanopharmaceuticals that have been evaluated by the EMA to date. Furthermore, the presentations of a key representative of the EMA at the second Nanotechnology Safety for Success Dialogue of the European Commission (2008), the ETPN Conference (2010) and the CLINAM (2011) dealt with the appropriateness of the existing pharmaceuticals regulation. With regard to nano-enabled medical devices, the N& ET Working Group is continuously evaluating the medical devices regulation. Considering the development of the governance process related to therapeutic nanoproducts we observe ongoing tests of the robustness of the medical products regulation system as well as ongoing monitoring of scientific development.

However, to date the medical products regulation system has not yet been changed to cope with the implementation problems that have been identified in the evaluations. It seems that regulatory action is still in the stage of reflection and preparation. Regarding the knowledge gaps on the benefits and risks of nano(medical) products, as well as the lack of validated risk assessment methods, appropriate regulatory adaptation that is based on evidence is not possible. What has been done by the regulators is preparing nano-specific safety and quality standards and guidance by collecting scientific expertise as well as by evaluating the experience of the competent bodies. In the area of nanopharmaceuticals the key European regulatory bodies seem to focus on learning from nanoscientific research and development activities. Through the EMA's SME facilities, companies are encouraged to share their knowledge with the competent authority. The EMA proactively seeks collaboration with the competent bodies of the Member States and other countries. It has built up an extensive European regulatory network including various groups of experts. These experts support the Agency's activities by providing specialist input on new scientific knowledge. They help with the review of guidelines on nanomedicines and the inclusion of international expertise.

In conclusion, the EU strategy to underpin necessary adaptation of existing medical products regulation and the modes that regulatory bodies have developed seem to be highly responsive.

Stakeholder legitimacy

Regarding *stakeholder legitimacy* the analysis explores whether all relevant stakeholders participate and how they are involved in the governance activities. Above we mentioned that a couple of stakeholders do not participate in the governance activities related to therapeutic nanoproducts. In light of their standardization tasks, earlier activities and competence it is striking that the ICH and the European Directorate for the Quality of Medicines and Health Care are not (yet) actively involved in the preparation of safety and quality standards for nanomedical products. It is striking that technology users (doctors and patients) do not have an active role in the reflection on existing regulation and the preparation of adaptation. This may be partly due to the closeness of certain expert workshops but also, in the case of patients, to a lack of financial resources, organization and interest.

Some of the governance activities were only by invitation or only open for the members of a committee or working group. The 2010 EMA Workshop was open to broad participation. The 200 participants who attended the workshop came from 27 countries and represented universities, companies, competent bodies of the Member States and other countries. However, doctors and patients were poorly represented. The speakers were recruited from the EMA, DG Health and Consumers, the competent bodies of the Member States and other countries, universities and other research organizations. The annual Nanotechnology Safety for Success Dialogue of the European Commission is open to broad participation. All stakeholders listed above (except doctors) attended the meetings and all of them were actively involved in the workshop programmes. The EMA 2006 reflection paper was released by the CHMP, which is composed of a chair, one member and an alternate nominated by each of the 27 Member States; one member and an alternate nominated by Iceland and by Norway; and up to five co-opted members who are expected to provide additional expertise in a particular scientific area (at present statistical, advanced therapies, non-biological and pharmacovigilance expertise). The CHMP ad hoc expert group on nanomedicines includes selected experts from academia and the EMA regulatory network. The EMA Innovation Task Force is composed of scientific and legal administrators appointed from different sectors of Human Units, Directorate and Inspection services. In the activities of the N& ET Working Group the competent bodies of the Member States are involved. SCENIHR members are scientific experts. The Committee's opinions are the subject of consultation and its conferences are open to participation.

It seems that only some stakeholders (the EMA, DG Health and Consumers, many experts and some technology suppliers) participate intensively and actively in the governance activities related to therapeutic nanoproducts. The EMA seems to be the key player in this regulatory area of nanomedicine. Technology users such as patients and doctors are underrepresented and are not actively involved in these activities. Since the EMA's proposed Road Map to 2015 emphasizes the growing importance of the structural involvement of patients and health care professionals in its activities (EMA 2010a), it is striking that doctors and patients are not represented in the CHMP and that they have not been more actively involved in the workshops and other activities.

Consequently, stakeholder legitimacy does not seem to be high in the area of regulatory governance of therapeutic nanoproducts.

Scientific legitimacy

With regard to scientific legitimacy, the analysis explores which experts and scientific committees are involved in regulatory governance of nanotherapeutics, whether their expertise covers all relevant areas and whether they appear to be independent. To reduce the complexity of the exploration we focus on core governance activities which have been initiated by the EMA and SCENIHR. In the EMA CHMP (which composed the reflection paper on nanotechnology-based medicinal products) the experts of the 27 Member States and the co-opted members cover a huge range of areas of expertise, including pharmacology, toxicology, pharmacokinetics, oncology, clinical trials, surgery, infections, metabolism, clinical medicine, physiology, neurology, cell replacement therapy, safety, quality and efficacy, transplant techniques, methodology, medical statistics, pharmacovigilance and pathology.[21] At the 2010 workshop the invited experts were a neuroscientist, an expert of (nano)material science, several pharmacists, a toxicologist, a chemist, an expert of immunology, a physical chemist, two experts of risk management and one expert of pharmacovigilance.[22] All EMA experts have a high profile. It seems that the expertise of experts that are involved in the EMA activities cover the relevant multidisciplinary areas of therapeutic nanoproducts.

The 16 members of SCENIHR are recruited from universities and other research organizations. They have expertise in many areas (amongst which risk assessment, toxicology, chemistry, biochemistry, epidemiology, genetics, physical chemistry, general medicine).[23] The breadth of expertise involved seems to cover all areas that are relevant for the governance activities of SCENIHR related to nanomaterials. SCENIHR members are recruited from universities and other research organizations. All CHMP and SCENIHR members have declared their interests and that they follow the guidance in case of conflicts of interests.[24] They seem to be independent.

To conclude, therefore, our (limited) study indicates that scientific legitimacy is high. In the governance activities related to therapeutic nanoproducts (including the SCENIHR activities) the involved experts have a high profile. Their expertise seems to cover all relevant areas. The publicly accessible declarations of interest provide indications for independence.

Conclusion

This chapter seeks to provide lessons that can be learnt to govern promising but speculative technologies. The paper assumes that responsive regulation, combined with high stakeholder legitimacy and high scientific legitimacy, can enhance the effectiveness and legitimacy of regulation. The case study of therapeutic nanoproducts shows how responsive regulation can be realized in regulatory practice. It points to shortcomings of stakeholder legitimacy. It provides indications of high scientific legitimacy. The exploration of current nanotechnological governance and the analysis of regulatory activities related to therapeutic nanoproducts lead to the following lessons.

1. Uncertain risks and benefits call for a preparatory and collaborative mode of regulation

The activities of the European Medicines Agency to govern therapeutic nanoproducts are an interesting example of responsive preparatory governance. They show that regulators do not need to wait when risks and benefits are uncertain. They can establish a sophisticated regulatory network with experts and other stakeholders to get insights into the properties and effects of existing and coming products. Generally, the regulatory activities related to nanosciences and nanotechnologies indicate that uncertain effects may require prudent waiting with launching new legislation in order to avoid effectiveness problems. However, it does not seem appropriate to be prudent and wait to come up with a definition of nanomaterials and combined therapeutic nanoproducts. The lack of legal definitions leads to legal uncertainty which may stifle investment and innovation.

2. Uncertain risks and benefits require experimentation with soft regulation

The overviews of the applicable regulations show that most regulatory gaps refer to the implementation of existing legislation. Implementation gaps can be reduced by guidance documents, standards, benchmarks and best practices. To cope with the uncertainties of measurement these forms of soft regulation can be launched as provisional and pragmatic instruments. The flexibility of soft instruments allows for quick updates according to scientific and technological progress.

3. Specific efforts should be made to involve technology users more actively in regulatory activities

The analysis shows that patients, doctors and medical staff are not actively involved in the governance of therapeutic nanoproducts. Regarding the importance of stakeholder legitimacy in European governance strategies the enhancement of technology users' participation should be given a high priority.

4. Scientific committees like SCENIHR and CHMP can enhance scientific legitimacy

According to the analysis, these scientific committees seem to be successful in involving independent experts with high-level expertise. Transparency about conflict of interest declarations, expertise and curriculum vitae provides valuable indications of scientific legitimacy.

Finally, we conclude that coping with the challenges of uncertain risks and benefits by using various tools of regulation has to be put into perspective. In the context of uncertainties, 'coping through regulation' does not mean problem-solving. Due to the evidence-based character of regulation, uncertain governability problems are highly resistant to regulatory solutions. Considering the huge demand for certainty in regulatory practice, one of the core tasks of the responsive approach may be to stress the preliminary character of regulation in order to forestall a false sense of certainty.

Notes

1 'Nanosciences' are the result of the interdisciplinary co-operation between physics, chemistry, biology, biotechnology, material sciences and engineering in studying assemblies of atoms and molecules (International Risk Governance Council [IRGC] 2006: 19). 'Nanotechnologies' refer to the development and application of structures, materials, devices and systems with fundamentally new properties and functions which derive from their size in the range of about 1 to 100 nanometers (Siegel *et al.* 1999).

2 For the discussion on nanotechnological governance it is important to distinguish between engineered nanoparticles/nanomaterials and non-intentional release into the environment. Nanoparticles originate from natural sources (e.g. sea-air, volcanic ashes) and/or artificial sources, such as technical products and by-products, cigarette smoke and diesel engine exhaust. The discussion on risks and regulatory governance focuses on engineered nanoparticles and nanomaterials.

3 This definition is used in the European Medicines Agency, Committee for Medicinal Products for Human Use, 'Reflection Paper on Nanotechnology-based Medicinal Products for Human Use', EMEA/CHMP/79769/2006. It refers to the definition of the European Science Foundation (ESF 2005).

4 On ecotoxicology, see Handy 2008.

5 Organizational legitimacy is defined as 'a generalized perception or assumption that the actions of an entity are desirable, proper or appropriate within some socially constructed system of norms, beliefs, and definitons' (Suchman 1995: 574).

6 The distinction between input and output legitimacy has been introduced by Scharpf (1999). The terminology of throughput legitimacy is used by Hahn and Weidtmann in their investigation on the legitimacy of International Organization for Standardization (ISO) standardization (Hahn and Weidtmann 2010; see, also, Forsberg 2011).

7 By 'stakeholder' we understand a person or organization that has legitimate interests in a project or entity (Freeman and David 1983). In this context 'legitimate interest' means that the life of the actor(s) is affected by activities of nanosciences and nanotechnologies.

8 Commonly, regulation is understood as the control of conduct or social affairs through rule-making, implementation, oversight and enforcement. This understanding refers to the influential definition of Julia Black (2002).

9 For a definition, see Senden 2004; Zumbansen 2011.

10 Regulation (EC) No 1907/2006, *OJ* 2006 L 396/1-849.

11 See http://chemicalwatch.com/7085/nano-food-labelling-falls-foul-of-eu-failure-to-agree-novel-foods-regulation, accessed 4 April 2012.

12 The general drugs regulation is mainly composed of Directive 2001/83/EC; Regulation EC/726/2004; and the Directives 2001/20/EC (Good Clinical Practice), 2003/94/EC (Good Manufacturing Practice), 2005/28/EC (Good Clinical Practice – investigational medicinal products).

13 A *medicinal product for human use* is defined as any substance having properties for treating or preventing diseases in human beings or that may be used in or administered to human beings with a view to restoring, correcting or modifying physiological functions by exerting principally a pharmacological, immunological or metabolic action (Art. 1, 1b 2 Directive 2004/27/EC).

14 *Advanced therapies medicinal products* mean any medicinal products for human use that include gene therapy medicinal products, somatic cell therapy products and tissue engineered products (Art. 2 Regulation 1394/2007/EC).

15 *Medical device* means any instrument, apparatus, appliance, software, material or other article, whether used alone or in combination, together with any accessories, including the software intended by its manufacturer to be used specifically for diagnostic and/or therapeutic purposes and necessary for its proper application, intended by the manufacturer to be used for human beings for diagnostic or other purposes (Art. 1.1 Directive 2007/47/EC). It achieves its principal intended action in or on the human body by mechanical means.

16 The medical devices regulation contains Directives for active implantable devices (90/385/EEC), medical devices (93/42/EEC) and in vitro medical devices (98/79/EC). It was the subject of a recast procedure that was expected to be finalized in early 2012.

17 D'Silva and Van Calster (2009: 261). See also Dorbeck-Jung and Chowdhury 2011.

18 *Guide for Safe Manufacture and for Activities Involving Nanoparticles at Workplaces in BASF* (http://basf.com/group/corporate/de/function/conversions:/publish/content/sustainability/dialogue/in-dialogue-withpolitics/nanotechnology/images/BASF_Guide_to_safe_manufacture_and_for_activities_involving_nanoparticles.pdf, accessed 4 June 2012).

19 See EU-OSHA 2008: 9.

20 See www.nanomedroundtable.org, accessed 4 June 2012.

21 See www.ema.europa.eu/ema/index.jsp?curl=pages/contacts/2010/02/people_listing_000002.jsp&murl=menus/about_us/about_us.jsp&mid=WCb01ac0580028c7c, accessed 4 June 2012.

22 See www.ema.europa.eu/docs/en_GB/document_library/Report/2010/10/WC500098380.pdf,accessed 4 June 2012.
23 See http://ec.europa.eu/health/scientific_committees/emerging/members_committee/index_en.htm, accessed 4 June 2012.
24 See, notes 21 and 23.

References

Ayres, I. and Braithwaite, J. (1992) *Responsive Regulation: Transcending the Deregulation Debate*, Oxford: Oxford University Press.

Bergeson, L. and Auer, C. (2011) 'Nano Disclosures: Too Small to Matter or Too Big to Ignore?', *Natural Resources & Environment*, 25(3), www.actagroup.com/other_pdfs/0007-0483.pdf.

Black, J. (2002) 'Critical Reflection on Regulation', *Australian Journal of Legal Philosophy*, 27: 1–35.

Black, J. and Baldwin, R. (2010) 'Really Responsive Risk-based Regulation', *Law & Policy*, 32: 181–213.

Borrás, S. (2006) 'Legitimate Governance of Risk at EU level? The Case of GMOs', *Technological Forecasting and Social Change*, 73(1): 61–75.

CRNNI – Committee to Review the National Nanotechnology Initiative (2006) *A Matter of Size*, Washington, DC: The National Academic Press.

Curtin, D.M. and Wessel, R.A. (eds) (2005) *Good Governance and the European Union: Reflections on Concepts, Institutions and Substance*, Antwerp: Intersentia.

Dorbeck-Jung, B.R. (2007) 'What can Prudent Public Regulators Learn from the United Kingdom Government's Nanotechnological Regulatory Activities?', *Nanoethics*, 1: 257–70.

——(2008) 'Challenges to the Legitimacy of International Regulation: The Case of Pharmaceuticals Standardisation', in A. Follesdal, R. Wessel and J. Wouters (eds), *Multilevel Regulation and the EU: The Interplay between Global, European and National Normative Processes*, Leiden: Martinus Nijhoff Publishers, pp. 55–71.

——(2011) 'Soft Regulation and Responsible Nanotechnological Development in the European Union: Regulating Occupational Health and Safety in the Netherlands', *European Journal of Law and Technology*, 2(3): 1–14.

Dorbeck-Jung, B.R. and Chowdhury, N. (2011) 'Is the European Medical Products Authorisation Regulation Equipped to Cope with the Challenges of Nanomedicines?', *Law & Policy*, 33(2): 276–303.

D'Silva, J. and Bowman, D. (2011) 'The Regulation of Nanomedicine', in R. Hunter and V. Preedy (eds), *Nanomedicine in Health and Disease*, New Hampshire: Science Publishers, pp. 20–42.

D'Silva, J. and Van Calster, G. (2009) 'News and Views: Taking Temperature – A Review of European Union Regulation in Nanomedicine', *European Journal of Health Law*, 16: 249–69.

EC – European Commission (2000) 'Communication from the European Commission on Precautionary Principle' (COM 1 Final), Brussels: EC.

——(2001) White Paper on Governance (COM 1 Final), Brussels: EC.

——(2005) 'Nanosciences and Nanotechnologies: An Action Plan for Europe 2005–2009', Brussels: EC.

——(2008a) Communication, 'Regulatory Aspects of Nanomaterials' and the accompanying Commission staff document, 'Summary of Legislation in Relation to

Health, Safety and Environment Aspects of Nanomaterials, Regulatory Research Needs and Related Measures', www.kowi.de/Portaldata/2/Resources/fp7/coop/eu-nano-policy-2004-08-en.pdf, accessed 5 August 2011.

——(2008b) 'Recommendation on a Code of Conduct for Responsible Nanoscience and Nanotechnologies Research' (COM 7.2.2008), Brussels: EC.

——(2009a) 'Nanosciences and Nanotechnologies: An Action Plan for Europe 2005–2009: First Implementation Report 2007–2009' (COM, 2007, 505 final), Brussels: EC.

——(2009b) 'Nanosciences and Nanotechnologies: An Action Plan for Europe 2005–2009: Second Implementation Report 2007–2009' (COM, 2009, 607 final), Brussels: EC.

——(2011) 'Recommendation of 18 October 2011 on the Definition of Nanomaterial' (2011/696/EU), *Official Journal of the European Union*, L 275/38.

EGE – European Group of Ethics in Science and New Technologies (2007) *Opinion on the Ethical Aspects of Nanomedicine*, Brussels: European Commission.

EMA – European Medicines Agency (2006) 'Nanotechnology-based Medicinal Products for Human Use', Reflection paper EMA/CHMP/79769/2006, London: EMA.

——(2010a) 'The European Medicines Agency Road Map to 2015: The Agency's Contribution to Science, Medicines, Health', *Draft for Public Consultation*, EMA/299895/2009, London: EMA.

——(2010b) '1st International Workshop on Nanomedicines 2010', Summary Report EMA/ 538503/2010.

ESF – European Science Foundation (2005) *ESF Forward Look on Nanomedicine*, Strasbourg Cedex: ESF, www.esf.org/publications/214/Nanomedicine.pdf, accessed 9 January 2010.

EU-OSHA – European Agency for Safety and Health at Work Literature Review (2008) 'Workplace Exposure to Nanoparticles', edited by J. Kosk-Bienko, European Agency for Safety and Health at Work (EU-OSHA).

Everson, M. and Vos, E. (eds) (2009) *Uncertain Risks Regulated*, Abingdon: Routledge-Cavendish.

Forsberg, E-M. (2011) 'Standardisation in the Field of Nanotechnology: Some Issues of Legitimacy', *Sci. Eng. Ethics*, 1–21.

Franzius, C. (2001) 'Technikermöglichungsrecht', *Die Verwaltung*, 34: 487–516.

Freeman, E. and David, L. (1983) 'Stockholders and Stakeholders. A New Perspective on Corporate Governance', *California Management Review*, 25(3): 88–106.

Gaspar, R. (2010) 'Therapeutic Products: Regulating Drugs and Medical Devices', in G. Hodge, A. Maynard and D. Bowman (eds), *International Handbook on Regulating Nanotechnologies*, Cheltenham: Edward Elgar, pp. 291–320.

Geertsma, R.E., de Bruijn, A. and Hilbers-Modderman, E.S.M. (2007) *New and Emerging Medical Technologies: A Horizon Scan of Opportunities and Risks*, Bilthoven: RIVM, www.rivm.nl/bibliotheek/digitaaldepot/ New_emerging_medical_technolo-gies.pdf.

Hahn, R. and Weidtmann, C. (2010) 'The Legitimacy of ISO 26000 as Standard for Social Responsibility', Paper presented at the annual meeting of the Theory vs Policy? Connecting Scholars and Practioners, New Orleans.

Handy, D.R. (2008) 'The Ecotoxicology of Nanoparticles and Nanomaterials: Current Status, Knowledge Gaps, Challenges and Future Needs', *Ecotoxicology*, 17: 315–25.

Haum, R., Petschow, U. and Steinfeldt, M. (2004) 'Nanotechnology and Regulation Within the Framework of the Precautionary Principle', Berlin: IÖW.

Héritier, A. and Lehmkuhl, D. (2008) 'Introduction: The Shadow of Hierarchy and new Modes of Governance', *Journal of Public Policy*, 28(1): 1–17.

Hodge, G., Bowman, D. and Ludlow, K. (2007) *New Global Regulatory Frontiers in Regulation: The Age of Nanotechnology*, Cheltenham: Edward Elgar.

——(2010) 'Introduction: The Regulatory Challenges for Nanotechnologies', in G. Hodge, A. Maynard and D. Bowman, *International Handbook on Regulating Nanotechnologies*, Cheltenham: Edward Elgar, pp. 3–24.

IRGC – International Risk Governance Council (2006) *Nanotechnology, Risk Governance*, White Paper No. 2, Geneva: IRGC.

Kandlikar, M., Ramachandran, G., Maynard, A., Murdock, B. and Toscano, W. (2007) 'Health Risk Assessment for Nanoparticles: A Case for Using Expert Judgement', *Journal of Nanoparticle Research*, 9: 137–56.

Kearnes, M. and Rip, A. (2009) 'The Emerging Governance Landscape of Nanotechnology', in S. Gammel, A. Lösch, and A. Nordmann (eds) *Jenseits von Regulierung: Zum Politischen Umgang mit der Nanotechnologie*, Berlin: Akademische Verlagsgesellschaft, pp. 97–121.

Kloepfer, M. (2002) *Technik und Recht im wechselseitigen Werden – Kommunikationsrecht in der Technikgeschichte*, Berlin: Duncker Humblot.

Levi-Faur, D. and Comaneshter, H. (2007) 'The Risk of Regulation and the Regulation of Risks: The Governance of Nanotechnology', in G. Hodge, D. Bowman and K. Ludlow (eds), *New Global Regulatory Frontiers in Regulation: The Age of Nanotechnology*, Cheltenham: Edward Elgar, pp. 149–65.

Linkov, I., Satterstrom, F.K. and Corey, L.M. (2008) 'Nanotoxicology and Nanomedicine: Making Hard Decisions', *Nanomedicine: Nanotechnology, Biology and Medicine*, 4: 167–71.

Lundqvist, M., Stigler, J., Elia, G., Lynch, I., Cedervall, T. and Dawson, K. (2008) 'Nanoparticle Size and Surface Properties Determine the Protein Corona with Possible Implications for Biological Impacts', *PNAS*, 105.

Masis (2009) 'Challenging Futures of Science in Society: Emerging Trends and Cutting-edge Issues', Report (EUR 24039 EN), Brussels: EC.

N& ET Working Group (2007) 'Nanotechnology to the Medical Devices Expert Group: Findings and Recommendations', Report from the Working Group New and Emerging Technologies in Medical Devices.

Nel, A., Xia, Tian, Mädler, L. and Li, Ning (2006) 'Toxic Potential of Materials at the Nanolevel', *Science*, 311: 622–27.

Nonet, P. and Selznick, P. (1978) *Law and Society in Transition. Towards Responsive Law*, New York: Harper.

Poland, C.A., Duffin, R., Kinloch, I., Maynard, A., Wallace, W., Seaton, A., Stone, V., Brown, S., MacNee, W. and Donaldson, K. (2008) 'Carbon Nanotubes into the Abdominal Cavity Display Asbestos-like Pathogenic Behaviour in a Pilot Study', *Nature Nanotechnology*, 3: 423–28.

Roco, M.C. and Bainbridge, W.S. (eds) (2001) 'Societal Implications of Nanoscience and Nanotechnology', Report NSET Workshop, Virginia, March 2001, based on NSF Workshop in September 2000, Dordrecht: Springer (formerly Kluwer).

——(2005) 'Societal Implications of Nanoscience and Nanotechnology – Improving Benefits to Humanity', Report NSET and NSF, Arlington, VA, Dordrecht: Springer (also at www.nano.gov).

Rosenbaum, A. and Shepherd, A. (2000) 'IASIA Symposium on Governance, Responsibility and Social Enhancement: Governance, Good Government and Poverty Reduction', *International Review of Administrative Sciences*, 66(2): 269–84.

SCENIHR – Scientific Committee on Emerging and Newly Identified Health Risks (2007) 'Opinion on the Appropriateness of the Risk Assessment Methodology in Accordance with the Technical Guidance Documents for New and Existing Substances for Assessing the Risks of Nanomaterials', Brussels: DG Health and Consumers.

——(2008) 'Opinion on the Scientific Aspects of the Existing and Proposed Definitions Relating to Products of Nanoscience and Nanotechnologies', Brussels: DG Health and Consumers.

——(2010) 'Opinion on the Scientific Basis for the Definition of the Term "Nanomaterial"', Brussels: DG Health and Consumers.

Scharpf, F.W. (1999) *Governing in Europe: Effective and Democratic?*, Oxford: Oxford University Press.

Schmitter, P. (2001) 'What Is There to Legitimise in the European Union … and How Might This Be Accomplished?', *Max Planck Projektgruppe Recht der Gemeinschaftsgüter*, Bonn, 2.

Schomberg, R. von (2011) 'Prospects for Technology Assessment in a Framework of Responsible Research and Innovation', in M. Dusseldorp and R. Beecroft (eds), *Technikfolgen abschätzen lehren: Bildungspotenziale transdisziplinärer Methoden*, Wiesbaden: Vs Verlag.

Selznick, P. (1992) *The Moral Commonwealth: Social Theory and the Promise of Community*, Berkeley, CA: University of California Press.

Senden, L. (2004) *Soft Law in European Community Law*, London: Hart Publishing.

Siegel, R.W., Hu, E. and Roco, M.C. (eds) (1999) *Nanostructure Science and Technology*, Dordrecht: Springer (also at www.wtec.org/loyola/nano).

Suchman, M.C. (1995) 'Managing Legitimacy: Strategic and Institutional Approaches', *Academy of Management Review*, 20(3): 571–610.

Trubek, L.G., Rees, J.V., Hoflund, A.B., Farquahr, M. and Heimer, C.A. (2008) 'Health Care and New Governance: the Quest for Effective Regulation', *Regulation and Governance*, 2: 1–8.

van Kersbergen, K. and van Waarden, F. (2004) 'Governance as a Bridge between Disciplines, Cross-disciplinary Inspiration regarding Shifts in Governance and Problems of Governability, Accountability and Legitimicy', *European Journal of Political Research*, 43: 143–71.

Vos, E. (1999) *Institutional Frameworks of Community Health and Safety Regulation – Committees, Agencies and Private Bodies*, Oxford: Hart Publishing.

Wagner, V., Dullaart, A., Bock, A.K. and Zweck, A. (2006) 'The Emerging Nanomedicine Landscape', *Nature Biotechnology*, 24(10): 1211–17.

Woodrow Wilson Centre (2011) 'Updates', www.nanotechproject.org/inventories/consumer/up-dates/, accessed 21 July 2011.

Woods, N. (2000) 'The Challenge of Good Governance for the IMF and the World Bank Themselves', *World Development*, 28(5): 823–42.

Zijverden, M. van and Sips, A.M. (eds) (2008) *Nanotechnology in Perspective: Risks for Man and the Environment*, Bilthoven: RIVM.

Zumbansen, P. (2011) 'Neither "Public" nor "Private", "National" nor "International": Transnational Corporate Governance from a Legal Pluralist Perspective', *Journal of Law and Society*, 38(1): 50–75.

6 Climate change, targets and trade

An EU law perspective on the preferential treatment of international competing industries

Marjan Peeters[1]

Introduction

Binding targets for the absolute reduction of greenhouse gases are the backbone of European Union (EU) climate policy. Such targets limit the total amount of greenhouse gas emissions that might be produced in a defined area during a defined period. The EU currently follows a target of 20 per cent reduction of greenhouse gas emissions in 2020 compared to the level of emissions in 1990. In order to reach this target, the EU relies to a large extent on the market-based regulatory approach known as emissions trading. This basically means that trading in emission rights, which are provided for through EU secondary law, is allowed among Member States themselves and among EU industries, which are covered by the so-called EU emissions trading scheme (EU ETS).[2] The EU has, in fact, conducted an impressive experiment by establishing internal greenhouse gas emissions trading schemes. Moreover, the EU regulatory frameworks through which emissions reduction targets and subsequently emission trading possibilities are defined are evolving at great speed. The first 'cap and trade' approach was adopted in 2003 with Directive 2003/87/EC, requiring Member States to adopt: 1) implementing legislation in only a few months; and 2) important decisions, among which a national allocation plan, only a few months later. This emissions trading system obliged industries to surrender yearly an amount of emission rights (referred to as 'allowances') at least equal to their factual emissions. The emission rights were allocated – mostly for free to industries – by the Member States through so-called national allocation plans and subsequent national allocation decisions (Peeters 2003; Faure and Peeters 2008). After a few years the European Commission considered this emissions trading system insufficient, which led in January 2008 to a proposal dramatically to amend the cap and trade system. With astonishing speed, the proposed new regulatory structure received political support from the European Parliament and the Council in December 2008, followed by a formal adoption of the amending directive by the Council in April 2009 (Peeters and Weishaar 2009). The new framework for the EU ETS sets the legal requirements for the next emissions trading period, running from 2013–2020, and beyond.

Given the fact that climate change is a global problem, unilateral action may meet fierce opposition from international industries, established within the rapidly evolving legal regime in the EU. Hence, a delicate issue with which the EU and every other regional organization or State wanting to carry on with unilateral greenhouse gas emissions reduction action must deal, is that international industries might complain about the damaging competitive effects of unilateral emission reductions requirements. The EU acts as a frontrunner and has introduced the most far reaching greenhouse gas emissions reduction target worldwide, which entails obligations for industries in the EU that compete internationally. How was the EU able, on the one hand, to reconcile its wish to take unilateral responsibility with regard to the climate change problem, with the competitive concerns of the EU-based international industry on the other? This chapter will explain that the EU legal framework gives preferential treatment to internationally competitive sectors based in the EU by means of allocating free allowances. The Court of Justice of the European Union (CJEU), however, has formulated an important rationale for EU climate law, which is that, in principle, emitters have to be treated on an equal footing and that, consequently, differential treatment has to be justified on the basis of objective and transparent criteria (a discussion of this case law follows below).[3] But how is the EU legislator, who has already expanded the EU ETS to international aviation, applying this rationale founded in the principle of equal treatment? It will be discussed whether the EU ETS might be vulnerable to legal challenges from industries, including aviation operators, trying to defend their economic position by arguing that: 1) unjustified differential treatment has occurred; or 2) the equal treatment of seemingly equal operators might be unjustified due to the different circumstances in which the operators find themselves.

The structure of this chapter is as follows: the next section provides an introduction on the emission reduction target set by the EU, showing that the specific design of the target is already a sensitive matter in view of global competition. Then the specific design of the EU ETS will be disussed, after which it will be analysed how the EU has dealt with the competitive concern of its international industries, including aviation. The last section ends with concluding observations.

The EU greenhouse gas target

Targets: political choices with consequences for the emitting sources

An emissions trading system rests on a predefined greenhouse gas emission reduction target, often called a 'cap'. Such greenhouse gas emission reduction targets need to be developed in the context of natural, technological and socio-economic uncertainties. Science cannot predict with precision which target should be set in order to avoid serious or less serious damages. Moreover, if science could predict the extent to which emissions should be reduced globally in a given year, like 2020, 2030 or 2050, it remains a question of international politics as to how to distribute this target among all relevant countries. The United Nations Framework Convention on Climate Change (UNFCCC) currently has 195 parties, and the burden to reduce emissions is intended to be distributed among these parties, thereby following the principle of common but differentiated responsibilities, which means, in effect, that the largest efforts should be undertaken by developed countries.[4] In this vein, the Kyoto Protocol contains a list of emission reduction targets that only apply to developed countries. However, no precise legal criteria exist to form the basis of a definition of the emission reduction targets for States. The process for setting emissions reduction criteria is highly political, and guidance is found in very vague principles, such as the already mentioned (Note 4) 'common but differentiated responsibilities' and 'the polluter pays principle'. Recently, 'equitable access to sustainable development' has also been added to this guidance framework.[5] The parties to the UNFCCC have not yet managed to agree on the definition of objective and transparent criteria for the definition of emissions reduction targets for States, not even for the period starting after the first Kyoto Protocol emission reduction period that ran from 2008 to 2012.

Negotiations among UNFCCC parties with regard to new emission reduction targets proceeded in the course of the Ad Hoc Working Group on Long-term Cooperative Action established in Bali in 2007, followed in 2011 by the establishment of a new sub-working group, the Ad Hoc Working Group on the Durban Platform for Enhanced Action.[6] However, there is not even an agreement about the specific form of the targets. China, for instance, chooses to base its greenhouse gas reduction policy on carbon intensity targets (Zhang 2011: 3–4), while the Kyoto Protocol and the EU rely on absolute emission reduction targets. An important difference is that in the latter case a cap is put on the total amount of emissions, while in the former case this cap is lacking. Here the amount of emissions relates, for instance, to each unit of production, making clean growth possible but also, if economic development does occur, increasing the total amount of emissions. This different perspective on the definition of the target is usually defended on the basis of the principle of common but differentiated responsibilities.

The EU target and its implications for industries competing internationally

The fact that the EU adhered to the Kyoto Protocol and hence is legally bound to reduce its emissions by 8 per cent in 2008–2012 compared to 1990 can be traced back to a political choice. The specific target of 8 per cent is not well explained on the basis of explicitly mentioned and objective distributive criteria, and is more to be seen as an outcome of political negotiations. Such a legally binding target, however, ultimately influences the legal position of private actors operating emitting sources situated in the EU, as it is clear that the EU and its Member States have to steer the emissions within their territory in order to achieve compliance with the international binding target.

The refusal of the United States to ratify the Kyoto Protocol, as well as the withdrawal of Canada from the Kyoto Protocol as announced in December 2011, illustrate that other powerful developed countries do not want to impose such a burden on their economic operators.

The EU is therefore gradually becoming isolated by virtue of it taking the Kyoto Protocol seriously and more so by virtue of the fact that it has already imposed a unilateral target of 20 per cent to be achieved in 2020. The fact that the EU wants to achieve such targets has consequences for EU-based industry that competes internationally. A large number of these industries already fall within the EU-wide emissions trading scheme, in particular as a result of the expansion of the scope of Directive 2009/29/EC. Objections from industries competing internationally to greenhouse gas emission reduction obligations under the emissions trading system, for example, took the form of legal claims by the largest global steel industry, having sites in several EU countries. This steel industry appealed both to the national administrative court in France and the EU Court of First Instance (now called the General Court), arguing in the latter case for the partial annulment of the EU emissions trading directive and claiming damages. The appeal before the French court led to the submission of preliminary questions to the European Court of Justice (ECJ, now the Court of Justice of the European Union: CJEU).[7] The decisions from both the CJEU and the General Court contain a very interesting fundamental consideration with regard to the meaning of the equal treatment principle and the polluter pays principle, which might have consequences for future case law. Both the CJEU and the General Court observed that the different sources of greenhouse gas emissions relating to economic activities are in principle comparable, since all emissions of greenhouse gases are liable to contribute to dangerous interference with the climate system. This means that these sources should be treated equally unless there is an adequate reason for justifying different treatment. To quote the CJEU:

> a difference in treatment is justified, if it is based on an objective and reasonable criterion, that is, if the difference relates to a legally permitted aim pursued by the legislation in question, and it is proportionate to the aim pursued by the treatment.[8]

The CJEU and then the General Court found it reasonable that the EU legislator took a step-by-step approach, so that not all polluters would be covered from the very start by the same legislative instrument. This step-by-step approach was found reasonable, particularly in view of the challenge of developing such a complex instrument as emissions trading in such a complex policy field as climate change.

Thus, it was justified for the legislator not to include all (competing) industries within the emissions trading system at the same time. So, particularly in the starting phase, there was policy room for differential treatment among greenhouse gas emitting sources by covering only some of the sources within the EU ETS.

Nevertheless, as time passes and experience is gained, the legislator can be expected to take further steps for the improvement and expansion of its legislative framework. In that respect, the policy discretion given by the court to the legislator may decrease, since – time having passed – it might no be longer valid to argue that differential treatment is a consequence of the start-up of the development of a complex legislative framework.[9]

The consideration of the EU courts with regard to the relevance of the principle of equal treatment for the legality of greenhouse gas emission reduction legislation is not unfamiliar to that of national courts, at least not to the French Constitutional Council.[10] The Consitutional Council followed the same reasoning in a case where differential treatment was proposed by the French national government between, on the one hand, sources covered by the EU emissions trading regime and, on the other hand, other sources not covered by the emissions trading regime. The aim was to impose a greenhouse gas emissions tax upon sources not covered by the EU ETS. EU ETS sources, however, would be exempted from this taxation obligation. Particularly referring to the fact that the EU ETS sources receive their tradable emission rights (referred to as 'allowances') for free until 2013, the tax obligation for the non-EU ETS sources was found by the Constitutional Council to breach the principle of '*égalité devant les charges publiques*', a principle resembling the equal treatment principle.[11] These basic considerations with regard to equal treatment of greenhouse gas emitters – backed up by the polluter pays principle – of both the EU courts and the French Constitutional Council can be seen as core to the basic rationale of EU climate law, against which future legislative and administrative acts may also be tested.

First, however, we must look at the unilateral EU target for the period 2013–2020. The final climate policy goal that the EU is seeking to achieve is to prevent the overall global annual mean surface temperature increasing beyond 2°C above pre-industrial levels. This means that from now on temperature increases should be limited to approximately 1.5°C, since temperature has already increased since the start of industrialization. The 2°C target, and the need to consider a change to a 1.5°C target (which would mean that the temperature increase should be limited to 1°C), is recognized by the parties to the UNFCCC.[12] Obviously, as soon as the overall target changes (e.g. from 2°C to 1.5°C), the legal obligations upon the emitters have to be strengthened too.

The 2°C target is only intended to avoid a *dangerous* anthropogenic interference with the climate system.[13] This means that the level of protection is limited: non-dangerous interference such as economic damage, or perhaps even the need to relocate, fall outside the scope of regulation.[14] The Communication of the European Commission from early 2010, on the options for an EU vision and a target for biodiversity beyond 2010, stated that 'a 2 degree rise in global temperature above pre-industrial levels would lead to catastrophic climate change'.[15] This illustrates that the target as endorsed by the EU is, according to at least the Commission, the borderline between catastrophic and non-catastrophic climate change.[16]

Moreover, one might also wonder whether the EU target is a sufficient contribution in order to achieve the 2°C threshold. To implement the goal of limiting global warming to 2°C, the EU legal framework currently aims at a 20 per cent emission reduction approach, to be reached in 2020. In contrast, the Intergovernmental Panel on Climate Change (IPCC) has indicated a 25 to 40 per cent reduction target, to be reached in 2020 compared to the emissions in 1990 by developed countries, and Annex I to the UNFCCC has listed the developed countries, and they are usually called Annex I countries.[17] Thus the EU, which adheres to the UNFCCC, is also cautious with regard to its minimum reduction target of 20 per cent, even if it is at the same time very ambitious compared to the other UNFCCC Treaty parties, particularly the Annex I countries.[18]

The intention of the IPCC that Annex I countries should make reductions of between 25 and 40 per cent in 2020 and between 80 and 95 per cent in 2050, again compared to 1990 emissions, can be found in chapter 13 of the 807-page report of Working Group III called 'Mitigation of Climate Change'. This intention has not been repeated in the integrated Fourth Assessment Report (the synthesis report), nor in the related Summary for Policymakers. The projection of between 25 and 40 per cent reduction in 2020 is furthermore linked to the goal of 450ppm (parts per million) CO_2 equivalent. A less stringent goal of 550ppm CO_2 equivalent is linked to a 10 to 30 per cent emission reduction goal for developed countries in 2020. The IPCC indicates that the relevant table has been based on studies covering multiple approaches to allocating emissions between regions, and thus claims that the table presents an aggregate range. It clarifies that each approach makes different assumptions about the pathway chosen, specific national efforts and other variables. Furthermore, the IPCC report states that 'the ranges presented … do not imply political feasibility, nor do the results reflect cost variances'.[19] Quite surprisingly, however, this 25 to 40 per cent target to be reached by developed countries in 2020 has been frequently repeated by governments, including the EU.[20] For example, the European Commission in the Communication for Copenhagen stated that:[21]

> The EU has proposed that developed countries, as a group, should reduce their emissions by an amount consistent with the 2° objective. The 4th Assessment report by the Intergovernmental Panel on Climate Change (IPCC) indicates that this would require emission reductions for developed countries in the range of 25–40% by 2020 and 80–95% by 2050. Developed countries should be able to achieve their reduction targets in part through domestic action and in part by using credits resulting from emission reductions in developing countries.

This shows that the EU connects to the '25–40 per cent target' while linking it to trading with developing countries as part of the achievement of this target (using credits from developing countries).[22]

This concise discussion shows that an indication made by the IPCC (between 25 and 40 per cent reduction in 2020 to be reached by developed countries) has become important in the development of EU policies. It seems as if the policy side has simply taken over the IPCC indication of distribution of commitments among developed and developing countries. Further debate is needed here about the IPCC policy interface: to what extent should a distributional statement by scientists saying that there should be a 25 to 40 per cent reduction in 2020 by Annex I countries be followed by politicians, and might the statement with the 25–40 per cent aggregated range have any value in a court case considering the stringency of climate law? In other words, if an industry were to contest the stringency of greenhouse gas emission reduction obligations, or if an environmental non-governmental organization (NGO) were to argue that the ambition of the proposed measures is not stringent enough, what value would the court then give to the distributional observations by the IPCC and/or the fact that the EU has – simply – followed this? It is interesting to note that, it is apparent in the case law within the EU thus far, the stringency of greenhouse gas reduction measures is not contested. Of course, the chance for a successful claim may be rather low given the usual deference that courts give to highly political decisions as well as the fact that the precautionary principle has been codified in EU environmental law.[23] But this does not necessarily mean that claims about the stringency of climate legislation would always be unsuccessful.[24]

Targets: not (yet) an issue for the CJEU

It is quite surprising that in the Arcelor case – where the steel industry tried to get the directive partially annulled – the need for the government, including the EU legislator, to take greenhouse gas emissions reduction measures was not contested by the appellant. This might have been attempted in order to test whether such measures or their intensity were justified. Particularly at the time of the claim, in 2003, the IPCC reports were more moderate in their demands for governmental policy compared to 2007. One might conjecture that the lawyers advising the industry were already anticipating the fact that the court usually gives a large margin of appreciation in such complex social-economic cases to the legislator.[25] Also, case law in the EU generally does not (yet) deal with the first step of climate change policies, which boils down to the question of whether governmental action towards the reduction of greenhouse gases is needed and, if so, with what aim. One can, however, expect that, if certain industries are not satisfied with the regulatory approach imposing obligations on them, they will seek out legal arguments to contest the need and the intensity of the regulatory action in question. It will be particularly interesting to see whether cases will emerge that question the need to have an ambitious unilateral target, while other countries fail to adopt binding frameworks, even exiting from the Kyoto Protocol or adopting frameworks with less ambitious targets.[26] The final question, however, is one of how EU courts proceed in scientifically complex cases concerning climate change and the need to take governmental action, particularly in view of the precautionary principle, as codified within Article 191 TFEU (Treaty on the Functioning of the European Union). Furthermore, if governmental action as such can be deemed justifiable, which specific emission reduction target would then be acceptable? For instance, is the UNFCCC threshold (the avoidance of only dangerous interference) acceptable, given the high level of environmental protection that should be pursued by the EU institutions according to Article 191 TFEU? Usually, the EU courts give a broad discretion to the EU legislator, but this does not mean that no judicial testing takes place at all. Moreover, proof of insufficient scientific approaches concerning the climate change projections, or even wrong calculations on important matters, could strengthen claims against EU greenhouse gas reduction measures.[27] To date, however, in the EU – the region in which the globally most stringent target has been set – the need for and intensity of the emission reduction target, including the reliability of the scientific reports that support the emission reduction legislation, have not yet been challenged before the court.[28]

EU emissions trading

The present regulatory framework

EU climate law has already become very complex, comprising many directives, regulations and decisions. It is not easy to understand the whole package, including the interlinkages and possible interactions between the several regulatory instruments. The EU ETS is not the only regulatory instrument. In the period 2005–2012 the EU ETS covers approximately only 40 per cent of the EU greenhouse gas emissions. Following the expansion of the coverage with Directive 2009/29/EC, the EU ETS in 2012–2020 will cover a larger part of the total EU greenhouse gas emissions, although a large number of emissions will still be covered by other instruments, in particular the so-called EU Effort Sharing Decision. This decision contains an emission reduction for the period 2012–2020 for each EU Member State.[29] In fact, EU climate law can be distinguished in two large emission bubbles, one for the industries covered by the EU ETS and one for the sources not covered by that system. This 'non-EU ETS bubble' is divided into 27 different emissions reduction obligations for the Member States. This implies that Member States have to develop policies and, if needed, legislative approaches in order to ensure that the total emissions from the non-EU ETS do not exceed the prescribed national emission reduction obligation.

In the course of developing the greenhouse gas emission reduction legislation, the EU legislator already incorporated a differential treatment of the EU ETS and the non-EU ETS sources: the package puts a larger emission reduction obligation on the EU ETS sources (21 per cent compared to 2005 emissions) compared to the non-EU ETS sources (10 per cent compared to 2005 emissions). Sources which are covered by the EU ETS might address the court for contesting that they are treated differently by means of a higher emissions reduction target compared to non-EU ETS sources.

Regulatory action by Member States

Consequently, the step-by-step approach that the EU legislator follows in order to build a regulatory approach towards greenhouse gas emitting sources has led to two major tracks being followed: one addressing sources with emissions trading, asking from these sources an effort of 21 per cent reductions in 2020 compared to 2005; and the other non-EU ETS sources, being addressed by national policies of the Member States. In total, these sources will need to deliver a 10 per cent emission reduction in 2020 compared to 2005. The intensity of the effort among comparable sources in different Member States can be, potentially, quite different because the emission reduction commitments for the Member States range between minus 20 per cent to plus 20 per cent emissions reductions in 2020 compared to 2005. In practice, this could mean that the agricultural sector in one country will be faced with further emission reduction efforts than the same sector in another country. While the EU ETS provides a harmonized system for the allocation of allowances to the covered industries, particularly for the period starting in 2013 (see next paragraph), the non-EU ETS sources need to be addressed by the Member States in order to achieve the applicable national emission reduction target as prescribed by the Effort Sharing Decision. Consequently, Member States have to make a distributional choice with regard to dividing the large national bubble of emissions among all relevant non-EU ETS sources in their country. A question arises here: according to which legal principles will these national regulatory approaches be developed? Since the regulatory measures are needed in order to comply with the Effort Sharing Decision, one should not overlook the fact that not only national law but also EU principles have to be met. Next to the principle of proportionality, this also concerns the principle of equal treatment in connection with the polluter pays principle. If a national government were to develop a national mitigation policy for some sectors or sources with heavier burden than others, legal cases might be considered. It will be interesting to see whether such legal cases will indeed be brought and, if so, whether the meaning of legal principles, particularly the principle of proportionality and the principle of equal treatment, will be further developed in EU and national climate law.[30]

Instead of imposing the full emission reduction requirement on the non-EU ETS sources, Member States may also decide to make use of the so-called flexibility mechanisms provided by the Effort Sharing Decision. This basically means that part of the allowed amount of national emissions can be sold to or bought from other Member States. The Effort Sharing Decision provides for various such flexible possibilities, ranging from trade between Member States to buying emission credits from developing countries. A Member State could then decide to mitigate the costs for their sources by making full use of the possibility to buy compensatory emission rights from other countries. Another way imaginable would mean a Member State imposing certain ambitious efforts on a certain sector, like the agricultural sector, with the resulting over-compliance being sold on to other countries. In such a case, the sources might complain that their obligation is disproportionate since it is not needed in order to comply with the Effort Sharing Decision, and that the extra effort benefits the State budget but does not contribute to the prevention of the climate problem, as the overall emissions in the EU will not decrease simply because the emissions saved will be used by others outside the country. Thus, as soon as a certain industry feels that disproportionate efforts are being imposed on it and it is subjected to unjustified differential treatment compared to other emitters, it may revert to the courts to seek less stringent – or more comparable – costs. In sum, the national policies that need to be developed under the Effort Sharing Decision can potentially be a learning source about which emission reduction policies are justifiable in view of legal principles. Much will of course depend on how much regulatory discretion in that respect will be given by the courts.

The position of international competing industries within the EU ETS framework

Differential treatment of emitters

For the EU ETS trading periods 2005–2007 and 2008–2012, Member States had the competence to decide how to treat the carbon emissions of internationally competitive industries. Through their national allocation plans and subsequent national allocation decisions, they decided on the amount of allowances to be issued to each industrial installation. With Directive 2009/29/EC an important shift took place: the power to decide on the rules for the allocation of the allowances was transferred to the EU level. This new system means that all industries in the EU receive allowances in line with rules set at the EU level.[31] Furthermore, only one EU-wide cap applies. This total amount of tradable greenhouse gas allowances will be lowered by 1.74 per cent every year in order to contribute to the overall goal of minus 20 per cent emissions in 2020.[32]

Consequently, the method for allocating the greenhouse gas allowances to industrial actors has changed dramatically. The European Commission has the power to establish through the comitology procedure the allocation procedures and rules for the period 2013–2020 and beyond, notably the rules for auctioning and free allocation, and the Member States have the task of applying those rules. The allocation for industrial operations can be divided into three categories, each using a separate allocation method. These categories can briefly be summarized as follows:

1 the power industry, which will have to buy the emission allowances at an auction organized by Member States in accordance with harmonized

rules adopted at the EU level in the EU ETS directive and subsequent decision-making from the European Commission;[33]

2 internationally competitive industry, receiving all allowances for free from the Member States, which issue those allowances in accordance with harmonized rules adopted at the EU level in the EU ETS directive and subsequent decision-making by the European Commission;[34]

3 the other industrial sectors, only entitled to receive part of their emissions allowances for free and having to buy the other needed allowances at the auction or on the secondary market. The need to buy allowances at the auction or through the secondary market will gradually increase. The first year (2013) starts with a 20 per cent auction or an 80 per cent free allocation approach, while for the last year of the trading period 2013–2020 a 30 per cent free allocation or a 70 per cent auctioning approach applies.[35] The free allowances will be allocated by the Member States, issuing those allowances in accordance with harmonized rules adopted at the EU level in the EU ETS directive and subsequent decision-making by the European Commission.

A fourth, distinctive category has been introduced by Directive 2008/101/EC, which has brought aviation into the scope of the EU ETS. From the start of 2012, emissions from all domestic and international flights arriving in or departing from an EU airport will be covered by the EU Emissions Trading System. The aviation sector will receive most of the allowances for free in 2012. The sector may not buy EU ETS allowances allocated to industries but they are allowed to sell their allowances to other EU ETS sources. The inclusion of aviation in the EU ETS is a very sensitive political matter: a group of American and British air companies have appealed to a court in the UK, which subsequently submitted preliminary questions to the CJEU asking for guidance on the interpretation of the international legal context for this EU action.[36]

The CJEU, in its decision of 21 December 2011, sees no reason to approve the legal arguments from the appellants but it does not seem that this European Court decision prevents further international protests against the EU ETS. Some Chinese companies have already announced that they are considering a procedure before a German court.[37] Moreover, several countermeasures have been announced and have already begun to take effect. In the USA, the House of Representatives has approved a draft law, named the 'European Union Emissions Trading Scheme Prohibition Act of 2011', that forbids American air companies from taking part in the EU ETS.[38] The Russian government has announced that it is considering increasing Trans-Siberian air transit fees for European air companies. These examples show that the unilateral inclusion of aviation – including non-EU-based civil aircraft companies – in the EU ETS has led to angry international reactions, court procedures and countermeasures. The EU continues to argue that, given the lack of a global agreement on aviation emissions, it is justified in imposing greenhouse gas reduction measures.

From the viewpoint of equal treatment, one can see that the regulatory framework treats the EU-based air companies on the same footing as other air companies: all air companies have to operate within their emissions allowances, which extend to cover all of their flights, including non-EU flights arriving in or departing from the EU. The Court has concluded that the uniform application of the EU ETS to all flights departing from or arriving in the EU is consistent with provisions designed to prohibit discriminatory treatment between aircraft operators.[39] In this respect, one cannot distinguish any differential treatment among them. In practice, however, this may be the case. For example, non-EU-based companies would be in a position to better profit from the trading opportunities, where they put their cleanest planes on the EU flights and their dirtiest planes on non-EU flights.[40] These air operators might generate a surplus of emission allowances to be sold on the EU ETS market. In this respect, EU-based air companies could attempt to develop an argument that the inclusion of all flights, including those outside the EU, leads to an unfair differential treatment of the EU-based air companies compared to their non-EU-based competitors.[41]

A closer look at international competing industries

Under the EU ETS, internationally competing industries enjoy preferential treatment since they will still receive their allowances for free. Being cautious because of possible repercussions at World Trade Organization (WTO) level, the EU legislator did not choose to impose carbon-related import measures, which would mean that importers of goods should surrender EU allowances (or pay a tax) in order to cover the carbon emissions for the production of the goods should these emissions not be regulated comparably in the home country of that industry. This would qualify as a unilateral border adjustment.[42] France has firmly argued that such a trade measure should be applied in the form of a tax to be raised on imported goods.[43] Although there are some indications that such a trade measure could be compatible with WTO law, the EU has chosen the free allowances approach to the carbon leakage sector, thus subsidizing EU-based international industry while imposing a carbon cost on other EU-based emitters.[44] Such a free allocation was already common practice in the period 2005–2012, being made mandatory by the EU ETS directive. Only 5 per cent (later 10 per cent) of the available allowances could be auctioned by the Member States.[45] In this vein, the free allocation of allowances is nothing new; what is new, however, is that from 2013 onwards other sources fall wholly or in part under an auction regime. It might be that revenues from the auction will be redistributed by Member States to (part of) the EU ETS industries, as long as this is in line with state aid provisions. The spending of the auction revenues has to be reported by the Member States to the European Commission. At the time of writing of this contribution, this data was not yet available.

In order to get a better understanding of the specific treatment of the international competing industry, four key issues need to be highlighted: 1) the determination of which industries are being significantly damaged by international competition (also called the carbon leakage sector); 2) the benchmark for the free allocation; 3) the use of internationally tradable rights; and 4) financial support measures by Member States.

Determination of the carbon leakage sector

The option of free allocation is only open for sectors or subsectors 'determined to be exposed to a significant risk of carbon leakage', more briefly referred to as the 'carbon leakage sector'. The core of the problem for industries suffering from carbon leakage is that they cannot pass on the price of the allowances in their products that they had to buy from an auction.[46] Leakage means that emissions shift from countries with carbon regulations to countries with no or relatively weak carbon regulation as production is cheaper in countries that impose no or relatively minor carbon costs on their industries. Hence, not only may the emissions shift, but the economic profits also. Moreover, unilateral greenhouse gas reduction measures will reduce demand for fossil fuels, with the result that prices for fossil fuels will decline. This will increase demand and therefore raise emissions in regions without comparable reduction measures, which is called 'the fossil fuel price channel'.[47]

To avoid the problem of carbon leakage, the EU has decided to allocate the allowances for free to the sectors concerned. The sensitive thing, of course, is how to define which industries qualify for this free allocation. Directive 2009/29/EC contains, in Article 10(a) 13 to 18, a detailed instruction for the determination of the carbon leakage sector, which is the competence of the European Commission. The determination can be done through a quantitative and, in addition, a qualitative assessment. The basic rule is:

> A sector or subsector shall be deemed to be exposed to a significant risk of carbon leakage if:
>
> (a) the sum of direct and indirect additional costs induced by the implementation of this Directive would lead to a substantial increase of production costs, calculated as a proportion of the gross value added, of at least 5%, and;
> (b) the intensity of trade with third countries, defined as the ratio between the total value of exports to third countries plus the value of imports from third countries and the total market size for the Community (annual turnover plus total imports from third countries), is above10 %.[48]

In addition to this quantitative assessment some alternative approaches for determining carbon leakage, including a qualitative approach, are provided for.[49] As can be seen in the definition given above, the determination is of a technical-administrative nature, and the Commission has the task of determining the Community-wide sectors or subsectors that will be suffering from carbon leakage according to the given criteria.[50] Consequently, the Commission adopted its Carbon Leakage Decision on 24 December 2009.[51] The determination of the carbon leakage sectors is not of a static character: trade relations can change, and other countries can adopt greenhouse gas reduction measures which would remove the ground for the EU to issue the allowances for free. The directive prescribes that, by 31 December 2009 and every five years thereafter, after discussion in the European Council, the Commission shall determine a list of the sectors or subsectors.[52] Moreover, every year the Commission may, at its own initiative or at the request of a Member State, add a sector or subsector to the list referred to in the first subparagraph if it can be demonstrated, in an analytical report, that this sector or subsector satisfies the criteria following a change that has a substantial impact on the sector's or subsector's activities.[53] Strikingly, the adverse modus, meaning that the Commission may remove sectors from the list, is not explicitly addressed in the EU ETS directive. If one assumes that this belongs to the competence of the Commission, then most likely a sector may only be removed from the list following a transition period and a proper preparatory procedure.

The benchmark

The allowances will be allocated for free on the basis of administrative criteria defined by the European Commission.[54] The free allocation does not mean that industries receive all the allowances they need: based on the administrative criteria, which serve as a benchmark, industries receive a certain amount of allowances, and only the 10 per cent best performing industries, in terms of efficient emissions output, will receive enough allowances to cover their emissions. For those industries that fall short on their allowances for covering their emissions (the other 90 per cent), the operators should either invest in new emissions-reducing technologies or buy emissions from the auction or the secondary market.

The starting point for the benchmarks is the average of the 10 per cent most efficient installations, in terms of greenhouse gases, in a sector and they shall take into account the most efficient techniques, substitutes and alternative production processes. The number of allowances a firm will receive for free is calculated based on the historic capacity use or production levels, the emission rate per unit of product and factors that are needed to ensure compliance with the annually declining total cap.[55] The carbon leakage sector will receive relatively more free allowances than other sectors. For the sectors exposed to a significant risk of carbon leakage, the free allocation will be multiplied by a factor of 1 (100 per cent), while for other sectors the allocation will be multiplied by a lower figure (0.80 in 2013 and reduced every year to reach 0.30 in 2020).[56] This illustrates that the rules for free allocation allow for differential treatment between the sectors exposed to carbon leakage and other industries that will get part of their allowances for free.

The European Commission refers explicitly to equal treatment in its website explanation in view of the product-based (and not industry-based) character of the benchmarks:

> It should be stressed that the free allowances will be product-based, not sector-based. All products of the same kind should get an equal treatment in terms of carbon leakage. All relevant products will be classified as exposed to carbon leakage or not, based on the list of sectors. Therefore, it is not because an installation mainly produces products exposed to a significant risk of carbon leakage that all products produced in such an installation will receive a favourable carbon leakage treatment.[57]

In this way the Commission attempts to respect the principle of equal treatment. Meanwhile, it is not excluded that industries will try to get the rules tested in court, in which case the appellant must provide arguments showing why, in practice, the rules imply an unjustified differential treatment. Under the umbrella of the EU-wide EU ETS, all the industries covered have become competitors on the secondary market for tradable emission rights. If a certain industry finds that another EU ETS industry should not have received a certain number of allowances for free because the criteria or the application of the criteria on which the free allocation is based cannot be justified, it may revert to court action claiming a breach of the principle of equal treatment. Industry might, for instance, try to argue that the threat of carbon leakage is rather illusionary and that the differential allocation towards the carbon leakage sector is unjustified.[58] If such cases do arise, the courts need to consider the extent to which the administration may be deferred to and whether intervention is justified within the complex technical-administrative judgments about carbon leakage and free allocation.

International project-based emissions trading

Clearly, if an industry emits more than is allowed according to the allowances that it has received for free, it has to buy additional allowances from the auction or the secondary market. This secondary market also includes rights that can be bought through the flexibility mechanisms from the Kyoto Protocol, which are the clean development mechanism (CDM) and joint implementation (JI).[59] The carbon leakage sector has the possibility of using this international trading mechanism as a means of reducing costs: generally, these rights are cheaper than the EU ETS allowances.[60]

Of course, other companies – like electricity companies – will try to get those cheaper CDM rights as well. It will be interesting to see how this market will develop and whether carbon leakage industries, for example, invest in the CDM. The CDM rights gained may be used by the carbon leakage company to cover its emissions under the EU ETS rights, while it can sell the allowances that it got for free against the (possibly higher) EU ETS market price.

Financial support measures by Member States

Since fossil fuel-powered electricity production will be covered with the auction, the prices of the allowances that power companies have to buy cause electricity prices to rise, which can have a negative impact on electricity-consuming industries, particularly industry that competes internationally. Article10(a)(6) of the EU ETS directive opens the possibility for Member States to adopt financial measures in favour of the carbon leakage sector in order to compensate for costs that relate to greenhouse gas emission costs passed on through electricity prices. These national financial compensation measures need to be in accordance with state aid rules.[61]

These four specific technical, regulatory elements dealing with the carbon leakage sector show that the real effect of the EU ETS on the carbon leakage sector is not easy to understand. In practice, EU ETS industries will investigate how the allocation approach impacts upon their economic position. If they conclude that unjustified preferential treatment is given to a certain industrial sector that qualifies as a carbon leakage sector, they may revert to court action. Now that industries have become competitors on the EU ETS allowance market, they have a financial concern as to how the allowances are distributed.[62] After all, the industries – in conjunction with carbon consultants – are expected to be the experts on the EU ETS, and they will be the first to explore whether there is any need to address the court, in particular in any case of assumed disproportional measures or unequal treatment.

A first case with the General Court was initiated by Eurofer. This organization represented the steel industry in the EU and initiated action for the annulment of Commission Decision 2011/278/EU containing rules for free allocation of emission allowances. This is clearly an attempt by a specific carbon leakage sector to argue that the benchmarking for the free allocation of the allowances is too strict, stating that the Commission decision is in breach of Article 10(a) of the EU ETS directive. The appellant tried to get access to the General Court on the basis of Article 263 TFEU, fourth sentence, which provides access to the court if a regulatory act is of direct concern – but without imposing the requirement of individual concern. In its decision of 4 June 2012, the General Court found the case inadmissible on the grounds that implementing measures are required for the free allocation of allowances.[63] This means that the national court has to be addressed if the company wants to proceed with its claim. Such an action could, in particular, be initiated against the individual decision that any Member States may have to take in order to issue the allowances to each specific industry.[64] A national court can then decide to address the CJEU with a preliminary question.

Eurofer's basic argument is that the benchmark for so-called 'hot metal' is set at a technically unachievable level. It wants the benchmark set at a higher (for the industry, more profitable) level, which would mean more allowances being freely allocated to the sector. This case illustrates how the court might be confronted with a highly technical question. The EU ETS directive does not provide any EU agency or other institution with a formal task to provide technical advice on the matter. It is the Commission that decides on the free allocation rules after consultation with stakeholders. One can expect that the court will largely defer to the Commission, with the result that potentially 'unjustifiable' differential treatment could hardly be addressed through the courts. Most likely, the industries will then try to defend their interests by lobbying throughout the decision-making process.

Whether any legal action will be initiated by the non-carbon leakage sector (which is subject to 20 per cent auctioning in 2013 and which will increase to 70 per cent auctioning in 2020) remains to be seen. According to an assessment, almost 75 per cent of the product benchmarks are classified as carbon leakage. Therefore, it could be that the relatively minor contingent of industries not qualifying as a carbon leakage sector would find itself at a disadvantage as quite a large number of allowances will be allocated for 100 per cent, while they will only get 80 per cent for free in 2013 and 30 per cent in 2020.

Regulatory developments in other countries

The carbon leakage approach cannot be seen in isolation from what other countries do. The globally competitive position of EU industries clearly depends on how non-EU competitors are regulated or subsidized. Quite apart from the question of whether any WTO conflicts might arise, the justification for differential treatment among different EU ETS sources gets flawed if the carbon leakage sector is not really suffering when countries like China impose burdens (like export taxes) on their carbon-emitting industries (see below). The difficulty with defining carbon leakage in the EU derives from the fact that the disadvantageous effects of unilateral measures depend on the (lack of) measures in countries where competitors operate. Those other countries show a differentiated picture with regard to their regulatory greenhouse gas reduction approach: some countries might raise export taxes, while others might impose greenhouse gas emission reduction obligations. Obviously, an overall assessment of the real occurrence of carbon leakage can only be undertaken following extensive research. Take China, for example, where the government chose to levy export taxes on international industries such as the cement sector. This is not a purely environmental measure as it is taken in the course of industrial policies to reduce the national trade surplus and to save energy resources for China. From 2006, the Ministry of Finance in China started to levy export taxes on a variety of energy and resource-intensive products, so that the international competitive position of these industries dropped (Zhang 2011: 28). It is even argued that the costs of CO_2 levied through export taxes are very much in the same range as the average price of EU allowances over the same period.[65] Moreover, China has developed and continues to develop measures to improve energy intensity, which may also impact upon the production costs of the internationally competing Chinese industries. Of course, only after close examination of the real costs may further conclusions be drawn. This example of only one country shows, however, that a precise assessment of the likelihood of carbon leakage is a very complex one.

Even if countries agree on emission reduction commitments under the umbrella of the UNFCCC – a process that is currently undertaken by the Ad Hoc Working Group on the Durban Platform for Enhanced Action – the question of how to get internationally competing industries on the same footing remains. Suppose that the EU agrees to a 35 per cent reduction target in 2030, while China commits itself to a reduction of 20+ per cent compared to 1990. This most likely implies that much more room for emissions can be given to the international sector in China compared to competing industries in the EU. Hence, only sectorial approaches – like a sectorial protocol for cement or steel – can pinpoint such differences. As long as competing industries are not put on a comparable footing at international level with regard to their emissions, differential treatment among the carbon leakage sector and the non-carbon leakage sector remains part of the legal debate in the EU.

Concluding observations

Within the context of some remaining uncertainty surrounding climate change and almost no progress at the international level in reaching a meaningful agreement about emission reduction obligations, the EU acts as a global frontrunner by having adopted an internal legal framework that aims at 20 per cent greenhouse gas emission reduction in 2020 compared to 1990. This implies that private actors in the EU are confronted with restrictions on their greenhouse gas-emitting activities. The logical first question that arises in this context is one of whether court cases have arisen, or will arise, in which private actors contest the necessity and stringency of a unilateral climate change law which limits their economic activity, thereby also contesting the input of science, by means of the IPCC, into legislative decision-making in the EU. Until now the question of whether unilateral climate change measures are justified and, if so, to what extent, has not been put before the courts in the EU. Given that the CJEU usually affords much deference to the political organs adopting binding legislation, and also the fact that the precautionary principle has been codified in EU environmental law, economic operators are most likely to be hesitant in raising this issue before the judges. The 20 per cent reduction target for 2020 is moreover lower than the IPCC has indicated, such that approaches to the courts are more likely to come from environmental NGOs, which would like to have more stringent climate legislation. These organizations, however, suffer from very limited access to the CJEU. Consequently, the debate on the necessity and stringency of unilateral climate action by the EU has thus, this far, taken place outside the courtroom.

This situation, however, is dramatically different in the context of the distribution of commitments among economic operators. The courts, particularly the CJEU, already play a meaningful role in this regard, having formulated the rationale that economic operators who emit greenhouse gases must be treated on an equal footing. Consequently, the legal discussion focuses on the reasons why differential treatment, particularly also the preferential treatment of international competing industries, can be justified. Since all industries covered by the EU ETS are competitors on the EU allowance market, a too generous allocation to one sector implies fewer allowances (and higher costs) for another sector because, after all, the absolute cap of 20 per cent greenhouse gas emission reduction must be reached. The fact that all EU ETS sources are connected to one EU allowance market might stimulate intersectorial concerns about too generous allocation approaches or too strict allocations to a certain sector. In order to be politically able to undertake unilateral action, the EU legislator chose to establish the so-called carbon leakage sector, which is an international sector which will receive allowances for free according to a defined benchmark. This leads to an internal EU legal question: whether this preferential treatment is justified. Such claims, however, will only arise if the industries that do not receive this preferential treatment feel harmed by the approach. Since the application of the carbon leakage qualification turns out to cover most of the EU ETS operators, preferential treatment benefits most industries.

The subsequent question of whether the benchmark on the basis of which the allowances will be freely allocated is set too high (or too low) concerns complex technical decision-making. The EU lacks a scientific body with the mandate to provide advice to the Commission on these highly complicated and sensitive matters. Time will tell whether industries have enough reason to address national and European courts and, if so, how courts will deal with this highly complex regulatory framework. Much will depend on the restrictiveness of the judges when addressing a claim, such as the action for annulment put forward by Eurofer. On the one hand, the tendency of the courts to defer to Commission decisions implementing the EU ETS framework post-2012 may enhance certainty within the allowance market (Ghaleigh 2009). Indeed, if we suppose that, after a claim before a national court, the CJEU were to answer, for instance in 2015, that the allocation criteria of the Commission on the basis of which allowances have been allocated by a national administration cannot be justified, this would have potentially far reaching repercussions for the EU-wide emissions trading scheme that is already up and running. On the other hand, however, perceived inequalities about the distributional elements of the system might harm support for market-based regulation and appreciation of the European Commission as the climate policy leader of the EU – and the EU as the emissions-trading leader of the world. This said, it is recommended to deepen the debate as to how the rationale that polluters have to be treated, in principle, on an equal footing can be applied in a meaningful way, and what role the courts may have in that respect.

Notes

1 This contribution was concluded on 3 August 2012.
2 Two main instruments that provide for emissions trading are: 1) The effort-sharing decision: Decision 406/2009/EC (European Parliament and Council) of

23 April 2009 on the effort of Member States to reduce their greenhouse gas emissions to meet the Community's greenhouse gas emission reduction commitments up to 2020, *Official Journal* (*OJ*) 2009 L 140/136 (with trading arrangements for Member States); and 2) the EU ETS directive: Directive 2003/87/EC (European Parliament and Council) of 13 October 2003 establishing a scheme for greenhouse gas emission allowance trading within the Community, *OJ* 2003 L 275/32, as amended, inter alia, with Directive 2009/29/EC of the European Parliament and of the Council of 23 April 2009, *OJ* 2009 L 140/63. See the consolidated version at: http://eur-lex.europa.eu/LexUriServ/LexUriServ.do?uri=CELEX:02003L0087-20090625:EN:NOT, accessed 2 August 2012. This contribution focuses on the EU ETS. For effort-sharing decision and trading provisions, see Peeters and Stallworthy 2012.

3 (European Court of Justice) ECJ, Case C-127/07, decided on 16 December 2008 (*Société Arcelor Atlantique et Lorraine and Others v. Premier ministre, Ministre de l'Écologie et du Développement durable, Ministre de l'Économie, des Finances et de l'Industrie*), at para. 34. Interestingly, the Court established this fundamental rationale before the new regime, with the favourable treatment to international competitive industries, was formally adopted: the co-decision procedure for Directive 2009/29/EC was at that time running.

4 The CBDR (common but differentiated responsibilities) principle is highly debated, and a lot of literature has been discussing this principle. For a very balanced approach, see Honkonen 2009, and for a very critical approach, see Stone 2004; Sarkar 2009: 57–64, 110–119.

5 See UNFCCC COP16, 'Outcome of the Work of the Ad Hoc Working Group on Long-Term Cooperative Action on the Convention and Adopted by the Conference of the Parties to the UNFCCC', Section 2.

6 See press release from the UNFCCC secretariat, 'Durban Conference Delivers Breakthrough in the International Community's Response to Climate Change', 11 December 2011, available at: www.unfccc.int, accessed 3 August 2012.

7 ECJ, Case C-127/07 and CFI, Case T-16/04; see also Peeters 2011: 19–36.

8 ECJ, Case C-127/07, at para. 47.

9 Directive 2009/29/EC has indeed now expanded the coverage of the EU ETS.

10 Another example is given by Poncelet 2011: 245–253 and particularly 248, where he refers to the Belgian Constitutional Court following the similar reasoning in a decision from 7 June 2006 where the courts found that the principle of equal treatment was respected because the different treatment was held as proportionate.

11 Conseil Constitutionnel, Décision 2009-599 DC du 29 Décembre 2009, available in French at: www.conseilconstitutionnel.fr, accessed 3 August 2012.

12 The Copenhagen Accord from 2009 recognizes the need to consider the strengthening of the long-term goal towards 1.5°C. That assessment should be done in 2015.

13 Art. 2 UNFCCC.

14 There is not yet a binding definition of the threshold 'dangerous anthropogenic interference'.

15 European Commission, *Communication from the Commission to the European Parliament, the Council, the European Economic and Social Committee and the Committee of the Regions, Options for an EU Vision and Target for Biodiversity Beyond 2010*, COM (European Commission) (2010) 4 final of 19 January 2010. See also the EU Council Conclusions of the 3002nd Environment Council of 15 March 2010, which, among other things:

> WELCOMES the recognition in the Copenhagen Accord of the scientific view that the increase in global temperature should be kept below 2°C compared to the pre-industrial level; REITERATES that, according to the IPCC, to stay

below 2°C requires that global greenhouse gas emissions peak by 2020 at the latest and are reduced by at least 50% compared with 1990 by 2050 and continue to decline thereafter.

16 One can question whether 'catastrophic' is comparable to the UNFCCC objective, which is the avoidance of 'dangerous interference'. Do both terms aim at the same level of protection or is 'catastrophic' interchangeable with 'dangerous interference'?

17 See the Fourth Assessment Report of the IPCC, Working Group III, IPCC (2007), at chapter 13, box 13.7, p. 776 (Metz *et al.* 2007), to be found at: www.ipcc.ch/publications_and_data/publications_ipcc_fourth_ assessment_report_wg3_report _mitigation_of_climate_change.htm, last accessed 8 January 2012.

18 On the uncertainty management by the IPCC and the need for improvement of the communication to the users of the assessment, see Swart *et al.* 2009: 1–29.

19 See Metz *et al.* 2007.

20 The EU does not have full participant status in the IPCC and is only an observer, while the Member States are parties; see Lefevere 2009.

21 *Communication from the Commission to the European Parliament, the Council, the European Economic and Social Committee and the Committee of the Regions, Towards a Comprehensive Climate Change Agreement in Copenhagen*, Brussels, COM (2009) 39 of 28 January 2009, p. 3.

22 The table of the IPCC with the 25–40 per cent reduction for developed countries, however, does not provide an explicit link to trading. This issue should be further examined.

23 See for the large deference: ECJ, Cases C-341/95, *Bettati* and C-284/95, *Safety Hi-Tech*, both decided on 14 July 1998. The precautionary principle is codified in Art. 191 TFEU (Treaty on the Functioning of the European Union).

24 See for a successful request for regulatory action under the USA Clean Air Act the Supreme Court decision, *Massachusetts v. EPA* (No. 05-1120; argued 29 November 2006; decided 2 April 2007), where States and NGOs asked the US Environmental Protection Agency (EPA) to issue legislation for greenhouse gas emissions from cars.

25 *Op. Cit.*, n. 22.

26 Such questions can be found in US case law, in particular in the Supreme Court decision *Massachusetts v. EPA*, *Op. Cit.*, n. 27.

27 Attempts to address criminal courts claiming that scientists committed fraud could also play a role in this regard. There is apparently an attempt in preparation in order to build a complaint against individual scientists to get them sued by prosecutors. If such an action indeed happens, the criminal courts will be confronted with the question whether scientists did act in good faith when developing their research. See www. climatedepot.com/a/14156/Fmr-Thatcher-advisor-Lord-Monckton-to-pursue-fraud-charges-against-Climategate-scientists-Will-present-to-police-the-case-for-numerous-specific-instances-of-scientific-or-economic-fraud, accessed 15 December 2011

28 The author did not do comprehensive research into the case law of the 27 Member States. According to her knowledge, cases in which the target as such has been contested in the EU have not yet been reported in the legal literature.

29 Decision 406/2009/EC of the European Parliament and of the Council of 23 April 2009 on the effort of Member States to reduce their greenhouse gas emissions to meet the Community's greenhouse gas emission reduction commitments up to 2020, *OJ* 2009 L 140/136.

30 See on the principle of equal treatment in EU renewable energy law, ECJ, Case C-2/10, at para. 64.

31 But an exemption has been made for fossil fuel power installations in East-European countries, see Art. 10c, EU ETS Directive. Hence, this is a form of differential treatment.

32 Commission Decision 2010/384/EU of 9 July 2010 on the Community-wide quantity of allowances to be issued under the EU Emission Trading Scheme for 2013 and Commission Decision 2010/634/EU of 22 October 2010 adjusting the Union-wide quantity of allowances to be issued under the Union Scheme for 2013 and repealing Decision 2010/384/EU. For 2013, the total absolute Union-wide quantity of allowances referred to in Arts. 9 and 9a(1) and (2) of Directive 2003/87/EC amounts to 2,039,152,882 (more than 2 billion allowances).

33 Art. 10(a)(1) third paragraph, last sentence: 'No free allocation shall be made in respect of any electricity production, except for cases falling within Article 10c and electricity produced from waste gases'; see also art. 10(a)(3). See for the auction regulation, Commission Regulation 1031/2010 of 12 November 2010 on the timing, administration and other aspects of auctioning of greenhouse gas emission allowances pursuant to Directive 2003/87/EC of the European Parliament and of the Council establishing a scheme for greenhouse gas emission allowances trading within the Community (see for the *OJ* references, footnote 2).

34 Art. 10(a)(12).

35 Art. 10(a)(11).

36 ECJ, Case C-366/10.

37 According to the Dutch Secretary of State for Infrastructure and Environment; see the official documents for the Dutch Parliament: Tweede Kamer, vergaderjaar 2011–2012, 31 936 nr. 102, p. 3.

38 Bill HR2594; see for a summary and status, http://thomas.loc.gov/cgi-bin/bdquery/z?d112:h.r.2594, last accessed 22 December 2011. The bill has been referred to the Senate.

39 It is interesting to see that a variation of the principle of equal treatment is included in Art. 2 of the Open Skies Agreement, headed 'Fair and equal opportunity', which states: 'Each Party shall allow a fair and equal opportunity for the airlines of both Parties to compete in providing the international air transportation governed by this Agreement'. The CJEU, in its decision of 21 December 2011 in Case C-366/10, however, did not come to a specific consideration in order to test whether, in practice, given the most likely effects of the rules, differential treatment occurs as a consequence of the rules. In section 155–156, the Court referred to the 'uniform application of the allowance trading scheme to all aircraft operators' and that the EU has sought 'to comply strictly with the non-discrimination provisions of bilateral air service agreements with third States, like the provisions in Articles 2 and 3(4) of the Open Skies Agreement'.

40 Furthermore, air operators conducting long flights may decide to make an extra stop just outside the EU, before entering the EU, in order to avoid the major part of the flight being covered by the EU ETS.

41 See for a comment on the fact that the EU treats all aviation operators equally, which could be criticized from the perspective of the international principle of CBDR, Scott and Rajamani (2012).

42 See *Trade and Climate Change*, WTO-UNEP 2009. See for a short assessment of the WTO compatibility of import allowance requirements, Zhang 2011: 113. For a pragmatic justification of the need for border adjustments, see Moser 2011.

43 A tax on imported products would not solve the competitive disadvantage that EU industries potentially face with their export of products if they were burdened with greenhouse gas costs but other competitors outside the EU were not.

44 This contribution does not discuss whether the EU approach would lead to any WTO problem (or a problem with Art. 3.5 of the UNFCCC which states that trade measures cannot be taken if they are intended to protect domestic

industry), but rather looks at the differential treatment made within EU climate law. See for a WTO analysis Bartels (2012).

45 Directive 2003/87/EC, Art. 10.

46 However, under the free allocation approach, industries also try to pass on the so-called opportunity costs, which are the costs that industries forgo if they do not sell the allowances but use them to cover their emissions. The carbon leakage sector, however, is expected not to be able to pass on such opportunity costs.

47 Bollen *et al.* (2011).

48 Art. 10(a) 15

49 See Art. 10(a) 16–18.

50 Art. 10(a)12 provides that:

> The Commission shall assess, at Community level, the extent to which it is possible for the sector or subsector concerned, at the relevant level of disaggregation, to pass on the direct cost of the required allowances and the indirect costs from higher electricity prices resulting from the implementation of this Directive into product prices without significant loss of market share to less carbon efficient installations outside the Community. These assessments shall be based on an average carbon price according to the Commission's impact assessment accompanying the package of implementation measures for the EU's objectives on climate change and renewable energy for 2020 and, if available, trade, production and value added data from the three most recent years for each sector or subsector.

51 See Commission Decision 2010/2/EU, followed by Decisions 2011/278/EU and 2011/745/EU, as regards the sectors and subsectors which are deemed to be exposed to a significant risk of carbon leakage.

52 Art. 10a(15) as introduced with Directive 2009/29/EC.

53 See also Art. 10(a)(3).

54 Commission Decision 2011/278/EU of 27 April 2011 determining transitional Union-wide rules for harmonized free allocation of emission allowances pursuant to Art. 10a of Directive 2003/87/EC of the European Parliament and of the Council. See also for an explanation, European Commission climate action website: http://ec.europa.eu/clima/policies/ets/leakage/index_en.htm, last accessed 19 December 2011.

55 See for a discussion of the benchmark approach, Bollen *et al.* 2011: 16–17, also pointing to considerable distributional effects related to the specific choices made within the benchmark design.

56 See Art. 10(a)(11) and (12) of the consolidated version of the EU ETS directive (see footnote 2).

57 See the European Commission climate action website: http://ec.europa.eu/clima/policies/ets/leakage/index_en.htm, last accessed 19 December 2011.

58 The report by Bollen *et al.* discusses the impacts of the EU ETS and climate policies in other countries on competitiveness and on leakage in 2020, and argues that the direct impacts are relatively minor if other countries follow up on the Copenhagen pledges (which are non-binding emission reduction statements). Production leakage for energy-intensive industries in developed countries is rather limited. The indirect impact, which is the decrease in fossil fuel prices which leads to higher demand in countries without greenhouse gas emissions reduction measures, is, however, considerable: see Bollen *et al.* (2011). They moreover argue that border measures are much less effective in reducing carbon leakage because the fossil fuel price channel rather than the trade channel is the dominant cause of leakage.

59 This possibility was introduced through the so-called linking directive, Directive 2004/101/EC. The Kyoto framework does not enable emission reduction units

(ERUs) to be created from 2013 onwards without new quantified emission targets being in place for host countries. CDM credits can potentially continue to be generated (see Recital 28 to the Preamble to Directive 2009/29/EC).

60 For the aviation sector, a maximum of 15 per cent of the number of allowances they are required to surrender is set in Directive 2008/101/EC (new Art. 11a(1)(a)). For other industries, Member States had the power to define to what extent these industries may use such rights in the period 2008–2012; a transitional provision is provided in Art. 11(b) as introduced by Directive 2009/29/EC, basically meaning that rights that have not been used up in 2008–2012 may be exchanged for allowances for the period 2013–2020. Furthermore, the Commission may determine the level of the use of new project-based emission rights in the period 2013–2020; see the detailed and complicated rules in Art. 11(b), in particular paras 8 and 9. For a calculation of the profits of this CDM possibility for the carbon leakage sector, see Bollen *et al.* (2011).

61 Draft Environmental State Aid Guidelines have been published for consultation from 21 December 2011 to 31 January 2012.

62 The directive has already recognized that a consideration by the Commission of the distributional effects is necessary in view of the portion that will be allocated to the industries, and the portion of allowances that remains for the power industry, see Art. 10(b)(2) as introduced with Directive 2009/29/EC.

63 Case T-381/11. The application to suspend the execution (see Arts 278 and 279 TFEU) has been dismissed on substantive grounds by order of 15 September 2011.

64 Art. 11 of the EU ETS directive (as amended by Directive 2009/29/EC).

65 Zhang 2011: 28, 120. The EU allowance price mentioned by the author is, however, rather high, which would mean that the carbon costs in China are even higher than in the EU.

References

Bartels, L. (2012) ‘The WTO Legality of the Application of the EU’s Emission Trading System to Aviation’, *The European Journal of International Law*, 23(2): 429–467.

Bollen, J., Koutstaal, P. and Veenendaal, P. (2011) ‘Trade and Climate’, CPB Netherlands Bureau for Economic Policy Analysis, http://trade.ec.europa.eu/doclib/docs/2011/may/tradoc_147906.pdf, last accessed on 26 November 2012.

European Commission (2009) *Communication from the Commission to the European Parliament, the Council, the European Economic and Social Committee and the Committee of the Regions, Towards a Comprehensive Climate Change Agreement in Copenhagen*, Brussels, COM (2009) 39 of 28 January.

——(2010) *Communication from the Commission to the European Parliament, the Council, the European Economic and Social Committee and the Committee of the Regions, Options for an EU Vision and Target for Biodiversity beyond 2010*, COM (2010) 4 final of 19 January.

Faure, M. and Peeters, M. (2008) *Climate Change and European Emissions Trading: Lessons for Theory and Practice*, Cheltenham: Edward Elgar.

Ghaleigh, N.S. (2009) ‘Emissions Trading before the European Court of Justice: Market Making in Luxembourg’, Edinburgh, University of Edinburgh School of Law Working Paper, Series 2009/12.

Honkonen, T. (2009) *The Common but Differentiated Responsibility Principle in Multilateral Environmental Agreements: Regulatory and Policy Aspects*, The Hague: Kluwer Law International.

Lefevere, J. (2009) 'A Climate of Change: An Analysis of Progress in EU and International Climate Change Policy', in J. Scott (ed.), *European Law and Governance*, Oxford: Oxford University Press, pp. 171–212.

Metz, B., Davidson, O.R., Bosch, P.R., Dave, R. and Meyer, L.A. (eds) (2007) *Contribution of Working Group III to the Fourth Assessment Report of the Intergovernmental Panel on Climate Change*, available at www.ipcc.ch/publications_and_data/publications_ipcc_fourth_assessment_report_wg3_report_mitigation_of_climate_change.htm, last accessed on 8 January 2012.

Moser, A.J. (2011) 'Pragmatism Not Dogmatism: The Inconvenient Need for Border Adjustment Tariffs Based on What is Known about Climate Change, Trade and China', *Vermont Journal of International Law*, 12: 676–711.

Peeters, M. (2003) 'Emissions Trading as a New Dimension to European Environmental Law: The Political Agreement of the European Council on Greenhouse Gas Allowance Trading', *European Environmental Law Review*, 12(3): 82–92.

——(2011) 'The EU ETS and the Role of the Courts: Emerging Contours in the Case of Arcelor', *Climate Law*, 2: 19–36.

Peeters, M. and Stallworthy, M. (2012) 'Legal Consequences of the Effort Sharing Decision for Member State Action', in M. Peeters, M. Stallworthy and J. de Cendra (eds), *Climate Law in EU Member States*, Cheltenham: Edward Elgar, pp. 15–38.

Peeters, M. and Weishaar, S. (2009) 'Exploring Uncertainties in the EU ETS: "Learning by Doing" Continues Beyond 2012', *Carbon and Climate Law Review*, 1: 88–101.

Poncelet, C. (2011) 'The Emissions Trading Directive: Analysis of Some Contentious Points', *European Energy and Environmental Law Review*, 245–253.

Sarkar, R. (2009) *International Development Law Rule of Law, Human Rights and Finance*, Oxford: Oxford University Press.

Scott, J. and Rajamani, L. (2012) 'EU Climate Change Unilateralism', *The European Journal of International Law*, 23(2): 469–494.

Stone, C.D. (2004) 'Common but Differentiated Responsibilities in International Law', *American Journal of International Law*, 98: 276–301.

Swart, R., Bernstein, L., Ha-Duong, M. and Petersen, A. (2009) 'Agreeing to Disagree: Uncertainty Management in Assessing Climate Change, Impacts and Responses by the IPCC', *Climatic Change*, 92: 1–29.

Zhang, X. (2011) *Energy and Environmental Policy in China*, Cheltenham: Edward Elgar.

Part IV

Role of courts

7 The role of science in mediating the conflict between free trade and health regulation at the WTO

The *EC – Biotech Products* dispute

*Denise Prévost**

Introduction

There are inherent difficulties in the use of science by the rules of the World Trade Organization (WTO) to mediate the conflict between free trade and non-trade concerns in the area of health. These are most clearly illustrated by the long-awaited decision of the WTO Panel in the *EC – Biotech Products*[1] dispute.

This politically charged dispute involved a challenge by the United States, Canada and Argentina[2] to the measures of the European Communities (EC)[3] affecting the approval and marketing of biotech products.[4] This dispute was decided under the WTO's *Agreement on Sanitary and Phytosanitary Measures* (*SPS Agreement*), which uses scientific disciplines to distinguish legitimate health regulation from disguised protectionist measures. The Panel reports in this case were repeatedly delayed,[5] for reasons evincing the Panel's struggle to understand and work with the scientific data before it, including the substantive complexity of the case and the lengthy procedure for the selection of scientific experts to advise the Panel.

Since 7 February 2006, when the confidential interim Panel reports were issued to the parties and subsequently leaked to the public, the Panel's findings have been the subject of much public discussion. Some of this discussion is based on misunderstandings regarding the actual findings of the Panel and their implications for the scientific assessment of the EC measures regarding biotech products. For example, the United States Trade Representative (USTR) Susan Schwab stated, 'The WTO has ruled in favour of science-based policymaking over the unjustified, anti-biotech policies adopted in the EU', and US Agriculture Secretary, Mike Johanns, said,

> Today's decision affirms what the world's farmers have known about biotechnology for many years … . Biotechnology crops not only are helping to meet the world's food needs, they also are having a positive environmental impact on our soil and water resources.[6]

Friends of the Earth Europe claimed that the Panel 'has bluntly ruled that European safeguards should be sacrificed to benefit biotech corporations'[7] and the then-USTR, Rob Portman, issued a statement that 'the facts on agricultural biotechnology are clear and compelling. It is a safe and beneficial technology that is improving food security and helping to reduce poverty worldwide'.[8]The USA is reportedly using the outcome of this dispute to warn other countries, especially developing countries, against the use of regulatory barriers to biotech products.[9]

These responses reflect misapprehension regarding what the Panel's findings mean for the European regime on the approval and marketing of biotech products, and potentially for those of other countries.[10] More importantly, perhaps, they are a red herring, diverting attention from the real cause for concern in the Panel report, namely the manner in which the Panel dealt with scientific expertise in addressing those provisions of the *SPS Agreement* that use science to mediate the conflict between trade and health regulation.

It is useful to examine the findings of the Panel in detail, to understand the role that science can play in reconciling trade and non-trade concerns in WTO adjudication. The Panel's legal interpretations matter not only for future dispute settlement cases decided under the *SPS Agreement*, but also, perhaps more importantly, for 'settlements negotiated in the law's shadow' (Shaffer 2004: 471). A large part of *SPS Agreement* disputes are resolved through informal bilateral consultations rather than by resort to adjudication. These negotiated settlements are informed by the content given to the legal provisions in dispute settlement.

This chapter will examine the interpretation given by the Panel in *EC – Biotech Products* to the relevant scientific disciplines of the *SPS Agreement* raised in that dispute. Before doing so, however, it will briefly set out the background to the use of science by the *SPS Agreement* to discipline risk regulation. It will then proceed to delimit the ambit of the dispute before the Panel. Turning to the findings of the Panel, it will first examine the surprising interpretation given by the Panel to the scope of application of the *SPS Agreement*, which could have implications for the types of situations in which the scientific disciplines of the Agreement will be the tools used to mediate between trade and non-trade concerns. Subsequently, the manner in which the Panel deftly avoided having to address the controversial issue of the scientific basis for the EC's measures will be examined, illustrating the difficulty that panels face in applying scientific disciplines in these sensitive regulatory areas. The following three sections will take a close look at the interpretation given by the Panel to the scientific obligations of the *SPS Agreement* when addressing the safeguard measures of the relevant EU Member States. First, the Panel's understanding of the risk assessment requirement of the *SPS Agreement* will be addressed. Second, its findings on the scope for provisional measures in the face of insufficient scientific evidence will be examined. Third, its view regarding the role of international law, including the precautionary principle, in interpreting the scientific obligations of the *SPS Agreement* will be discussed. Further, a close look will be taken at the standard of review applied by the Panel to the scientific evidence before it, to highlight the problematic role of the Panel in reviewing regulatory determinations in the light of scientific disciplines. Finally, some conclusions will be drawn on the implications of the findings in this dispute for the future, if followed in later cases.

The role of science in disciplining health risk regulation

National sanitary and phytosanitary (SPS) health regulation is normally purported to be based on scientific findings, usually in the form of a risk assessment. Without such basis, regulatory measures would be subject to criticism at national level. In fact, it has been argued that science is used 'as a screening device to rationalise priorities in risk regulation and, in particular, to ensure that government resources and authority are directed toward substantial risks as opposed to small or trivial ones' (Wirth 1997: 335). Similarly, science is used at the international level, in particular by the rules of the WTO's *SPS Agreement*, to distinguish legitimate health regulations from disguised forms of protectionism by Members.

The use of science as a justificatory tool can usefully be understood from a social science perspective. Regulations gain authoritative validity through recourse to scientific justifications. This has been termed the 'meta-legal' authority of science (Joerges 1997: 320). Since the early 1970s, in developed countries national legislation governing the enactment of health regulations by agencies began explicitly to set scientific justification requirements against which the validity of these regulations can be tested. Scientific committees were created to provide the input into the regulatory process necessary for rational decision making. Currently, scientific assessments of risks to human, animal or plant life or health determine areas in which regulatory action is necessary, and science is also used to evaluate the efficacy of the various possible measures in order to design an appropriate regulation (Atik 1997: 736). Thus, it is clear that at national level science plays an important role in the regulatory process.

However, that is not the whole story. Social science analysis also helps to clarify the limits of science as a benchmark for regulatory legitimacy. In practice, regulatory design is more than just a scientific discipline. Public health measures also reflect social policy choices. One must bear in mind that regulators do not operate in a vacuum. Instead, regulations are drafted in a particular economic, social and political context. They reflect societal values and preferences regarding acceptable levels of risk, economic judgements regarding the feasibility of alternative SPS measures and their costs to society when compared to the benefits to be achieved by the regulation concerned, political pressures brought to bear upon regulators by powerful lobby groups and other such non-scientific factors. As a result, disparate regulatory measures are taken across national boundaries even where the scientific rationale for the measures is the same. Science does inform the process, but is not decisive in determining the regulatory outcome.

Even in the risk assessment part of the regulatory process, reliance on the neutrality of science should be approached with caution. The traditionally uncritical view taken of science by the law is no longer generally accepted. Starting in the 1950s, a new understanding of the limitations of science has gradually replaced the initial authoritative view of its claims to objective validity. There is currently a more critical understanding of scientific processes, and general recognition of the fact that science is not absolute but is characterised by gaps in knowledge and uncertainties.[11] This is particularly so in the field of health and the environment, due to the complexity of the human body and ecology.[12] Further, the exponential growth in scientific knowledge has made it clear that science is inherently evolving and that what is regarded as valid today may be substantially disproved tomorrow. Scientists deal with these realities by making use of basic assumptions, models, rules of thumb and extrapolations of conclusions from empirical data to similar areas for which insufficient data is available (Phillips 2001; Khachatourians 2001).[13] The choice of assumptions and models used to fill gaps in scientific knowledge involves subjective judgement which is based on the values[14] and the dominant paradigms and ideologies of the scientific community of which the scientist is part.[15] These discretionary elements of the risk assessment process are known as 'science policy' and are widely recognised in scientific discourse.[16] It is thus often the case that more than one scientifically valid conclusion can be drawn from the same data.[17] This is commonly known as the problem of 'duelling science'.[18] It is accordingly crucial to recognise that an element of subjectivity is present in most risk assessments. Aside from the uncertainty arising from these problems of insufficient evidence, measurement error, imperfect models and subjective evaluation, which Rosie Cooney and Andrew Lang refer to as 'epistemic uncertainty', in areas involving complex systems there is also what these authors call 'ontological uncertainty' (Cooney and Lang 2007: 529–530). This type of uncertainty is a result of the variability and unpredictability of the system under analysis. Unlike epistemic uncertainty, ontological uncertainty is inherent and persistent – it cannot be eliminated or reduced by additional research. It requires new approaches to risk management that take into account unpredictability and are responsive to systems-wide effects and interactions.[19] Here social science has a useful role to play in informing the use of science by law.

This fundamental change in thinking extends to the appreciation of the use of science in regulation as a tool to depoliticise regulatory decisions.[20] A substantial debate exists today, for the reasons set out above, concerning the limitations of use of science in law, particularly as regards the uncritical use of risk assessment as a criterion for regulatory validity. These limitations of science, however, do not imply that it is not still a useful tool in promoting greater rationality in decision making in the regulatory process and reducing the risks of protectionism due to private interest capture of the regulatory process. Requiring scientific justification from regulators at least improves the transparency of the regulatory process and forces regulators to produce the factual evidence on which they base their decisions (Green and Epps 2007: 303). However, account should be taken of the limitations of science by means of a more realistic and nuanced approach to its justificatory capacity by adjudicators applying scientific disciplines set out in legal rules to national SPS regulation.

A further, but related, limitation to the use of science as a basis for the evaluation of SPS regulation lies in the problem of scientific uncertainty. Rigorous scientific evidence requirements may limit the possibilities for governments to act in situations where science has not yet provided a definite answer regarding the existence, magnitude or probability of a risk. Increasing awareness of the limitations in the ability of science to accurately predict SPS risks, and to do so early enough to allow for effective action to prevent the risk (McIntyre and Mosedale 1997: 222), have led to a shift in approach 'in favour of a bias towards safety or caution' (Freestone 1994: 211). Particularly in high income countries where high levels of health protection have been achieved, resulting in longer life spans and greater attention to health risks that may only materialise in the long term, regulators are under pressure to err on the side of caution in decision making in situations of scientific uncertainty. Another development reinforcing this trend is growing use of new technologies in agricultural and food production (Craddock 2001: 82), such as the use of hormones in beef and milk production, the genetic modification of crops, the use of meat and bonemeal additives in cattle feed, the great increase in highly processed consumer-ready food and the concomitant increase in consumer fears regarding the safety of these products. Following highly publicised health risks, such as the BSE outbreaks in Europe or the dioxin scandal in Belgium, citizens demand regulatory action to protect them from possible risks from new technologies, even in those cases where there is no definitive proof of risk yet, as is the case with genetic modification (Khachatourians 2001: 17).[21]

The precautionary principle, or precautionary approach,[22] emerged in response to the concerns regarding scientific uncertainty in environmental regulation.[23] It can be seen as complementary to the preventive principle,[24] which is reflected in the idea that established hazards should be prevented before they occur. The precautionary principle goes beyond this, by dealing with the situation where there is a lack of scientific certainty regarding the risk that a hazard may occur or its magnitude. As explained by De Sadeleer:

> The distinction between the preventive principle and the precautionary principle rests on a difference of degree in the understanding of risk. Prevention is based on certainties: it rests on cumulative experience concerning the degree of risk posed by an activity (Russian roulette, for example, involves a predictable one-in-six chance of death). Therefore, prevention presupposes science, technical control, and the notion of an objective assessment of risks in order to reduce the probability of their occurrence. Preventive measures are thus intended to avert risks for which the cause-and-effect relationship is already known … . Precaution, in

> contrast, comes into play when the probability of a suspected risk cannot be irrefutably demonstrated. The distinction between the two principles is thus the degree of uncertainty surrounding the probability of risk. The lower the margin of uncertainty, the greater the justification for intervention as a means of prevention, rather than in the name of precaution. By contrast, precaution is used when scientific research has not yet reached a stage that allows the veil of uncertainty to be lifted.
>
> (De Sadeleer 2002:74)

The precautionary principle has gained wide acceptance at the international level,[25] particularly in the area of environmental protection,[26] in response to the increasing realisation of the prevalence of uncertainty in science.[27] Although there is still debate regarding whether the precautionary principle has gained the status of a principle of customary international law, and no generally accepted definition of the precautionary principle has yet emerged,[28] one can outline its 'core content' in broad terms. It comes down to the idea that a government may legitimately regulate against possible risks in situations where conclusive scientific evidence as to the existence or extent of the risk is still lacking. Thus, there are three components to this principle: 1) scientific uncertainty; 2) threat of harm; and 3) precautionary action (Barrieu and Sinclair-Desgagne 2003: 5).[29] Typically, certain thresholds or conditions are applied as limits to the possibility of relying on this principle, in order to prevent its misuse, but these vary in different formulations of the principle. According to one formulation, reliance on the precautionary principle is limited to situations where there are threats of serious or irreversible damage.[30] Other possible limits are the requirement that the threat of harm be based on 'reasonable grounds for concern, rather than mere conjecture'[31] and that the precautionary action be effective and proportional to the risk involved (Trouwborst 2006: 147–153).

While, in the area of SPS risk, the status and content of the precautionary principle remain controversial, it is not debated that precautionary approaches are embedded in the regulatory processes of many countries and are particularly prevalent in those where SPS risks are a regulatory priority.[32] It is beyond the scope of this contribution to engage in an analysis of the status and content of the precautionary principle in the area of SPS risk. Instead, brief reference is made to this principle to draw attention to the fact that SPS regulatory regimes currently take account, to a greater or lesser extent, of the fact that regulators may need to act to protect against harm in situations of scientific uncertainty. Precaution thus tempers the reliance on science as the final arbiter of the legitimacy of SPS regulation.

One example of a precautionary approach in the area of SPS regulation is the requirement of prior approval for the importation of a potentially risky product whose safety has not yet been determined, as is the case with the EC regime for approval of genetically modified organisms. Such a system relies on an *a priori* ban on certain category of products, pending a scientific determination of their safety.[33] It now falls to be determined whether the challenges to trade-restrictive measures taken in the context of this system in the *EC – Biotech Products* dispute were decided in a manner that reflects an understanding of the complexities of the use of science as a benchmark for regulatory validity, as discussed above.

Understanding the limited ambit of the dispute

To grasp accurately the ramifications of the *EC – Biotech Products* dispute for the role of science in policing health regulation under WTO law, it is useful to start by accurately sketching the ambit of this dispute and making clear what it did *not* address.[34]

It should be noted, as expressly stated by the Panel,[35] that the dispute did *not* concern the question of whether biotech products in general are safe or whether the conclusions of the EC scientific committees regarding the safety of specific biotech products are scientifically valid.[36] The Panel also did not address whether biotech products are 'like' their conventional counterparts. With regard to the EC regime for biotech approvals, the Panel did not examine whether the EC has a right to require premarketing approval of biotech products or whether the EC approval procedures requiring a product-by-product assessment of risks are WTO-consistent.[37] In addition, the dispute was not about the WTO consistency of current EC legislation regarding biotech products.[38]

Instead, the dispute concerned three types of measures:[39] 1) the general *de facto* EC moratorium on the approval of biotech products;[40] 2) certain EC measures affecting the approval of specific biotech products;[41] and 3) the safeguard measures of six EC Member States[42] prohibiting biotech products that had been approved at the European level.[43] These three measures were challenged under various provisions of the following WTO agreements: *SPS Agreement*, the *Agreement on Technical Barriers to Trade* (*TBT Agreement*), the *General Agreement on Tariffs and Trade* of 1994 (GATT 1994) and the *Agreement on Agriculture.* The Panel analysed the challenged measures under the *SPS Agreement* and, having found violations thereof, considered it unnecessary to rule on their conformity with the *TBT Agreement*, GATT 1994 or the *Agreement on Agriculture.*

The Panel's findings regarding the claims under the *SPS Agreement* present interesting issues that deserve careful analysis. This chapter will not attempt to provide a comprehensive discussion of all the Panel's findings, but will instead limit itself to selected issues of relevance to the role of science to mediate between the conflicting objectives of trade liberalisation and health protection.

Stretching the scope of application of the *SPS Agreement*

A surprising aspect of the Panel's findings is its interpretation of the scope of application of the *SPS Agreement*. These findings are particularly relevant in that they establish the range of measures by WTO Members that will be subject to the disciplines of the *SPS Agreement* and thus the situations of conflict between trade and health that will be resolved through the use of science.

The *SPS Agreement* is applicable to all 'SPS measures' which may, directly or indirectly, affect international trade,[44] in terms of Article 1.1 thereof. Therefore, the first issue before the Panel was the question of whether the relevant EC procedures for the approval of biotech products could be seen as 'SPS measures' as defined in Annex A(1) of the *SPS Agreement*.[45] The Complainants had alleged that the EC approval procedures were SPS measures and fell within the scope of the *SPS Agreement*, whereas the EC argued that these procedures fell in part within the scope, and in part outside the scope, of the *SPS Agreement*. In particular, the EC regarded the environmental objectives of its legislation on the approval of biotech products as falling outside the scope of the *SPS Agreement* and being instead covered by the *TBT Agreement*. The EC approval procedures, which are relevant to all three categories of challenged measures in this dispute, are found in Directive 2001/18 (and its predecessor Directive 90/220) on the Deliberate Release into the Environment of Genetically Modified Organisms and Regulation 258/97 concerning Novel Foods and Novel Food Ingredients.[46] The Panel emphasised, however, that it was not these procedures themselves that were being challenged by the Complainants, but rather the EC's *application* of these procedures.[47]

In order to determine whether the EC approval procedures could be regarded as SPS measures,[48] the Panel examined the definition of an SPS measure in Annex A(1) of the *SPS Agreement*, which provides:

> Sanitary or phytosanitary measure – Any measure applied:
>
> (a) to protect animal or plant life or health within the territory of the Member from risks arising from the entry, establishment or spread of pests, diseases, disease-carrying organisms or disease-causing organisms;
> (b) to protect human or animal life or health within the territory of the Member from risks arising from additives, contaminants, toxins or disease-causing organisms in foods, beverages or feedstuffs;
> (c) to protect human life or health within the territory of the Member from risks arising from diseases carried by animals, plants or products thereof, or from the entry, establishment or spread of pests; or
> (d) to prevent or limit other damage within the territory of the Member from the entry, establishment or spread of pests.
>
> Sanitary or phytosanitary measures include all relevant laws, decrees, regulations, requirements and procedures including, *inter alia*, end product criteria; processes and production methods; testing, inspection, certification and approval procedures; quarantine treatments including relevant requirements associated with the transport of animals or plants, or with the materials necessary for their survival during transport; provisions

on relevant statistical methods, sampling procedures and methods of risk assessment; and packaging and labelling requirements directly related to food safety.

The Panel found that there are three elements in this definition: 1) the *purpose* of the measure, as enumerated in sub-paragraphs (a) to (d); 2) the *form* of the measure, as described in the second paragraph ('all relevant laws, decrees, [and] regulations'); and 3) the *nature* of the measure, also set out in the second paragraph ('requirements and procedures, including … ').[49] These three elements will now be examined in turn.

As correctly identified by the Panel, the purpose of the measure, as enumerated in sub-paragraphs (a) to (d), is crucial to the classification of a measure as an SPS measure under this definition.[50] This list is exhaustive, designed to limit the application of the *SPS Agreement* to a specific category of measures, broadly speaking those that aim to protect human, animal or plant life or health, or the territory of a Member, from specified risks in food/feed or risks from pests or diseases of plants or animals. The Panel therefore had to determine if the EC approval procedures were aimed at one or more of the listed objectives. It examined, in turn, all the stated purposes of the approval legislation with regard to the deliberate release of biotech products into the environment (Directive 90/220 and its successor Directive 2001/18) and that with regard to novel foods (Regulation 258/97).

The stated objective of Directives 90/220 and 2001/18 is the protection of human health and the environment from the adverse effects that might arise from the deliberate release into the environment or the placing on the market of genetically modified organisms (GMOs).[51] While the Directives do not specifically set out which risks for human health or the environment they aim at, the Panel identified a series of such risks from their provisions on information requirements and risk assessment coverage. The Panel rejected the EC's argument that the *SPS Agreement* was not intended to cover measures aimed at risks to the environment in general, that are not linked to the health of humans, animals or plants.[52] It then proceeded to examine each of the sub-paragraphs (a) to (d) of Annex A(1) to establish whether certain potential adverse effects of GMOs identified in the Directives fall under these sub-paragraphs. It found that all the risks aimed at by the Directives were covered by one or more sub-paragraphs of Annex A(1). With regard to Regulation 258/97, the Panel noted that it had three purposes, namely, to prevent novel foods and food ingredients[53] from presenting a danger to the consumer, misleading the consumer and being nutritionally disadvantageous to the consumer.[54] It found the first purpose to fall under Annex A(1)(b) of the *SPS Agreement*, but the other two purposes not to be covered by any of the sub-paragraphs of Annex A(1).

In coming to these findings, the Panel's interpretation of the list of relevant purposes contained in sub-paragraphs (a) to (d) of Annex A(1) is so wide, however, that the scope of application of the *SPS Agreement* thereby is significantly extended. To name but a few examples, the Panel considered that in sub-paragraph (a) the term 'animal or plant life or health' includes non-target microorganisms;[55] the term 'establishment or spread of pests' includes risks of the development of resistance in already existing target pests;[56] and the term 'pests' includes cultivated genetically modified (GM) plants if they are growing where they are undesired, cross-breeds that result from unintentional gene-flow between GM plants and other plants, if they have undesired introduced traits, and pesticide-resistant target or non-target organisms that result from exposure to pesticide-producing GM plants.[57] Similarly, in sub-paragraph (b) the Panel regarded the term 'food, beverages or feedstuffs' as including GM crops not intended to be eaten by humans or animals but nevertheless consumed by them, as well as GM plants that are not eaten as such but are processed into food or feed;[58] the word 'additives' as encompassing genes internationally added for technological purposes to a GM plant that is eaten or processed into food;[59] and the term 'contaminants' as including proteins produced by GM plants through the unintended expression of modified genes.[60] With regard to sub-paragraph (c), the Panel regarded 'pests' as covering intentionally cultivated allergenic GM plants that have already been harvested.[61] Further, in sub-paragraph (d) the Panel interpreted 'other damage' to include not only economic damage or damage to property, but also damage to the environment (other than to the life or health of plants or animals) encompassing adverse effects on biodiversity, population dynamics of species or geochemical cycles. One may wonder if this extensive interpretation of the list of purposes of measures covered by the *SPS Agreement* was intended by the negotiators of this Agreement when they agreed to its rigorous scientific disciplines.[62]

In coming to these broad interpretations, the Panel often went beyond the internationally agreed-upon definitions of the pertinent terms developed by the relevant international standard-setting bodies referred to in the *SPS Agreement*.[63] The Panel itself had invited several international organisations to identify appropriate standard references (such as technical dictionaries, glossaries, standards and guidelines) which might be useful to it in determining the meaning of terms in the *SPS Agreement*.[64] In its arguments regarding the scope of application of the *SPS Agreement*, the EC repeatedly relied on definitions of terms used in Annex A(1), which have been developed by the international standard-setting bodies expressly referred to in the *SPS Agreement*. These are the Codex Alimentarius Commission (Codex) in the area of food safety, the World Organisation for Animal Health (OIE) in the area of animal health and the Secretariat of the International Plant Protection Convention (IPPC) in the area of plant health.

For example, the EC argued that the definition of a 'pest' in the IPPC of 1997 as a 'plant, animal or pathogenic agent injurious to plants or plant products' provides a context for the interpretation of the term in the *SPS Agreement*, requiring that the pest be a living organism and that it cause injury to a plant.[65] Similarly, it relied on the definition of 'additives' of the Codex, which refers to a substance intentionally added to food in the manufacture thereof for a technological purpose, for its argument that the substance must be added to food and not to a plant that may later find its way into food.[66] It also pointed to the Codex definition of 'contaminants' as 'any substance not intentionally added to food, which is present in the food as a result of the production – of such food' to argue that, as GMOs and the proteins they produce will be intentionally present in food, they cannot be contaminants.[67] The OIE definition of a 'disease' as 'the clinical and/or pathological manifestation of infection' was further pointed to by the EC in support of its contention that a GMO is not a disease.[68]

The Panel found that, while these internationally agreed definitions are informative,[69] they are not dispositive of the meaning of the relevant terms in the *SPS Agreement* since the international standard-setting bodies are not referred to in the Annex A(1) definition. It therefore felt free to deviate from these definitions and come to a more expansive interpretation of the relevant terms. The Panel appeared to prefer to rely on definitions in the *New Shorter Oxford English Dictionary* to determine the 'ordinary meaning' of the terms used in the *SPS Agreement.*[70] This approach does not seem in line with the *SPS Agreement*'s reliance on the work of the relevant international standard-setting bodies as establishing standards and guidelines that Members are encouraged to adopt.[71] It seems strange to promote the use of these international standards by Members, while the Panel can freely disregard their work in applying the provisions of the *SPS Agreement*. This approach has led to an understanding of the list of purposes of SPS measures set out in Annex A(1) that goes far beyond the meaning that is generally accepted by risk regulators.

In addition to its unusually broad interpretation of the 'purpose' element of the definition of an 'SPS measure', the Panel's identification of two additional separate elements (form and nature) in the second paragraph of the definition in Annex A(1) is rather unexpected. There seems to be no obvious reason to break up the relevant sentence in this definition in such an artificial way. In fact, in order to do so, the Panel had to insert the word 'and' between 'decrees' and 'regulations',[72] which seems contrary to the principle that a treaty interpreter must interpret the words actually used in the treaty, rather than add words it considers should have been used.[73] It would seem more in line with the natural meaning of the text to regard the second paragraph as providing a broad illustrative list of five types (or in the Panel's word *forms*) of measures that would be considered SPS measures, namely, all relevant laws, decrees, regulations, requirements and procedures. That this list is non-exhaustive is indicated by the use of the word 'include'. The purpose of the list, rather than to limit the scope of the *SPS Agreement* by adding specific form and nature requirements, seems to be to make clear the broad reach of the Agreement to all types of measures, whether legislative, administrative or otherwise, once it is established that they are imposed for one of the four purposes listed in the sub-paragraphs. The further list of various measures ('including, *inter alia*, end product criteria … ') is again a non-exhaustive illustration, this time of examples of specific SPS measures that would be regarded as 'laws, decrees, requirements, regulations and procedures' under this definition.[74]

The Panel's approach had practical implications for the application of the *SPS Agreement* to the measures in dispute, and in particular for the relevance of the scientific disciplines of the Agreement to these measures.[75] While the Panel recognised the broad ambit of the 'form' requirement,[76] it relied on the 'nature' requirement it had read into Annex A(1), and which it regarded as 'key' to its determination,[77] to find that the EC general *de facto* moratorium on biotech approvals did not fall under the definition of an SPS measure. The Panel regarded the general *de facto* moratorium as neither a 'requirement' nor a 'procedure', but rather as the 'application' of approval procedures.[78] As the second paragraph of Annex A(1) does not refer to the 'application' of requirements and procedures, the Panel saw its way clear to conclude that the moratorium was *not* an SPS measure.[79] Similarly, the Panel regarded the product-specific measures challenged as 'the alleged failure by the [EC] to consider particular applications for final approval'.[80] As this was likewise seen by the Panel to be neither a 'procedure' nor a 'requirement' but rather the 'application' of an approval procedure, it did not meet the Panel's 'nature' requirement and therefore did not fall under the definition of Annex A(1).[81]

This construction served a useful purpose for the Panel in this dispute. The finding that the moratorium and the product-specific measures were not SPS measures, but rather the application of SPS measures, allowed the Panel to limit its analysis to those procedural rules of the *SPS Agreement* that refer to the *application* of SPS measures rather than apply the substantive disciplines of the Agreement. In this way, the Panel avoided having to rule on controversial issues regarding the scientific basis for these two categories of measures.

However, these findings could have had unintended far-reaching effects for the coverage of the *SPS Agreement* if followed in future disputes.[82] Under the Panel's interpretation of Annex A(1), the determination of whether a measure falls within the *SPS Agreement* would turn on the rather technical criteria of its form and particularly its nature, rather than the more substantive (and arguably more important) criterion of its purpose. The Panel seemed to disregard the inclusive nature of the list in the second paragraph of Annex A(1) and, in effect, required all SPS measures to have the 'nature' of either 'requirements' or 'procedures'. This formalistic approach may create incentives for Members to draft legislation in a manner that avoids meeting the Panel's 'nature' criterion. By contrast, the overly-broad interpretation of the limited list of objectives of SPS measures is practically all-encompassing, reducing this list to inefficacy in delimiting the measures covered by the *SPS Agreement*.

As discussed above, this approach does not rest comfortably with the text of Annex A(1), which instead appears to restrict the *purpose* of an SPS measure to only the listed objectives, yet allow for the measures aiming at these objectives to be given a wide range of legal forms, providing only an illustrative list of possibilities to be included.[83] The Panel's expansive interpretation of the listed purposes, instead, may lead to an invasive application of the rigorous scientific disciplines of the *SPS Agreement* to matters not intended to fall within its ambit.[84] This interpretation could have far-reaching consequences. As pointed out by Doaa Motaal, and supported by the negotiating history of the *SPS Agreement*, the *SPS Agreement* is 'intended to deal with a limited set of measures' (Motaal 2004:856; Peel 2006: 1014). It is this limited scope of application that enabled Members to agree to the inclusion of strict scientific disciplines (Peel 2006: 1016). SPS measures, in the classical sense, most often directly regulate food or agricultural products, thus accounting for the need for strong disciplines to prevent protectionist abuses in the agricultural sector, which is traditionally difficult to liberalise. Other measures, aimed at broader concerns such as biodiversity and other environmental issues, in many cases have only incidental effects on trade in agricultural products. In addition, such other measures embody societal values of a different nature than those reflected in 'SPS measures' as traditionally understood. Whereas SPS measures address health protection at national level, environmental measures often address harm which has a long-lasting global impact.[85] Further, the appropriateness of the scientific disciplines of the *SPS Agreement* for the evaluation of environmental regulation is exceedingly doubtful. As convincingly argued by Jacqueline Peel, in contrast to the strong reliance in SPS regimes on a scientific basis for regulation, 'environmental regimes invariably couple a requirement for reliance on scientific information with an instruction to act with caution in the face of scientific uncertainty' (Peel 2006: 1017). This broad acceptance of precautionary action in the field of environmental protection is in marked contrast to the weak and limited scope for precautionary measures in the *SPS Agreement*.[86] This variance in the role of science in these two regimes reflects 'the different nature of available scientific knowledge regarding most environmental problems, as opposed to those associated with quarantine pests or diseases, or toxins of concern for human health' (Peel 2006: 1017).[87]

The implications of the Panel's extremely broad interpretation of the purposes covered by the definition of an SPS measure, and of the relationship between the measure and such purpose, for Members, and particularly for those at lower levels of development, should not be underestimated.[88] For example, Members that are trying to establish a regulatory regime for biotech products are now faced with the situation that their biotech regulations, often motivated by environmental concerns in general[89] and, more pragmatically, by the need to ensure that their agricultural products continue to have access to the EC market, may now unexpectedly be subject to the strict scientific disciplines of the *SPS Agreement*.[90] For all Members, but particularly for those that face capacity constraints in the area of scientific risk assessment, such a result may have an inhibiting effect on regulatory initiatives. A similar concern can be raised with regard to efforts by Members to implement their obligations under multilateral environmental agreements, such as the *Basel Convention on Hazardous Waste* and the *Cartagena Protocol on Biosafety*. Measures to implement these environmental treaties may have trade effects, and may now fall under the expanded definition of SPS measures. Although poorly suited to this purpose, the *SPS Agreement* would then discipline these measures. Most Members would be hard pressed to defend such environmental measures from a challenge under the scientific obligations of the *SPS Agreement*, but this would be even more notably the case for Members at lower levels of development.

Side-stepping the scientific obligations

In addressing the measures in dispute under the obligations set out in the *SPS Agreement*, the Panel's reluctance to address the sensitive issue of the scientific justification for the EC measures under consideration, namely the general *de facto* moratorium and the product-specific measures, is apparent. It is interesting to examine how the Panel managed to avoid tackling this matter head on.

The Panel examined first the Complainants' claim that the general *de facto* moratorium violated Article 5.1 of the *SPS Agreement*. Article 5.1 requires that Members ensure that their SPS measures are based on a risk assessment. Stringent requirements are laid down for a risk assessment in Annex A(4), as clarified in the case law thus far.[91] Therefore, if the Panel had found the general moratorium on biotech approvals to constitute an SPS measure, it would have had to assess whether such moratorium was based on a proper risk assessment meeting the requirements of Annex A(4). As discussed above, the Panel held that the moratorium was not an SPS measure as defined in Annex A(1) of the *SPS Agreement* as it did not meet the 'nature' requirement. Instead, it could be seen as the 'application' of SPS measures, i.e. the application of the EC biotech approval procedures.

To determine whether this 'provisional conclusion' under Annex A(1) was appropriate, the Panel examined Article 5.1 as the 'specific context' within which the term 'SPS measure' appears.[92] It expressed the view that the term 'SPS measure' in Article 5.1 should be interpreted to refer to a measure applied to achieve a Member's appropriate level of SPS protection.[93] As the moratorium was merely a procedural decision to delay final approval decisions, it could not be said to achieve or imply a particular level of protection according to the Panel.[94] It therefore held that the moratorium was not an 'SPS measure' for purposes of Article 5.1, and thus Article 5.1 was not applicable to it.[95] In the same way, the Panel found the moratorium not to be an 'SPS measure' for purposes of Articles 2.2, 2.3, 5.5 and 5.6 of the *SPS Agreement*,[96] thereby deftly avoiding ruling on the conformity of the moratorium with the substantive obligations of the *SPS Agreement* which require a scientific basis for SPS measures and an absence of arbitrary or unjustifiable discrimination. In addition, as the moratorium was held not to be an SPS measure, the Panel found the transparency obligations in Article 7 and Annex B(1) inapplicable.[97]

Rather than address these difficult and controversial issues, the Panel focused on the challenge under the procedural disciplines of Article 8 and Annex C(1)(a) of the *SPS Agreement*, which prohibit undue delays in control, inspection and approval procedures.[98] Reiterating its finding that the EC approval procedures are SPS measures in the form of procedures to check and ensure the fulfilment of SPS measures as referred to in Annex C(1), the Panel found Annex C(1)(a) applicable to these procedures. Thus, the EC was obliged to ensure its biotech approval procedures were 'undertaken and completed without undue delay'. The Panel noted that what matters is not the length of the delay, but rather whether there is a legitimate reason or justification for it.[99] The Panel examined and rejected the EC's arguments that the delays were justified by the perceived inadequacy of its existing legislation and the prudent and precautionary approach it applied due to the fact that the relevant science was evolving and in a state of flux.[100] While the Panel agreed that limited availability of scientific evidence may mean that deferring decisions might allow for better decisions to be taken, it pointed out that the core obligation of Annex C(1)(a) is for Members to come to a substantive decision. This decision need not give 'a straight yes or no answer to applicants'. Instead, a Member, for example, may reject an application subject to later review, or give a time-limited approval. The Panel then examined a particular approval procedure for a biotech product to determine if the moratorium had led to undue delay and readily found this to be the case. It therefore found that the general *de facto* moratorium constituted a violation of the procedural prohibition in Annex C(1)(a) and consequently of Article 8 of the *SPS Agreement*.

However, the practical effect of the Panel's findings and recommendation for the EC's *de facto* moratorium is negligible. Although, in its final report, the Panel refrained from finding that the moratorium had ceased to exist, this does seem to be the case from the subsequent approvals of biotech products.[101] Thus, nothing more is needed to bring this measure of the EC into compliance with the *SPS Agreement*.

Similarly, with regard to the product-specific measures, namely, the failure to consider for final approval applications concerning certain specified biotech products, the Panel took the same procedural approach as it did with regard to the general moratorium, which allowed it to sidestep the substantive issues. Once again it determined that the measures at issue were not 'SPS measures' as defined in Annex 1(A) of the *SPS Agreement*, but were rather the application of SPS measures.[102] Thus, Articles 2.2, 2.3, 5.5, 5.6 and 7 and Annex B(1) of the *SPS Agreement*, which lay down substantive disciplines on SPS measures, including the requirement of sufficient scientific evidence for the maintenance of a measure and its basis in scientific principles, were not applicable.

The Panel consequently focused its examination on the procedural question whether Article 8 and Annex C(1)(a) had been violated. The Panel examined the procedures followed with regard to the 27 products specified in the dispute and determined that there had been 'undue delay' in 24 of the 27 cases, contrary to Article 8 and Annex C(1)(a).[103] Therefore, the Panel recommended that the EC bring these measures into compliance with its WTO obligations.

The consequence of these findings on the product-specific measures for the EC is, once again, fairly limited. To comply with the Panel's recommendations, the

EC must complete the application procedures for these 24 products without undue delay. However, the outcome of the approval procedures is left up to the EC. It is *not* required that the EC *approve* the biotech products for use in the EC. Therefore this finding does not lead to politically charged consequences for the EC.

The scientific assessment of the EC Member States' safeguard measures

The third category of measures in this dispute was the WTO consistency of the nine safeguard measures taken by six EU Member States[104] with regard to certain biotech products that had already been approved at the European level for use in the EC. The Complainants did not challenge the EC legislation that allows the use of safeguard measures where a Member State has justifiable reasons to consider that an approved product constitutes a risk to human health or the environment.[105] Instead, they challenged the safeguard measures themselves.

The Panel examined the purpose of each of the nine safeguard measures and found that they were 'SPS measures' as defined in Annex A(1).[106] Therefore the substantive rules of the *SPS Agreement* raised in the Complainants' claims had to be addressed by the Panel in respect of these measures.

The challenges to the Member States' safeguard measures were made on the grounds that they were not based on a risk assessment and scientific principles as required by Articles 2.2 and 5.1 of the *SPS Agreement* and embodied arbitrary or unjustifiable distinctions in levels of protection against risk resulting in discrimination or disguised trade restrictions contrary to Articles 2.3 and 5.5 of the *SPS Agreement*. This contribution will focus on the challenges that related to the scientific basis for the safeguard measures, namely the claims of violation of Articles 2.2 and 5.1. As a violation of the more specific obligation of Article 5.1 necessarily implies a violation of the more general scientific obligation of Article 2.2, the Panel's analysis centred on the claim under Article 5.1.[107]

Article 5.1 of the *SPS Agreement* requires Members to ensure that their SPS measures are based on a risk assessment as appropriate to the circumstances. The risk assessment obligation of the *SPS Agreement* can be seen as an attempt to ensure rational, science-based decision making in national SPS regulation and thereby to prevent private-interest capture of the regulatory process (Howse 2000). As noted by Jacqueline Peel: 'the very fact of having to take a risk assessment into account and respond to its findings could have the salutary effect of forcing national regulators "to articulate objectives, to assess means, and to rationalize results", a substantial improvement for the regulatory processes of many nations' (Peel 2004: 57).[108]

Article 5.1 thus sets science as the touchstone against which SPS measures are judged for validity. However, once one recognises the fallacy inherent in a notion of universal science, as discussed above,[109] it becomes necessary to ask:

Whose science must measures be tested against? The same factual situation can lead to different scientific conclusions. These different scientific conclusions may be arrived at due to different choices between various scientifically plausible alternatives. This is particularly true when the science-policy decisions inherent in the assumptions, rules-of-thumb and models used to fill gaps in data differ. The science policy choices made in conducting national risk assessments reflect subjective values as risk assessors reflect on how the scientific information before them must be understood (Green and Epps 2007: 304). Therefore the risk orientation prevalent in a Member will influence the outcome of a risk assessment, leading to the possibility that different conclusions may be drawn from the same scientific data. This situation is sometimes referred to as the problem of 'duelling science' as discussed in the section on 'The role of science in disciplining health risk regulation', above. It is therefore interesting to see to what extent the interpretation of the scientific obligations of the *SPS Agreement* by the Panel in *EC – Biotech Products* acknowledges this reality.

The requirements of Article 5.1 can be divided into two elements, which will be examined successively below. First, Article 5.1 requires the existence of a risk assessment as appropriate to the circumstances. Second, it requires the regulating Member to base its SPS measure on such a risk assessment.

What is meant by a 'risk assessment' is defined in Annex A(4) of the *SPS Agreement*, which sets out two separate definitions, depending on the risk at issue. The interpretation of these definitions in the case law is important in assessing what is required of Members that impose SPS measures. The rigour of these requirements determines the possibilities for Members to apply and maintain SPS measures.

The first type of risk assessment, which must be conducted where the risk at issue is from pests or diseases, contains three requirements. Such a risk assessment must:

- identify the pests/diseases whose entry, establishment or spread a Member wants to prevent, as well as the potential biological and economic consequences associated with the entry, establishment or spread of such pests/diseases;
- evaluate the likelihood of entry, establishment or spread of these pests/diseases and the associated biological and economic consequences; and
- evaluate such likelihood according to the SPS measures that might be applied.[110]

The second type of risk assessment, relevant to risk to human or animal health from food or feed, comprises two requirements, namely that the risk assessment must:

- identify the adverse effects on human or animal health (if any) arising from the additive, contaminant, toxin or disease-causing organism in food/beverages/feedstuffs at issue; and

- if such adverse health effects exist, evaluate the potential or probability of occurrence of these effects.[111]

The Panel in *EC – Biotech Products* examined the risk assessments submitted in support of the safeguard measures. It first noted that the risk assessments conducted by the relevant EC scientific committees had found no risks from the approved products, either before approval or when reviewing the safeguard measures. Therefore these assessments could not form the basis for the nine safeguard measures applied by EC Member States to ban biotech products that had already been approved at EC level.[112]

It then examined the other scientific studies relied upon as the basis for the safeguard measures. Here, an important aspect of the evaluation by the Panel of risk assessments falling under the first definition, i.e. those addressing risks from pests or diseases, was the question whether the studies assessed the 'likelihood' of the risk occurring. In past case law, 'likelihood' in the first definition was interpreted to mean 'probability' as opposed to 'possibility', which was the meaning given to 'potential' in the second definition.[113] The Panel used the probability assessment element of the first definition of a risk assessment to reject several of the studies as not meeting the requirements of a risk assessment for purposes of the *SPS Agreement*. For example, when looking at Austria's safeguard measure on T25 maize, the Panel rejected Austria's contention that a scientific report, known as the Hoppichler study,[114] constituted a risk assessment under Article 5.1.[115] According to the Panel, the Hoppichler study did not identify the relative probability of the risks it identified, but only referred to the possibilities of the risks, or to the inability to determine probabilities.[116] It therefore did not meet the requirements of the first definition of a risk assessment.[117] Similar findings were made in respect of the studies relied upon as the basis for several of the other safeguard measures at issue in this dispute.[118]

The requirement that SPS measures be based on a risk assessment is qualified by the phrase 'as appropriate to the circumstances'. It was therefore necessary to determine what this qualification entails to determine whether circumstances such as scientific uncertainty might ease the strict requirements relating to risk assessments. The Panel in *EC – Biotech Products* had to address the question whether the term 'as appropriate to the circumstances' allows a Member to take into account as a relevant 'circumstance' the level of protection it has chosen and the uncertainties in science. The EC argued that an importing Member may reject an existing risk assessment as not 'appropriate to [its] circumstances' on the grounds that the risk assessment identified constraints or uncertainties such that the risk assessment would not enable the Member to determine with a sufficient degree of precision whether an SPS measure would achieve its appropriate level of protection.[119] The Panel rejected this argument, finding that the appropriate level of protection of a Member and the uncertainties or constraints identified in a risk assessment do not play a role in determining whether there is a risk assessment as appropriate to the circumstances. Rather, they are only factors to be considered by a Member in determining the SPS measure to be applied for achieving its appropriate level of protection,[120] i.e. in the risk management phase of regulation.

The Panel also had to address the question of whether the safeguard measures were 'based on' risk assessments. The Complainants argued that, although the Member States concerned had offered reasons for their measures, pointing to shortcomings in the risk assessments conducted as part of the EC approval process or expressing general concerns with regard to risks to human health or the environment arising from the relevant biotech products, they had not put forward risk assessments meeting the requirements of Annex A.4. Instead, the only risk assessments available were those conducted by the EC scientific committees and lead Competent Authorities,[121] which were favourable to the biotech products at issue. Consequently, the safeguard measures could not be said to be 'based on' these risk assessments.[122] To the contrary, the EC argued, *inter alia*, that the risk assessments carried out at the time of approval of the biotech products 'could serve, at least temporarily, as a basis both for the original Community consent, and for the Member States' provisional [safeguard] measures'.[123] This argument was based on the EC's view that, as the requirement for a measure to be 'based on' a risk assessment does not mean that the measure must 'conform to' that risk assessment, the same risk assessment can 'sufficiently warrant' or 'reasonably support' more than one possible SPS measure.

It was common ground between the parties that the assessments conducted by the EC scientific committees and the lead Competent Authorities were risk assessments within the meaning of Annex A.4 and Article 5.1.[124] The question was thus whether the safeguard measures were 'based on' these assessments.[125] The Panel agreed with the EC that the words 'based on' in Article 5.1 do not mean the same as 'conform to'.[126] It accepted that a particular risk assessment can form the basis for different types of measures, in cases where a risk is determined to exist.[127] It also acknowledged that the determination of whether a measure is 'based on' a risk assessment may be influenced by the fact that a Member has chosen to follow a precautionary approach in the face of uncertainties or constraints identified in the risk assessment.[128] However, the Panel noted that this does not mean that 'Members are free to adopt any kind of SPS measure provided there exists a risk assessment for the product subject to the SPS measure'.[129] It recalled that the term 'based on' has been interpreted by the Appellate Body to mean 'sufficiently warranted by', 'reasonably supported by' or 'rationally related to'.[130] The Panel held therefore that the 'based on' requirement in Article 5.1 'is plainly a substantive requirement and not simply a formal requirement to accompany an SPS measure by a risk assessment'.[131]

However, in previous case law it was acknowledged that a Member need not follow mainstream scientific opinion, but may base its SPS measure on what at a given time may be a divergent opinion, coming from qualified and respected sources.[132] The question then arose as to whether an SPS measure could be said to be based on a 'divergent opinion' in a risk assessment if that risk assessment set out a single opinion with which the Member concerned disagrees, as in this case. The Panel clarified that, to the extent that Members disagree with some or all of the conclusions contained in such a risk assessment:

> it would in [the Panel's] view be necessary for Members to explain, by reference to the existing assessment, how and why they assess the risks differently, and provide their revised or supplemental assessment of the risks.[133]

However, the Panel found that the Member States' safeguard measures at issue simply disregarded the favourable risk assessments by the EC scientific committees.[134] They did not identify uncertainties or constraints and explain how these justified the safeguard measures.[135] According to the Panel, if it were to allow this, it would turn the conduct of risk assessments into 'a mere formality'.[136]

The Panel held, therefore, that the Member States' safeguard measures could not be regarded as being based on risk assessments, as required by Article 5.1, as the Member States did not come up with alternative studies, aside from those conducted by the EC scientific committees, conforming to the requirements of the definition of a 'risk assessment' in Annex A(4).

Dealing with scientific insufficiency and precaution

The EC argued that the Member States' safeguard measures fell to be assessed under Article 5.7 of the *SPS Agreement*, which allows Members to take provisional measures in cases of insufficient scientific evidence. The Panel in *EC – Biotech Products* emphasised that the trigger for the applicability of Article 5.7 is the insufficiency of the scientific evidence, not merely the provisional nature of the measure at issue.[137]

In the case law thus far it has been established that scientific evidence is 'insufficient' when it is does not allow, in quantitative or qualitative terms, the performance of a proper risk assessment as required under Article 5.1 read together with the definition in Annex A(4) of the *SPS Agreement*.[138] According to the requirements of Article 5.7, such provisional measures taken in cases of insufficient scientific evidence must be based on the available pertinent information and be reviewed within a reasonable period of time. In addition, the Member concerned is obliged to seek to obtain additional information necessary for a proper risk assessment. By laying down specific requirements for the exercise of the right to take provisional measures, Article 5.7 operates to avoid abuse of this right. It ensures that a framework is in place within which risk management decisions taken in the face of insufficient scientific evidence can be disciplined, to promote rationality.

The question of the relationship between the scientific disciplines of Articles 2.2 and 5.1 of the *SPS Agreement* on the one hand, and the scope for provisional measures under Article 5.7 on the other, arose in the *EC – Biotech Products* case. The Panel, relying on the test used by the Appellate Body in *EC – Tariff Preferences* to distinguish between exceptions and exemptions,[139] agreed with the EC that Article 5.7 is an exemption, creating an autonomous right, and not merely an exception from the general scientific obligation under Article 2.2 and the obligation to base a measure on a risk assessment in Article 5.1.[140] Thus, a measure falling under Article 5.7 is *excluded* from the scope of application of the scientific obligations in Article 2.2 and Article 5.1.[141] This, as recognised by the Panel, has implications for the burden of proof regarding a violation of Article 5.7. The party claiming a violation of Article 2.2 (the Complainant) bears the burden of proving that the challenged measure is inconsistent with Article 5.7.[142] If it does not succeed in doing so, the measure is not caught by the scientific obligations of Articles 2.2 and 5.1.

It is surprising to note that this safe haven from the scientific disciplines of Articles 2.2 and 5.1 of the *SPS Agreement* has been held to apply only to SPS measures that meet *all four* requirements of Article 5.7.[143] In line with this approach, the Panel in *EC – Biotech Products* held that, if a challenged SPS measure is not consistent with one of the requirements of Article 5.7, the situation is not 'as provided for in Article 5.7' and thus Article 2.2 applies.[144] A similar finding was made by this Panel in respect of Article 5.1, due to its view of Article 5.7 as a 'qualified exemption' from Article 5.1.[145] Thus, according to the case law, all four conditions of Article 5.7 must be met in order to avoid the scientific disciplines of Articles 2.2 and 5.1 of the *SPS Agreement*.

It can be questioned whether this line of case law is correct. A preferable approach, as argued by Andrew Lang, would be to regard the right to take provisional measures as existing in *all* cases where the scientific evidence is insufficient for the conduct of a risk assessment. In such cases, as explained below, it is *impossible* for Members to comply with the scientific disciplines of Articles 2.2 and 5.1. The remaining three obligations of Article 5.7 should not be seen as *conditions* for the existence of the right to take provisional measures, but rather as *substantive requirements* triggered by the exercise of this right (Lang 2008: 8). If these requirements are not met, the measure is in violation of Article 5.7 of the *SPS Agreement*. To instead 'send the panel back' to Articles 2.2 and 5.1 in such cases makes no sense, once it is recognised that Article 5.7 applies only in cases where the insufficiency of the scientific evidence is such as to hinder compliance with Articles 2.2 and 5.1. In addition, as stated by Lang, 'at the level of principle: there is something objectionable in principle about a situation in which the right to take protective measures can become legally unavailable, even where a clearly legitimate reason exists for such measures' (Lang 2008: 9).

Be that as it may, in the case at hand the Panel found that the scientific evidence was not 'insufficient', as enough evidence was available to permit a risk assessment as required under Article 5.1. This was evinced by the fact that the EC scientific committees had conducted risk assessments before approving the biotech products at issue and had reviewed these risk assessments after the adoption by the Member States of the safeguard measures at issue. The Panel disagreed with the EC that the insufficiency of the scientific evidence must be assessed in relation to the appropriate level of protection of the importing Member, but reiterated that it relates to the sufficiency of the scientific evidence to permit the performance of a risk assessment as defined in Annex A(4).[146] It held:

> The protection goals of a legislator may have a bearing on the question of which risks a Member decides to assess with a view to taking regulatory action, if necessary. And a legislator's protection goals are certainly relevant to the determination of the measure … to be taken for achieving a Member's level of protection against risk. Yet there is no apparent link between a legislator's protection goals and the task of assessing the existence and magnitude of potential risks.[147]

Thus, it held that the situation before it was not the kind of situation where Members are allowed to adopt provisional measures. In doing so, the Panel disregarded the fact that 'insufficiency' cannot be objectively assessed but depends on the societal context within which the risk regulator acts.[148] The latter is an intrinsic part of the risk assessment process and therefore affects the question whether the science available permits the conduct of a risk assessment (including the underlying values, assumptions, safety factors and rules of thumb that are inherent to it).[149] Therefore, the fact that the EC scientific committees were able to perform a risk assessment should not operate to exclude the possibility that EC Member States that apply a higher level of protection, and which may therefore not regard the available scientific evidence as sufficient to assess the risk to the extent necessitated by their chosen level of protection, could rely on Article 5.7. The Panel's approach, instead, was based on a uniform and objective view of science, divorced from its societal context. It therefore found 'insufficiency' of scientific evidence not to exist in this case.

Consequently, the Panel found a violation of Articles 5.1, 2.2 and 5.7 of the *SPS Agreement* and recommended that the Member States bring their safeguard measures into conformity with the Agreement. This recommendation entails that the Member States should either withdraw their safeguard measures or provide proper risk assessments to support them. Such an outcome should not have been too difficult for the EC to accept, since the Commission had been trying, and failing, to get the relevant Member States to remove their safeguard measures for some time.[150]

Interestingly, in response to public comment on its leaked interim report, the Panel clarified some of its findings on the issue of insufficient scientific evidence, under Article 5.7, in a letter to the parties.[151] It made clear that insufficiency can be quantitative or qualitative. It also emphasised that in applying the concept of insufficiency it had borne in mind the Appellate Body's statement in *EC – Hormones* that the risk to be assessed is real world risk, rather than only risk ascertainable in a laboratory under controlled conditions. Further, it noted that its findings preserve the freedom of Members to take prompt protective action in case new scientific evidence becomes available that affects their risk assessments. It pointed out that the possibility remains open that scientific evidence which is sufficient for a risk assessment at one time may later be considered insufficient. This would be the case if new scientific evidence negates the validity of the existing risk assessment but is itself insufficient to permit the performance of a new risk assessment. It appears that the Panel was concerned that its findings (in the leaked interim report) had been misconstrued, leading to public concern regarding the scope for government action in areas where science is in a state of flux.

While Article 5.7 has been held in previous case law to reflect the 'precautionary principle',[152] it is useful to note that scientific uncertainty does not only exist in limited cases of insufficient evidence, which can be dealt with by means of temporary solutions until certainty is achieved, as provided for under Article 5.7. The true state of affairs is that uncertainty is a more common situation than certainty in scientific affairs, as elucidated by the social science perspectives on the role of science discussed in the section on 'The role of science in disciplining health risk regulation', above. Uncertainty is often incorporated into assumptions or rules of thumb used in risk assessments where gaps in evidence exist. In this way, the biases underlying these assumptions remain hidden. It is argued that it would be better to deal openly with the uncertainties inherent in scientific analysis. By recognising the pervasive nature of uncertainty and the gaps in information inherent in scientific analysis and by allowing Members to explicitly take account of these problems through conservative or prudent approaches to risk regulation, using the flexibilities in the *SPS Agreement* to do so, panels and the Appellate Body could contribute to greater transparency in SPS regulation and a more realistic and informed use of science as a justificatory instrument.

Disregarding the relevance of other rules of international law

The EC raised the question of the relevance of other rules of international law to the interpretation of the *SPS Agreement*, including its scientific provisions, in this dispute. It relied on the provisions in the Vienna Convention on the Law of Treaties (VCLT) requiring a treaty interpreter to take account of relevant rules of international law. In particular, the EC referred to multilateral environmental agreements, especially the Convention on Biological Diversity (CBD) of 1992 and the Cartagena Protocol on Biosafety of 2000,[153] and the precautionary principle as international law rules to which the Panel must have regard.

The Cartagena Protocol to the CBD is highly relevant as it deals with transboundary movement of living modified organisms. It contains provisions dealing with approval procedures, laying down a time line and addressing factors that could cause delays in such procedures (in Articles 9–11 thereof). It also contains provisions on risk assessment (in Article 15 and Annex III) and the precautionary approach (Articles 1, 10.6 and 11.8 and Annex III). The EC argued that the Cartagena Protocol and the *SPS Agreement* should be interpreted and applied consistently as far as possible. It claimed that there are no *a priori* inconsistencies between the two treaties and that the Protocol's provisions on risk assessment and the precautionary principle inform the meaning and effect of the relevant provisions in the *SPS Agreement*.[154]

The Panel noted that Article 3.2 of the WTO's *Dispute Settlement Understanding* requires it to interpret WTO Agreements 'in accordance with customary rules of interpretation of public international law'. As acknowledged in previous WTO case law, these customary rules are reflected in Articles 31 and 32 of the VCLT. The Panel focused on Article 31.3(c) of the VCLT, which deals with the relevance of other international law rules to the interpretation of a treaty. It provides:

> There shall be taken into account, together with the context:
>
> (c) any relevant rules of international law applicable in the relations between the parties.

The Panel noted that the use of the word 'shall' indicates that Article 31.3(c) *mandates* a treaty interpreter to take account of other international law rules, rather than merely gives the interpreter the option of doing so.[155] Thereby, this Article enhances the consistency of international law rules applicable to the relevant States parties and contributes to avoiding conflicts between those rules.[156]

The Panel examined the term 'rules of international law' in Article 31.3(c) and noted that it is broad enough to encompass 'all generally accepted sources of public international law' including treaties and customary international law rules.[157] Further, it noted that in *US – Shrimp*, the Appellate Body had made clear that general principles of international law also fall under Article 31.3(c).[158] Thus, if the precautionary principle is a general principle of public international law, it could also be considered to fall under this provision.[159]

However, the Panel pointed out that Article 31.3(c) of the VCLT contains an important limitation, namely that only those rules of international law 'applicable in the relations between the parties' are to be taken into account.[160] The Panel held 'the parties' to mean those states that have consented to be bound by the treaty being interpreted (i.e. *all* WTO Members).[161] After examining the environmental agreements at issue, the Panel found that, while the EC, Argentina and Canada are parties to the CBD (having signed and ratified it), the USA is not.[162] Further, the Cartagena Protocol has been signed and ratified by the EC only. Argentina and Canada have signed but not ratified it, and the USA has neither signed nor ratified it.[163] Thus, according to the Panel, these two treaties cannot be regarded as falling within the scope of 31.3(c) of the VCLT. Therefore they did not have to be considered as part of the context for interpretation of the *SPS Agreement*.

This finding would seem to practically exclude the possibility of a Panel being obliged to have regard to other treaties in the interpretation of WTO Agreements, since it is improbable that all 159 WTO Members would be parties to another treaty. As is stated in the report of the study group set up by the United Nations International Law Commission (ILC) to address the issue of the fragmentation of international law[164] (expressly criticising this finding by the Panel in *EC – Biotech Products*):

> Bearing in mind the unlikeliness of a precise congruence in the membership of most important multilateral conventions, it would become unlikely that *any* use of conventional international law could be made in the interpretation of such conventions. This would have the ironic effect that the more the membership of a multilateral treaty such as the WTO covered agreements expanded, the more those treaties would be cut off from the rest of international law. In practice, the result would be the isolation of multilateral agreements as 'islands' permitting no references *inter se* in their application.[165]

The ILC Study Group finds it a better solution to allow reference to another treaty under Article 31.3(c) of the VCLT, provided that the *parties in dispute* are also parties to that other treaty. The resulting possibly divergent interpretations would respect party will, which is inherently divergent according to the Study Group. Further, it advocates taking into account the extent to which the other treaty can be regarded as implicitly accepted or tolerated by other parties in the sense that it can be considered to reflect the common understanding of Members as to the meaning of the relevant term.[166] In the same vein, in the conclusions of the Study Group, the particular relevance of other treaty-based rules to the interpretation of a treaty under Article 31.3 (c) of the VCLT is noted, *inter alia* where 'they provide evidence of the common understanding of the parties as to the object and purpose of a treaty under interpretation or as to the meaning of a particular term'.[167]

The Panel's finding seems to be a step backwards from the progressive approach of the Appellate Body in *US – Shrimp*. In that case, the Appellate Body had reaffirmed that WTO law is not to be read 'in clinical isolation from public international law'.[168] It followed an evolutionary interpretation of the relevant treaty terms, taking into account the 'contemporary concerns of the community of nations'[169] as reflected in other treaties. In so doing, it relied on treaties that were not binding on all the parties to the dispute, let alone all WTO Members.[170] However, the Panel in *EC – Biotech Products* considered that its approach was consistent with that followed by the Appellate Body in *US – Shrimp*. According to the Panel, the Appellate Body in the latter case 'drew on other rules of international law because it considered that they were informative and aided it in establishing the meaning and scope of the term'[171] rather than because it was obliged to refer to these other rules under Article 31.3(c) of the VCLT. The Panel pointed out that, under Article 31.1 of the VCLT, a treaty must be interpreted in accordance with the ordinary meaning of its terms, in their context and in the light of its object and purpose. It regarded, in addition to dictionaries, other relevant rules of international law as aids for a treaty interpreter to establish the ordinary meaning of words in their context. Thus, the treaty interpreter may rely on such other rules when he/she considers them informative, but need not do so, particularly if the ordinary meaning of the treaty terms can be otherwise ascertained.[172] In this case, the Panel apparently did not regard the CBD or Cartagena Protocol to be 'informative' for the interpretation of the *SPS Agreement*.[173] This was despite the fact that the Cartagena Protocol directly addresses risk assessments with respect to living modified organisms and precautionary approaches, which are core issues in the application of the *SPS Agreement* to the safeguard measures at issue in this dispute.

With regard to the precautionary principle, the Panel rejected the EC's argument that it has now become a fully fledged and general principle of international law.[174] It referred to the Appellate Body's finding in January 1998, in the *EC – Hormones* case, that the status of the precautionary principle was still subject to debate and that it was 'unnecessary and probably imprudent' for the Appellate Body to take a position on that question.[175] The Panel noted that this legal debate is still ongoing and that, despite the precautionary principle's incorporation in numerous international conventions and declarations, mainly in the area of the environment, its precise definition, content and legal status remain an open question. Due to considerations of prudence, the Panel declined to resolve this complex issue, noting further that it was unnecessary to do so.[176] While one can understand the Panel's reluctance to rule upon this controversial issue, it is difficult to see how it could be regarded as 'unnecessary' in this dispute. As pointed out by the Panel itself, if the precautionary principle has become a general principle of law, or a rule of customary international law, it *must* be taken into account in the interpretation of the *SPS Agreement* under Article 31.3(c) of the VCLT. It therefore seems imperative for the Panel to decide whether the precautionary principle has achieved this status, in order for it to know whether it is obliged to have regard to this principle.

The narrow view of the Panel regarding the role of other international law in the interpretation of WTO agreements is lamentable. The Panel fruitfully could have had recourse to relevant multilateral environmental agreements and general principles of international law (if found to exist) to inform certain terms in the *SPS Agreement*, such as 'risk assessment' and 'insufficient scientific evidence'. In this way, the Panel would have promoted the coherence of the international law system, in line with the progressive approach of the Appellate Body in *US – Shrimp*.

One ray of light in the Panel report relating to the precautionary principle can be found in an *obiter dictum* statement of the Panel. In response to the claims by the USA, Canada and Argentina that the safeguard measures applied by the EC Member States were in violation of Article 5.1, the EC argued that these measures were based on the precautionary principle.[177] While refraining from referring here to the question whether the 'precautionary principle' has achieved any particular status in international law, as mentioned above, the Panel agreed that the fact that a Member chooses to follow 'a precautionary approach' could have a bearing on the assessment by a panel of whether the SPS measure at issue was 'based on' a risk assessment under Article 5.1.[178] More specifically, the Panel considered that, if there are factors, such as the limited body of scientific evidence available, that affect scientists' confidence in the risk assessment they have conducted, a Member may in principle take this into account in determining the SPS measure to be applied to achieve its appropriate level of protection. Therefore, when faced with a risk assessment that 'identifies uncertainties or constraints' a Member following a precautionary approach may apply a stricter measure than another Member to address the same risk, or may decide to apply an SPS measure where another Member might decide not to do so.[179] However, the SPS measure at issue must still be 'based on' (i.e. reasonably supported by) a risk assessment.[180] In this case, the EC had not identified uncertainties or constraints in the risk assessments at issue, nor had it explained how the safeguard measures were reasonably supported by the relevant risk assessments, which were favourable to the biotech products.[181] Therefore the argument regarding the 'precautionary approach' of the relevant Member States did not persuade the Panel that this approach had been applied consistently with Article 5.1.

Although not addressing the precautionary principle as such, this finding seems to indicate a welcome openness of the Panel to interpret the obligation to base an SPS measure on a risk assessment in a manner that respects the right of Members to choose a precautionary approach in their risk management decisions. Notably, this does not mean that the existing scientific obligations of the *SPS Agreement* are overridden. Instead, in the application of these disciplines, a panel would be guided by the recognition of precaution as a legitimate risk management option and would therefore not expect as close a correlation between the SPS measure applied and the relevant risk assessment in order for the former to be 'reasonably supported' by the latter as has been the case to date. This is precisely the effect that the use of the precautionary principle as an interpretative tool in disputes under the *SPS Agreement* could have, were it to be found to have emerged as a principle of customary international law. The advantage of basing such an interpretation on a principle of international law is that a normative basis is provided for the flexibility inherent in this approach, thereby enhancing its legitimacy.

Standard of review

The question of the level of scrutiny to be applied by a panel in reviewing the scientific determination of a Member's regulatory authority, commonly termed the 'standard of review', is a key issue for the role of science as a benchmark for regulatory legitimacy. It has a significant role to play in the allocation of authority to make policy choices balancing competing trade and health interests. The particular standard of review applied determines the extent to which the WTO panels are entitled to interfere in Members' regulatory determinations. On either end of the spectrum of possible standards of review are deference to national regulatory decisions and *de novo* review, allowing the adjudicator to replace national regulatory decisions with its own assessment. The question of where on this spectrum the appropriate standard of review lies in SPS disputes is crucial to the limits of policing national regulatory choices in favour of trade liberalisation and therefore to the trade/health balance achieved in the implementation of the rules of the *SPS Agreement*. Considering the fact that SPS disputes largely turn on determinations regarding the scientific disciplines of the Agreement, the importance of ensuring that the standard of review applied reflects the balance aimed at by the Agreement cannot be overstated.

As noted by Shaffer, through its determination of the applicable standard of review, the adjudicatory body 'can effectively allocate decision making over policy matters brought before it to alternative decision-making processes, each of which favours different actors to varying extents' (Shaffer 2005: 159).[182] A deferential approach effectively allocates the competence to balance the competing interests of trade liberalisation and health protection to national authorities. This has the advantage of giving greater policy space to domestic regulators, enabling them to give effect to democratically determined preferences.[183] The application of a *de novo* standard of review would instead allocate the balancing competence to the adjudicatory body itself, replacing the regulatory choices of the national regulator with its own. While this has the benefit of incorporating the trade interests of the exporting Member, as reflected in WTO disciplines, in the balancing exercise, it creates legitimacy problems.[184] There are many subjective elements to the risk analysis process, in particular with regard to the evaluation of scientific evidence and the choice amongst equally plausible alternative risk assessments, which are best left to democratic decision-making processes. It would therefore seem that neither complete deference nor *de novo* review is the appropriate standard of review to be applied by WTO adjudicators.[185]

Despite its importance, the standard of review to be applied by panels is not explicitly addressed in the *SPS Agreement* or in the *Dispute Settlement Understanding* (*DSU*). It has therefore been elaborated in the case law. In *EC – Hormones*,[186] the question of the appropriate standard of review for SPS disputes was first dealt with. The EC in that case argued that the Panel had failed to apply the appropriate standard of review, which it asserted to be a 'deferential reasonableness standard'.[187] Instead of adopting the deferential standard proposed by the EC, the Appellate Body focused on the need to maintain the balance between the competences that WTO Members retain and those that they transferred to the WTO, as reflected in the *SPS*

Agreement itself.[188] The Appellate Body found that the standard of review applicable to 'both the ascertainment of facts and the legal characterization of such facts' in disputes under the *SPS Agreement* is to be found in Article 11 of the *DSU.* Article 11 of the *DSU* provides that 'a panel should make an objective assessment of the matter before it, including an objective assessment of the facts of the case and the applicability of and conformity with the relevant covered agreements'.[189] Examining this provision, the Appellate Body held:

> So far as fact-finding by panels is concerned, their activities are always constrained by the mandate of Article 11 of the *DSU*: the applicable standard is neither *de novo* review as such, nor 'total deference', but rather the 'objective assessment of the facts'. Many panels have in the past refused to undertake *de novo* review, wisely, since under current practice and systems, they are in any case poorly suited to engage in such a review. On the other hand, 'total deference to the findings of the national authorities', it has been well said, 'could not ensure an "objective assessment" as foreseen by Article 11 of the *DSU*'.[190]

The Appellate Body's finding that neither a panel nor the Appellate Body is authorised to change the balance of jurisdictional competences agreed to by the Members and embodied in the *SPS Agreement* is undoubtedly correct. However, it could be argued that *where* this balance lies is not always made explicit in the *SPS Agreement* and there is thus room for interpretation. The standard of review applied by a panel will have important consequences for the allocation of the authority to make policy choices balancing competing trade and health interests.[191] The extent to which a panel may examine the substantive choices made by a Member, including in its assessment of scientific evidence, is crucial in establishing the nature of this balance. An examination of previous case law shows that, while expressly recognising that their task is not to conduct their own risk assessments or impose a particular scientific view on the respondent Member,[192] panels in practice apparently do substitute their judgements for that of the respondent Member in the evaluation of scientific evidence,[193] despite their lack of 'technical expertise' in reviewing such evidence and their possible miscomprehension of the advice of the panel experts. This could lead to arbitrary results when one bears in mind the complexity of scientific evidence in the area of health and the conflicting opinions that often exist. It is therefore useful to examine the standard of review applied by the Panel in *EC – Biotech Products* to the scientific evidence before it.

An examination of the way in which the Panel addressed the claims regarding the Member States' safeguard measures under 5.7 of the *SPS Agreement* is useful in illustrating its intrusive standard of review. In examining the argument that the scientific evidence was insufficient under Article 5.7, the Panel clearly substituted its own view for that of the regulating Member. It did not limit its enquiry to the question as to whether the scientific data on which the EC based its conclusion of 'insufficiency' reasonably supported this conclusion. Instead it chose among competing scientific opinions regarding the sufficiency of the available evidence for the performance of a risk assessment. For example, in examining the safeguard measure taken by France in respect of oilseed rape MS1/RF1, the Panel gave most weight to the opinion of one of the Panel experts, Dr. Nutti. He regarded the available scientific evidence as sufficient to conduct a risk assessment, as evinced by the positive assessment of the UK's Competent Authority and the EC Scientific Committee on Plants, which had conducted the risk assessment at EC level. In doing so, it disregarded the statements of the remaining three Panel experts and the French Biomolecular Engineering Committee, all of which pointed to various insufficiencies in the available evidence.[194] Therefore the Panel clearly regarded it as its task to assess the weight to be given to the various scientific opinions before it and to come to its own scientific conclusions on that basis.

As can be seen from this discussion, in practice the Panel in *EC – Biotech Products,* like other panels addressing claims under the *SPS Agreement*, did not merely police the trade/health balance as established by the rules of the *SPS Agreement*. Instead it appropriated one of the aspects of this balance left by the Agreement in the competence of Members, namely the competence to evaluate the scientific evidence in a way that reflects the science policy choices of that Member, provided that the requirements set out in the Agreement are met.[195] Instead of reviewing the Member's assessment of the available science for compliance with the requirements of the *SPS Agreement*, the Panel directly reviewed the available science to establish its sufficiency. In doing so, it has gone further than allowed by the 'objective assessment' standard of review and has allocated to itself the competence to conduct a scientific assessment of the available data to determine its sufficiency for the purposes of the conduct of a risk assessment.[196]

Conclusion

From the above discussion, it is apparent that the practical implications of the Panel's findings for the European regime for biotech products were minimal, contrary to much of the alarmist commentary at the time. As aptly noted by a Commission spokesperson, the outcome of the Panel findings in the *EC – Biotech Products* dispute 'will not alter the system or framework within which the EU takes decisions on GMOs'.[197] None of the findings of the Panel supports the contention that WTO Members may not have in place strict regulatory systems for the premarketing approval of biotech products, provided that these systems are applied in a way that avoids undue delays.[198] In fact, the Panel carefully avoided having to rule on the scientific basis for the general *de facto* moratorium and product-specific measures maintained by the EC. The USA may have won this battle, but it seems to have lost the war.[199]

However, one should not underestimate the implications of the Panel report *outside* the context of this particular dispute. The Panel's interpretation of certain provisions of the *SPS Agreement* in the *EC – Biotech Products* dispute has potentially important consequences for future cases in this area. The Panel seems to have inadvertently threatened the delicate balance between trade and health achieved by the *SPS Agreement*. Five main concerns can be raised in this regard.

First, by extending the scope of application of the *SPS Agreement* to areas not originally envisioned to come within its ambit, the Panel has expanded the scientific disciplines to complex situations that are not appropriately dealt with under these rules. Second, in assessing the term, 'as appropriate to the circumstances', in Article 5.1, the Panel's rejection of the view that a Member may take into account as a relevant 'circumstance' the level of protection it has chosen and the uncertainties in science severely restricts the potential flexibility in this article to make provision for the inherent complexity of science. Third, the Panel's view of science as a universal and objective benchmark for regulatory legitimacy is out of touch with the current understanding of science, reflected in social science literature, as intrinsically contextual and value driven. Fourth, the Panel's interpretation of the scientific provisions of the *SPS Agreement* in a way that is divorced from the international legal context, and in particular the precautionary principle, undermines the potential for current understandings among states as to the role of science in risk regulation to inform these provisions. Fifth, the intrusive standard of review applied by the Panel in assessing the factual evidence before it to assess its sufficiency has the unfortunate consequence of placing the Panel in the shoes of the national regulator and replacing the latter's assessment with its own. This allows the Panel to cherry-pick among the various scientific views before it, including those of the Panel experts, to choose that which it considers most convincing. This role is clearly one for which the Panel, composed of trade experts, is not well suited.

In conclusion, it appears that the Panel's interpretations are not informed by social science understandings of the role of science as an instrument of regulatory justification. The Panel's findings may consequently make the disciplines of the *SPS Agreement* unworkable restrictions on the policy space of Member governments in the area of SPS regulation.

Notes

* This contribution is based on an earlier article by this author (Prévost 2007). It also draws upon this author's doctoral dissertation (Prévost 2009).

1 Panel reports, *European Communities – Measures Affecting the Approval and Marketing of Biotech Products*, WT/DS291/R, WT/DS292/R, WT/DS293/R (hereinafter Panel reports, *EC – Biotech Products*). A single Panel was established on 29 August 2003 to hear the three complaints by the USA, Argentina and Canada against the EC, and the Panel issued its three reports in a single document, comprising some common parts and some parts specific to each report. The final reports were adopted on 21 November 2006. The reports were not appealed against.

2 The complainants are among the four biggest growers of biotech crops. In 2005, the USA accounted for 55 per cent of the global area planted with biotech crops

(49.8 million hectares), Argentina for 19 per cent (17.2 million hectares) and Canada for 6 per cent (6.1 million hectares), according to the International Service for the Acquisition of Agri-biotech Applications. See 'Global Status of GM/ Biotech Crops in 2005: Executive Summary', ISAAA Briefs No. 34-2005.

3 It is useful to note that, until 30 November 2009, the European Union was formally called the 'European Communities' for the purposes of WTO matters, and that name still appears in older materials including in the Panel report in *EC – Biotech Products.* Since the entry into force of the Lisbon Treaty, however, the term European Union (EU) is used in the WTO.

4 As in the Panel reports, the terms 'biotech products' and 'genetically modified organisms' (GMOs) will be used interchangeably here.

5 The Panel reports, initially scheduled for March 2005, were delayed six times before they were finally circulated on 29 September 2006. This means that the proceedings from the time of composition of the Panel on 4 March 2004 until the issuing of the final Panel reports to the parties on 10 May 2006 took more than two years, whereas the WTO Dispute Settlement Understanding provides, in Art. 12.9, that in no case should the period from the establishment of a panel to the circulation of the Panel report to the WTO Members exceed nine months.

6 See 'U.S. Trade Representative Susan Schwab and U.S. Agriculture Secretary Mike Johanns Announce Favorable Ruling in WTO Case on Agricultural Biotechnology', Press Release, Office of the United States Trade Representative, 29 August 2006.

7 This statement was made by Adrian Bebb, campaigner on genetically modified organisms for Friends of the Earth, Europe (see 'Unyielding Stances on Biotech', *International Herald Tribune*, 9 February 2006) and was quoted in Peter Van den Bossche, 'Preliminary Conclusions of the Panel in the EC – Biotech Products Dispute: Much Ado about Very Little?', posted on the *International Law and Policy Blog*, available at *http://worldtradelaw.typepad.com/ielpblog/*, accessed 18 July 2006.

8 This statement was reported in 'Unyielding Stances on Biotech', *International Herald Tribune*, 9 February 2006 and was quoted in Peter Van den Bossche, 'Preliminary Conclusions of the Panel in the EC – Biotech Products Dispute: Much Ado about Very Little?', posted on the *International Law and Policy Blog*, available at *http://worldtradelaw.typepad.com/ielpblog/*, accessed 18 July 2006.

9 The USA has long been trying to gain acceptance of its biotech products into developing country markets. The *Guardian Unlimited* reports,

> It is now clear that the real reason the US took Europe to the WTO court was to make it easier for its companies to prise open regulatory doors in China, India, south-east Asia, Latin America and Africa, where most US exports now go. This is where millions of tonnes of US food aid heads, and where US GM companies are desperate to have access, buying up seed companies and schmoozing presidents and prime ministers.

(See 'America's Master Plan is to Force GM Food on the World', *Guardian Unlimited*, 13 February 2006.) According to Friends of the Earth, US officials stated that the EU lost this case and other countries around the world should learn the lesson. These officials claimed that the ruling 'sends an important warning to other parts of the world – particularly nations in Africa and Asia – against following the European lead in throwing up bans or partial bans against genetically modified crops'. See 'Looking Behind the US Spin: WTO Ruling does not Prevent Countries from Restricting or Banning GMOs', Friends of the Earth International Briefing Paper, February 2006. See also 'Real Impact of GMO Decision Will Be Felt in Developing Countries', *Financial Times*, 13 February 2006.

10 While the recommendations and rulings contained in adopted Panel reports are binding only on parties to the dispute, and the WTO does not have a formal precedent system, in practice, later panels follow adopted findings in previous disputes. This is due to the legitimate expectations that previously adopted reports create among WTO Members, as well as the need to ensure the security and predictability of the multilateral trading system under Art. 3.2 *Dispute Settlement Understanding* (*DSU*) (for more on this issue see Panel report, *United States – Measures Relating to Zeroing and Sunset Reviews*, WT/DS322/R, footnote 733). Thus, the relevance of the findings in this case extends beyond the present dispute.

11 Walker identifies three main categories of uncertainty in risk assessment, namely measurement uncertainty, uncertainty associated with the use of scientific models and uncertainty associated with gaps in data (Walker 1998: 258).

12 Atik states:

> In general, the science which underlies regulation, including SPS regulation, is science applied to immense complexity. The human body, the ecology of a particular locale and the interplay of social factors are all enormously complex systems, about which strong scientific assertion breaks down. Heuristics (rules-of-thumb) replace direct observation and synthesis in guiding the formation of scientific consensus and introduce the possibility of multiple outcomes.
>
> (Atik 1997: 747–748)

Stark notes that, while risk assessment was first developed by the insurance industry to determine life expectancies, it has developed into a highly sophisticated technique for establishing risks from chemicals in food and the environment. However, it is much less developed when it comes to assessing biological hazards, such as risks of the spread of exotic insect species (Stark 2000).

13 The tools used to infer risks from data that are incomplete are termed 'inference options' and provide flexibility in the risk assessment process (Motaal 2005: 495).

14 The fact that science incorporates cultural and social biases is demonstrated by the disparate scientific consensuses that exist across countries (Atik 1997: 739 and note 711).

15 For an enlightening discussion of the cultural theory of risk analysis, which posits that the principles inherent in a particular institution or organisation determines how risks are perceived, defined and managed, see Rayner 1992: 412.

16 Vern Walker notes that science policies are the guidance followed by risk assessors in their choices on how to proceed when they are faced with specific types of scientific uncertainty (Walker 2003: 211–216; Walker 1998: 304).

17 Harry Otway refers to a comparison of ten studies regarding risks to people living in proximity to liquefied natural gas terminals carried out in Germany, the UK, the Netherlands and the USA. Although the technical facilities in the studies were alike, the risks established by these studies varied over a factor of 100 million, due to the assumptions and methods used by the analysts in making their quantitative assessments (Otway 1992: 412).

18 Carolyn Raffensperger and Joel Tickner note that:

> [a] typical risk assessment relies on at least 50 different assumptions about exposure, dose-response, and relationships between humans and animals. The modelling of uncertainty also depends on assumptions. Two risk assessments conducted on the same problem can vary widely in results.
>
> (Raffensperger and Tickner 1999: 2)

19 In this respect, Cooney and Lang refer to the approach called 'post-normal science' (Cooney and Lang 2007: 530). See further Funtowicz and Ravetz 1993: 739–755;

1992: 412. These authors argue that a new conception of science is emerging to address prevailing circumstances where traditional scientific methodologies are ineffective. These are circumstances of high levels of uncertainty or high 'decision stakes' (referring to the costs, benefits and value commitments involved in the issue through various stakeholders). In such situations, the traditional methods of science of managing uncertainties automatically and, leaving values unspoken, is inappropriate. In terms of the new methodology of science, 'uncertainty is not banished but is managed, and values are not presupposed but are made explicit' (Funtowicz and Ravetz 1993: 740).

20 For an interesting discussion on the attempts to use of science and scientific committees to 'take the politics out of policy making' and thereby to legitimate regulation in the USA, see Jasanoff 1990. Jasanoff argues that:

> [t]he notion that the scientific component of decision making can be separated from the political and entrusted to independent experts has effectively been dismantled by recent contributions to the political and social studies of science. With the accumulation of evidence that 'truth' in science is inseparable from power, the idea that scientists can speak truth to power in a value-free manner has emerged as a myth without correlates in reality.
>
> (*Ibid.*, 16–17)

21 Khachatourians gives another example, namely that of rBST, a hormone used in milk production, which is banned in both Canada and the EC following expert advice that approval of a licence for the use of this hormone not be granted until the long-term effects of rBST are studied.

22 There is considerable debate on the nature of this concept between the EC, which sees it as a 'precautionary principle', and the USA, which instead regards it as a 'precautionary approach'. Nevertheless, both these Members, and many others, typically act with precaution when faced with serious, but uncertain, health risks. Catherine Button notes that; '[w]hile the US has not embraced the precautionary principle in the WTO, it would be wrong to assume that its domestic regulations are necessarily less protective than those of the EU'. She recommends moving beyond the caricature of Europeans as 'paranoid Luddites opposed to science and innovation' and of the USA as 'forward-looking and risk-taking', to a recognition that in both jurisdictions the approach taken depends on the particular health risk at stake (Button 2004: 126).

23 It is generally accepted that the origins of the precautionary principle lie in the principle of precautionary action established in German environmental law in the 1970s and 1980s (*Vorsorgeprinzip*) (Von Moltke 1996: 102). See also McIntyre and Mosedale 1997: 221. McIntyre and Mosedale cite the following: Boehmer-Christiansen 1994; and Von Moltke 1998, Appendix 3.

24 This point has been made by Alessandra Arcuri (Arcuri 2004: 16). Arcuri further notes that the prevention principle is tempered by the proportionality principle. Requiring that all risks be prevented would mean that most industrial activities (which are otherwise beneficial to society) should be banned. The proportionality principle, instead, brings in an element of cost-benefit analysis and trade-off which are part of a rational regulatory process.

25 The precautionary principle is recognised in the following international instruments amongst others: the *Treaty on the European Community*, as amended by the *Treaty on the European Union* 1992 (Art. 174, previously Art. 130r, with regard to environmental protection), the *Framework Convention on Climate Change* (1992 31 I.L.M. 849 in Art. 3.3), Agenda 21 of the *United Nations Conference on the Environment and Development* (1992, in para. 17.21), the *Rio Declaration on Environment and Development* (1992 31 I.L.M. 876 in Principle

15) and the *Cartagena Protocol on Biosafety*, UNP/157, adopted 29 January 2000, entry into force 11 September 2003, in Art. 10.5.

26 There is an extensive body of literature on the precautionary principle in environmental law, only a few examples of which are mentioned here for further information on this issue (Cameron 1999: 239–269; Cameron and Abouchar 1991; Cameron and Abouchar 1996; Coutrelis 2000: 1; Fisher 2002; Freestone and Hey 1996; Hey 1992).

27 For a law-and-economics analysis of the precautionary principle, based on a broad interpretation of scientific uncertainty that includes not only situations where the probability of a risk cannot be ascertained but also situations of ambiguity and ignorance in risk appraisals, see Wibisana 2008. Andri Wibisana notes: 'By recognizing the intrinsically subjective and political nature of risk regulations, the precautionary principle has a potential to reveal assumptions and reasons behind a particular policy or technological choice' (*Ibid.*, 295).

28 In the field of environmental protection, a convincing argument has been made by Trouwborst that the precautionary principle has evolved into a principle of customary international law, and he has conducted a thorough study into the content of the principle in this field. See Trouwborst 2006.

29 These three elements are elaborated on in detail in Trouwborst 2006.

30 This limitation is found in the formulation used in the *Rio Declaration*.

31 This implies more than a theoretical possibility of harm, but does not go as far as requiring proof of the existence and magnitude of the risk. See Trouwborst 2006: 115–117.

32 Although it is often believed that 'precaution is for Europeans' and that the USA takes a more rational, cost/benefit approach to risk regulation, due to certain widely publicised controversies regarding US criticism of precautionary European regulations, studies have shown that both the EC and the USA have highly precautionary regulatory regimes. Where they differ is on the question of which risks to prioritise as significant enough for precautionary action, and this has often led to transatlantic tensions (see Wiener 2003: 45; Rogers and Wiener 2002). An example of a precautionary approach in US food regulation can be found in its statutes on pesticide residues, food additives, colourants and veterinary drug residues. The USA takes the approach that all these substances are unsafe unless proven safe and consequently applies a premarketing approval requirement. To obtain such approval, convincing evidence must be presented to the US Food and Drug Administration that no harm will result from the intended use of the product (Walker 2003: 217–218). For a discussion of the application of the precautionary principle in the area of food and agricultural policy to avoid SPS risks, see Turvey and Mojduszka 2005.

33 An example of the use of precaution (partly) in the area of SPS risk at international level is the *Cartagena Protocol on Biosafety* to the *Convention on Biological Diversity*, UNP/157, adopted 29 January 2000, entry into force 11 September 2003. Art. 10.6 of the *Cartagena Protocol* provides:

> Lack of scientific certainty due to insufficient relevant scientific information and knowledge regarding the extent of the potential adverse effects of a living modified organism on the conservation and sustainable use of biological diversity in the Party of import, taking also into account *risks to human health*, shall not prevent that Party from taking a decision, as appropriate, with regard to the import of the living modified organism in question … to avoid or minimize such potential adverse effects (emphasis added).

34 This point was made in Peter Van den Bossche, 'Preliminary Conclusions of the Panel in the EC – Biotech Products Dispute: Much Ado about Very Little?'

posted on the *International Law and Policy Blog*, available at *http://worldtrade-law.typepad.com/ielpblog/*, accessed 18 July 2006.

35 See Panel reports, *EC – Biotech Products*, para. 8.3. The Panel noted that most of the issues it did not address were not raised by the complainants. Although the complainants did raise the question of likeness of biotech and conventional products, the Panel found it unnecessary to address this issue.

36 The only scientific issue raised was the scientific basis for the objections of some EC Member States, and it was in connection with this issue that the Panel consulted scientific experts.

37 It is interesting that the premarketing approval system itself was not challenged (as noted by the Panel more than once, see Panel reports, *EC – Biotech Products*, paras 7.1353 and 7.1693) despite the fact that such a system sits uncomfortably with the disciplines of the *SPS Agreement*. The *SPS Agreement* requires that a risk assessment must exist on which the relevant SPS measure (such as a marketing prohibition) is based. A premarketing approval system, however, prohibits the marketing of a product until such time as its safety is proven by means of a risk assessment. It can be seen as a provisional ban pending a risk assessment. However, as most countries maintain premarketing approval systems for particular products, it is possible that the Complainants wished to avoid opening this can of worms.

38 The dispute was brought before the new EC legislation came into force and therefore addressed issues arising under the old legislation. The current regime is embodied in *Regulation on Traceability and Labelling of Genetically Modified Organisms and the Traceability of Food and Feed Products Produced from Genetically Modified Organisms and Amending Directive 2001/18/EC* No. 1830/2003/EC and *Regulation on Genetically Modified Food and Feed* No. 1829/2003/EC.

39 See Panel reports, *EC – Biotech Products*, para. 7.98.

40 All three Complainants challenged the general EC moratorium.

41 Different Complainants challenged different specific measures in this category. These measures relate to approval procedures concerning 30 different biotech products.

42 Nine separate safeguard measures were taken by six EC Member States, namely Austria, France, Germany, Greece, Italy and Luxembourg. In each case, the relevant scientific committee of the EC found that there was no scientific basis for the use of the safeguard.

43 Despite the fact that these measures were taken by Member States, the EC as a whole was the responding party in respect of the challenges to these measures. This is due to the fact that the Complainants directed their complaints against the EC, and the EC did not contest that, for purposes of this dispute, the relevant Member State measures were attributable to it. See Panel reports, *EC – Biotech Products*, para. 7.101.

44 The uncontroversial issue of whether the measures 'may directly or indirectly affect international trade' was dealt with briefly. As did previous panels faced with this question, the Panel in this case noted that it is not necessary to prove that an SPS measure has an actual effect on trade, but only that it may do so. It therefore readily found that as the EC approval procedures lay down requirements for premarketing approval that also apply to imported biotech products, they may affect international trade. Further, as the procedures themselves are lengthy and impose information and documentation requirements, they may directly or indirectly affect international trade. See Panel reports, *EC – Biotech Products*, para. 7.435.

45 See Panel reports, *EC – Biotech Products*, para. 7.103.

46 The Panel briefly described the EC approval procedures in this legislation (see Panel reports, *EC – Biotech Products*, paras 7.106–7.146). For more information

regarding the EC regulatory regime for GMOs and the nature of the '*de facto* moratorium', see Prévost and Van Calster 2004 and Wüger 2006.

47 Panel reports, *EC – Biotech Products*, para. 7.103.

48 The Panel also examined the question of whether a law or a requirement contained therein could be regarded as embodying an SPS measure as well as a non-SPS measure. It found that, where two different objectives are sought by a measure embodied in a single document, one of which falls within the definition of an SPS measure and the other of which does not, there are in effect two separate measures which fall to be examined under different WTO Agreements. The Panel therefore had to determine whether the EC approval procedures are SPS measures and, if so, if they are *only* SPS measures. See Panel reports, *EC – Biotech Products*, paras 7.150–7.174.

49 See Panel reports, *EC – Biotech Products*, para. 7.149.

50 The importance of the purpose of the measure in categorising it as an SPS measure was confirmed by the Appellate Body in the later case of *Australia – Apples*. According to the Appellate Body, for a given measure to fall within the scope of the *SPS Agreement*, scrutiny of the measure's stated purpose and the text, structure and context of the measure 'must reveal a clear and objective relationship between that measure and the specific purposes enumerated in Annex A(1)(a)' (see Appellate Body report, *Australia – Measures Affecting the Importation of Apples from New Zealand*, WT/DS367/AB/R, paras 171–173).

51 See Directive 90/220, Art. 1.1, second tiret and Directive 2001/18, Art. 1, second tiret.

52 The Panel found that, as part of the Directives' purpose of protecting the environment, they addressed the protection of the health of animals and plants. Further, to the extent that they addressed environmental damage not affecting plants or animals, the Directives might fall under the objective of preventing 'other damage within the territory' in paragraph (d). Consequently, to the extent that the Directives aimed at environmental protection, they were not *a priori* excluded from the scope of application of the *SPS Agreement*. See Panel reports, *EC – Biotech Products*, paras 7.197–7.211.

53 Novel foods and food ingredients include foods and food ingredients containing or consisting of GMOs and those produced from, but not containing, GMOs.

54 These objectives are set out in Art. 3(1) of Regulation 258/97.

55 The EC had argued that GMOs could affect ecosystems without affecting animals or plants by affecting microorganisms in soil or water that are specialised in biophysical or biochemical processes. The Panel considered that the fact that a footnote to Annex A(1) clarifies that the words 'animal' and 'plant' include wild fauna and wild flora indicates that the phrase 'animal or plant life or health' is intended to be comprehensive in coverage, encompassing microorganisms and non-target organisms. See Panel reports, *EC – Biotech Products*, paras 7.219–7.220.

56 The Panel considered that the development of resistance could lead to the existing pest becoming 'established' or spreading to new areas. See Panel reports, *EC – Biotech Products*, para. 7.232.

57 See Panel reports, *EC – Biotech Products*, paras 7.241 and 7.244.

58 The EC had argued that food and beverages are things intentionally ingested by humans for nutritional purposes, and a feedstuff is something animals are intentionally permitted to ingest for nutritional purposes. The Panel, instead, held that a GM crop not grown as fodder for animals but which is nevertheless eaten by animals (including wild animals), or the pollen of which is consumed by insects, can be considered to be feedstuff. Further, it held that GM seeds intended for sowing that are spilt and eaten by birds are also animal feedstuff. See Panel reports, *EC – Biotech Products*, para. 7.292.

59 See Panel reports, *EC – Biotech Products*, paras 7.295–7.301.

60 See Panel reports, *EC – Biotech Products*, para. 7.313.

61 At issue here was the potential of GM plants to produce allergenic effects other than as foods, for example in persons working with or otherwise coming into contact with GMOs. The Panel found that pests need not be living, so that GM plants that cause harmful effects in persons handling them during harvesting, transport or processing, can be regarded as pests. See Panel reports, *EC – Biotech Products*, para. 7.351.

62 The Panel's determination to find that all the objectives of the approval legislation fell under sub-paragraphs (a)–(d) of Annex A(1) appears to be motivated by its desire to limit its examination to the *SPS Agreement*. However, it seems unnecessary to stretch the enumerated purposes of an SPS measure to cover all the objectives of the EC approval legislation, since once some objectives fall under the definition in Annex A(1), the measure is at least to that extent an SPS measure. A finding of violation of the *SPS Agreement* would still allow the Panel to use judicial economy to avoid ruling on claims of violation of other WTO agreements (as it did with regard to Regulation 258/9).

63 The EC pointed to the strong relationship between the *SPS Agreement* and these international bodies, which are expressly referred to in Annex A(3) of the *SPS Agreement* as the relevant standard-setting bodies for purposes of the harmonisation obligations in Art. 3. Further, it noted that Art. 12.3 of the *SPS Agreement* refers to the objective of securing from the relevant international organisations the best available scientific and technical advice for the administration of the *SPS Agreement* (by the SPS Committee). See Panel reports, *EC – Biotech Products*, para. 4.749.

64 See Panel reports, *EC – Biotech Products*, paras 7.19 and 7.31. The Panel consulted the parties on the choice of organisations and decided to seek information from the secretariats of the CBD (Convention on Biological Diversity), Codex, FAO (Food and Agriculture Organization), IPPC, OIE, UNEP (United Nations Environment Programme) and WHO (World Health Organization).

65 See Panel reports, *EC – Biotech Products*, para. 7.241.

66 See Panel reports, *EC – Biotech Products*, para. 7.295.

67 See Panel reports, *EC – Biotech Products*, para. 7.314.

68 See Panel reports, *EC – Biotech Products*, para. 7.276.

69 The Panel, in its findings on the relevance of other international law as evidence of the ordinary meaning of terms used in a treaty, noted that the reference materials obtained from the relevant international organisations had been 'taken into account by [the Panel] as appropriate'. See Panel reports, *EC – Biotech Products*, para. 7.96.

70 For example, the Panel noted that the IPPC definition did not support part of its interpretation of the term 'pest' but, as it did not regard the IPPC's definition as dispositive, it did not regard it as detracting from the Panel's view that plants may be considered pests even if they are not injurious to other plants (see Panel reports, *EC – Biotech Products*, para. 7.241). Likewise, the Panel, while noting that the word 'manufacture' in the Codex definition of 'additives' does not fit well with the situation where GM plants are grown for food purposes and the gene is added in the development of the seeds, preferred to rely on the dictionary definition of this term. It thus held that genes intentionally added to food for a technological purpose are to be considered 'additives in food' (see Panel reports, *EC – Biotech Products*, para. 7.301). Further, the Panel preferred to make use of the wider definition of 'disease' in the *New Shorter Oxford English Dictionary* rather than rely on that of the OIE, although it refrained from finding that GMOs are themselves diseases (see Panel reports, *EC – Biotech Products*, para. 7.277). Similarly, with regard to 'contaminants', after examining the *New Shorter Oxford English Dictionary*, the Panel agreed that intentionally added genes and the proteins produced by GM plants that are intended, are not contaminants.

However, it regarded proteins that are an unintended expression of the intentionally added genes as contaminants if they infect or pollute the food product (see Panel reports, *EC – Biotech Products*, para. 7.313).

71 Many of the definitions at issue are contained in actual 'standards' developed by the relevant organisations. While Art. 3 of the *SPS Agreement* does not oblige Members to adopt international standards, guidelines or recommendations, it provides a strong incentive for doing so by providing a presumption of conformity with the *SPS Agreement* and GATT 1994 for measures conforming to international standards and requiring that deviation be justified by means of a risk assessment (see Art. 3.1–3.3 of the *SPS Agreement*, as clarified by the Appellate Body in *EC – Hormones*, paras 173–177).

72 See Panel reports, *EC – Biotech Products*, para. 7.422.

73 As the Appellate Body held in *US – Patents*:

> The duty of a treaty interpreter is to examine the words of the treaty to determine the intentions of the parties. This should be done in accordance with the principles of treaty interpretation set out in Art. 31 of the *Vienna Convention*. But these principles of interpretation neither require nor condone the imputation into a treaty of words that are not there or the importation into a treaty of concepts that were not intended.

(See Appellate Body report, *United States Patent Protection for Pharmaceutical and Agricultural Chemical Products* WT/DS50/AB/R, adopted on 16 January 1998, paras 46–47.) This principle was reiterated in *EC – Hormones*, where the Appellate Body stated, 'The fundamental rule of treaty interpretation requires a treaty interpreter to read and interpret the words actually used by the agreement under examination, not words the interpreter may feel should have been used' (see Appellate Body report, *EC Measures Concerning Meat and Meat Products (EC – Hormones)*, WT/DS26/AB/R, WT/DS48/AB/R, adopted on 13 February 1998, para. 181).

74 The Panel regarded this illustrative list of specific SPS measures in the last part of Annex A(1) as relating only to the words 'requirements and procedures' and as setting out 'a number of substantive requirements (prescribed end-product criteria, prescribed quarantine treatments, certain packaging and labelling requirements, etc.) and procedures (testing procedures, inspection procedures, certification procedures, approval procedures, etc.)'. The Panel did note that the term 'requirements' is broad, including both an authorisation to market a particular product and a ban on marketing a particular product. See Panel reports, *EC – Biotech Products*, para. 7.1334.

75 The Panel readily found that the EC approval procedures in the relevant Directives and Regulation were SPS measures. As discussed above, the Panel interpreted the objectives laid down in sub-paragraphs (a)–(d) of Annex A(1) broadly to cover the aims of these approval procedures. As the relevant Directives and Regulation were legislative acts that were legally binding and attributable to the EC, the Panel regarded them as 'laws' meeting the 'form' requirement it had identified. Since they laid down approval procedures (as clarified in Annex C(1)), they met the Panel's 'nature' requirement (see Panel reports, *EC – Biotech Products*, paras 7.422–7.431). However, as stated above, the Complainants did not challenge the approval procedures themselves, as laid down in the Directives and Regulation, but rather the general *de facto* moratorium, the product-specific measures and the Member States' safeguard measures.

76 The Panel noted the use of the word 'include' and found that 'the reference to "laws, decrees [and] regulations" should not be taken to prescribe a particular

legal form. Rather we consider that SPS measures may in principle take a variety of legal forms'. See Panel reports, *EC – Biotech Products*, paras 7.422–423.

77 See Panel reports, *EC – Biotech Products*, para. 7.1338.

78 The Panel found that the general moratorium should be characterised as a decision to delay the decision on final approval of specific applications until certain conditions were met. It rejected the argument that the moratorium should be seen as an across-the-board marketing ban on biotech products requiring approval, and thus as a 'requirement'. The Panel correctly noted that the premarketing approval system itself imposes a provisional ban on biotech products for which approval is sought, pending the final approval decision, yet the Complainants chose not to challenge the premarketing approval system (on this point see note 15 above). The Panel also disagreed that the moratorium could be seen itself as a 'procedure' by setting out a particular mode or course of action to be followed by the Commission and Group of Five Member States delaying applications. Instead, the Panel found that the EC continued to apply its existing approval procedures, but intentionally did not make full use of these procedures to complete the approval process. See Panel reports, *EC – Biotech Products*, paras 7.1338–7.1378

79 See Panel reports, *EC – Biotech Products*, para. 7.1382.

80 See Panel reports, *EC – Biotech Products*, para. 7.1690.

81 The Panel rejected the argument that the failure to consider particular applications for final approval amounted to a ban, and was thus a 'requirement' under Annex A(1). It also disagreed with the allegation that the EC's failure to consider particular applications for final approval was in itself a 'procedure' as it modified the approval procedure with respect to the biotech product in question. See Panel reports, *EC – Biotech Products*, paras 7.1690–7.1697 (with regard to the US claim). The Panel rejected the claims of Canada and Argentina in this regard on the same reasoning (see Panel reports, *EC – Biotech Products*, paras 7.1701–7.1704 and 7.1711–17.12).

82 It should be noted that in the only SPS dispute to date decided by the Appellate Body since the Panel's findings in *EC – Biotech*, namely in the *Australia – Apples* case, the Appellate Body fortunately did not follow the *EC – Biotech* Panel's approach. It noted that the first part of the relevant sentence in the definition of SPS measures 'contains a list of legal instruments linked by the conjunction "and" (laws, decrees, regulations requirements and procedures)' and that the words 'include' and 'all relevant' 'suggest that measures of a type not expressly listed may nevertheless constitute SPS measures when they are 'relevant', that is, when they are 'applied' for a purpose that corresponds to one of those listed in subparagraphs (a) through (d). Further, it pointed out that, in the second part of that sentence, the list of measures 'covers a broad range of measures that are identified with varying degrees of specificity' and is thus 'a list of examples of measures that may fall within the definition of an SPS measure, provided always that the measure manifests a clear and objective relationship with (is 'applied' for) at least one of the purposes set out in subparagraphs (a) through (d)' (see Appellate Body report, *Australia – Apples*, paras 175–176).

83 This approach was followed in later cases, which deviated from the interpretation given by the Panel in *EC – Biotech Products*. In *Australia – Apples*, the Appellate Body regarded the definition of an SPS measure to contain a limited 'purpose' requirement, which it saw as a 'fundamental element' of the definition, and an illustrative and expansive list of 'types' of SPS measures. See Appellate Body report, *Australia – Apples*, paras 172–176.

84 Christiane Conrad argues convincingly in this regard that, in view of the fact that the *SPS Agreement* imposes stricter disciplines on health measures than those applicable under the GATT 1994 and the *TBT Agreement*, the interpretative

principle *in dubio mitius* would require an interpretation of ambiguous terms in the definition of SPS measures in a narrow way so as to limit the applicability of the *SPS Agreement* in favour of the application of the 'softer' disciplines of the GATT 1994 or *TBT Agreement* (Conrad 2006: 29–30).

85 Conrad suggests a normative approach which would recognise the existence of 'a different and possibly higher category of value' that an environmental measure seeks to protect (Conrad 2006: 18).

86 Unlike the *SPS Agreement*, environmental regimes do not limit the possibility for precautionary measures to cases of insufficient scientific evidence, but cover a broad range of situations of scientific uncertainty. For a brief discussion of the precautionary principle, see section on 'The role of science in disciplining health risk regulation'.

87 Peel points to the extensive and well-developed nature of scientific research on food safety risks and risks from quarantine pests or diseases with the potential to cause economic losses to agricultural production: 'knowledge of ecosystems interactions and other environmental problems is more often patchy' (Peel 2006: 1017).

88 This issue has been addressed in Palmer 2006; Oliva and Zarrilli 2007.

89 Gregory Jaffe has pointed out that: 'many developing countries are focusing their Biosafety systems on environmental issues surrounding release of GMOs into the environment and have not established clear pathways for the food-safety assessment and approval process surrounding GMOs' (Jaffe 2004: 191).

90 For example, a regulation on traceability and segregation of biotech products to prevent their adventitious presence in non-biotech food exports to the EC, and thereby secure access for these exports to the EC market, may be deemed, indirectly, to prevent a risk from a 'contaminant' in food if some of those food products are also sold on the domestic market. This is despite the fact that such a regulation may not be imposed to prevent food-safety risks at all, but only indirectly has that effect.

91 The requirements for a risk assessment are discussed further in the section on 'The scientific assessment of the EC Member States' safeguard measures'.

92 See Panel reports, *EC – Biotech Products*, para. 7.1387.

93 See Panel reports, *EC – Biotech Products*, paras 7.1388–7.1389. This finding was based on the somewhat tenuous argument that Art. 5.1 refers to the obligation to base an SPS measure on a risk assessment, and Art. 5.3 establishes a link between a risk assessment and the appropriate level of protection; thus, the SPS measure must be applied to achieve the appropriate level of protection. Further, Art. 5.6 requires that, when establishing or maintaining SPS measures to achieve their appropriate level of protection, Members must ensure that their measures are not more trade restrictive than required. Thus, to be an SPS measure, a measure must be applied to achieve the Member's appropriate level of protection.

94 See Panel reports, *EC – Biotech Products*, para. 7.1391.

95 See Panel reports, *EC – Biotech Products*, para. 7.1393.

96 See Panel reports, *EC – Biotech Products*, paras 7.1396–7.1448.

97 See Panel reports, *EC – Biotech Products*, para. 7.1462. Annex B(1) refers to SPS regulations, defined in a footnote to mean SPS measures such as laws, decrees or ordinances which are generally applicable.

98 The EC argued that 'undue delays' refer to a period of time lost due to inaction or inability to proceed, which is unjustifiable. It claimed that there was no general suspension of the approval process, and that, where delays occurred in individual instances due to requests for additional information, these were justified by the nature of the request. It argued that it is legitimate to request additional information necessary for the completion of a risk assessment or for compliance with certain standards of risk management or risk communication as set out by the regulator. See Panel reports, *EC – Biotech Products*, paras 4.363–4.365.

99 This must be determined on a case-by-case basis. Logically, a Member is only responsible for delays that are attributable to it (thus not for delays caused by the applicant). The Panel considered that Members applying approval procedures must be allowed to take the time reasonably needed to determine with adequate confidence that their SPS requirements are met. See Panel reports, *EC – Biotech Products*, paras 7.1496–7.1498.

100 See Panel reports, *EC – Biotech Products*, paras 7.1511–7.1530.

101 Applications for approval of Bt-11 sweet maize (food) and NK603 maize (food) were definitively granted in 2004 under Directive 2001/18 and Regulation 258/97 respectively.

102 See Panel reports, *EC – Biotech Products*, paras 7.1697–7.1700 (with regard to the US claim), paras 7.1704–7.1705 (with regard to Canada's claim) and paras 7.1712–7.1713 (with regard to Argentina's claim).

103 Since it had already found a violation of the *SPS Agreement*, the Panel exercised judicial economy with regard to the claims under the GATT and the *TBT Agreement*.

104 Austria, Belgium, France, Germany, Italy and Luxembourg.

105 Safeguard measures by individual Member States are allowed under Art. 12 of Regulation 258/97 and Art. 23 of Directive 2001/18 (a similar provision was contained in Art. 16 of Directive 90/220). These measures may only be maintained provisionally, pending a full assessment on the EC level. The safeguard is notified to the Commission, which must consult the relevant scientific committee and take a decision thereon resulting either in the modification of the EC marketing approval, or the termination of the safeguard measure. Although for each safeguard measure at issue, the relevant scientific committee reaffirmed its previous assessment, or that of another EC committee, that the biotech products at issue presented no risk to health or the environment, no decision was taken at the EC level in this regard. The EC asserts that the Commission called upon all six Member States to withdraw their safeguard measures. However, the Member States have not done so and the Commission did not use the power given to it under Art. 226 of the EC Treaty to initiate enforcement proceedings against these Member States.

106 The Panel noted that, since Annex A(1) refers to the purposes for which an SPS measure is 'applied', it could consider not only the objectives for which the measures were adopted, but also those for which they were maintained. It further held that it was not barred from considering purposes that were not articulated by the Member States when adopting the safeguard measures. It referred to the Appellate Body's findings (in *Japan – Alcoholic Beverages II*, pp. 27–28 and *US – Offset Act (Byrd Amendment)* para. 259) that panels need not seek the subjective intent of the legislators/regulators but should determine the purpose of a measure on the basis of objective considerations, such as the structure of the measure and the objective relationship between the stated objectives and the text of the measure. See Panel reports, *EC – Biotech Products*, para. 7.2558. After identifying the objectives of each safeguard measure, the Panel applied the same broad interpretation to Annex A(1) (a)–(d) to find that the objectives of each safeguard measure fell thereunder. It further found that the measures met the form and nature requirements it had read into Annex A(1). The Panel held that the form requirement allows SPS measures to take many legal forms, and the nature requirement is met, as the prohibition on the marketing of a product can be considered a 'requirement'.

107 Panel reports, *EC – Biotech Products*, para. 7.3396.

108 The citation referred to by Peel comes from Horn and Weiler 2003.

109 See section on 'The role of science in disciplining health risk regulation'.

110 This three-pronged test was set out by the Panel and endorsed by the Appellate Body in *Australia – Salmon*. See Appellate Body report, *Australia – Salmon*,

para. 121. The test was confirmed in Appellate Body report, *Japan – Agricultural Products*, para. 113 and used again in Panel report, *Australia – Salmon* (*Art. 21.5 – Canada*), para. 7.41.

111 These requirements are generalised on the basis of the findings of the Panel in *EC – Hormones* as modified by the Appellate Body in that case. Panel report, *EC – Hormones (Canada)*, para. 8.101; Panel report, *EC – Hormones (US)*, para. 8.98; and Appellate Body report, *EC – Hormones*, paras 184–186.

112 This issue is discussed in more detail below.

113 Appellate Body report, *EC – Hormones*, paras 184–186; Appellate Body report, *Australia – Salmon*, paras 123–124.

114 The study by Hoppichler, entitled 'Concepts of GMO-free Environmentally Sensitive Areas', was commissioned by the Austrian Federal Ministry of Women's Affairs and Consumer Protection.

115 The first definition of a risk assessment was at issue to the extent that Austria's measure was aimed at addressing concerns regarding the spread of pollen to surrounding cultivated fields, long-term ecological consequences and the development of resistance to toxins in insects. Panel reports, *EC – Biotech Products*, para. 7.3039.

116 *Ibid.*, para. 7.3044.

117 *Ibid.*, para. 7.3046.

118 The lack of an evaluation of likelihood or probability was identified as a defect in the scientific studies relied upon in respect of several other safeguard measures to which the first definition of a risk assessment applied. See for example *Ibid.*, paras 7.3078 (with regard to Austria's measure on Bt-176 maize), 7.3094 and 7.3098 (with regard to Austria's measure on MON810 maize), paras 7.3145 and 7.3151 (with regard to Germany's measure on Bt-176 maize), para. 7.3170 (with regard to Greece's measure on Topas oilseed rape), para. 7.3186 (with regard to Italy's measure onT25 maize, MON810 maize, MON809 maize and Bt-11 maize) and para. 7.3205 (with regard to Luxembourg's measure on Bt-176 maize). Other flaws in the scientific studies relied upon were also identified by the Panel in rejecting these studies as proper 'risk assessments'. For example, some of the studies relied upon by the Member States as risk assessments did not meet the requirement that they 'evaluate the likelihood of entry, establishment or spread of a pest or disease … and of the associated biological and economic consequences' laid down in the definition of a risk assessment in Annex A(4) of the *SPS Agreement*. See for example on Germany's safeguard measure on Bt-176 maize, Panel reports, *EC – Biotech Products*, paras 7.3145 and 7.3151.

119 Panel reports, *EC – Biotech Products*, para. 7.3244.

120 *Ibid.*

121 The lead Competent Authorities were the authorities of the Member State to which the application for approval of the relevant biotech product was originally submitted.

122 Panel reports, *EC – Biotech Products*, paras 7.3012–7.3013.

123 *Ibid.*, para. 7.3015.

124 *Ibid.*, para. 7.3027. The Panel agreed with the parties on this point.

125 This question was addressed with regard to each of the safeguard measures at issue. However, as the same arguments were presented by the EC in this regard, the Panel addressed the arguments in respect of the first safeguard measure that it addressed, Austria's ban on T25 maize, and referred back to these findings, *mutatis mutandis*, in its analysis of the other safeguard measures.

126 Panel reports, *EC – Biotech Products*, para. 7.3067.

127 *Ibid.*, para. 7.3064.

128 *Ibid.*, para. 7.3065. In these cases, the Panel held that the Member might decide to apply an SPS measure even if another Member might not do so on the basis

of the same risk assessment; or it might decided to apply a stricter SPS measure than that applied by another Member to address the same risk.

129 Panel reports, *EC – Biotech Products*, para. 7.3067.

130 Appellate Body report, *EC – Hormones*, 194.

131 Panel reports, *EC – Biotech Products*, para. 7.3067.

132 Appellate Body report, *EC – Hormones*, para. 193.

133 Panel report, *EC – Biotech Products*, para. 7.3062.

134 At issue here was the safeguard measure imposed by Austria with respect to T25 maize, which was adopted in disregard of the risk assessment conducted by the EC Scientific Committee on Plants and that conducted by the lead Competent Authority.

135 Panel reports, *EC – Biotech Products*, para. 7.3066.

136 *Ibid.*, para. 7.3067.

137 The Panel noted that the provisional adoption of an SPS measure is not a precondition for the application of Art. 5.7. Instead, the provisional adoption of an SPS measure is permitted by the first sentence of Art. 5.7 (if certain conditions are met). See Panel reports, *EC – Biotech Products*, para. 7.2939.

138 Appellate Body report, *Japan – Apples*, para. 179.

139 Appellate Body report, *European Communities – Conditions for the Granting of Tariff Preferences to Developing Countries* (*EC – Tariff Preferences*), WT/DS246/AB/R, adopted on 20 April 2004, para. 88.

140 See Panel reports, *EC – Biotech Products*, paras 7.2969 and 7.2976. This finding is contrary to the finding of the Panel in *Japan – Apples*, which held that the burden of proof under Art. 5.7 is on the respondent. The Appellate Body in that case noted that this finding was not appealed against, which the Panel in *EC – Biotech Products* took as expressing the Appellate Body's reservation with regard to this allocation of the burden of proof (see Panel reports, *EC – Biotech Products*, para. 7.2979). For a thoughtful look at the burden of proof issue, See Grando 2006.

141 This finding makes it rather strange that the Panel then started its analysis with examining whether Art. 5.1 was violated, rather than first determining whether the requirements of Art. 5.7 were met, in which case Art. 5.1 would not be applicable. See Panel reports, *EC – Biotech Products*, para. 7.3007.

142 This finding is contrary to the finding of the Panel in *Japan – Apples*, which held that the burden of proof under Art. 5.7 is on the respondent. The Appellate Body in that case noted that this finding was not appealed against, which the Panel in *EC – Biotech Products* took as expressing the Appellate Body's reservation with regard to this allocation of the burden of proof (see Panel reports, *EC – Biotech Products*, para. 7.2979). For a thoughtful look at the burden of proof issue, see Grando 2006.

143 Already in *Japan – Agricultural Products II*, the Appellate Body had rejected Japan's argument that an SPS measure that is adopted in conformity with the requirements of the first sentence of Art. 5.7 (i.e. in a situation of 'insufficient' scientific evidence and on the basis of available pertinent information), is automatically freed from the requirements of Art. 2.2 and can only be tested against the obligations of Art. 5.7. It disagreed with Japan that the words 'except as provided for in Art. 5.7' in Art. 2.2 refer only to the first sentence of Art. 5.7, holding that the text of Art. 2.2 does not support this proposition as it refers to Art. 5.7 as a whole. Appellate Body report, *Japan – Agricultural Products II*, para. 90.

144 Panel reports, *EC – Biotech Products*, para. 7.2975.

145 Panel reports, *EC – Biotech Products*, para. 7.2998.

146 See Panel reports, *EC – Biotech Products*, para. 7.3239. In addition, the Panel held that the insufficiency of the scientific evidence must be assessed at the time when the provisional measure was adopted. See Panel reports, *EC – Biotech Products*, para. 7.3253.

147 Panel reports, *EC – Approval and Marketing of Biotech Products*, para. 7.3238. This finding was cited and followed in Panel report, *US – Continued Suspension*, para. 7.609; Panel report, *Canada – Continued Suspension*, para. 7.587.

148 See in this regard Gruszczynski 2008: 117–123.

149 As noted by Winickoff *et al.*, 'evidence deemed reliable enough to generate a sufficient risk assessment in one regulatory context may fail in other contexts because of the different concerns, risk frames and particular circumstances' (Winickoff *et al.* 2005: 114).

150 The Commission initiated separate cases against Austria, France, Luxembourg and Germany for refusing to lift bans on gene-altered products, including Switzerland-based Syngenta AG's Bt11 pest-resistant corn. In the meantime, Austria appealed against a European Court of Justice ruling against the country's planting ban, and Greece was resisting a Commission order to allow for sowing Monsanto's MON810 corn, which was approved before 1998.

151 This letter is appended to the Panel report in *EC – Biotech Products* as Annex K.

152 Appellate Body report, *EC – Hormones*, para. 124.

153 The Cartagena Protocol on Biosafety is a protocol to the UN Convention on Biological Diversity. It currently has 135 contracting parties (as of 5 October 2006).

154 See Panel reports, *EC – Biotech Products*, para. 7.55.

155 See Panel reports, *EC – Biotech Products*, para. 7.69. The Panel pointed out that, although this obligation is limited to taking account of other international law rules and no particular outcome is prescribed, the principle of good faith would require that where more than one interpretation is possible, the treaty interpreter applying Art. 31.3(c) of the VCLT must choose the alternative that is more in accord with the other rules of international law.

156 See Panel reports, *EC – Biotech Products*, para. 7.70.

157 See Panel reports, *EC – Biotech Products*, para. 7.67.

158 The Panel here referred to the finding of the Appellate Body in *US – Shrimp*, WT/DS58/AB/R, para. 158 and note 157.

159 See Panel reports, *EC – Biotech Products*, para. 7.67.

160 See Panel reports, *EC – Biotech Products*, para. 7.68.

161 See Panel reports, *EC – Biotech Products*, para. 7.67. To support its finding, the Panel noted that Art. 31.3(c) does not refer to 'one or more parties' or 'the parties to the dispute'. Further, it pointed to the definition of 'party' in Art. 2.1(g) of the VCLT as 'a State that has consented to be bound by the treaty and for which the treaty is in force' and derived from this definition the conclusion that 'parties' in Art. 31.3(c) refers to states which have consented to be bound by the treaty that is being interpreted and for which that treaty is in force.

162 The USA signed the CBD in 1993 but never ratified it.

163 Although the Panel limited its examination to the four parties to this dispute, this should not give the impression that it had departed from its view that the other rules of international law must be applicable to *all* WTO Members. Instead, the Panel stated that, if a rule of international law is not applicable to one of the four parties to this dispute, it is not applicable to the relations between all WTO Members. Thus, although the Panel declined to take a position on this, it appears that even if the relevant international law rules raised in this dispute had been applicable to all four parties, but had not been applicable to another WTO Member, they would still not have to be taken into account by the Panel under Art. 31.3(c) of the VCLT. See Panel reports, *EC – Biotech Products*, paras 7.71–7.72.

164 International Law Commission, 58th Session, *Fragmentation of International Law: Difficulties Arising from the Diversification and Expansion of International Law*, Report of the Study Group of the International Law Commission, finalised

by Martti Koskenniemi, A/CN.4/L.682, 13 April 2006. This report contains an analytical study finalised by the Chairman of the ILC Study Group. A set of 42 conclusions adopted by the Study Group is published separately as an appendix. The ILC took note of the conclusions and commended them to the UN General Assembly. The Study Group emphasised that conclusions are based on the analytical study and must be read together with it. It is interesting that this report expressly addresses the findings of the Panel in *EC – Biotech Products* although at that stage only the interim Panel report had been issued and was officially confidential.

165 International Law Commission, 58th Session, *Fragmentation of International Law: Difficulties Arising from the Diversification and Expansion of International Law*, Report of the Study Group of the International Law Commission, finalised by Martti Koskenniemi, A/CN.4/L.682, 13 April 2006, para. 471 (footnote omitted).

166 International Law Commission, 58th Session, *Fragmentation of International Law: Difficulties Arising from the Diversification and Expansion of International Law*, Report of the Study Group of the International Law Commission, finalised by Martti Koskenniemi, A/CN.4/L.682, 13 April 2006, para. 472. Here the ILC refers to the approach taken in Appellate Body report, *US – Shrimp*, WT/DS58/AB/R, para. 130.

167 These conclusions are contained in the following document: International Law Commission, 58th Session, *Fragmentation of International Law: Difficulties Arising from the Diversification and Expansion of International Law*, Report of the Study Group of the International Law Commission, A/CN.4/L.702, 18 July 2006, para. 21.

168 This finding reiterates that of the Appellate Body in *US – Gasoline.* See Appellate Body report, *United States – Standards for Reformulated and Conventional Gasoline,* WT/DS2/AB/R, adopted on 20 May 1996.

169 The Appellate Body was interpreting the term 'exhaustible natural resources', which it regarded as by definition evolutionary, necessitating regard to modern environmental treaties. See Appellate Body report, *United States – Import Prohibition of Certain Shrimp and Shrimp Products (US – Shrimp)*, WT/DS58/AB/R, adopted 6 November 1998, paras 129–130.

170 It is interesting that in *US – Shrimp*, the Appellate Body referred to the CBD in support of the arguments of the USA, which had itself neither signed nor ratified that convention.

171 See Panel reports, *EC – Biotech Products*, para. 7.94.

172 See Panel reports, *EC – Biotech Products*, paras 7.92–7.93.

173 The Panel stated that it 'did not find it necessary or appropriate' to rely on the CBD or Cartagena Protocol in interpreting the WTO agreements at issue. See Panel reports, *EC – Biotech Products*, para. 7.95.

174 The EC pointed to several international instruments incorporating the precautionary principle and noted that the approval systems in many countries are based on the need to take precautionary action. See Panel reports, *EC – Biotech Products*, para. 7.78.

175 Appellate Body report, *EC – Hormones*, para. 121, cited in Panel reports, *EC – Biotech Products*, para. 7.87.

176 See Panel reports, *EC – Biotech Products*, para. 7.89. According to the Panel, it was not necessary for it to take a position on the question of whether the precautionary principle is a recognised principle of general or customary international law, in order for it to dispose of the legal claims before it.

177 Panel reports, *EC – Biotech Products*, para. 7.3065.

178 *Ibid.*

179 *Ibid.*

180 *Ibid.*

181 *Ibid.*, para. 7.3066.

182 Shaffer analyses the *US – Shrimp* dispute and identifies five different options for the standard of review that could have been applied. These overlap to some extent with some of the discussion below.

183 Shaffer notes that participation in democratic decision-making is of a higher quality at national level than at international level due to the closer relation between the citizen and the state, the sense of a common identity and communal cohesiveness, and the reduced costs of organisation and participation (*Ibid.*, 143).

184 In respect of the *US – Shrimp* dispute, involving a conflict between trade and environmental objectives, Shaffer notes that the Appellate Body was

> reluctant to allocate substantive decision-making authority to itself due to the realisation that it lacked the legitimacy to engage in a delicate balancing of the priorities of constituencies from countries of widely disparate levels of development under open-ended standards. Although, as any court, WTO judicial bodies are not elected, they are even more subject to legitimacy challenges than domestic courts because of the more fragile social acceptance of their decisions.
>
> (Shaffer 2005: 153)

185 Some have suggested that, instead, a process-based review would be best, limited to establishing whether the procedural requirements have been complied with. See for example Cooney and Lang 2007: 544. Cooney and Lang advocate procedural rather than substantive review, not primarily to ensure against interference with democratic decisions at national level but rather in order to use the trade regime in a positive way to facilitate and encourage appropriate governance frameworks on national level by promoting transparent, accountable and reasoned use of science and risk assessment. However, as the *SPS Agreement* does not lay down procedures for the conduct of a risk assessment or the establishment of sufficient scientific evidence, such a limited review seems inappropriate. See on this point Ehlermann and Lockhart 2003: 291. These authors note that, while the *SPS Agreement* identifies the substantive issues to be considered in a risk assessment, it does not lay down procedures for how the risk assessment is to be conducted. There is no requirement to carry out an investigation, engage in formal fact finding or publish a report explaining the justification for the SPS measure adopted. See further on this point Button 2004: 182–185.

186 Appellate Body report, *EC – Hormones*, para. 133.

187 According to the EC, which based its argument on the standard of review set out in the WTO's *Anti-Dumping Agreement*, under such a standard, the Panel should not interfere in the investigation conducted at national level which led to the establishment of the measure. If the Member has properly established the facts and conducted an objective, unbiased examination thereof, its conclusions should be deferred to by the Panel, even if it would have come to a different conclusion on the facts. Instead, the EC argued that the Panel had undertaken a *de novo* standard of review, under which it has complete freedom to examine the factual and procedural validity of the decision and to come to a different conclusion.

188 Appellate Body report, *EC – Hormones*, para. 115.

189 The utility of this 'objective assessment' standard has been criticised on the grounds that it far from clarifies the required standard of review. See Desmedt 1998: 698. See also Palmeter 2006: 229.

190 Appellate Body report, *EC – Hormones*, para. 117. A footnote to this sentence refers to Panel report on *US – Underwear*, para. 7.10.

191 Natalie McNelis argues that, regardless of the expressed terminology for the standard of review to be applied by an adjudicator, the real standard of review is

determined by the relationship between the adjudicator and the actor that is judged (as reflected by the different standards of review applied when WTO adjudicators judge the acts of WTO Members, when the ECJ judges an act of a European institution and when the ECJ judges an act of an EU Member State). She cautions that, as the WTO adjudicators do not have the same legitimacy with regard to WTO Members as the ECJ has with regard to EU Member States, WTO adjudicators should be less interventionist in reviewing health measures or will risk strident opposition from citizens (McNelis 2003: 234 and 237–239).

192 See, for example, Panel report, *EC – Hormones (Canada)*, para. 8.104; Panel report, *EC – Hormones (US)*, para. 8.101; Panel report, *Japan – Agricultural Products II*, para. 8.32; Panel report, *Australia – Salmon*, para. 8.126; Panel report, *US – Continued Suspension*, para. 7.443; and Panel report, *Canada – Continued Suspension*, para. 7.432.

193 See, for example, Panel report, *Japan – Agricultural Products II*, para. 7.10; Panel report, *Japan – Apples*, paras 8.123–8,128; Panel report, *Japan – Apples (Art. 21.5 – US)*, paras 8.140–8.144; Panel report, *US – Continued Suspension*, para. 7.538; and Panel report, *Canada – Continued Suspension*, para. 7.510.

194 One Panel expert, Dr Andow, regarded the evidence on pollen dispersal as insufficient to assess accurately the probability of such dispersal. He also viewed the assessment of the risk of the development of resistance in weeds and the data on non-target effects as insufficient. Another Panel expert, Dr Snow, also noted the insufficiency and noted that there were valid reasons for France to conduct further research to supplement existing data. A further expert, Dr Squire, confirmed the insufficiency of knowledge to predict accurately the rate and spread of pollination from genetically modified rapeseed to non-genetically modified rapeseed. This was reiterated by the Biomolecular Engineering Committee of France. See *EC – Biotech Products*, Annex H, paras 780–791.

195 On the subjective elements inherent to a risk assessment that reflect science policy choices, see section on 'The role of science in disciplining health risk regulation'.

196 The issue of the standard of review that a panel must apply when reviewing a risk assessment under Art. 5.1 of the *SPS Agreement* was addressed by the Appellate Body in *US/Canada – Continued Suspension*, where it identified two aspects of a panel's scrutiny of a risk assessment. These are: 1) scrutiny of the underlying scientific basis; and 2) scrutiny of the reasoning of the risk assessor based upon such underlying science. In the former, the Appellate Body saw the panel's role as limited to reviewing whether the scientific basis constitutes 'legitimate science according to the standards of the relevant scientific community'. The latter aspect of a panel's review was held by the Appellate Body to involve an assessment of whether the reasoning of the risk assessor is objective and coherent, that is, whether the conclusions find sufficient support in the scientific evidence relied upon. Thus a different standard applies to the two aspects of the risk assessment (see Appellate Body reports, *US/Canada – Continued Suspension of Obligations in the EC – Hormones Dispute*, WT/DS320 & 321/AB/R, adopted 14 November 2008, para. 591, as referred to in Appellate Body report, *Australia – Apples*, para. 215).

197 This statement was made by Commission trade spokesman Peter Power and quoted in Peter Van den Bossche, 'Preliminary Conclusions of the Panel in the EC – Biotech Products Dispute: Much Ado about Very Little?', posted on the *International Law and Policy Blog*, available at http://worldtradelaw.typepad.com/ielpblog, accessed 18 July 2006.

198 It is important to be accurate in identifying the practical implications of the Panel's findings. Misleading and alarmist comments on the outcome of this dispute are counterproductive and may serve to dissuade developing countries from having in place regulatory systems for biotech products. This would be regrettable and

would have a negative impact on their ability to access the EC market for their agricultural products.

199 In addition, a subsequent challenge to the current EC legislation on traceability and labelling of GMOs and on GM food and feed may be brought and perhaps decided on more substantive grounds.

References

Arcuri, A. (2004) 'The Case for a Procedural Version of the Precautionary Principle Erring on the Side of Environmental Preservation', Global Law Working Paper 09/04, New York, Hauser Global Law School, available at: www.nyulawglobal.org/workingpapers/documents/GLWP0904Arcuri.pdf, accessed on 12 May 2005.

Atik, J. (1997) 'Symposium – Institutions for International Economic Integration: Science and International Regulatory Convergence', *Journal of International Law and Business*, 17: 736–758.

Barrieu, P. and Sinclair-Desgagne, B. (2003) *The Paradox of Precaution*, Montreal: CIRANO, available at: www.cirano.qc.ca/pdf/publication/2003s-63.pdf, accessed on 15 June 2004.

Boehmer-Christiansen, S. (1994) 'The Precautionary Principle in Germany – Enabling Government', in T. O'Riordan and J. Cameron (eds), *Interpreting the Precautionary Principle*, London: Cameron May, pp. 31–60.

Button, C. (2004) *The Power to Protect. Trade, Health and Uncertainty in the WTO*, Oxford/Portland, OR: Hart Publishing.

Cameron, J. (1999) 'The Precautionary Principle', in G.P. Sampson and W. Bradnee Chambers (eds), *Trade, Environment, and the Millennium*, Tokyo: United Nations University Press, pp. 239–269.

Cameron, J. and Abouchar, J. (1991) 'The Precautionary Principle: A Fundamental Principle of Law and Policy for the Protection of the Global Environment', *Boston College International and Comparative Law Review*, 14(1): 1–27.

——(1996) 'The Status of the Precautionary Principle in International Law', in D. Freestone and E. Hey (eds), *The Precautionary Principle and International Law: The Challenge of Implementation*, The Hague/London/Boston, MA: Kluwer Law International, pp. 29–52.

Conrad, C.R. (2006) 'PPMs, the EC – Biotech Dispute and Applicability of the SPS Agreement: Are the Panel's Findings Built on Shaky Ground?', Research Paper No. 8-06 (International Law Forum of the Hebrew University of Jerusalem, Jerusalem), August, 29–30, available at: http://papers.ssrn.com/sol3/papers.cfm?abstract_id =920742#PaperDownload, accessed on 12 May 2008.

Cooney, R. and Lang, A.T.F. (2007) 'Taking Uncertainty Seriously: Adaptive Governance and International Trade', *European Journal of International Law*, 18(3): 523–551.

Coutrelis, N. (2000) 'Le Principe de Précaution: Aspects Juridiques', *Revue de l'Actualité Juridique Française*, 16 May.

Craddock, N. (2001) 'Risk, Precaution, and the Food Business', in P.W.B. Phillips and R. Wolfe (eds), *Governing Food: Science, Safety and Trade*, Montreal: McGill-Queen's University Press, pp. 75–88.

Cross, F.B. (1996) 'Paradoxical Perils of the Precautionary Principle', *Wash & Lee Law Review*, 53(3): 851–925.

De Sadeleer, N. (2002) *Environmental Principles: From Political Slogans to Legal Rules*, Oxford: Oxford University Press.

Desmedt, A.G. (1998) 'Hormones: "Objective Assessment" and (or as) Standard of Review', *Journal of International Economic Law*, 1(4): 695–698.

Ehlermann, C.-D. and Lockhart, N. (2003) 'Standard of Review in WTO Law', in M. Hoskins and W. Robinson (eds), *A True European: Essays for Judge David Edwards*, Portland, OR: Hart Publishing, pp. 267–296.

Fisher, E. (2002) 'Precaution, Precaution Everywhere: Developing a Common Understanding of the Precautionary Principle in the European Community', *Maastricht Journal of European and Comparative Law*, 9(1): 7–28.

Freestone, D. (1994) 'The Road to Rio: International Environmental Law after the Earth Summit', *Journal of Environmental Law*, 6: 193–218.

Freestone, D. and Hey, E. (1996) 'Implementing the Precautionary Principle: Challenges and Opportunities', in D. Freestone and E. Hey (eds), *The Precautionary Principle and International Law: The Challenge of Implementation*, The Hague/London/Boston, MA: Kluwer Law International, pp. 249–268.

Funtowicz, S.O. and Ravetz, J.R. (1992) 'Three Types of Risk Assessment and the Emergence of Post-Normal Science', in S. Krimsky and D. Golding (eds), *Social Theories of Risk*, Westport, CT: Praeger, pp. 251–273.

——(1993) 'Science for the Post-Normal Age', *Futures*, 25(7): 739–755.

Grando, M.T. (2006) 'Allocating Burden of Proof in WTO Disputes: A Critical Analysis', *Journal of International Economic Law*, 9(3): 615–658.

Green, A. and Epps, T. (2007) 'The WTO, Science, and the Environment: Moving Towards Consistency', *Journal of International Economic Law*, 10(2): 285–316.

Gruszczynski, L. (2008) 'SPS Measures Adopted in Case of Insufficiency of Scientific Evidence: Where do we stand after the EC – Biotech Products case?', in J. Chaisse and T. Balmelli (eds), *Essays on the Future of the World Trade Organization*, Vol. II, London: Cameron May, pp. 91–140.

Hey, E. (1992) 'The Precautionary Concept in Environmental Policy and Law: Institutionalizing Caution', *Georgetown International Environmental Law Review*, 4: 303–318.

Horn, H. and Weiler, J.H.H. (2003) 'European Communities – Trade Description of Sardines: Textualism and Its Discontent', *The WTO Case Law of 2002: The American Law Institute Reporter's Studies*, 1: 248–275.

Howse, R. (2000) 'Democracy, Science, and Free Trade: Risk Regulation on Trial at the World Trade Organization', *Michigan Law Review*, 98: 2329–2357.

Jaffe, G. (2004) 'Biosafety Regulation in the North and South', in *Proceedings of the Eighth International Symposium on the Biosafety of Genetically Modified Organisms*, Montpellier: International Society for Biosafety Research, pp. 190–194, available at: www.isbr.info/symposia/docs/proceedings_montpellier2004.pdf, accessed on 19 May 2008.

Jasanoff, S. (1990) *The Fifth Branch: The Science Advisers as Policymakers*, Cambridge, MA/London: Harvard University Press.

Joerges, Chr. (1997) 'Scientific Expertise in Social Regulation and the European Court of Justice: Legal Frameworks for Denationalized Governance Structures', in Chr. Joerges *et al.* (eds), *Integrating Scientific Expertise into Regulatory Decision-Making: National Traditions and European Innovations*, Baden-Baden: Nomos, pp. 295–323.

Khachatourians, G.G. (2001) 'How Well Understood is the "Science" of Food Safety?', in P.W.B Phillips and R. Wolfe (eds), *Governing Food: Science, Safety and Trade*, Montreal: McGill-Queen's University Press, pp. 13–23.

Lang, A.T.F. (2008) 'Provisional Measures under Article 5.7 of the WTO's Agreement on Sanitary and Phytosanitary Measures: Some Criticisms of the Jurisprudence So Far', LSE Legal Studies Working Paper No. 11/2008 (London School of Economics,

London), 30 June, 8, available at: http://ssrn.com/abstract=1153660, accessed on 18 August 2008.

McIntyre, O. and Mosedale, Th. (1997) 'The Precautionary Principle as a Norm of Customary International Law', *Journal of Environmental Law*, 9(2): 221–241.

McNelis, N. (2003) 'The Role of the Judge in the EU and WTO: Lessons from the BSE and Hormones Cases', in T. Cottier and P.C. Mavroidis (eds), *The Role of the Judge in International Trade Regulation: Experience and Lessons for the WTO*, Ann Arbor, MI: University of Michigan Press, pp. 225–246.

Motaal, D.A. (2004) 'The "Multilateral Scientific Consensus" and the World Trade Organisation', *Journal of World Trade*, 38(5): 855–876.

——(2005) 'Is the World Trade Organization Anti-Precaution?', *Journal of World Trade*, 39(3): 483–501.

Oliva, M.J. and Zarrilli, S. (2007) *WTO Panel Report on The 'EC – Biotech' Case: Considerations for Trade and Development*, TD/B.COM.1/CRP.4 (Trade and Development Board, Commission on Trade in Goods and Services, and Commodities, Geneva), 19–23 March.

Otway, H. (1992) 'Public Wisdom, Expert Flexibility: Toward a Contextual Theory of Risk', in S. Krimsky and D. Golding (eds), *Social Theories of Risk*, Westport, CT: Praeger, pp. 215–228.

Palmer, A. (2006) *The WTO GMO Dispute: Implications for Developing Countries and the Need for an Appeal* (GeneWatch UK, The RSPB, Forum for Biotechnology and Food Security and the GM Freeze, Buxton), available at: www.genewatch.org/uploads/f03c6d66a9b354535738483c1c3d49e4/WTO_Biotech_case_dcsummaryfinal_1.pdf, accessed on 19 May 2008.

Palmeter, D. (2006) 'The WTO Standard of Review in Health and Safety', in G.A. Bermann and P.C. Mavroidis (eds), *Trade and Human Health and Safety*, Cambridge: Cambridge University Press, pp. 224–234.

Peel, J. (2004) 'Risk Regulation under the WTO SPS Agreement: Science as an International Normative Yardstick?', Jean Monnet Working Paper 02/04 (NYU School of Law, New York), June, 57, available at: www.jeanmonnetprogram.org/papers/04/040201.pdf, accessed on 14 September 2004.

——(2006) 'A GMO by Any Other Name … Might Be an SPS Risk! Implications of Expanding the Scope of the WTO Sanitary and Phytosanitary Measures Agreement', *European Journal of International Law*, 17(5): 1009–1031.

Phillips, P.W.B. (2001) 'Food Safety, Trade Policy and International Institutions', in P.W.B Phillips and R. Wolfe (eds), *Governing Food: Science, Safety and Trade*, Montreal: McGill-Queen's University Press, pp. 27–48.

Prévost, D. (2007) 'Opening Pandora's Box: The Panel's Findings in the EC – Biotech Products Dispute', *Legal Issues of Economic Integration*, 34(1): 67–101.

——(2009) *Balancing Trade and Health in the SPS Agreement: The Development Dimension*, Nijmegen: Wolf Legal Publishers.

Prévost, D. and Van Calster, G. (2004) 'The EU Legislation Regarding GMOs and its Implications for Trade', in OECD, *Challenges and Risks of Genetically Engineered Organisms*, pp. 51–59.

Raffensperger, C. and Tickner, J. (1999) 'To Foresee and to Forestall', in C. Raffensperger and J. Tickner (eds), *Protecting Public Health and the Environment: Implementing the Precautionary Principle*, Washington, DC: Island Press, pp. 1–12.

Rayner, S. (1992) 'Cultural Theory and Risk Analysis', in S. Krimsky and D. Golding (eds), *Social Theories of Risk*, Westport, CT: Praeger, pp. 83–115.

Rogers, M.D. and Wiener, J.B. (2002) 'Comparing Precaution in the United States and Europe', *Journal of Risk Research*, 5(4): 317–349.

Shaffer, G. (2004) 'Recognizing Public Goods in WTO Dispute Settlement: Who Participates? Who Decides?', *Journal of International Economic Law*, 7: 459–482.

——(2005) 'Power, Governance, and the WTO: A Comparative Institutional Approach', in M. Barnett and R. Duvall (eds), *Power in Global Governance*, Cambridge: Cambridge University Press, pp. 130–160.

Stark, J.D. (2000) 'An Overview of Risk Assessment', in National Research Council Board on Agriculture and Natural Resources (ed.), *Incorporating Science, Economics, and Sociology in Developing Sanitary and Phytosanitary Standards in International Trade: Proceedings of a Conference*, Washington, DC: National Academy Press, pp. 51–64, available at: www.nap.edu/openbook/0309070902/html/199.html, accessed on 25 June 2007.

Trouwborst, A. (2002) *Evolution and Status of the Precautionary Principle in International Law*, The Hague/Boston, MA/London: Kluwer Law International.

——(2006) *Precautionary Rights and Duties of States*, Doctoral Thesis, Utrecht University, Faculty of Law, Leiden/Boston, MA: Martinus Nijhoff Publishers.

Turvey, C.G. and Mojduszka, E.M. (2005) 'The Precautionary Principle and the Law of Unintended Consequences', *Food Policy*, 30: 145–161.

Von Moltke, K. (1996) 'The Relationship between Policy, Science, Technology, Economics and Law in the Implementation of the Precautionary Principle', in D. Freestone and E. Hey (eds), *The Precautionary Principle and International Law: The Challenge of Implementation*, The Hague/London/Boston, MA: Kluwer Law International, pp. 97–108.

——(1998) *The Vorsorgeprinzip in West German Environmental Policy*, 12th Report, London: Royal Commission on Environmental Policy.

Walker, V.R. (1998) 'Keeping the WTO from Becoming The "World Trans-Science Organization": Scientific Uncertainty, Science Policy, and Fact-finding in the Growth Hormones Dispute', *Cornell International Law Journal*, 31: 251–320.

——(2003) 'The Myth of Science as a "Neutral Arbiter" for Triggering Precautions', *International & Comparative Law Quarterly*, 26: 197–228.

Wibisana, M.R.A.G. (2008) *Law and Economics Analysis of the Precautionary Principle*, Doctoral Thesis, Maastricht University, Faculty of Law, Maastricht: Universitaire Pers.

Wiener, J.B. (2003) 'Whose Precaution after All? A Comment on the Comparison of Civil Justice Systems', *Duke Journal of Comparative and International Law*, 13: 207–262.

Winickoff, D., Jasanoff, S., Busch, L., Grove-White, R. and Wynne, B. (2005) 'Adjudicating the GM Food Wars: Science, Risk, and Democracy in World Trade Law', *Yale Journal of International Law*, 30(1): 81–123.

Wirth, D.A. (1997) 'International Trade Agreements: Vehicles for Regulatory Reform?', *The University of Chicago Legal Forum*, 331–373.

Wüger, D. (2006) 'Biotech Products WTO Panel Report', *ASIL Insight*, 10(5), 8 March, available at: www/asil/org/insights060308.cfm, accessed on 27 June 2007.

8 EU risk regulation reviewed by the European Courts

*Ellen Vos**

Scientification of EU risk regulation and judicial review by the Court

It is generally agreed that the BSE ('mad cow') and other food crises have been instrumental in shaping the way that the EU deals today with science underlying its decision-making. These crises have led to a fundamental change in our view of the legitimacy of government use of science, resulting in a quest for a higher quality of scientific advice used to verify agricultural production and food-processing methods together with increased transparency and broader participation in science-based decision-making. Today, the issue is not merely one of how to ensure that the science used in governance is sound, but it also encompasses the way that scientific opinion is balanced with wider ethical and social values. New approaches introduced by the EU in the wake of the BSE crisis sought to repair the deficiencies in EU risk regulation to make a clearer separation between risk assessment and risk management, clarify which portions of risk policy should be attributed to scientists and public administrations, and define new rules for the production of scientific advice, the introduction of the precautionary principle and increasing openness and participation (Everson and Vos 2009).

This has resulted in what we have called the 'scientification' of risk regulation in view of the heavy reliance by the European Commission and, to a lesser extent, the other EU institutions on science and the scientific advice delivered by the European Food Safety Authority (EFSA) (Everson and Vos 2009: 1–17), revealing a tendency by regulators to perceive and/or use science as an objective and neutral source to validate their decisions. This tendency raises important questions about the role of science in decision-making, the quality of science and science-making and principles of good governance. Due to the important role ascribed to science, disputes about science-based measures do not only involve legal questions but also touch upon the science underpinning disputed measures. As a matter of fact, the authority ascribed to science by the law and decision-makers, referred to as the 'meta-legal authority of science' by Christian Joerges (Joerges 1997: 320), can also be identified in the case law of the EU Courts,[1] which, like their counterpart courts elsewhere (Foster 2011), visibly struggle to deal with the technicalities of such cases (Foster 2011;

Tai 2009). These issues are at times so complex that the question arises as to whether the EU Court, and courts in general, have the necessary legitimacy to deal with such issues (Barbier de la Serre and Sibony 2008: 941). What precisely should be the role of the Court in adjudicating these kinds of conflicts? Should the Court merely address the various stages of the decision-making process, or should it assess the quality of the scientific analysis conducted or even review the latitude afforded to policy as opposed to science?[2]

The scientification of risk regulation is therefore not only problematic in terms of decision-making but also impacts on judicial review by the Court. Without a doubt, the standards applied by the Courts when reviewing measures is of utmost importance, as they determine the allocation of regulatory powers on science-related matters. Analysis of the Court's case law reveals that, in sharp contrast to its approach towards measures adopted by Member States, the Court has been habitually respectful of the discretionary powers of the EU institutions and deferential towards measures adopted by them (Scott and Vos 2002).[3] Today, notwithstanding the Court's insistence on the limits of its review of measures involving complex and uncertain matters, as it is 'not entitled to substitute its assessment of the facts for that of the Community institutions',[4] it increasingly pays attention to the science underlying the decision-making.[5] We can thus observe a change in the Court's behaviour from a rather deferential to a more proactive approach to setting the standard of review, paying much more attention to the question of whether authorities relied on a sufficiently rigorous assessment and applying the established grounds for review with much more intensity than before (Chalmers, Davies and Monti 2010: 898).

This has resulted in the Court still formally upholding the same wording and examining whether the exercise of discretionary powers by the EU institutions 'is vitiated by a manifest error or a misuse of power'.[6] Yet, in practice, the Court has stretched this to include a review of the adequacy and quality of the informational basis of science-based measures. This new approach of the Court, however, raises the question of how comprehensive the Court's review should be.

Cases like *Pfizer* provoke concerns as to whether the Court is not straying beyond the limits of its judicial function. In *Pfizer* the Court had to rule on the validity of the EU ban on the use of four antibiotics as growth promoters in feedingstuffs.[7] Upholding the EU ban, the Court arguably went further in this case than beyond its role of informational catalyst and delved into the science underlying the EU ban, thus acting as a kind of 'super expert'. This case illustrates perfectly the echo of the scientification of EU risk regulation in the judicial review of relevant measures, with the Court increasingly dictating the parameters of science and risk assessment (Stokes 2008). While the Court's more intense standard of review is to be welcomed in principle, we argue against too interventionist a role for the Court and its becoming immersed in the quagmires of scientific uncertainty and complexity that may surround a dispute. In this chapter we discuss the delicate dilemma of how the Court should balance deferential and interventionist review in cases of scientific uncertainty and complexity.

To this end, the chapter will first discuss the Court's standard of review in respect of measures that involve scientific or technical complexity used in its early case law. It then examines the Court's recent approach to its limited review developed in the famous case *Technische Universität München*. It will subsequently analyse the *Pfizer* judgment to reveal how the EU Court clearly overstepped its mandate. It finally discusses the fundamental question as to which role the EU Courts should have in conflicts involving science and the role that science and experts should play in litigation.

The Court's review of science-based measures in its early case law

From the 1970s to the 1990s in conflicts on the free movement of products in relation to Member State measures in the context of Articles 34–36 TFEU (Treaty on the Functioning of the European Union), the Court refrained from going into detail. It preferred simply to confirm the Member States' powers to decide the level of protection 'insofar as uncertainties persist in the present state of scientific research'.[8] Member States were thereby required to look at the results of findings of international scientific bodies, such as the Codex Alimentarius Commission and the EU's Scientific Committee of Foodstuffs on food-related issues (Joerges 1997). Therefore, Member States have often been afforded a large amount of discretion 'in [the] absence of harmonisation'.[9] This kind of case law has in turn led to a host of regulatory activities in relation to health and safety protection at the EU level. As for the review of measures of the EU institutions, we observe a similar attitude. A traditional standard formula used by the Court reads that the EU Court determines the existence of discretionary powers of the EU institutions in the field so that the legality of the relevant measure can only be affected if this measure is 'manifestly inappropriate having regard to the objective which the competent institution is seeking to pursue'.[10] This allows the Court to carry out a relatively 'tolerant level of scrutiny' (Jacobs 1999: 4).

The case law of the Court in the beef hormones controversies of the early 1990s perfectly illustrates the Court's reluctance to make an in-depth review of substantive issues. *Fedesa* concerned a challenge of the validity of the Second Hormones Directive,[11] which prohibited the use of certain hormones in livestock farming. The EU's controversial regime on the use of hormones in the production of beef was first established in 1981 and revised in 1988 (Scott 2001). In its proposal of 1984 to revise the regime and prohibit the use of certain substances having a hormonal or thyrostatic action in stock farming, the Commission concluded on the basis of scientific advice that the use of the relevant hormones 'would not present any harmful effects to the health of the consumer nor harm the consumer by altering the characteristics of meat when used under the appropriate conditions'.[12]

The Commission thus proposed to allow Member States to authorise the use of these hormones for fattening purposes.[13] This proposal was strongly opposed by the Parliament and the Economic and Social Committee on the grounds of consumer anxieties concerning hormone-treated meat, and the Commission decided to follow their concerns. Thus, on the basis of the same scientific evidence, instead of allowing the use of hormones for fattening purposes, in 1988 the Commission and the Council adopted a ban of the relevant hormones with explicit reference to consumer anxieties and expectations.[14] This ban was challenged before the Court.[15] In *Fedesa*, the European Federation for Animal Health – a representative body of companies engaged in animal health products – challenged the national implementation of the 1988 Hormones Directive, also questioning the directive itself.

Before the Court, the EU ban on hormone-produced meat got away with little legal reasoning (Slootboom 2003: 592). Here the Court had no difficulties in keeping away from (scientific) substance and limited its review to examine 'whether the measure in question is vitiated by a manifest error or misuse of powers, or whether the authority in question has manifestly exceeded the limits of its discretion'.[16] The Court found that this was not the case. For the Court it was clear that the claim based on the existence of scientific evidence demonstrating the safety of the five hormones could not be upheld.[17] Although the applicant argued that the directive lacked any scientific basis justifying the public health considerations and consumer anxieties,[18] the Court did not find it necessary to order any measures of inquiry to verify the accuracy of that allegation.

As a result, the Court not only took account of the divergent appraisals of the Member States on the question of the safety of hormones, but it also looked at 'the concerns expressed by the European Parliament, the Economic and Social Committee and by several consumer organisations'[19] in relation to the Commission's 1984 proposal to relax the EU's hormone regime and allow the use of the hormones for fattening purposes. It concluded that the Council had remained within the limits of its discretionary power in deciding to adopt the solution of prohibiting the hormones in question, considering that 'in view of the divergent appraisals which had been made, traders were not entitled to expect that a prohibition on administering the substances in question to animals could be based on scientific data alone'. It therefore upheld the measure.[20]

Hilson argues that, in view of the fact that the divergent national appraisals that the Court refers to were non-scientific and based on national public concern, this ruling explicitly supports the consideration of public concern over science (Hilson 2005: 325; Scott and Vos 2002: 284–285) and even results in 'lending support to a reliance on broad EU public opinion *in place of* science' (Hilson 2005: 325). Although the Court indeed listened to social and political conceptions of risk (Scott 2001), at the same time it shied away from engaging critically with the statements put forward by the various organisations, the Parliament and the Committee (Scott and Vos 2002; Scott 2007). The Court's mere reference to the concerns of the various actors is in line with its limited approach to the review of legislative acts adopted within the framework of the common agricultural policy and the multiple aims pursued by the directive (Scott 2001), having no desire to address the factual basis of EU action (Button 2004: 136).

The Court's review of science-based measures in its more recent case law

Technische Universität München

A quick glance at the Court's case law after *Fedesa* might prompt the reader to believe that little has changed (Craig 2006: 446). The Court indeed still speaks in deferential language and continues relentlessly to repeat the standard formula that in cases of wide discretion the Court exercises a mere limited review, in particular in cases where the EU institution is faced with complex scientific, technical or economic data.[21] Yet a closer look reveals that the Court today is much more willing, and at times required, to go into the substance of the case, scrutinising in detail the informational basis for the decisions at hand. Thus, a year after the *Fedesa* ruling, in the landmark case *Technische Universität München*[22] we see a clear shift in the Court's approach to the standard of review. This case has been considered a turning point in the philosophy underlying both judicial review of administrative discretion and, more specifically, judicial control on procedural grounds (Nehl 1999: 133). In this case the Court even appeared ready to look 'behind the veneer of apparent expertise to check its adequacy in relation to the matter at hand' (Scott and Sturm 2006: 584).

Technische Universität München concerned the import of an electronic microscope from Japan by the applicant, Technische Universität München. Its application for a customs exemption had been rejected by the European Commission upon consultation of a group of experts on the grounds that an apparatus of equivalent scientific value, capable of being used for the same purposes, was produced in the EU. It is noteworthy that, up until that moment, in similar cases, the Court had always minimised judicial protection in the face of the administrative discretion offered to the EU institutions (Craig 2006).

In its reference to the Court, the *Bundesfinanzhof* expressed its strong doubts as to whether the Court's traditionally limited review could be maintained, that traditionally limited approach being that the Court had

> only a limited power of review in relation to disputes concerning the duty-free importation of scientific apparatus and, given the technical nature of the questions which arise, the Court may only declare a decision of the Commission invalid where there has been a manifest error of appraisal or a misuse of power.[23]

The implicit threat of the German Court to engage in a constitutional or supremacy quarrel with the European Court by involving the *Bundesverfassungsgericht* was well understood by the European Court (Nehl 1999: 133).

The European Court thus engaged in a more intense scrutiny of the Commission's decision. It recognised that, in cases involving complex technical evaluations, respect for the rights of individuals is to be ensured *inter alia* by the duty of the relevant institution 'to examine carefully and impartially all the relevant aspects of the individual case, the right of the person concerned to make his views known and to have an adequately reasoned decision'.[24] The Court added its readiness to examine also the factual elements of the case by stressing that 'only in this way can the Court verify whether the factual and legal elements upon which the exercise of the power of appraisal depends were present'.[25] This led the Court to examine attentively the composition of the group of experts that the Commission had consulted: a group that had been of decisive importance for the negative outcome of the decision. The Court found the expertise held by the group members (who had not been advised by others having the requisite knowledge) to be insufficient and that the Commission had infringed the duty to examine carefully and impartially all the relevant aspects of the case in point.[26] This principle of care or diligence or good or sound administration has been applied in subsequent case law.

A more proactive standard of review

Consequently, *Technische Universität München* introduced a shift in the Court's standard of review from one of deference to a more proactive one. In what Craig coins its 'modern' case law, the Court applies the established grounds for review with greater intensity than before (Craig 2006: 446–447). Some have referred to this as a new kind of 'proceduralist' test that the Court carries out and argue that this test has increasingly been used in answer to progressing knowledge leading to increased uncertainty as well as the realisation that science is not capable of providing zero risk (Chalmers *et al.* 2010: 898). When labelling this as a 'proceduralist' test, one must nevertheless keep in mind that the Court's current role and position involves much more than carrying out a formal check on whether the correct procedures to reach a decision have been followed. Following *Technische Universität München*, the Court currently examines the adequacy of the information on which the decision is based and seeks to ensure that decision-makers have the right information at their disposal in view of the underlying objective used and the applicable legal provisions (Scott and Sturm 2006: 570, 582).

Pfizer: informational catalyst and super-expert

The long and complex judgment of the General Court in the *Pfizer* case of 2002[27] is an example of the Court's more intense approach to judicial review and hence confirms the approach followed in *Technische Universität München* (see below). At the same time, however, the Court does much more than that and appears eager to get its teeth into scientific substance and act itself as a kind of 'super-expert' (see below) (Van Asselt and Vos 2006).

The case

In *Pfizer*, the producer of an antibiotic called virginiamycin, Pfizer (and Alpharma[28]) challenged the Council's decision to prohibit the use of this and three other antibiotics as additives in feedingstuffs before the General Court.[29] These antibiotics were used as a growth promoter for poultry and pigs. The Council's decision was based on the precautionary principle as there was a risk of the transfer of a streptogramin or vancomycin resistance from organisms of animal origin to those that reside in the human digestive tract. Virginiamycin is an antibiotic belonging to the streptogramin class, used exclusively as a growth promoter for animals, and had been authorised up to the Council's ban in 1999 as an additive in feedingstuffs for certain poultry and pigs. Denmark however, notified the European Commission through the safeguard clause that it had banned the use of virginiamycin as it had evidence that there was a risk of the transfer of the resistance of antibiotics from animals to humans. This evidence was provided by the Danish National Veterinary Laboratory. The Commission submitted this scientific report to the EU's Scientific Committee on Animal Nutrition for advice. This Committee concluded that the use of virginiamycin as a growth promoter did not constitute an immediate risk to public health in Denmark. Yet, notwithstanding this scientific advice, and following a failure to adopt an opinion through comitology, the Council decided to ban the use of the four antibiotics as additives in animal feedingstuffs for health protection reasons. Pfizer immediately challenged the ban, which was nevertheless upheld by the General Court.

The Court's more intense standard of review: the Court as an informational catalyst

As pointed out, on the one hand, the Court's judgment can be regarded as an illustration of the Court's modern approach to the standard of review. It reveals the Court's role to be what Scott and Sturm have coined an 'informational catalyst': the role of the Court to review the adequacy and quality of the informational basis of science-based measures and hence, also, to scrutinise the informational basis for the decisions at hand in detail (Scott and Sturm 2006: 583). Noteworthy, in sharp contrast with rulings of both the Court of Justice and the General Court in their early case law, is the length of this judgment: 519 paragraphs compared to, for example, the 50 paragraphs of the *Fedesa* judgment. This length, although surely not being representative of the average length of a 'modern' judgment, is already telling of the level of detail that the Court has demonstrated itself to be ready to engage in. The complexity of the case took the Court 72 paragraphs just to account for the facts, background and the procedure leading to the case. Finding the application admissible, the Court starts the examination of the substance, perfectly in line with the deferential language of its early case law, by pointing to the wide discretion that the EU institutions enjoy in matters concerning the common agricultural policy regarding the definition of the objectives to be pursued and choice of the appropriate means of action, and that judicial review must be limited.[30]

In *Pfizer* the Court is both ready and forced to scrutinise in detail the adequacy of the decision-making procedure to produce the kind and quality of information that is needed to reach a decision on the matter (Scott and Sturm 2006: 583). Yet, as tradition demands, the Court persistently repeats throughout the whole judgment its traditional formula of its classical deferential approach pointing out to the limits of judicial review.

Nevertheless, this language did not stop the Court from examining in some detail the extent to which the institutions had committed errors when assessing the risks and judging the validity of the parties' arguments, thus also embarking on a substantive review (Craig 2006: 726). First, the Court, right after having stressed that it can carry out only a limited review, follows the line set in *Technische Universität München*, and underlines the importance of, in particular, the duty of the competent institution to examine carefully and impartially all the relevant aspects of the individual case.[31] This means first that, in situations that involve extremely complex scientific and technical assessments over which scientists have widely diverging views, the EU institutions are under an obligation to carry out a risk assessment prior to adopting precautionary measures.[32] The Court's view is that

> a risk assessment carried out as thoroughly as possible on the basis of scientific advice founded on the principles of excellence, transparency and independence, is an important procedural guarantee whose purpose is to ensure the scientific objectivity of the measures adopted and preclude any arbitrary measures. The statement of reasons must be of a scientific level at least commensurate with that of the opinion in question.[33]

It is in this light that the Court examines the risk assessment carried out by the institutions. The Court not only insists on the quality of risk assessment that the Commission and the Council had to rely on, but also on the manner by which they reached the decision and which elements were taken into account. The Court thereby requires experts who carry out a risk assessment to provide the competent public authorities with 'sufficiently reliable and cogent information to allow it to understand the ramifications of the scientific question raised and decide upon a policy in full knowledge of the facts'.[34] Importantly, where an EU committee or body has been set up by the EU institutions to provide it with scientific advice, the Court insists that the EU institutions may 'only in exceptional circumstances and where there are adequate guarantees of scientific objectivity in cases of particularly complex scientific facts', adopt a precautionary measure without obtaining an opinion from the relevant scientific committee that was set up for that purpose.[35] Moreover, the Court holds that, where the EU institution disregards the opinion of this advisory body, 'it must provide specific reasons for its findings by comparison with those made in the opinion and its statement of reasons must explain why it is disregarding the latter'.[36]

That being said, regrettably the Court failed to apply all the parameters it set for the adequacy of the informational basis of decision-making to the specifics of the case at hand. It ruled that precautionary measures should be based on a risk assessment, thereby confirming the approach taken by the Commission in its communication on the precautionary principle[37] and even admitting that the Court should examine whether the institutions were entitled to conclude 'on the basis of as thorough a risk assessment as possible and taking account of the best scientific data available', but it subsequently failed to examine whether 'as thorough a risk assessment as possible' had been carried out and whether the Commission had taken account of the 'best scientific data available'. Another example can be found in the Court's readiness to accept little evidence that the risk be 'adequately backed up' by the scientific data available at that time,[38] where in this case the institutions had been able to refer to one case of potential transferral of the virginiamycin resistance (a Dutch farmer) and an experimental study produced by the Danish authorities. According to the Court, this justified the conclusions of the EU institutions that there was 'sufficiently reliable and cogent scientific evidence for them to conclude that there was a proper scientific basis for the ban of the antibiotics'.[39] The Court thereby took particular account of the documents which had been submitted to it, from which it derived that other scientists and specialist bodies[40] had taken a different view from that of the Scientific Committee on Animal Nutrition (SCAN) and the experts relied on by Pfizer.[41] The Court was, however, completely silent as to the requirement of adequate guarantees of scientific objectivity. Here one would have expected that the Court would have examined whether the advice or studies relied on by the EU institutions fulfilled the requirements of excellence, independence and transparency, as it views these principles to be of 'the utmost importance in risk assessment', to guarantee that the regulatory measures have a 'proper scientific basis' and that the institutions were able to 'examine carefully and impartially all relevant evidence'.[42] In this sense, the Court can be criticised for having been too lenient, potentially allowing for cherry-picking 'convenient' science.[43]

The Court's substantive review: the Court as a 'super-expert'

The role of an informational catalyst that the Court has assumed in *Pfizer* and other cases also has a more normative underpinning, and we suggest that this role should be undertaken by the Court (see below) (Scott and Sturm 2006). In our view this means that the Court has rightly been demanding as regards the evidence submitted and the procedures followed, so as to assess the adequacy of the decision-making procedure, as required by *Technische Universität München*. We can observe that indeed in the aftermath of *Pfizer* the Court continued to unfold the parameters of the application of the precautionary principle and applied a more procedural interpretation of the precautionary principle, focusing on the decision-making process and the procedures followed (Stokes 2008; Alemanno 2008), although the Court is not always very consistent in its case law in this perspective (Janssen and Van Asselt 2012).

Yet, equally, *Pfizer* demonstrates the Court's eagerness to delve into the substance of the case, clearly extending its role by assuming the role of an expert, hence doing too much (Craig 2006: 448). It is true that the Court was also forced to get engaged in the scientific debate by the grounds invoked by Pfizer, the evaluation of manifest errors of assessment and the breach of the precautionary principle. The Court visibly struggles to shape the relationship between scientific evidence, uncertainty and the precautionary principle (Janssen and Van Asselt 2012). Collaborative research with Marjolein van Asselt on the *Pfizer* case shows that the Court tries to be a super-expert as it not only requires the adequacy of the information underlying the Council's decision but actively engages in the scientific merits of the case. We have argued that the Court got stuck in the deadlock of being forced to do what it may not (evaluating science) and is unable to do (evaluating science).[44] First, it is beyond the Court's competence to go into the scientific merits and validity, as it admits itself. Second, it presupposes that the Court is a super-expert, who would be able to resolve scientific disputes. By pronouncing itself on the scientific merits of the plausibility discourses brought forward by the various parties, the Court unconsciously pretends to be the super-expert that it cannot be (Van Asselt and Vos 2006). Without a doubt, it is neither possible nor desirable for the Court to fulfil such a role.

There are abundant examples of the Court trying to act as an expert to be found throughout the whole judgment. The Court finds, for instance, that:

> The various experiments and observations … were not mere conjecture but amounted to sufficiently reliable and cogent scientific evidence for them to conclude that there was a proper scientific basis for a possible link between the use of virginiamycin as an additive in feedingstuffs and the development of streptogramin resistance in humans.[45]

While the Court insists that it 'is not for the Court to assess the merits of either of the scientific points of view argued before it and to substitute its assessment for that of the Community institutions',[46] it nevertheless finds itself competent to conclude that the parties' arguments, 'supported in each case by the opinions of eminent scientists', show that there was great uncertainty at the time of adoption of the contested regulation, about the link between the use of virginiamycin and the development of the resistance in humans.[47]

The Court moreover views that the institutions 'could reasonably take the view that they had a proper scientific basis for a possible link', and that 'the mere fact that there were scientific counter arguments does not establish that they exceeded the limits of their discretion'.[48] A prominent example of the Court's own interference with the scientific validity of the arguments raised and the measure is the Court's own examination of four reports issued by the World

Health Organization (WHO), the Dutch Health Council, the Copenhagen Recommendations, the Swedish authorities and the House of Lords (Van Asselt and Vos 2006: 325). It thus spends six paragraphs of the judgment in quoting relevant passages from the four reports.[49] It is moreover quite remarkable that the Court explicitly points out that, in relation to the report issued by House of Lords Select Committee on Science and Technology, this Committee had 'heard a large number of experts, some of whom represented the industry concerned (one of them was in fact employed by Pfizer)'.[50] The Court concluded that Pfizer had not established that the EU institutions had erred when they did not take over SCAN's opinion and that, on the contrary, the institutions 'could properly find that there were serious reasons … concerning human health for restricting streptogramins to medical use'.[51] This is a clear example of the Court's analysing itself the available scientific evidence instead of reviewing the parties' arguments and their assessment of the evidence so as to produce a judgment on the informational quality of the contested decision.

Moreover, we have observed that the Court used the differences in scientific arguments brought forward as well as the Commission's and Council's reliance on the precautionary principle, merely to conclude that there are contrasting scientific opinions, which it takes as enough evidence of uncertainty. The Court 'saved' itself by using one version of uncertainty for something it can observe itself, i.e. contrasting opinions between experts whom it has considered as being qualified. As the Court cannot balance the scientific arguments, it is arguably inclined to assume equal standing of scientific opinions and counter-opinions. We thus concluded that the Court seemed to construct a situation of scientific uncertainty: it employed the scientific evidence submitted by the various parties to demonstrate uncertainty, which, in turn, it used to validate the resort to the precautionary principle. In this way, the Court upheld the Council's ban (Van Asselt and Vos 2006).

In this context we observe that the Court, too, falls victim to what we have called the 'uncertainty paradox', meaning that, although uncertainty is acknowledged by both the regulators and the Court, the role of science and experts is always framed in terms of providing certainty about uncertain risks (Van Asselt and Vos 2006). The Court on the one hand surely recognises that science cannot provide decisive evidence on uncertain risks and that there is great uncertainty and on the other hand finds sufficiently reliable and cogent scientific evidence and a proper scientific basis. Thus, although uncertainty is recognised, science is still expected to speak the truth about uncertain risks. This gives reason for concern not only in view of various academic insights proving this paradigm to be a 'myth' (Jasanoff 1990: 16–17), but also because, visibly, the Court is unable to understand the scientific merits, which follows painfully from the following discussion between a judge and a scientist during the hearing in this case before the Court:[52]

> *Scientist*: You get the organisms in chickens; the organisms are transmitted to man and the rest of it flows. If you cannot demonstrate the rest of it, the

> whole thing comes to a stop. I do insist that no harm has been done. You have the potential and the hazard but it is not translated into a risk. That is my understanding of all the scientific evidence I have read.
>
> *Judge*: Is that not to some extent playing on the words? You say it is a hazard and we had this morning the distinction between hazard and risk. If you have a hazard, it may become a risk. Is that not playing on the words?
>
> *Scientist*: No. I do not believe it is. If you are defining your risk as the use of growth promoter in animals leading to resistance in animals, the hazard is translated into a risk. If you are saying 'has that hazard ever been translated into the transmission?', on very rare occasions that has been demonstrated to be the case, so you are demonstrating risk there. What happens to those organisms once they contaminate food, once they are cooked, once they are ingested by man, all has to be assessed before you say that you can turn the hazard into what is the risk, to me, which is the infection in man. I thought that was what we were talking about.
>
> *Judge*: That latter aspect is more a legal question than a scientific question. Where do you place the bar before jumping? Does it suffice to have a hazard, which might turn into a risk, or should you have some sort of calculable risk? Is that part of science for you?
>
> *Scientist*: It is part of science to do a risk assessment. It is then society's role, the law's role, to decide what risk is acceptable? (Van Asselt and Vos 2006).

This is not only a clear example of science and law speaking two different languages, but it also indicates the clear limits of the Court's role and the role of science before courts. We will therefore need to reflect upon the Court's role and the role of science and experts before the Courts.

Reconceptualising the role of the Courts and the role of science before the EU Courts

The Court's case law in context

Pfizer and other rulings touch upon the fundamental questions as to which role the EU Courts should have in conflicts involving science and which role science and experts should play in litigation. While this question has been, and still is, quite extensively debated in the USA and internationally, especially the World Trade Organization (WTO) context (Cottier and Mavroides 2003; Feldman 2009; Faigman 1999; Foster 2011; Jasanoff 1995), it hardly gets attention in the EU.[53] Our discussion of the Court's review in the *Pfizer* case underlines the need to rethink the role of the Court as well as the role of science and experts before the Court. As set forth in the introduction, the Court's more interventionist role in reviewing science-based measures must be considered first, against the background of the scientification of regulation which can be observed in the EU in the BSE aftermath and, second, to some extent also in the context of the Sanitary and Phytosanitary (SPS) agreement on science and the interpretation of that agreement by the WTO panel and Appellate Body in the *Hormones* case.

As regards the first point, we have already observed that, in the aftermath of the BSE crisis, where the independence and objectivity of scientists and scientific advice had been clearly undermined, science underlying decision-making has become of ever increasing importance (Vos 2000). While it is true that the social construct of science and the legend of 'science telling truth to power' (Jasanoff 1990: 16–17) have become more evident, both regulators and judges still behave according to that outdated model of an unquestionable authority of science, reifying the uncertainty paradox. At the same time, as Lee convincingly argues, the need for regulators to justify their decisions at many levels (local, national, EU and WTO), and to a variety of stakeholders and citizens, enhances both legal and political pressures to explain their decisions through risk, a trend reinforced by the deferential review exercised by the Courts at the various levels (Lee 2010: 267–276).

As regards the second point, the shift of the Court from its deferential approach to informational catalyst can be argued to be a response to litigation before the WTO, in particular the WTO panel's rulings in the *EC – Hormones* case (Slootboom 2003: 593–594; Stokes 2008: 504). These cases moreover show that the question of how scientific evidence and expertise is to be used by courts is surely not limited to the EU Courts. In the *Hormones I* case, in striking contrast to the complete disregard of scientific evidence by the European Court in *Fedesa*, the WTO panel thoroughly scrutinised a large number of scientific reports and interviewed scientists, subsequent to which it concluded that the European ban on hormone-treated meat that was earlier upheld by the European Court in *Fedesa* was incompatible with the WTO's SPS rules.[54] Yet, like the Court in *Pfizer*, the WTO panels, too, have been overstepping their mandate and substituting their opinions for that of the WTO members.[55] In the *EC – Biotech* case, for example, Prévost argues that the Panel 'appropriated one of the aspects of [the trade/health] balance left by the [SPS] Agreement in competence of Members, namely, the competence to evaluate the scientific evidence in a way that reflects the science policy choices of that Member' (Prévost 2013). In this case, the Panel had directly reviewed the available science to establish its sufficiency, thus overstepping the traditional 'objective assessment' standard of review and itself conducting a scientific assessment of the available data (Prévost in this volume). In *Hormones II*, the Panel was reproached by the Appellate Body for having applied the standard of review erroneously and, in reviewing the scientific experts' opinions, 'somewhat peremptorily decided what it considered to be the best science, rather than following the more limited exercise that its mandate required'.[56] The standard of review carried out by the Panel, therefore, reminds the Appellate Body, is not to establish the correctness of the risk assessment of a Member, 'but rather to determine whether that risk assessment is supported by coherent reasoning and respectable scientific evidence and is, in this sense, objectively justifiable'.[57]

Re-thinking the roles of the EU Courts, science and experts

How, then, should the Court approach conflicts about measures involving scientific uncertainty and complexity? Clearly, the traditionally deferential approach adopted by the Court in its case law pre-*Technische Universität München* is not suitable for reviewing measures that involve scientific uncertainty and complexity. The habitual static role of courts' being responsible for the elaboration and enforcement of public norms is unsatisfactory as it gives leeway to 'arbitrary and capricious' (Marchant and Mosman 2004) decision-making, with public authorities not being required to respond to and/or account for decisions that they have adopted. It at the same time negates the responsibility of the Courts. This holds particularly true for cases where decision-makers have broad discretionary powers in an area such as risk regulation. The Courts therefore cannot hide behind a deferential standard of review and should engage intensely in scrutinising the adequacy of the informational basis of contested measures.

In *Pfizer*, the Court seeks to ensure that decision-makers have at their disposal the type and quality of information they need to reach a decision that is consistent with the underlying objective and, with the relevant legal norms, thus taking on the role of an informational catalyst, as Scott and Sturm have argued (Scott and Sturm 2006: 582). This role of the Court seems to be especially pertinent in cases of scientific uncertainty like the one at hand, where the traditional deferential approach would not do justice to the complexity of the case. As Ladeur already forcefully argued, 'the reductionist approach following the traditional limited court control in complex technical matters such as the control of "*erreur manifeste d'appréciation*" is no longer acceptable' (Ladeur 2003: 1478).

The scrutiny of the informational basis of measures is one aspect of the reconceptualisation of the role of courts by Scott and Sturm in relation to new governance, in addition to providing for full and fair participation and fostering principled decision-making (Scott and Sturm 2006). While this concept as a normative framework needs further elaboration, the attractiveness of it is apparent: it requires courts to prompt and to actively engage in normatively motivated and accountable inquiry (Scott and Sturm 2006: 571, 593). Courts would so review whether decision-makers have the right type and quality of information at their disposal to make decisions that are consistent with the goal sought and the relevant legal norms. Reconceptualising courts as informational catalysts[58] would, moreover, prompt them to reassess settled but perhaps untested assumptions or prejudices and expose them to the full consequences of their decisions (Scott and Sturm 2006: 582). In this manner it is necessary that no decisions escape scrutiny, as decision-makers are forced to link the reasons for their decisions to the available information closely: this would ultimately lead to a higher quality of decisions based on all relevant information.[59] This would allow the Courts to closely scrutinise the distinct parts of the reasoning of the decision-makers and to assess whether their conclusions are convincing in the light of the information at hand and the reasoning provided (Craig 2006: 479).

The catalyst function of courts should also make it possible to circumvent situations whereby regulators would, through a light judicial review, be encouraged even more to rely on science to explain a political decision. Proper explanation of reasons for the adoption of a decision thus allows those reasons to be challenged, both in the political or judicial process (Lee 2010: 276–277). As the Court acknowledged in *Pfizer*, 'scientific legitimacy is not a sufficient basis for the exercise of public authority'.[60] Consequently, it is important to ensure that the EU Courts are and remain 'institutions of justice, not institutions of science' (Jasanoff 1997: 19). As Jasanoff forcefully argues:

> Judges need to reject mythical versions of both 'pure science' and 'junk science'. … Most of all, they need to retain the conviction that courts are not a forum for resolving scientific disputes definitively, but rather for doing justice on a case-by-case basis with the aid of all available scientific knowledge that meets threshold tests of relevance and reliability.
>
> (Jasanoff 1997)

Hence, judges should remain judges. They should not become 'amateur scientists' (Scallen and Wiethoff 1998: 1145). The recognition that science is not a monolithic kind of activity and that a risk assessment is not neutral, but is a social construct and as such a political act (Van Asselt *et al.* 2012), is therefore key. With science and law in the courtroom speaking two different languages, it is necessary that they understand each other.[61] The question therefore arises as to whether courts need to be assisted by court-appointed experts or whether there is a need for specialised courts in order to better understand the underlying science, but not to adjudicate it.[62] Until now the Courts have been reluctant to use court-appointed experts in cases surrounding scientific uncertainty and complexity as they fear relinquishing power to external experts and the delegation of adjudication to experts.[63] However, 'since, by definition, the EC Courts do not master the technical discipline at issue, there could be no guarantee that their opinion on the existence of a manifest error is not purely arbitrary' (Barbier de la Serre and Sibony 2008: 957). This, together with the findings that the case law of the Courts and especially in trade mark cases, is full of examples of verdicts based on the EU judges' personal experience (Barbier de la Serre and Sibony 2008: 959), would argue in favour of having such experts informing the EU Courts. Yet, the use of court-appointed experts would further encourage a scientification of judicial review and might give rise to a 'battle of experts', outcomes which have surely to be avoided. These questions therefore still beg further reflection.

Concluding remarks

The increasing scientific complexity of cases before the EU Court underlines that the traditionally deferential court control pre-*Technische UniversitätMünchen* is no longer appropriate. The shift to a more intensely interventionist review by the Court in *Technische Universität München* is therefore to be welcomed. While *Pfizer* is a prominent example of this new approach, at the same time it reveals the Court's struggle with scientific uncertainty. The Court immersed itself in the scientific merits of the case, clearly overstepping its mandate. Scott and Sturm's reconceptualisation of the Court's role as an informational catalyst would be of great interest in the formulation of a normative framework for how the Court should operate, in particular in the face of uncertainty and complexity. Courts need to actively engage in normatively motivated and accountable inquiry and decision-makers need to be forced to reveal all reasoning in their decisions. Ultimately this will lead to better-informed decisions that do not escape judicial scrutiny. The focus on scientific justifications of decisions by EU regulators, however, has resulted in science increasingly featuring in the courtrooms and framing the Court's reasoning. The scientification of risk regulation echoes in the courtroom, with the consequence that the Court might actively engage in substantive review. Our analysis demonstrates that this kind of review is highly problematic. The question of how the EU Court should deal with conflicts that involve scientific uncertainty requires a more in-depth reflection on the scientification of EU risk regulation. It requires a careful scrutiny of which criteria and parameters can and should be set by the Court in order to make sure that science-based measures can be adequately reviewed, and all the while respecting the discretionary powers of the EU decision-makers and making sure that the Court remains a court rather than an institution of science. This necessitates further interdisciplinary research.

Notes

* The author would like to thank Marjolein van Asselt for her invaluable comments on an earlier version.

1 In this contribution we will refer to the EU Court, European Court or the Court as encompassing both the General Court and the Court of Justice of the European Union (CJEU), unless otherwise specified.

2 Opinion of Advocate General M. Poiares Maduro to European Court of Justice (ECJ), Case C-41/02, para. 32.

3 This would link up with the view of McNelis who, in her comparison of the WTO and EU courts, argues that the 'real standard of review lies in the relationship between judging entity and the actor "judged"'. See McNelis (2003: 234).

4 ECJ, Case C-269/90, *Technische Universität München v. Hauptzollampt München-Mitte*, [1991] ECR I-5469; Court of First Instance (CFI), Case T-13/99 *Pfizer Animal Health SA v. Council* [2002] ECR II-03305, at para. 169.

5 See, for instance, ECJ, Case C-331/88, *The Queen v. The Minister for Agriculture, Fisheries and Food and the Secretary of State for Health, ex parte: Fedesa and other (Fedesa)* [1990] ECR I-4023; ECJ, Case C-405/92, *Établissements Armand*

Mondiet SA v. Armement Islais SARL (Mondiet) [1993] ECR I-6133; ECJ, Case C-280/93, *Germany v. Council* [1994] (European Court Reports) *ECR* I-4973. See Stokes (2008).

6 See e.g. ECJ, Case C-157/96, *National Farmers' Union and Others* [1998] ECR I-2211, at para. 39, referring to a classic case in this respect, ECJ, Case 98/78 *Racke v. Hauptzollamt Mainz* [1979] ECR 69, at para. 5.

7 CFI, Case T-13/99, *supra* n. 4.

8 See, *inter alia*, Case 227/82 *Van Bennekom* [1983] ECR 3883 and Case 174/82 *Sandoz BV* [1983] ECR 2445.

9 See, *inter alia*, Case 104/75, *De Peijper* [1976] ECR 613; Case 132/80, *NV United Foods and PVBA Van den Abeele v. Belgian State* [1981] ECR 995; Case 272/80, *Biologische producten* [1981] ECR 3277; *Sandoz, Van Bennekom*, ECJ; Case C-293/94, *Brandsma* [1996] ECR I-3159, ECJ; Case C-400/96, *Harpenies* [1998] ECR I-5121 and ECJ Case 55/99 *Commission v. France* [2000] ECR I-11517.

10 Case C-331/88, *supra* n. 5, at para. 14.

11 Council Directive 88/146/EEC prohibiting the use in livestock farming of certain substances having a hormonal action, *OJ* 1988 L 70/16.

12 See the 7th recital to the Proposal for a Council Directive amending Directive 81/602/EEC concerning the prohibition of certain substances having a hormonal action and of any substances having a thyrostatic action, *OJ* 1984 C 170/04.

13 Art. 1, Commission proposal, *supra* n. 12.

14 See the 2nd recital to Council Directive 85/649/EEC prohibiting the use in livestock farming of certain substances having a hormonal action, *OJ* 1985 L 382/228–231.

15 Before this, in 1985 the ban was adopted by the Council in the Hormones Directive of 1985, but this directive was declared void by the Court for breach of essential procedural requirements. See Case 68/86 *UK v. Council*, ECR 1988, p. 855. Shortly after this ruling, the Council quickly adopted a similar directive, repairing the procedural defects of the first directive soon after the Court's ruling in 1988 (Council Directive 88/146/EEC prohibiting the use in livestock farming of certain substances having a hormonal action, *OJ* 1988 L 70/16). See Scott (2001).

16 Case C-331/88, *supra* n. 5, para 8.

17 Case C-331/88, *supra* n. 5, para 9.

18 Case C-331/88, *supra* n. 5, para 7.

19 Case C-331/88, *supra* n. 5, para 9.

20 Case C-331/88, *supra* n. 5, para. 10.

21 E.g. CFI, Case T-13/99, *supra* n. 4, para. 169.

22 See Case C-269/90, *supra* n. 4.

23 Case C-269/90, *supra* n. 4, para. 9.

24 Case C-269/90, *supra* n. 4, para 14.

25 Ibid.

26 Case C-269/90, *supra* n. 4, para 22.

27 See CFI, Case T-13/99, *supra* n. 4.

28 See CFI, Case T-70/99, *Alpharma* [2002] ECR II-03495. See, for a brief discussion of this case, Vos (2004). See also Janssen and Van Asselt (2012).

29 Council Regulation 2821/98/EC amending, as regards withdrawal of the authorisation of certain antibiotics; Directive 70/524/EEC concerning additives in feedingstuffs, *OJ* 1998 L 351/4.

30 Case T-13/99, *supra* n. 4, para. 166.

31 Case T-13/99, *supra* n. 4, para. 170.

32 Case T-13/99, *supra* n. 4, paras. 155–157.

33 Case T-13/99, *supra* n. 4, para. 172.

34 Case T-13/99, *supra* n. 4, para. 162.
35 Case T-13/99, *supra* n. 4, para. 270.
36 Case T-13/99, *supra* n. 4, para. 199.
37 See 'Communication on the Use of the Precautionary Principle', COM (2000) 1, 2 February 2000.
38 See Case T-13/99, *supra* n. 4, para. 144.
39 Case T-13/99, *supra* n. 4, para. 389. See also para. 393 where the Court finds that the EU institutions 'could reasonably take the view that they had a proper scientific basis'.
40 Namely, the World Health Organization (WHO) Report, the Copenhagen Recommendations, the Swedish Report, the Report of the Netherlands Health Council and the House of Lords Report.
41 Case T-13/99, *supra* n. 4, paras. 394–400.
42 Case T-13/99, *supra* n. 4, para. 268.
43 See for a further analysis Vos (2004). Also, the Court of Justice in its more recent ruling, *Gowan*, has been criticised for not applying the procedural guarantees such as the duty of careful examination and the obligation to give reasons. See Alemanno (2008).
44 In this subsection I draw mainly on the findings of the research that I carried out with Marjolein van Asselt. See, for an in-depth analysis of the case, Van Asselt and Vos (2006).
45 CFI, Case T-13/99, *supra* n. 4, para. 389.
46 CFI, Case T-13/99, *supra* n. 4, para. 391.
47 CFI, Case T-13/99, *supra* n. 4, para. 393.
48 Ibid.
49 CFI, Case T-13/99, *supra* n. 4, paras. 396–400.
50 CFI, Case T-13/99, *supra* n. 4, para. 400.
51 CFI, Case T-13/99, *supra* n. 4, paras. 401–402.
52 Transcript of the hearing, as quoted by M. Everson, see Van Asselt and Vos (2006).
53 With the exception of the literature mentioned in this contribution.
54 Appellate Body Report, *EC – Hormones*. For a discussion of this case, see e.g. Scott (2001).
55 Examples include: Panel report Japan – Agricultural Products II, para. 7.10; Panel report Japan – Apples, paras. 8.123–8.128; Panel report Japan – Apples (Art. 21.5 US), paras. 8.140–8.144; Panel report, US/Canada, Continued suspension WT/DS320 and 321 para. 7.538 res para. 7.510. See Prévost (2013).
56 US/Canada – Continued Suspension, *supra* n. 55, para. 612.
57 US/Canada – Continued Suspension, *supra* n. 55, para. 590.
58 It seems to me that, in many cases, the two other aspects, participation and principled decision-making, could also ultimately be considered to fall under this aspect.
59 As Scott and Sturm note, it is well known that the amount of information that is available to decision-makers is decisive for decisions reached. Scott and Sturm (2006: 582 also 83), referring to Holder (2004).
60 Case T-13/99, *supra* n. 4, para 201.
61 Scallen and Wiethoff emphasise the importance of an expert's ethos whereby 'analyzing and understanding the conceptual frameworks within which expert witnesses express their opinions is as essential as evaluating the basic reliability of any scientific theories on which they rely' (Scallen and Wiethoff 1998: 1168).
62 See for a discussion Barbier de la Serre and Sibony (2008).
63 Barbier de la Serre and Sibony (2008: 949). In an American study amongst 108 judges, all 108 judges disfavoured court-appointed experts. See *The 1997 Forum for State Court Judges*, Roscoe Pound Foundation, Washington (1997).

References

Alemanno, A. (2008) 'The Shaping of European Risk Regulation by Community Courts', Jean Monnet Working Paper, No. 18/08.

Barbier de la Serre, E. and Sibony, A. (2008) 'Expert Evidence before the EC Courts', *Common Market Law Review*, 45(4): 941–985.

Button, C. (2004) *The Power to Protect: Trade, Health and Uncertainty in the WTO*, Oxford: Hart Publishing.

Chalmers, D., Davies, G. and Monti, G. (2010) *EU Law*, Cambridge: Cambridge University Press.

Cottier, T. and Mavroides, P. (2003) *The Role of the Judge in International Trade Regulation*, Ann Arbor, MI: University of Michigan Press.

Craig, P. (2006) *EU Administrative Law*, Oxford: Oxford University Press.

Everson, M. and Vos, E. (2009) 'Scientification of Politics and Politicisation of Science', in M. Everson and E. Vos (eds), *Uncertain Risks Regulated*, London: Routledge/Cavendish Publishing, pp. 1–17.

Faigman, D. (1999) *Legal Alchemy: The Use and Misuse of Science in the Law*, New York: W.H. Freeman and Co.

Feldman, R. (2009) *The Role of Science in Law*, Oxford: Oxford University Press.

Foster, C. (2011) *Science and the Precautionary Principle in International Courts and Tribunals: Expert Evidence, Burden of Proof and Finality*, Cambridge: Cambridge University Press.

Hilson, C. (2005), 'Beyond Rationality? Judicial Review and Public Concern', *Northern Ireland Legal Quarterly*, 56(3): 320–341.

Holder, J. (2004) *Environmental Assessment: The Regulation of Decision-Making*, Oxford: Oxford University Press.

Jacobs, F.J. (1999) 'Recent Developments in the Principle of Proportionality in the European Community', in E. Ellis (ed.), *The Principle of Proportionality in the Laws of Europe*, Oxford: Hart Publishing, pp. 1–22.

Janssen, A.M. and Van Asselt, M.B.A. (2012) 'The Precautionary Principle in Court: An Analysis of Post-Pfizer Case Law', in M.B.A. van Asselt, E. Versluis and E. Vos (eds), *Balancing Between Trade and Risk: Integrating Legal and Social Science Perspectives,* London: Taylor and Francis.

Jasanoff, S. (1990) *The Fifth Branch. Science Advisers as Policymakers*, Cambridge, MA/London: Harvard University Press.

——(1995) *Science at the Bar: Law, Science and Technology in America*, Harvard, MA: Harvard University Press.

——(1997) 'Judging Science: Issues, Assumptions, and Models', in Roscoe Pound Foundation, *Report of the 1997 Forum for State Court Judges, Scientific Evidence in Courts: Concepts and Controversies*, pp. 9–26.

Joerges, C. (1997) 'Scientific Expertise in Social Regulation and the European Court of Justice: Legal Framework for Denationalised Governance Structures', in C. Joerges, K.H. Ladeur and E. Vos (eds), *Integrating Scientific Expertise into Regulatory Decision-Making – National Experiences and European Innovations*, Baden-Baden: Nomos, pp. 295–324.

Ladeur, K.H. (2003) 'The Introduction of the Precautionary Principle into EU Law: A Pyrrhic Victory for Environmental and Public Health Law? Decision-Making under Conditions of Complexity in Multi-Level Political Systems', *Common Market Law Review*: 1455–1479.

Lee, M. (2010) 'Beyond Safety? The Broadening Scope of Risk Regulation', in C. O'Cinneide (ed.), *Current Legal Problems 2009*, Oxford: Oxford University Press, pp. 267–276.

McNelis, N. (2003) 'The Role of the Judge in the EU and WTO: Lessons from the BSE and Hormone Cases', in T. Cottier and P. Mavroides (eds), *The Role of the Judge In International Trade Regulation*, Ann Arbor, MI: University of Michigan Press, pp. 225–247.

Marchant, G.E. and Mosman, K.L. (2004) *Arbitrary and Capricious: The Precautionary Principle in the European Courts*, Washington, DC: AEI Press.

Nehl, H. (1999) *Principles of Administrative Procedure in EC Law*, Oxford: Hart Publishing.

Roscoe Pound Foundation (1997) *Report on the 1997 Forum for State Court Judges, Scientific Evidence in Courts: Concepts and Controversies*, Washington, DC: Roscoe Pound Foundation.

Scallen, E. and Wiethoff, W. (1998) 'The Ethos of Expert Witnesses: Confusing the Admissibility, Sufficiency and Credibility of Expert Testimony', *Hastings Law Journal*, 49: 1143–1468.

Scott, J. (2001) 'On Kith and Kine (and Crustaceans), "Trade and Environment in the EU and WTO"', in J.H.H. Weiler (ed.), *The EU, the WTO, and the NAFTA*, Oxford: Oxford University Press, pp. 125–167.

——(2007) *The WTO Agreement on Sanitary and Phytosanitary Measures: A Commentary*, Oxford: Oxford University Press.

Scott, J. and Sturm, S. (2006) 'Courts as Catalysts: Re-Thinking the Judicial Role in New Governance', *Columbia Journal of European Law*, 13: 565–594.

Scott, J. and Vos, E. (2002) 'The Juridification of Uncertainty: Observations on the Ambivalence of the Precautonary Principle within the EU and the WTO', in C. Joerges and R. Dehousse (eds), *Good Governance in Europe's Integrated Market*, Oxford: Oxford University Press, pp. 253–286.

Slootboom, M. (2003) 'Do Public Health Measures Receive Similar Treatment in European Community and World Trade Organisation Law?', *Journal of World Trade Law*: 553–996.

Stokes, E. (2008) 'The EC Courts' Contribution on Refining the Parameters of Precaution', *Journal of Risk Research*: 491–507.

Tai, S. (2009) 'Uncertainty about Uncertainty: The Impact of Judicial Decisions on Assessing Scientific Uncertainty', *Journal of Constitutional Law*, 11(3): 671–727.

Van Asselt, M.B.A. and Vos, E. (2006) 'Precautionary Principle and the Uncertainty Paradox', *Journal of Risk Research*: 313–36.

Van Asselt, M., Fox, T., Versluis, E. and Vos, E. (2012) 'Synthesis', in M.B.A. van Asselt, E. Versluis and E. Vos (eds), *Trade, Health and the Environment*, London: Taylor and Francis.

Vos, E. (2000) 'EU Food Safety Regulation in the Aftermath of the BSE Crisis', *Journal of Consumer Policy*: 227–255.

——(2004) 'Antibiotics, the Precautionary Principle and the Court in First Instance', *Maastricht Journal of European and Comparative Law*: 187–200.

Part V

Role of stakeholders

9 Involving stakeholders in risk governance

The importance of expertise, trust and moral emotions

Sofia Kaliarnta, Maria Hage and Sabine Roeser

Introduction

As global trade increases with exploding speed, so do attempts to regulate the production and distribution of countless products, ranging from medication and cosmetics to chemical solvents and food additives. The challenge for regulators is to find a delicate balance between promoting trade values, such as product distribution and market access, and non-trade values, such as health and safety of the general public who will consume such goods. The European Union has taken a leading role here by appointing authorities, both at a Member State level and at a pan-European level. The goal of these authorities is to regulate the EU internal and external markets by authorizing the introduction of new products and also by performing quality controls on all products distributed in the EU, with the final aim of safeguarding public health and the environment. However, this task becomes increasingly challenging due to the multitude of such authorities at various levels of governance as well as the conflicting interests and goals of non-EU members and manufacturers. At this critical juncture, the contribution of the various stakeholders who are involved in the assessment and regulation of goods can provide a much needed inside perspective on several pressing issues. The specialized knowledge and different perspectives provided by different stakeholders can lead to a deepened knowledge and better informed final decisions. Involving the general public in the stakeholder process is also a way of contributing to a more inclusive participation procedure.

In April 2010, Maastricht University held a conference titled 'European Integration between Trade and Non Trade', with the aim to 'provide more insight in the difficulties for regulators and scientists in their struggle to encourage trade and further integration, whilst protecting important societal values such as health and safety and the environment'. The lead conference organizers were Ellen Vos, Professor of European Union Law at Maastricht University, Marjolein B.A. van Asselt, Professor of Risk Governance at Maastricht University, and Michelle Everson, Professor of European Law in the School of Law at Birkbeck, University of London. In order to further stimulate the discussion and exchange between the academic participants and stakeholders, two workshops were organized where various stakeholders could talk about their experience as representatives of governmental authorities, non-governmental organizations (NGOs) or industry members. One of the workshops was entitled 'The Role of Stakeholders in Protecting Market and Non Market Values'. The other workshop focused on insights into stakeholder involvement from a participant's point of view. During these workshops, a broad spectrum of stakeholders was present, ranging from representatives of EU regulatory bodies to national Member State authorities and industry representatives. The issues discussed spanned an array of matters, such as regulation procedures, the length of procedures, usefulness (or desirableness) of the public's participation in the stakeholders' process and the trust and uncertainty arising in the context of risk regulation. The main issues posed by the workshop chair were: the dilemmas of free trade versus the protection of human health and environment; expectations from stakeholder participation with regard to the types of policy dossiers; and the role of scientific uncertainty and expertise. The workshops yielded significant insights into a wide range of topics regarding regulation and stakeholder participation. In this essay we will analyse the most important issues that were discussed. Most importantly, the importance of trust in risk governance was emphasized. We will argue that trust can be a legitimate moral emotion that ought indeed to have a prominent place in risk governance. Furthermore, we will argue that moral emotions in general can be helpful in making trade-offs between various values. However, we will first discuss some general key issues underlying stakeholder participation and expand upon them by using insights provided by the workshop participants.

Stakeholder participation

We will use the *Stakeholder Participation Guidance of the Netherlands Environmental Assessment Agency* (Hage and Leroy 2008) to structure the issues discussed in the workshops. This *Stakeholder Participation Guidance* is intended to guide and support project leaders in their choices in the area of stakeholder participation. But it is also suited as a tool for analysing and evaluating participatory practices. The Guidance is organized around the following central questions:

- Why provide for participation?
- What should participation be about?
- How much participation should there be?
- Who should be involved?

We use the structure of the Guidance for analysing the debate at the workshop. To that end, we will discuss the concepts and ideas that lie behind these questions. We will introduce them one by one and then structure the discussions from the workshop (see section on 'Stakeholder participation: views from the workshop participants') around these questions.

Why provide for participation?

The vast literature on stakeholder participation in the area of environmental knowledge production and decision making (see for instance: Funtowicz and Ravetz 1993; Gibbons *et al.* 1994; Irwin 1995; Renn *et al.* 1995; Wynne 1996; Thompson Klein *et al.* 2001; Pellizoni 2003; Joss and Bellucci 2002; Kates *et al.* 2001; Kasemir *et al.* 2003; Rowe and Frewer 2000; Reed 2008) lists a multitude of aims and motives which, in practice, overlap and coincide (Hage *et al.* 2010). It is fair to distinguish them into four main categories: instrumental aims, quality aims, democratic aims and emancipatory aims.

Instrumental aims focus on the acceptance of a procedure, product or institution. Participation here is meant to help gain public support for certain risk practices and strengthen the image of the organizing institution. Another instrumental aim is the wider distribution of a given content, such as scientific evaluation reports among decision makers, which in turn may contribute to its actual impact in decision-making processes.

Quality aims of participation concern either quality control of the used knowledge and used methods or filling in knowledge gaps. Where there is a large degree of uncertainty, due to the nature of the issue at stake or because it is a 'new' problem, stakeholder participation can be used to legitimize knowledge. This involves identifying and defining problems from different perspectives, but also formulating research questions and bringing in hands-on knowledge.

Democratic aims envisage participation for its own sake. The consideration here is that stakeholders are entitled to participate in decision-making processes that affect them. That is often the case with risk governance issues where value conflicts play a role (e.g. safety versus security, environment versus safety, etc.).

Emancipatory aims concern processes of mutual learning, creating networks of expertise and supporting less privileged groups with knowledge and capacity building (empowerment). Emancipatory aims may overlap with democratic aims because empowerment enables unorganized groups, like consumers or farmers in developing countries, to engage in the process.

What should participation be about?

What should be the scope of the participatory process and which parts of the process are or are not open to stakeholder participation? Some procedures are more policy-oriented, while others are more science-oriented. Participatory processes differ in their political context, their geographical and administrative scale and the degrees of freedom of the organizing institution in which to manoeuvre. With regard to an issue's complexity, some scholars such as

Ezrahi (1980); Funtowicz and Ravetz (1993); and Hisschemöller and Hoppe (1996) have all classified emerging societal problems in two axes: one axis regards the availability and (un)certainty of knowledge on the issue; the second regards the ethical or political consensus or controversy of or on the issue. As a consequence, the scope, need and possible added value of participation (or 'extended peer review', as Funtowicz and Ravetz call it) will differ accordingly. The classification into categories of knowledge problems and value conflicts appears simple on paper. In practice, however, actors do not agree on the category into which 'their' problem falls: they tend either to estimate the knowledge base or the norms and values consensus higher than they actually are or they put the emphasis on gaps in knowledge and uncertainty and call for more research on strategic or political grounds. We will return to the issues of uncertainty of knowledge and values later on (see sections on 'Scientific uncertainty and the role of expertise' and 'Stakeholders, emotions and trust in risk debates', below).

How much participation should there be?

As stakeholder participation is a very broad instrument having diverse aims, it occurs in different forms and at different levels of inclusion: from an informative meeting about research findings as a form of participation to allow stakeholders to be actively involved in the analysis, to giving stakeholders an actual say on the outcomes of the process. To indicate different degrees of participation, scholars often use the metaphor of a ladder, a metaphor initiated by Arnstein (1969) and frequently elaborated upon since (see Klinke and Renn 2002), indicating the levels of ambition for participation from low to high. However, the ladder metaphor does not necessarily imply 'the more participation, the better'. Different degrees of participation may be appropriate depending on the aims, context of the problem and resources available.

Who should be involved?

This question presupposes an answer to the first question on aims and motives of the stakeholder involvement broken down into instrumental aims, quality aims, democratic aims and emancipatory aims. When the aim is to gather knowledge (quality aim), then a broad selection of scientists, policy makers and societal representatives is desirable, while if the aim is to generate support (instrumental aim), then the influence and power position of stakeholders is an important criterion for selection. Participation of the broader public is associated with the democratic and emancipatory aim that every citizen should have a say in the process. It builds on the idea that participation should contribute to a further democratization of society by including all voices and all arguments on the issue that are given by the stakeholders. In the context of risk governance, the question of power becomes an issue when we think about how to offer access to all interested parties. The question arises as to who or what should be included in the process: citizens, consumers, specific interest groups, different perspectives and/or different sources of knowledge? When we deal with professional interest groups, it is not always clear who is represented by whom.

Stakeholder participation: views from the workshop participants

We will now analyse salient ideas that were discussed at the workshops. We will relate them to the framework on stakeholder participation discussed in the previous section. Next to the aspects of the framework of stakeholder participation, a few additional concepts were discussed, namely the roles of expertise and of trust. These notions will be discussed in more detail in the section on 'Scientific uncertainty and the role of expertise'.

Why participation?

How were the aims of stakeholder participation perceived by the workshop participants? And how does that relate to the previously mentioned aims: instrumental, quality, democratic and emancipatory aims? It will be shown that all these aims were indeed deemed to be important by the workshop participants.

First, participants spoke of 'quality improvement' as an important aim of stakeholder participation. A more inclusive stakeholder participation process can assist with providing knowledge about the impact of decision making on societal actors and what the effects of the proposed regulations can be on different societal groups. One workshop participant said: 'The added value is to have a different voice, so not only the scientific voice'. Regulatory authorities use stakeholder participation to get to know what is going on in the field and what will be the impact of their decisions. Stakeholders from industry may suggest slight legislative changes that will improve their manufacturing process since the outcome of the regulatory process can lead to adjustment of rules and legislation. Stakeholders such as scientists employed by industry or NGOs can contribute specialized scientific knowledge in hearings and consultation rounds.

Second, participants pursue a 'democratic aim' (which also involves emancipatory aims): especially workshop participants who represent organized stakeholders from industry, as well as from NGOs, stated that they want to 'get heard in the legislation process'. They insisted on 'getting engaged [at] a very early stage and not to miss any stakeholder [out]'. Giving all stakeholders, including members of the public, the chance to be heard could potentially increase legitimacy and societal support for the outcome of the stakeholder participation process. One participant mentioned that stakeholder participation could be an important tool in order to 'build trust in the system', although it is unclear whether the aim of trust building is instrumental in avoiding public unrest or is perceived as the result of stakeholder participation. This might indicate a general ambiguity or even tension between instrumental and genuinely democratic and emancipatory aims.

What should participation be about? How much participation should there be?

These questions were so intermingled that they are best discussed together. Stakeholder participatory processes can be very different depending on the scope and the orientation of the procedure. The participants of the workshops generally underlined the idea of different degrees of participation, depending on the purpose and issue at stake. From the point of view of the workshop participants, broader participation is welcomed when the issue is about a new emerging technology or product. According to one of them:

> If you go for new areas, like nanotechnology, where you need new legislation, where you need to discuss, to debate with each other what might be the risks, who is concerned about risks and who is exposed to risks. I completely agree with you that we should do it in a participatory process.

Broad stakeholder participation appears to be the most accepted approach among the workshop participants. As one adviser at EU level stated, 'It is very important that all stakeholder interests are engaged at a very early stage and not to miss any stakeholder. That means taking into account all possible views, and also to base regulation on sound science and risk regulation.'

Within participatory regulation procedures, participation is strictly regulated. The government is the final actor to decide after a regulatory process. According to workshop participants, stakeholders should be aware that, in the end, the responsibility lies with the government: 'So participation does not have to mean that their views will be adopted and I think that must be very clear'.

A slightly different perspective can be detected on participation by 'organizers' of participatory processes on the one hand and by 'stakeholder participants' of processes on the other hand. As a stakeholder, a 'participant' expects that, 'we are involved in the different steps of the legislative process and also have a voice and are able to state our interests. … We believe it is a way to enhance discussions and to reach a balanced approach to these different views'. However, according to the 'organizers' of participatory procedures this is different when the subject is or has become an established technology or procedure.

> When the legislation is in place this comes to an end, then we start our daily work. Even if there is an exceed of a standard, there is not much we can do … . If someone expects that shareholder participation should be part of my daily work, then I'll say: 'Wait a moment'. It might not be necessary each time, because people only want to hear from us that the food is safe.

One civil servant agreed that '80 per cent to 90 per cent of our daily work can be done without participation. In my work, most of the time we do our job without any participatory process.' A risk governance student framed this discussion as an issue of trust: 'if you are sure that with a risk based approach the public trusts in you and stakeholders completely agree with you, then you should not involve stakeholders'.

These views correspond with the idea of structured problems (Hisschemöller and Hoppe 1996) as worked out by the *Guidance for Stakeholder Participation* (Hage and Leroy 2008): in cases of sufficient certainty of knowledge and reasonable consensus as to the norms and values at issue, there is little need for stakeholder participation. In cases of 'unknown areas' like new technologies or procedures with need for scientific, practical and ethical knowledge to be developed, stakeholder participation is an instrument to broaden the knowledge base. We will discuss these issues in more detail in the following sections.

Whom to involve?

If stakeholder involvement is relevant, the question arises as to which stakeholders should be included and who are the stakeholders in the first place. In the view of one participant: 'Stakeholders are the full range of social actors who stand to be affected by decision making'.

That includes stakeholders from industry, NGOs, and consumer and patient organizations as unorganized stakeholders, also known as 'the general public' or citizens.

Regulatory authorities find it sometimes difficult to define who exactly the stakeholders are and what their true interests are. Some umbrella organizations only represent a small common interest: a small supermarket chain can have completely different interests compared to a large multinational in the same sector. The same question arises with consumer and patient organizations: who are they representing and should they be entitled to take part in the process? As one of the workshop participants formulated it: 'Are we talking to the right parties?' The discussion at the workshop regarding the possible participation of the public as a legitimate stakeholder resulted in the general consensus that including the public is desirable. However, regulatory authorities have difficulties in reaching the general public. They encounter a lack of interest or lack of public debate, or they face difficulties in finding the right communication channels. Their experience is that only 'the usual suspects' turn up on the day.

Second, there seems to be an issue of being well informed in order to participate in stakeholder debates, and members of the general public are considered not to have the knowledge necessary to contribute in a meaningful way. Some of the workshop participants made a distinction between 'qualified' and 'unqualified' stakeholders. Lack of knowledge seems the most important threshold for 'unqualified' stakeholders to participate in procedures. In cases of very specific statutory procedures where there is very little spare time for consultation, there is no time for educating stakeholders in a way that they can understand and contribute to the procedure. As one civil servant said,

> the pitfall is that when we start implementation or the negotiation process, we have a heavy time constraint, so if we were to use stakeholder involvement, we expect from the stakeholders a level of knowledge, that makes it extremely difficult. But if they have good knowledge, then we can work very fast because we communicate in the same language. That is a pitfall, the fact that stakeholders want to be involved but do not have a clue of what they are talking about. I am willing to educate these people but I do not have a year: I only have one day.

In practice, that might lead to the exclusion of members of the general public due to lack of specific expertise. The participants agreed that the general public should be more involved, but were unsure as to which issues should be opened up to broad public participation and to what extent. According to another civil servant, representing a food and safety authority, 'We hardly communicate with final consumers. We mostly talk to producers, inspection services, etc.' A representative from industry agreed, pointing out that they also have to deal with very different types of consumer, some being more involved and more knowledgeable already and others less so. This is perceived as a significant problem in communication. Even though consulting the public is considered important, it was not clear from the discussion what the added value of engaging the general public would be. In the discussion this was framed as the 'paradox of the general public'. As described by one NGO representative:

> There is a paradox in the idea of involving the general public. What do you expect from this? Because if you want someone from the general public to really be engaged to enter into a subject and to grow in his competence on the subject, then he becomes organised and is no more part of the general public.

There is an interesting discussion in both workshops on the role of the general public. Participants share the feeling that 'the public' should be included and be able to contribute to participatory processes in the area of risk governance, but that also in some way they are not able to specify the form that their contribution might take. We will come back to this question in the section on 'Stakeholders, emotions and trust in risk debates', below, where we will propose that involving the public in the stakeholder process can contribute specifically to addressing moral aspects of risk governance.

Another issue discussed during the workshops was the (in)dependence and neutrality of the process. The inclusion of very influential and knowledgeable stakeholders and industry is perceived as controversial, especially when it comes to the role of the chair:

> My expectations are that the role of the chair needs to be very clear. It really needs to be an independent chair without an own agenda. However, we have seen in many stakeholder approaches … that it was

> chaired by a former [employee of a renowned multinational]. That does not seem like a very independent chair. They have their own agenda, even if they [have left the company], so that is a major flaw.

It appears that it is not always easy to find a neutral chairperson due to the very technical subjects that risk regulation is dealing with. The people who are able to follow the discussion are mostly those who are professionally involved and have an interest. This principle applies in particular to the chairperson: 'I can understand that it is hard to balance this, the interest, the former interest and the expertise a chair should have'.

As a rule, it is considered that, even though including the public as a stakeholder is desirable, there are several issues connected to this: first, there is a difficulty in defining the general public precisely. Some failed attempts to include the general public in the stakeholder process have generated scepticism regarding the feasibility for the general public to be included. Second, it seems to be questionable that members of the general public are well enough informed to participate in stakeholder debates. Many of the workshop participants considered members of the general public not to have the knowledge necessary to contribute to the stakeholder process in a meaningful way. Lastly, the inclusion of industry representatives, especially those in positions of authority, in the stakeholder process needs to be done in a way that balances technical knowledge with neutrality.

Scientific uncertainty and the role of expertise

A central topic at the workshop was the observation that the uncertainty inherent in risk governance leads to many controversies. Many of the risk governance practitioners that participated in the workshop mentioned science as the main way to be able to offer correct information. Science is also perceived as a basis on which to organize common ground between different countries and cultures in view of the ambition to reach a common decision. As one risk assessor stated:

> Depending on science is the only way to go. Certainly in a WTO world, science, risks, health effects are the only issues where you can find a baseline for some kind of common agreement, because we know our culture is different from culture in the Philippines. The only way to come to a common agreement is to use science.

Thus, science is viewed as a neutral mediator that may be acceptable to all parties. Science is also seen as an instrument to 'temper emotions', especially of the general public. Emotions are experienced as something that needs to be corrected with the right scientific information:

> I think the first role of science is to deal with a very emotive topic. Animal welfare brings a lot of emotions to the table and so the first role

> of science for us is in providing a basis for reasoned arguments in an arena often characterized by far too many emotions.

In the case of risk assessment, science has to deal with very complex long-term causal relationships, scientific models with underlying assumptions and so-called 'radical uncertainty' (Pellizoni 2003). As Van Asselt and Vos (2008: 282) state:

> In the case of uncertain risks, basic, seemingly simple, questions as to whether there is a real risk or whether there is enough safety cannot be answered by science. The presence of uncertainty challenges, or at least complicates, the role of experts as risk assessors.

For many of the practitioners in the workshop, scientific uncertainty is something they are aware of and they seemed to accept the inherently uncertain nature of science:

> I find scientific uncertainty a complete norm, a normative human condition. I think that everything changes on the planet at a greater speed than we necessarily recognize and I think the same is true for science. Therefore we can have certainty at a given moment in time, but perhaps within a week, within a month or within a year, that certainty will have disappeared as science moves on at a great pace. Whilst science is very important to us, we recognise that it has its limitations.

During the workshop, there seemed to be a marked difference between how regulation practitioners and politicians deal with scientific uncertainty, politicians accepting far lower margins of uncertainty when there is an important regulation decision to be made. One policy advisor commented:

> You need courage to make a decision and that is what at certain times is missing in politicians. They don't want to show any courage because they want to have the freedom to say: 'I cannot do anything else other than to accept the conclusion.' But that is not the politician's job. Therefore you need the courage to make a decision, notwithstanding the question of whether it's certain or not.

This view was also expressed by an NGO representative:

> My experience is that politicians often expect science to be 'one-armed', what I mean by that is that they want a certain result, they want clarity, so they do not feel comfortable with a scientist that says: 'on the one hand … , but on the other hand … '. That is why I say 'one-armed' scientist. I think the world is so complex these days, and people understand that, so to be clear about where you're certain and where you're not, a better clarity on that could really help improve the policy process as well.

As we can observe, then, while scientific uncertainty was acknowledged and accepted by some of the workshop participants as an inherent part of science, the view of science that it provides the necessary knowledge in order to create certainty is still upheld, particularly by political stakeholders. This pattern is also recognized as 'the uncertainty paradox': a paradoxical situation where 'on the one hand, it is increasingly recognised that science cannot provide decisive evidence on uncertain risks, while on the other hand policy-makers and authorities increasingly resort to science for more certainty and conclusive evidence' (Van Asselt and Vos, 2006: 317). To combat the effects of scientific uncertainty, one of the panellists advocated more inclusive stakeholder participation:

> When facing a situation with a high level of uncertainty or a high level of socio-political ambiguity, facing the situation of various visions on risks or benefits between social actors, then the problems cannot be solved by conventional science based [on] risk assessment alone. In those situations we need some kind of consultation, some kind of stakeholder participation to at least get to a common definition of what the problems are.

In conclusion, at the workshop different ideas about scientific expertise emerged, ranging from science as the ultimate authority to overcome public disputes, including value conflicts, to acknowledgment of scientific uncertainty. Ideas about trust also seemed to play a central role. In the first approach, science creates trust, while, in the second, stakeholder involvement is perceived as an instrument for creating trust to fill in the void that arises due to scientific uncertainty. We will discuss the relationship between expertise and trust and other emotions in the following section.

Stakeholders, emotions and trust in risk debates

The participants of the workshop emphasized the roles of trust, expertise and public participation in risk governance. In this section we will discuss how these various notions can be connected in a constructive way.

Trust in stakeholders and the regulation process

The issue of trust appeared important to all practitioners. In a regulatory process involving delicate negotiations and where different values and goals need to be balanced, trust must be cultivated between the participants. As one civil servant said:

> Trust is a process of interaction which is not only one-sided. And especially risk communication in terms of stakeholder involvement and gaining public trust is not the end step after risk communication and risk management has been concluded. As a general statement, talking about

> trust, what comes to my mind is this notion of trust being hard to gain but easily lost.

Another civil servant seemed to agree that trust

> is a problem all three of us have: risk communicators, risk managers and risk assessors. We have to do something to gain it. We do not have it. For us it is still very difficult. We need some kind of a sign or some kind of tool that can tell us to go with a participatory procedure.

The notion of trust seems to be linked to personal communication and contact: once trust has been established, it is even possible for stakeholders coming from completely different standpoints and representing different interests to achieve a more harmonious co-operation. In the words of one NGO representative:

> If you share a table with industry, normally you just exchange positions: 'I'm against nuclear, I'm pro-nuclear, full stop'. But if you have gotten to know each other a bit better, you also get an understanding of the interests of the other party. Sometimes you can even come together.

Entering a participatory procedure in order to create and establish trust was one of the proposed approaches mentioned by the workshop participants. A student present at the conference said:

> Risk assessors or regulators must always try to measure the extent of trust that exists between the public and you as risk assessors or regulators, and that also includes the stakeholders that are involved. If you realise that there is no maximum trust, then there is a need for you to involve stakeholders, but if you are sure that with a risk based approach the public trusts in you and stakeholders completely agree with you, then you should not involve stakeholders.

In other words, lack of trust in science or the regulators, or both, can provide motivation and a legitimate reason to enhance a more inclusive stakeholder involvement.

Trust and other emotions as aid in making value trade-offs

In this subsection, we will review various existing approaches as to how trust, expertise and public participation can interact in risk governance. We will distinguish the technocratic approach and various participatory approaches, which we subdivide into populist and deliberative approaches. We will reject the technocratic approach and the populist approach because they fail to take sufficient account of moral values. We will then propose an improved version of the deliberative approach by proposing a more prominent role for moral emotions than is currently the case. This requires a different understanding of emotions: not as opposition to, but as a specific form of, rationality.

On the technocratic approach to risk governance, scientists have the necessary expertise and should hence be in charge of decision making or advising regulators, taking the approach that the public should trust the scientists and advocating that there is neither need nor room for public participation.

Alternatively, there are various participatory approaches to risk governance, such as stakeholder involvement. Involving the public and other stakeholders can contribute to creating trust. Van Asselt and Renn (2011) make a nuanced discussion of this. The question is, What role expertise has within a participatory approach? According to some approaches, only scientists have relevant expertise, but the public should be included for democratic or instrumental reasons in order to achieve public support (Loewenstein *et al.* 2001). This can be referred to as the populist approach of risk governance.

In the populist approach, moral values either play no explicit role or are taken as subjective preferences that do not allow or require further deliberation and can at most be manipulated, as opposed to being reflected on critically. In the technocratic approach, moral values play an even less important role. Indeed, proponents of the technocratic approach praise it for being rational, objective and value neutral. In the technocratic approach, risk is defined as the probability of an unwanted effect, while cost-benefit or risk-benefit analysis is used to determine which of various alternative actions, policies or technologies would be preferable. However, determining what counts as an unwanted effect presupposes highly contestable value judgments. Does one only take into account fatalities alone or should injuries and illnesses that result from an activity, policy or technology also be considered (Asveld and Roeser 2009)? How should one measure, compare and balance these effects? How should one balance the positive effects of a policy or technology for one group with the negative effects for another group? What constitutes a fair distribution of risks and benefits in society (Hayenhjelm 2012)? Is it legitimate to impose risks on people and, if so, when (Asveld 2007)?

This is just a selection of moral considerations that matter when making decisions about risks, but which are either neglected by technocratic approaches or hidden within supposedly formal, value-neutral models. However, rather than implicitly include contestable moral values in a formal model, they should be made explicit as they require moral deliberation, reflection and discussion by all parties involved. This does not happen in the technocratic approach. But, in the populist approach, although the public is heard, there is no genuine dialogue and no explicit reflection about the moral values involved in risk decisions. What we need, then, are approaches to stakeholder participation that acknowledge the importance of explicit reflection and deliberation on moral values. Several scholars who argued in favour of participatory approaches have argued that the public should be included in risk governance because it adds an important perspective to decision making about risk, as their risk perceptions include moral and social values (see Slovic 2000; and

Jaeger *et al.* 2001). In such an approach, which we could call the deliberative approach, the public has moral expertise. Concerning moral expertise, the public is on an equal footing with scientists, since the unique expertise of the latter is confined to the scientific realm.

However, some scholars are concerned about the disruptive role that emotions might play in stakeholder involvement. This was also mentioned by some of the workshop participants. Emotions are taken to be a disturbing factor in sound decision making as they make people prone to various biases (Gilovich *et al.* 2002). Laypeople's risk perceptions are emotionally charged (see Slovic 2010) and seen as a problem or a reason to be hesitant to include the public in decision making about risks (Sunstein 2005).

Thus, the dilemma arises as to whether to ban the public from risk decisions – which might make it difficult to include a broad reflection and discussion of moral values – or include the public, which gives too much room for irrational emotions. One might think this dilemma could be solved by asking experts to reflect about ethical aspects of risk but psychometric research into risk perceptions of experts and laypeople shows that the public has a broader view of risks than experts who include moral values (Slovic 2000). Other studies show that gender and ethnicity of experts influence the risk perceptions of experts (Slovic 1999). Therefore, leaving the reflection and discussion of moral values to experts would seem inadequate. As for including the public as an opportunity for genuine moral reflection about the risks involved, there is, apparently, a high risk of emotional bias. But is it really true that emotions are likely to disturb moral decision making?

We are so used to the idea that emotions are irrational that this often becomes an assumption, something taken for granted, or even an uncontested assumption in a lot of academic research. However, many leading philosophers and psychologists who study emotions have challenged the dichotomy between reason and emotion. They emphasize that emotions involve cognitive aspects (Scherer 1984; Frijda 1987; Lazarus 1991; Solomon 1993; Damasio 1994; Nussbaum 2001). Emotions have affective and cognitive aspects that cannot be separated. They are two sides of the same coin (Zagzebski 2003; Roberts 2003). For example, having the emotion of guilt not only involves feeling the pangs of guilt but also holding the belief that one did something wrong (Roeser 2011). Emotions help us to detect moral aspects of situations that we would otherwise not notice (Little 1995; Blum 1994).

The neuroscientist Antonio Damasio (1994) has studied people with brain defects to their amygdala in the prefrontal cortex. It turns out that amygdala patients do not feel emotions any more and at the same time they lose their capacity to make practical and concrete moral judgments. Amygdala patients still perform purely cognitive tasks well and they still know general moral principles. However, in concrete circumstances, amygdala patients do not know how to behave. From normal, pleasant people, they change into rude, inconsiderate people. Amygdala patients also make decisions about risks that deviate from those of normal people. Amygdala patients are willing to take major risks that normal people find unacceptable (the so-called Iowa gambling task: Damasio 1994). Apparently, emotions are needed for (moral) risk judgments to be made.

These insights show that the apparent dilemma formulated before is actually grounded in a false dichotomy. The fact that including the public in decision making about risk also means including emotions, does not threaten moral deliberation about risks but actually may facilitate it. Emotions such as worry, enthusiasm, compassion, feelings of justice and responsibility, make people sensitive to important moral values that are not given explicit attention in formal approaches to risk. For example, enthusiasm for a technology can point to benefits to people's well-being, whereas fear and worry can indicate which public values and dimensions of individual well-being are at stake. Sympathy and empathy can provide insights into a fair distribution of risks and benefits, and indignation can be an indication of violations of autonomy by risks that are imposed against somebody's will (Roeser 2006). Reflecting upon and discussing moral emotions in deliberations about risks – which we refer to as the 'emotional deliberation approach' to risk governance – might allow us to avoid the technocratic and populist pitfalls, and paves the way for genuine ethical reflection. Emotions should not be neglected or seen as givens that cannot be investigated any further but, rather, as triggers for discussion. The arguments, reasons and considerations that are revealed by or underlie emotional responses to technological risks and benefits have to be taken seriously. The importance of moral reasons in politics has been emphasized in the literature on deliberative democracy (Rawls 1996; Habermas 1996; Bohman and Rehg 1997; Guttman and Thompson 2000). O'Neill (2002) argues that such accounts are overly rationalistic and should include emotions as sources of moral knowledge. What we need, then, is an approach to stakeholder involvement that explicitly encourages and includes moral emotions as indispensable sources of ethical insight.

Explicitly addressing emotions in debates about risky technologies will help to bring moral values out in the open. Of course, it is likely that people will have different emotions, values and concerns about risky technologies. But by making these concerns explicit, there is a chance for a genuine dialogue and for critical reflection. In stakeholder involvement one should accept the possibility of emotions diverging among people and discuss the concerns that lie behind them. Considering these diverging emotions and views can lead to more balanced judgments. Emotions are not infallible and, just like other sources of knowledge, emotions can also be mistaken. Emotions have to be critically assessed but they are an important source of second-order reflection about people's first-order emotions (Lacewing 2005). For example, an emotion such as sympathy can correct egoistic emotions such as in the NIMBY ('not in my back yard') problem (Roeser 2010). What are the concerns informing the moral emotions of the public, experts and policy makers? Those concerns need to be examined carefully and met with genuine arguments in public debates.

Stakeholder participation that explicitly addresses emotions might allow for a more balanced and morally better decision-making process. In addition, this might contribute to the trust between stakeholders. Including moral emotions in debates about risky technologies puts all stakeholders and participants on an equal footing, as there are no 'emotional experts' in the same sense as there are scientific experts. Due to the different interests and views between industry stakeholders and NGO stakeholders, trust between them can be difficult at times. However, because all stakeholders have an equal status in the moral debate, explicitly including moral emotions can contribute to lowering existing barriers and to fostering an open discussion and co-operation.

Consequently, the proposed approach helps to clarify the relationship between the salient notions that have emerged from the workshop with risk experts, NGOs and industry stakeholders. These notions were expertise, uncertainty, public participation and trust. These notions could be seen to be at odds with each other, constituting a dilemma between science and emotions. The notion that the public's emotions should be tempered by information emanating from scientific expertise, as was observed in the workshop, is based on a false dichotomy where emotion and rationality are two opposing concepts. Such a notion may stir up unnecessary worries about the potential participation of the public in the stakeholder process, while the potential moral expertise of the participants themselves and the added value of their views is not (sufficiently) recognized. By adopting a specific understanding of emotions, where emotions pinpoint morally salient aspects, such dilemmas regarding public participation in the stakeholder process can be corrected. Good stakeholder involvement involves expertise and trust, but moral expertise stands next to scientific expertise and can actually be provided by stakeholder involvement that takes people's emotions seriously. This provides for morally better-made decisions as well as for more trust between stakeholders.

Conclusion

In risk governance, difficult value trade-offs have to be made. In this chapter, we have reflected on the discussions of a workshop among stakeholders and experts about stakeholder involvement. Central to the discussion were notions of expertise and trust. In the workshop discussions, assumptions derived from the technocratic and populist approaches emerged, giving rise to false dichotomies, and unnecessary dilemmas and superfluous fears about participation resulted. It was also not recognized that moral expertise which is provided through emotions is necessary to decision making about risk. Participation can have added value in risk governance when moral emotions are genuinely reflected upon and discussed. The emotions and intuition of laypeople reflect a broader view of risks (Slovic 2000; Roeser 2007). Taking emotions seriously in risk governance can lead to a reassessment of emotional responses to risk by showing that certain concerns are unfounded. On the other hand, if emotional concerns are indeed well founded, they may lead to a shift in risk governance. We propose to respect the views of people by taking their emotional concerns seriously and we are convinced that this can contribute to better risk governance by making sure that all important ethical considerations receive sufficient attention in finding a delicate balance between different values. In addition, by contributing to a genuine dialogue between stakeholders, this approach might contribute to overcoming some predictable stalemates that currently often occur in debates about risks.

References

Arnstein, S.R. (1969) 'A Ladder of Citizen Participation', *Journal of the American Institute of Planners*, 35: 216–24.

Asveld, L. (2007) 'Autonomy and Risk: Criteria for International Trade Regimes', *Journal of Global Ethics*, 3(1): 21–38.

Asveld, L. and Roeser, S. (eds) (2009) *The Ethics of Technological Risk*, London: Earthscan.

Blum, L.A. (1994) *Moral Perception and Particularity*, New York: Cambridge University Press.

Bohman, J. and Regh, W. (eds) (1997) *Deliberative Democracy: Essays on Reason and Politics*, Boston, MA: MIT Press.

Damasio, A. (1994) *Descartes' Error*, New York: Putnam.

Ezrahi, Y. (1980) 'Utopian and Pragmatic Rationalism: The Political Context of Expert Advice', *Minerva*, 18: 111–41.

Frijda, N. (1987) *The Emotions*, Cambridge: Cambridge University Press.

Funtowicz, S.O. and Ravetz, J.R. (1993) 'Science for the Post-normal Age', *Futures*, 739–55.

Gibbons, M., Limoges, C., Nowotny, H., Schwartzman, S., Scott, P. and Trow, M. (1994) *The New Production of Knowledge: The Dynamics of Science and Research in Contemporary Societies*, London: Sage Publications.

Gilovich, T., Griffin, D. and Kahnemann, D. (eds) (2002) *Heuristics and Biases: The Psychology of Intuitive Judgment*, Cambridge: Cambridge University Press.

Guttman, A. and Thompson, D. (2000) *Democracy and Disagreement*, Cambridge: Harvard University Press.

Habermas, J. (1996) *Between Facts and Norms: Contributions to a Discourse Theory of Law and Democracy*, Oxford: Blackwell Press.

Hage, M. and Leroy, P. (2008) *Leidraad Stakeholderparticipatie voor het Planbureau voor de Leefomgeving*, Hoofddocument, Bilthoven: PBL/RU Nijmegen.

Hage, M., Leroy, P. and Petersen, A.C. (2010) 'Stakeholder Participation in Environmental Knowledge Production', *Futures*, 42(3): 254–64.

Hayenhjelm, M. (2012) 'What is a Fair Distribution of Risk?', in S. Roeser, R. Hillerbrand, P. Sandin and M. Peterson (eds), *Handbook of Risk Theory*, Dordrecht: Springer, pp. 909–29.

Hisschemöller, M. and Hoppe, R. (1996) 'Coping with Intractable Controversies: The Case for Problem Structuring in Policy Design and Analysis', *Knowledge and Policy: The International Journal of Knowledge Transfer and Utilization*, 8: 40–60.

Irwin, A. (1995) *Citizen Science: A Study of People, Expertise and Sustainable Development*, London: Routledge.

Jaeger, C.J., Renn, O., Rosa, E.A. and Webler, T. (2001) *Risk, Uncertainty, and Rational Action*, London: Earthscan.

Joss, S. and Bellucci, S. (eds) (2002) *Participatory Technology Assessment. European Perspectives*, London: CSD.

Kasemir, B., Jäger, J., Jaeger, C.C. and Gardner, M.T. (eds) (2003) *Public Participation in Sustainability Science. A Handbook*, Cambridge: Cambridge University Press.

Kates, R.W., Clark, W.C., Corell, R., Hall, J.M., Jaeger, C.C., Lowe, I., McCarthy, J.J., Schellnhuber, H.J., Bolin, B., Dickson, N.M., Faucheux, S., Gallopin, G. C., Grübler, A., Huntley, B., Jäger, J., Jodha, N.S., Kasperson, R.E., Mabogunje, A., Matson, P., Mooney, H., Moore III, B., O'Riordan, T. and Svedin, U. (2001) 'Environment and Development: Sustainability Science', *Science*, 292: 641–42.

Klinke, A. and Renn, O. (2002) 'A New Approach to Risk Evaluation and Management: Risk-Based, Precaution-Based, and Discourse-Based Strategies', *Risk Analysis*, 22: 1071–94.

Lacewing, M. (2005) 'Emotional Self-Awareness and Ethical Deliberation', *Ratio*, 18: 65–81.

Lazarus, R. (1991) *Emotion and Adaptation*, New York: Oxford University Press.

Little, M.O. (1995) 'Seeing and Caring: The Role of Affect in Feminist Moral Epistemology', *Hypatia*, 10: 117–37.

Loewenstein, G.F., Weber, E.U, Hsee, C.K. and Welch, N. (2001) 'Risk as Feelings', *Psychological Bulletin*, 127: 267–86.

Nussbaum, M. (2001) *Upheavals of Thought*, Cambridge: Cambridge University Press.

O'Neill, J. (2002) 'The Rhetoric of Deliberation: Some Problems in Kantian Theories of Deliberative Democracy', *Res Publica*, 8: 249–68.

Pellizoni, L. (2003) 'Uncertainty and Participatory Democracy', *Environmental Values*, 12: 195–224.

Rawls, J. (1996), *Political Liberalism*, New York: Columbia University Press.

Reed, M.S. (2008) 'Stakeholder Participation for Environmental Management: A Literature Review', *Biological Conservation*, 141: 2417–31.

Renn, O., Webler, T. and Wiedemann, P. (eds) (1995) *Fairness and Competence in Citizen Participation*, Dordrecht: Kluwer Academic Publishers.

Roberts, R.C. (2003) *Emotions. An Essay in Aid of Moral Psychology*, Cambridge: Cambridge University Press.

Roeser, S. (2006) 'The Role of Emotions in Judging the Moral Acceptability of Risks', *Safety Science*, 44: 689–700.

——(2007) 'Ethical Intuitions about Risks', *Safety Science Monitor*, 11: 1–30.

——(2010) 'Emotional Reflection about Risks', in S. Roeser (ed.), *Emotions and Risky Technologies*, Dordrecht: Springer, pp. 231–44.

——(2011) 'Nuclear Energy, Risk and Emotions', *Philosophy and Technology*, 24: 197–201.

Rowe, G. and Frewer, L. (2000) 'Public Participation Methods: A Framework for Evaluation in Science', *Science, Technology and Human Values*, 25(1): 3–29.

Scherer, K.R. (1984) 'On the Nature and Function of Emotion: A Component Process Approach', in K.R. Scherer and P. Ekman (eds), *Approaches to Emotion*, Hillsdale/London: Lawrence Erlbaum Associates, 293–317.

Slovic, P. (1999) 'Trust, Emotion, Sex, Politics, and Science: Surveying the Risk-Assessment Battlefield', *Risk Analysis*, 19: 689–701.

——(2000) *The Perception of Risk*, London: Earthscan.

——(2010) 'If I Look at the Mass I Will Never Act: Psychic Numbing and Genocide', in S. Roeser (ed), *Emotions and Risky Technologies*, London: Earthscan, pp. 37–59.

Solomon, R. (1993) *The Passions: Emotions and the Meaning of Life*, Indianapolis, IN: Hackett.

Sunstein, C.R. (2005) *Laws of Fear*, Cambridge: Cambridge University Press.

Thompson Klein, J., Grossenbacher-Mansuy, W., Häberli, R., Bill, A., Scholz, R.W. and Welti, M. (eds) (2001) *Transdisciplinarity: Joint Problem Solving among Science, Technology and Society*, Berlin/Basel: Birkhauser Publisher.

Van Asselt, M.B.A. and Vos, E. (2006) 'The Precautionary Principle and the Uncertainty Paradox', *Journal of Risk Research*, 9(4): 313–36.

——(2008) 'Wrestling with Uncertain Risks: EU Regulation of GMOs and the Uncertainty Paradox', *Journal of Risk Research*, 11(1–2): 281-300.

Van Asselt, M.B.A. and Renn, O. (2011) 'Risk Governance', *Journal of Risk Research, Special Issue Uncertainty Precaution and Governance*, 14(4): 431–49.

Wynne, B. (1996) 'May the Sheep Safely Graze?', in S. Lash, B. Szerzynski and B. Wynne (eds), *Risk, Environment and Modernity*, London: Sage, pp. 44–83.

Zagzebski, L. (2003) 'Emotion and Moral Judgment', *Philosophy and Phenomenological Research*, 66: 104–24.

10 The interplay between science, law, health and trade

A practitioner's perspective

Interview with Member of European Parliament, Kartika Liotard, by Jos Cortenraad

The introduction of new foods into the European Union has been subject to strict regulations since the introduction of the Novel Food Regulation in 1997. New products must undergo extensive scientific testing and may not present a danger to consumer health. This applies to genetically manipulated crops such as corn, bananas and soy beans, but also to all products containing animal or vegetable ingredients. A separate regulation was introduced for genetically modified organisms (GMOs) in 2001 and 2003.

Meat from cloned animals and products manufactured using nanotechnology or nanoparticles can be freely traded in the 27 EU Member States. Since 2008, the majority of the European Parliament has unsuccessfully advocated the introduction of comprehensive legislation. One such advocate is Dutch Member of European Parliament, Kartika Liotard: 'Our health is at stake'.

When the Novel Food Regulation was incorporated into EU legislation in 1997, animal cloning was still considered as something akin to science fiction, while nanotechnology was still in its infancy. 'That's why it wasn't included in the regulation', says Kartika Liotard, who began her second term as European Parliament member in 2009. 'Technical developments eventually caught up with us and cloning gained momentum, particularly in the United States. Manufacturers also began using nano particles in their food packaging materials. It soon became clear that we needed new legislation.'

In 2007, the European Commission moved towards a recast of the ten-year-old Novel Food Regulation, to the initial satisfaction of parliament.

> Of course, we don't know whether eating cloned animal products is harmful to our health. But at the same time, you can also argue the ethical aspects of cloning. Opinions are divided. We're also not sure whether packages containing nanoparticles affect the food they contain. Without making any value judgements: we need legislation. That's the opinion of a wide majority of members of parliament; it's our job to guarantee food safety. The following precautionary principle applies: first determine whether the food is safe; only then release it on the market. Not the other way around. This was established in the General Food Law Regulation 178/2002.

The first proposals for a modified Novel Food Regulation were submitted in 2008. 'In principle, we had plenty of time', Liotard says looking back, 'certainly in terms of introducing legislation for cloning animals. The United States was making headway in this area but had to stick to the *gentlemen's agreement* of not selling any cloned products for the time being.'

Trade war

This was easier said than done. Political divisions emerged within the European Commission and proposals ran aground due to bureaucratic entanglements or additional questions from the European Union. After years of meeting, lobbying and negotiating, the parties were unable to reach agreement. The battle was mainly fought between parliament and council, but the commission was always the troublemaker. The main stumbling block in this entire process was and remains the issue of cloning.

> The European Commission didn't want to apply the precautionary principle, but parliament did. We even proposed a temporary ban on products from cloned animals and their offspring until a definitive cloning regulation could be agreed upon. This would at least have allowed other rules within the Novel Food Regulation – such as nanotechnology – to be implemented. But the member states, including the Netherlands, rejected this proposal.
>
> That rejection can be ascribed to several politicians and civil servants within the commission led by Commissioner for Trade, Karel De Gucht. It was 2011 and the first cloned animal products from the US had already reached the European market. De Gucht warned of a trade war with the US if we decided to ban the import of cloned animals. We would be in violation of WTO and GATT. That's why the bill was rejected. De Gucht used an unfounded argument to scare member states. Economic motives should remain separate from the precautionary principle. In concrete terms this means we will lose control of new 'clone products' and foods produced using nanotechnology. We also have no legal claim for introducing safety regulations for packaging materials. It's very possible that shops are currently selling beef or dairy products derived from clone offspring, albeit in trace amounts.
>
> It's just a matter of time before more cloned products hit the shelves; without any safety guarantee. How do you explain why less than 10 per cent of cloned animals survive the first year after birth? Wouldn't that influence the quality of the meat? I'm not ruling it out. More importantly, the stalemate means that the most important topic can't be addressed: how do we feel about cloning? Now that we've opened the borders to these 'cloned products', we are implicitly accepting the fact that animals are being cloned for food production. And this comes after a Eurobarometer study revealed that 61 per cent of EU citizens morally object

> to cloning animals. Only nine per cent of respondents have no problem with cloning animals for food production.

As a staunch supporter of sustainable food production and a passionate animal rights activist, Liotard shares the opinion of the majority of EU citizens. 'That's right', she agrees.

> But parliament wants new and better legislation surrounding Novel Foods. It comes down to the safety of EU citizens. That was the main motivation in 1997 as well. Back then we were apprehensive about genetically modified food and additives such as aspartame sweeteners. First test it, then approve it. There's nothing wrong with wanting the same for nano products and cloned products. In my opinion, this has nothing to do with political preference. I don't even view myself as a politician, but rather as someone elected to safeguard the interests of the people. Safety is essential and I see objective science playing a key role in this. I'm not interested in electoral gain.

Precautionary principle

Kartika Liotard is a parliamentary spokesperson/reporter on behalf of various left-wing European parties for several key fields. She is also vice chair of the United Left political group and a member of ENVI, a parliamentary commission that deals with environmental protection, public health and food safety. For her European group, United Left, Liotard coordinates the ideal political path for these topics. She has spent the past few years immersing herself in everything food-related.

> If we're talking about food in relation to nanotechnology, I think there's still a lot we don't know. We don't know if packaging materials are bad for our health. We don't know whether nano materials are being used in new foods and what the consequences of this may be. We don't know this because there's no legislation; the current Novel Food Regulation doesn't provide for this. That's exactly why we need new regulations. The same applies to clone products. Nine out of ten animals die at birth and the ones that survive are not particularly healthy. What does this mean?

The precautionary principle should be the guiding topic of most discussions.

> Sound and independent scientific research should be the foundation of every approval procedure. That takes time, but thoroughness is the key. At the time, aspartame and Bisphenol A – an organic compound used to make the polycarbonate polymers found in plastics – were approved based on inadequate studies. And now it appears that these compounds may be linked to

> certain health conditions. After all these years, it's extremely hard, both legally and economically, to ban these products. So we need more thorough research. Luckily, new research techniques, such as in vitro, help save time.

Ethics

Ethical questions play a particularly significant role in the cloning debate.

> Should we be allowed to clone? Absolutely not, if you ask most religious people; decisions about life and death should be left to God. Others see it as a form of innovation that can't be stopped. I respect every opinion and think we should ask voters how they feel about it. That hasn't happened yet. Very little attention is being paid to animal welfare. One thing we do know for certain is that the animals suffer when giving birth.

The absence of legislation also has economic ramifications.

> On the one hand, it seems like companies can do whatever they want, which is bad news given that their first priority is making profit rather than ensuring the health of consumers. On the other hand, the manufacturers of new foodstuffs are taking huge risks. Ultimately, they are the ones responsible for any harmful substances the food may contain. Extensive research would benefit them as well. The stalemate is preventing companies from gaining innovative headway. At some point new legislation will be approved and it could mean a recall of certain products until they have been proven safe. That's not going to make investing in new products any easier.

The absence of legislation in the field of nanotechnology and cloning does not prevent individual countries from taking action.

> That's right. Every member state is free to fill that gap and draft their own legislation. But in practice this doesn't happen. Monitoring and enforcing it is very difficult because it's next to impossible to trace products made from cloned animals or their offspring. The ideal situation would be to introduce a uniform European regulation. We've had good experiences with this in the past. The EFSA oversees scientific research studies and monitors things such as packaging, food safety and certification. I hope and expect that wisdom will prevail and we'll see a new Novel Food Regulation in 2013.

Index

Please note that page numbers relating to Notes will have the letter ‘n’ following the page number. Page numbers in *italics* refer to figures on that page.

www.ingramcontent.com/pod-product-compliance
Ingram Content Group UK Ltd.
Pitfield, Milton Keynes, MK11 3LW, UK
UKHW010956180926
475701UK00004B/400

* 9 7 8 1 1 3 8 1 9 2 6 0 7 *